A LIFE OF DATES

DAVID S. FLORIG

To Charlie, Marge, Nancy, Dylan and the 1,045 others mentioned herein.

Contents

Foreword   IX

Chapter 1   I
    Tuesday, May 4, 1954

Chapter 2   19
    Friday, December 25, 1959

Chapter 3   33
    Friday, November 22, 1963

Chapter 4   36
    Sunday, February 9, 1964

Chapter 5   42
    Sunday, June 21, 1964

Chapter 6   48
    Monday, April 1, 1968

Chapter 7   53
    Wednesday, June 5, 1968

Chapter 8   59
    Wednesday, July 16, 1969

Chapter 9   65
    Sunday, July 20, 1969

Chapter 10   67

Thursday, October 1, 1970

Chapter 11   78
   Tuesday, May 4, 1971

Chapter 12   84
   Monday, November 8, 1971

Chapter 13   101
   Thursday, June 15, 1972

Chapter 14   116
   Sunday, July 2, 1972

Chapter 15   118
   Tuesday, November 7, 1972

Chapter 16   121
   Tuesday, October 15, 1974

Chapter 17   123
   Tuesday, December 6, 1977

Chapter 18   128
   Friday, June 15, 1979

Chapter 19   130
   Tuesday, October 21, 1980

Chapter 20   133
   Sunday, January 25, 1981

Chapter 21   140
   Monday, November 11, 1985

Chapter 22   142
   Sunday, September 14, 1986

Chapter 23   149
   Saturday, October 24, 1987

Chapter 24   154
   Thursday, December 24, 1987

Chapter 25   164
    Friday, January 15, 1988

Chapter 26   168
    Tuesday, February 23, 1988

Chapter 27   175
    Wednesday, December 21, 1988

Chapter 28   178
    Friday, September 29, 1989

Chapter 29   185
    Sunday, June 17, 1990

Chapter 30   188
    Tuesday, October 8, 1991

Chapter 31   194
    Saturday, October 24, 1992

Chapter 32   195
    Sunday, November 1, 1992

Chapter 33   197
    Friday, January 22, 1993

Chapter 34   204
    Saturday, November 5, 1994

Chapter 35   207
    Wednesday, April 12, 1995

Chapter 36   210
    Wednesday, July 31, 1996

Chapter 37   227
    Friday, August 8, 1997

Chapter 38   233
    Saturday, December 5, 1998

Chapter 39   235

Friday, November 10, 2000

Chapter 40   239
Sunday, December 31, 2000

Chapter 41   241
Tuesday, September 11, 2001

Chapter 42   242
Saturday, October 13, 2001

Chapter 43   245
Sunday, November 17, 2002

Chapter 44   252
Sunday, March 21, 2004

Chapter 45   254
Sunday, February 6, 2005

Chapter 46   259
Monday, August 29, 2005

Chapter 47   262
Saturday, March 17, 2007

Chapter 48   264
Sunday, May 4, 2008

Chapter 49   265
Sunday, May 25, 2008

Chapter 50   270
Saturday, August 30, 2008

Chapter 51   274
Wednesday, June 3, 2009

Chapter 52   276
Wednesday, June 23, 2010

Chapter 53   277
Monday, June 6, 2011

Chapter 54   297
   Friday, October 26, 2012

Chapter 55   319
   Friday, December 14, 2012

Chapter 56   321
   Saturday, January 25, 2014

Chapter 57   323
   Thursday, May 22, 2014

Chapter 58   326
   Thursday, November 6, 2014

Chapter 59   331
   Saturday, July 4, 2015

Chapter 60   334
   Monday, May 30, 2016

Chapter 61   337
   Friday, January 20, 2017

Chapter 62   338
   Saturday, September 16, 2017

Chapter 63   340
   Sunday, February 4, 2018

Chapter 64   344
   Friday, May 4, 2018

Chapter 65   346
   Saturday, February 9, 2019

Chapter 66   349
   Saturday, September 14, 2019

Chapter 67   351
   Thursday, September 26, 2019

Chapter 68   355

Friday, January 17, 2020

Chapter 69 356
 Wednesday, March 11, 2020

Chapter 70 358
 Tuesday, March 24, 2020

Chapter 71 364
 Saturday, May 9, 2020

Chapter 72 372
 Wednesday, January 6, 2021

Chapter 73 373
 Wednesday, January 20, 2021

Chapter 74 374
 Wednesday, March 10, 2021

Chapter 75 376
 Sunday, March 21, 2021

Chapter 76 379
 Friday, April 9, 2021

Chapter 77 381
 Saturday, November 6, 2021

Epilogue 383

Index of Dates Cited 387

Index of Names Cited 407

About the Author 414

FOREWORD

To the best of my knowledge, everything that follows is true. Truth, of course, being subjective. The other people who were involved in these events may have completely different recollections of when, how, where and even whether, they occurred. But this is how I remember things.

I didn't really set out to write this. For a long time, I had wanted to see if I could create a timeline of my life, trying to see if I could piece together what I was doing on each and every day from the day I was born. I imagined a wall covered with calendars from 1954 on, with each block filled in with what I was doing on that date. That, of course, would be impossible. How could I possibly know whether I was in second grade class at Strawbridge School on February 21, 1962, for example? I was supposed to be there, but was I absent because I was sick? Was it a school holiday? Were we on a field trip? Not to mention that I've been alive for nearly 25,000 days. So, the idea morphed into recounting specific events that I could recall, figuring out when and where they happened, and letting the memories of those dates take me wherever they went.

Memory is a wonderful, mysterious thing. Do I really remember something as it actually happened, or only because I saw a picture or heard a story about it? Did it really happen on that date, or at some other time? Do I truly remember which people were involved, or am I simply surmising who they were? Some of the things that I thought I remembered quite clearly have been contradicted by people with quite different recollections.

I have relied on many sources in addition to simply my memory in writing this. A diary or journal would have been an enormous help, but I have never kept either. The internet is great for finding calendars and dates and historical events and pictures, and I have used it for all of those things. I have kept, or inherited, a lot of papers, pictures, movies, documents and miscellaneous stuff, which have been invaluable in piecing together this timeline. How else would I know who my mother's fourth grade teacher was without her name being signed to a report card? Even simple things like bank or E-ZPass statements and receipts help. I have talked to, or emailed, some of the people involved to ask for their recollections and to provide detail and context. Nancy and Dylan have filled in some blanks, although their recollections often differ from mine. Surprisingly, I have been able to attach specific dates and, in some cases, even times, for hundreds of events.

This is most definitely not a list of everything that I have done or that has happened to me over 67 years, nor do I want it to be. Many things that I clearly recall are omitted, mainly because I simply don't want to write about them, but also because I have been unable to weave them into the story. Entire swaths of my life are excluded. This is not intended to be an autobiography, although it is autobiographical. An autobiography seems a little presumptuous, really. And if an autobiography seems a *little* presumptuous, a memoir sounds even *more* so, since there really is no overall theme or focus or story arc leading to some momentous insight or life lesson learned. Nor is it even a timeline, since much of it is not in chronological order. It is more of a stream of consciousness, with memories of events and people triggered by what happened on certain dates, places and times. I make no pretext of objectivity.

Above all else, this is not about any universal truths or great insights into life that I have learned and want to pass on. First, I'm not sure that there are any universal truths. Second, if there are, I think that I'm probably too young and witless to have discovered them yet. Third, even if I *have* stumbled upon any great insights into life, I'm not one to give advice without being asked. And no one asked. Most of my insights are into more practical things, like not climbing on roofs or not pulling out poison ivy with bare hands, anyway.

What this is mostly about is people. People who have been friends seemingly forever, people who were once friends but have disappeared from my life, people who made a difference to me without even knowing it, and most of all, family. In the end, it has been a perfectly average life, yet filled with moments of great joy, overwhelming sadness, and some extraordinary people. Every memory has led to another and another and another. Most things will be of absolutely no interest to anyone except me. I'm OK with that.

CHAPTER 1

TUESDAY, MAY 4, 1954

I don't personally remember being born, although some people claim that they can. According to my birth certificate, it was on TUESDAY, MAY 4, 1954, in Camden, New Jersey. I don't know who my biological mother is, or was, much less my biological father. What I do know is that Charles and Marjorie Florig, at the respective ages of 32 and 33, adopted me within a few days of my birth. Perhaps it was planned beforehand with the mother, or maybe it was just happenstance. For the sum of $125.00, a private adoption was arranged through the law office of John J. Finnegan, Jr. (phone number EMERSON 5-4896) in Camden and I went home to live with them at 741 Woodlynne Avenue in Woodlynne. My parents paid the bill, and Finnegan sent them a copy of my birth certificate on TUESDAY, OCTOBER 11, 1955, a year-and-a-half after my adoption.

Charlie and Marge had also adopted another boy, Charles Dennis, in 1950. He was always called "Dennis" or "Den" or "Denny," never some version of "Charles." Dennis was born on SUNDAY, JULY 23, 1950, in Philadelphia, or possibly Trenton, and I never learned anything about the circumstances surrounding his adoption. Dennis looked nothing like me or my adoptive parents, primarily because he was a redhead, which nobody else was. Not that I resembled my parents, either, particularly my father, who stood 6'4", while I topped out at 5'5". I looked much more like Marge, who was short and had blue eyes, like me, although any resemblance, obviously, was strictly coincidental. Charlie and Marge had been unable to have a child of their own. I think that Marge may have had at least one miscarriage, although it was never spoken of.

I've known that I was adopted for as long as I can remember. I don't know when I was told, or who told me, but I always knew. It was never really important to me or something that I have thought that much about - it just was. Not until much later in life did I learn a little about my natural mother. From what I gather, it was a teenage out-of-wedlock pregnancy, sometimes abbreviated "OW" on birth certificates back in those days. The mother might have been from Haddonfield. Maybe she was 16. Hopefully, the father was from a good neighborhood. In the mid-1950's, keeping me was not a very viable or appealing option for an unwed, presumably middle-class, teenage girl.

Only a few times have I actually considered trying to learn any more about my birth parents, but have never had enough interest to pursue it. As far as I know, they haven't made an effort to learn about me, either, and I say that without any malice or ill-will. I simply don't know whether either of them has made any attempt at locating me. I could probably find out who they are, or more likely were, if I really wanted to, since the laws around adoption records have been relaxed over the years, but I don't know what good (or bad) might come of that. I understand that New Jersey would send me a copy of my original birth certificate for $25.00, if I asked. It might or might not contain my birth mother's or birth father's names. Sometimes the names are redacted, sometimes not. They would be in their 80's by now. I don't know whether they are living or dead. I doubt that I will ever know.

My anti-vaccine friends may be disappointed to know that I received my smallpox vaccination on WEDNESDAY, APRIL 27, 1955, from Dr. Rade R. Musulin. I have the mark on my upper left arm to prove it. Amazingly, I never got smallpox. I completed my polio vaccine series on SATURDAY, FEBRUARY 9, 1957. Likewise, I never contracted polio. In fact, once the United States began a massive polio vaccination campaign, polio deaths dropped from 35,000 in 1953 to 161 just eight years later. Possibly a coincidence, but I don't think so. I also received the PDT three-in-one vaccine for pertussis, diphtheria and tetanus, with boosters, on SATURDAY, NOVEMBER 19, 1955, and SATURDAY, JANUARY 31, 1959.

Charlie and Marge had me baptized into the Methodist Church when I was 40 days old, on SUNDAY, JUNE 13, 1954. It was Children's Day at the church, and I'm guessing that I was sprinkled, not dunked, by Minister William R. McClelland of the Marshall Memorial Methodist Church in Woodlynne. On MONDAY, AUGUST 2, 1954, I officially became a member, being enrolled in the Cradle Roll Department. We remained members of Marshall Memorial until I was around 11 or 12 years old, when Charlie and Marge joined the First Baptist Church of Collingswood. The four of us were baptized together, by immersion, as American Baptists. I remember standing in the baptismal pool at the front of the church and being immersed by Pastor Floyd Brown. The water was warm.

We had continued as members at Marshall Memorial even after we moved from Woodlynne. Uncle Bill (one of Marge's three brothers) Scott and Aunt Joanne may have been members there, too, living only a block or two from the church. I clearly remember standing near the pulpit when I was maybe four or five years old and looking out at my parents sitting up front. I sang "At the Cross." I don't think that congregants clapped in church back then, but if they did, they surely would have. I'm not sure why or how I merited a solo at such a young age. Maybe it was Childrens' Day at the church.

Charlie and Marge were both born shortly after the end of World War I, and spent many of their formative years living through the Great Depression. They were part of the Greatest Generation that won World War II and built middle-class America.

My mother, Marjorie Lowden Scott, was born on WEDNESDAY, OCTOBER 20, 1920, in Camden, where I would also be born, to Thomas Scott (SUNDAY, SEPTEMBER 2, 1894 - SUNDAY, FEBRUARY 23, 1958) and Marjorie (*nee* Lowden) Scott (SATURDAY, JANUARY 13, 1894 - TUESDAY, SEPTEMBER 15, 1981). As World War I was winding down, Marge's parents were married in Philadelphia on WEDNESDAY, SEPTEMBER 25, 1918. A few weeks before their wedding, on THURSDAY, AUGUST 8, 1918, Thomas Scott had purchased a walnut bed, mattress, dresser, chiffonier, table and two chairs for the bedroom; a Jacobian buffet, server, china closet, table and six chairs for the kitchen; a three piece velour cane suite for the living room; and a kitchen table with four chairs from the Kensington Carpet Company on Market Street in Philadelphia. He paid the princely sum of $301 for everything. A bargain, even though $301 in 1918 equals about $5,700 today. Shortly after the wedding, Thomas Scott received a letter postmarked WEDNESDAY, DECEMBER 4, 1918, from an aunt in Belfast, Ireland, in which she referenced being the only member of the Scott family still in Ireland. She then wrote:

> *I am sure that you are just as glad as we are that the war is over after such a terrible loss of life and destruction of property. We live close to a hospital in which there are between 3 or 4 hundred soldier patients a good many of whom have lost arms or legs. It is very sad to see so many young people crippled for life.*

> *I would have written sooner only I was lying very ill when I received your letter and am still under Doctors treatment but thank God we have escaped the Influenza as I hope you have.*

Marge's maternal grandparents were Frederick Lowden (THURSDAY, DECEMBER 1, 1854 - TUESDAY, DECEMBER 21, 1915) and Anna Hazeltine Barnes Lowden (SATURDAY, NOVEMBER 16, 1861 - THURSDAY, JANUARY 15, 1953). Her maternal great-grandparents were Jacob L. Barnes (SUNDAY,

SEPTEMBER 1, 1822 - FRIDAY, FEBRUARY 14, 1890) and Hannah Barnes (SATURDAY, JUNE 14, 1823 - MONDAY, AUGUST 26, 1912).

Jacob Barnes wrote a letter to his wife during the Civil War, which I still have, which concluded:

> *We are within 16 miles of the enemy. Take care of yourself and your children for I may never see you more. I hope God & the People will protect you through life. Farewell. Address your letters as you did before. Think of me & hope that I will return. Your affectionate husband.*

Jacob Barnes did return home from the War, unlike more than 600,000 others. Years later, his death was reported in the newspaper this way, under the caption, "Death's Work":

> *The body of Jacob L. Barnes of Londonderry township, a man about 67 years of age, was found floating in the water of Hoy Creek, a tributary of the Schuylkill, at Birdsboro, Berks county on Friday evening. He took dinner on Friday with his son, Martin Barnes, in Coatesville, and started home from there for Birdsboro, where he had business to transact. It is supposed by his friends that he attempted to cross the stream while it was flooded and lost his life in the attempt. Deceased had spent much of his life in Londonderry township and was a blacksmith. He leaves to survive him a wife and seven children, four daughters and three sons. Two of his sons are railroad employees. Franklin is a conductor on the P&B Central road, and Joseph is a fireman on the West Chester and Philadelphia Railroad, and resides in West Chester. It was late on Saturday afternoon when he learned of his father's death. The deceased served in the army during the*

late war and was at the time of his death engaged in collecting testimony to secure a pension which was pending in the Pension Office.

The "late war," of course, was the Civil War, in which he served in the United States Army, Company K, 175th Regiment P.V. as a private from MONDAY, NOVEMBER 10, 1862, to FRIDAY, AUGUST 7, 1863.

Marge's other set of maternal great-grandparents were Charles Lowden (MONDAY, APRIL 17, 1815 - THURSDAY, FEBRUARY 18, 1904) and Hannah Fish Lowden (FRIDAY, FEBRUARY 20, 1818 - MONDAY, DECEMBER 29, 1902). According to a newspaper story from September 1900, Charles and Hannah had the longest-tenured marriage in Palmyra, New Jersey, if not in all of Burlington County, clocking in at 68 years and counting. Marge's paternal grandparents were Thomas and Mary Scott, immigrants from Northern Ireland.

Marge was baptized into the State Street Methodist Episcopal Church in Camden at eight months old by Pastor Herbert J. Belting on SUNDAY, JUNE 12, 1921. Reverend Belting was apparently an interesting fellow. In 1908, he had convinced the boys who were members of his church in New Brunswick, New Jersey - the Pitman Methodist Episcopal Church - to give up all sports for the summer in order to excavate a foundation for the new church that was being built. By hand, I would guess.

On SUNDAY, AUGUST 1, 1920, he delivered an evening sermon decrying gambling in the town of Red Bank, New Jersey, calling it "the worst menace in the community," and saying that "the popularity of this vice showed the moral sense of the community had been blunted." Reverend Belting went on to condemn the lack of action by the town and called the lack of action "a disgrace." Surely, Reverend Belting knew that Red Bank Mayor Arthur Allen Patterson was a member of the church. I can't say for sure if there was a connection between the sermon and the pastor's relocation to Woodlynne soon thereafter, but it wouldn't surprise me. Politics usually upstages religion, as we have all recently witnessed.

Marge had one older brother - Thomas B. Scott, who was born on TUESDAY, MAY 31, 1910, and passed away on SUNDAY, JANUARY 14, 1968, from chronic myelogenous leukemia (cancer of the bone marrow) - and three younger brothers - Robert ("Uncle Bob"), who was born on SATURDAY, JANUARY 7, 1922, and passed away on WEDNESDAY, DECEMBER 6, 2006; William ("Uncle Bill"), who was born on TUESDAY, JANUARY 25, 1927, and passed away on WEDNESDAY, SEPTEMBER 25, 2013; and James ("Uncle Jim"), who was born on SUNDAY, OCTOBER 21, 1928, and passed away on FRIDAY, JULY 1, 2016. Rose, Marge's only sister, passed away on FRIDAY, OCTOBER 29, 1999. Marge's parents were billed $25 by

Dr. Albert B. Davis for "confinement" services after Uncle Bob was born and were billed $33 by Dr. W. H. Haines for "confinement" services after Uncle Bill was born. No word on Uncle Jim's confinement.

At some point, Marge's parents moved to 249 Stratford Avenue in Haddon Township, New Jersey. She spent her elementary school years at Westmont School #5, which would later be known as Strawbridge School. Strawbridge School would play a very important role in both my childhood and my adult life. Marge's first grade teacher was Bertha Woodrow, who promoted her to second grade on FRIDAY, JUNE 10, 1927. Her second grade teacher was Dorothy Bowker (Bertha Woodrow was now the principal), who promoted her to third grade on FRIDAY, JUNE 8, 1928. Third grade was Dorothy Albrecht, who noted on Marge's report card that she was especially good in reading and spelling, and who also checked the box on the report card for "Whispers too Much." At least she didn't get a check mark for "Indolent," "Inclined to Mischief," or "Annoys Others." During third grade, Marge was promoted from the Primary Department of the First Methodist Episcopal Church in Westmont, which her family now belonged to, to the Junior Department on SUNDAY, OCTOBER 7, 1928, by Pastor Benjamin Allgood. What a great name for a pastor. Dorothy Albrecht promoted Marge to fourth grade on FRIDAY, JUNE 14, 1929. Fourth grade was Marion Ashmore, who promoted her to fifth grade on FRIDAY, JUNE 13, 1930. Fifth grade was Inez Lear (who advised her to "bring up arithmetic so you can be an honor student"), who promoted her to sixth grade on FRIDAY, JUNE 19, 1931. Sixth was Margaret Simpson, who gave her straight A's in spelling and promoted her to junior high school on FRIDAY, JUNE 17, 1932. Only women taught elementary school in those days, it seems, although I, too, only had women teachers throughout elementary school. During fourth and fifth grades, Marge was in the Camden County 4-H Club, from which she received an *Award of Merit* from the Camden County Home Economics Extension Service on TUESDAY, MAY 22, 1931:

Marjorie Scott having completed her second year of work as member of a Camden County 4-H Club, is commended for her high standards of work and achievement in homemaking activities and for her attitude and cooperative spirit in all Extension movements.

/s/_____

County Home Demonstration Agent

*/s/*_____

President, Camden County Home Economics Extension Service

Awarded May 22, 1931

During the summer after sixth grade, from MONDAY, JUNE 27, 1932, to FRIDAY, JULY 22, 1932, Marge attended Vacation Church School at St. Paul's Evangelical Lutheran Church on Park Avenue in Collingswood. She received a certificate for "regular attendance and faithful work in the Intermediate Department" from Pastor Ivan H. Hagedorn. Denominations seemingly didn't matter too much to Marge, since she had been baptized Methodist Episcopal, went to summer church school at an Evangelical Lutheran church, had me baptized as a Methodist, and spent most of her adult life as an American Baptist.

Haddon Township only had elementary schools until the 1960's, so in September, 1932, Marge started her post-elementary education at Collingswood Junior High. Haddon Township kids were shipped off to Haddonfield, Audubon or Collingswood for junior high and high school back then. Collingswood Junior High School consisted of 7th, 8th and 9th grades. For seventh grade, her homeroom (Room 313) teacher was Helen Thayer. Marge had two "absences not valid" days that year. Apparently, absences were taken much more seriously in the 1930's:

> *Teachers are required to obtain written excuses from parents for the absence or tardiness of pupils. The purpose of this rule is to prevent truancy and to enable the teacher, in case of valid absence, to cancel the regular deduction of 3 points made from the classstanding of a pupil for each absence from recitation. Except for personal illness, death of a near relative, or quarantine regulations, no excuse is made valid unless, in the judgment of the Principal of the building, the absence was due to urgent necessity.*

Helen Paxon was Marge's homeroom teacher for eighth grade (no "absences not valid," thankfully) and promoted her to ninth grade on FRIDAY, JUNE 15, 1934. Her best grades were still in spelling.

During ninth grade, on SATURDAY, JANUARY 26, 1935, Marge received a *Certificate of Superior Ability* from the Palmer Method of Business Writing, which read:

The Palmer Method of Business Writing

A.N. Palmer

Originator and Author

Advanced Course

This Certifies That

Marjorie L. Scott

Has completed the lessons in The Business and High School

Edition of The Palmer Method of Business Writing, and

having satisfactorily passed the required Examination, is

hereby awarded this

Certificate of Superior Ability

In Rapid Muscular Movement Commercial Penmanship

Given at New York, N.Y., on this 26th day of Jan., 1935

The good folks at the Palmer Method took penmanship extraordinarily seriously. The Palmer Method turned cursive writing into an exercise involving virtually the entire body:

Muscular movement writing means good, healthful posture, straight spinal columns, eyes far enough away from the paper for safety, and both shoulders of equal height. These features alone should be sufficient to encourage boys and girls to master a physical training system of writing . . . remembering that it is impossible to do good muscular movement writing in twisted, unhealthful positions, or with stiff and rigid muscles.

Harriet Smelker was homeroom teacher for ninth grade and promoted Marge to tenth grade on FRIDAY, JUNE 14, 1935. For reasons that I can't explain, and that I find totally out of character, her worst grades were in "Conduct," where she got straight C's. Maybe there was a wild girl inside that I never got to see. Two days prior, on WEDNESDAY, JUNE 12, 1935, she was granted a *Certificate of Admission* to high school, which read:

Collingswood Public Schools

Junior High School

Collingswood, New Jersey

This Certifies That

Marjorie Lowden Scott

Has successfully completed the prescribed work of the ninth

grade in the Collingswood Junior High School and is

therefore awarded this

Certificate of Admission

To the Senior High School, by authority of the Board of

Education, given at Collingswood, New Jersey this 12th day of

June, 1935

High school at Collingswood High School began on MONDAY, SEPTEMBER 9, 1935, where Marge's homeroom teacher was Ms. Kirk, and where her subjects included bookkeeping and typewriting, in which she obtained her two highest grades. I also took typing as an elective in high school and it turned out to be one of the most useful electives I ever took. I was one of two boys in a typing class of 25 students at Haddon Township High School. I doubt that there were very many, if any, boys in Marge's typing class, either.

Eleventh grade started on WEDNESDAY, SEPTEMBER 9, 1936, with Gladys Hillman for homeroom. Stenography had been added to the bookkeeping and typing courseload, and there were two more invalid absences (in the final marking period.) Marge was most definitely not the type to play hookey, so I can only assume that this was a failure to present the proper paperwork excusing the absence. On the other hand, I may be sensing a pattern here, with the bad marks in "Conduct" in ninth grade and the "absences not valid." During senior year, with Anna A. Latimer (B.A., Temple University) for homeroom, bookkeeping and typing were no longer taken, but stenography still was, with secretarial practice now added. And there was one final "absence not valid." Her 1938 yearbook, *The Knight*, lists her address as 88 Emerald Avenue in Westmont; her "likes" as dancing, skating and chocolate nut sundaes; "dislikes" as onions and hockey; and lists her activities in school as Play Usher 3; Play

Committee 4; and Glee Club 2, 3, 4. How she could have possibly disliked hockey and onions is lost to history.

On THURSDAY EVENING, JUNE 16, 1938, Marge and 334 of her classmates were part of the 29th graduating class of Collingswood High School. Her diploma reflects that she was in the "Secretarial Curriculum" and received 2 credits in English, 1 credit in French, 5 in Civics, 5 in Biology, 2.5 in Penmanship, 5 in Commercial Arithmetic, 5 in Junior Business Training, 1 in Bookkeeping, 2.5 in Economics, 2.5 in Commercial Law, 5 in Typewriting, 10 in Stenography, 2.5 in Secretarial Practice, 1 in Foods, 1 in Clothing, 4 in Music and 4 in Physical Training. How times have changed.

Charlie's childhood is much more of a mystery. He wasn't born in a regular hospital, but rather at 2639 South Hancock Street in Philadelphia, which I believe was then the Naval Shipyard, on WEDNESDAY, JUNE 1, 1921, to John (MONDAY, NOVEMBER 29, 1897 - MONDAY, SEPTEMBER 1, 1969) and Mary (*nee* Bernhardt) Florig (1899 - SATURDAY, SEPTEMBER 6, 1930). Charlie was a third generation American, his paternal grandparents, Adolph Florig (THURSDAY, FEBRUARY 11, 1866 - THURSDAY, MARCH 11, 1937) and Marie Florig having emigrated to the United States from Germany in the 1800's. Adolph arrived in New York in 1885. Charlie's maternal grandparents were Franz John Bernhardt (SUNDAY, APRIL 21, 1833 - SATURDAY, MARCH 18, 1905) and Anna Catharina Bedos (TUESDAY, FEBRUARY 9, 1836 - TUESDAY, OCTOBER 14, 1879), both of whom were also born in Germany, and Thomas Birrane (1840 - SATURDAY, MARCH 9, 1907) and Elizabeth McAndrew Birrane (1854 - ~1911), born in Ireland.

Charlie's paternal great-grandparents were Johann Adam Florig (born THURSDAY, MAY 19, 1836) and Henrike Ziegler (TUESDAY, JULY 27, 1841 - WEDNESDAY, APRIL 7, 1915).

John was 23 and Mary was 22 when Charlie was born. His full name was Charles Leon Florig. Under Question 7 on Charlie's birth certificate, the question "Legitimate?" was answered "Yes." For the father's information, John was listed as "Boiler Maker" under "Trade, profession, or particular kind of work, as spinner, sawyer, bookkeeper, etc." For the mother's information, Mary was listed as "Wife" under "Trade, profession, or particular kind of work done, as bookkeeper, typist, nurse, clerk, etc." Career options were very different for men and women in those days. Four days later, on SUNDAY, JUNE 5, 1921, Charlie was baptized at the Church of Our Lady of Mt. Carmel in Philadelphia, one week before Marge was baptized. I don't remember ever meeting Charlie's father, and his mother died long before I was born.

There were seven kids in Charlie's family, four boys and three girls, although only six lived to adulthood. Charlie's oldest brother, John Joseph Florig, was born in 1918, but died at the age of three on WEDNESDAY, MAY 18, 1921, of pneumonia and whooping cough, just two weeks before Charlie was born. I can barely imagine what that must have been like, to lose your first-born and welcome your second within two weeks. Next came Thomas John Florig (SATURDAY, FEBRUARY 24, 1923 - FRIDAY, APRIL 20, 2001), Agnes Florig Sheldon (1926 - FRIDAY, MAY 11, 2018), Stephen Florig (TUESDAY, FEBRUARY 11, 1930 - WEDNESDAY, SEPTEMBER 16, 2009), Theresa Florig Helmuth and Elizabeth Florig Hettmannsperger.

Charlie spent at least some of his childhood on a farm in Gloucester County, New Jersey. I know because I would sometimes hear about "sticking" pigs and draining their blood into a bucket so that Mary could make blood soup. During the depression, nothing could go to waste. I have never had blood soup, nor do I plan to any time soon. Apparently, though, it's a real thing, and you can find dozens of blood soup recipes online, should you care to. Other farm stories involved decapitated chickens. And apparently, someone in the family could make dandelion wine.

Charlie went to elementary school in West Deptford, New Jersey. He spent third grade at Verga School, which was for grades 3-8, with Emma Gleason as his teacher during the 1929-30 school year. Third-graders studied reading, writing, spelling, English, arithmetic, geography and nature, history and civics, physical education and art (drawing, handwork and music). Pretty much the same as they do today. By the end of third grade, his best subject was spelling.

In seventh grade, Charlie had Ruth Kille, who gave him his best grades in reading and his *worst* in spelling. "Carries work to completion" and "Begins work promptly" were noted as weaknesses. In eighth grade, it was Edna Brown, who wrote that working well with others, courtesy, school spirit, self-reliance and sportsmanship were strengths. Spelling was once again a weakness. In June, 1935, he finished Verga School and was promoted to high school, receiving his *County School Certificate* on THURSDAY, JUNE 6, 1935, which read:

State of New Jersey
Department of Public Instruction
County School Certificate
This certifies that Charles L. Florig has completed the course
of study prescribed for the Eighth Grade in Gloucester

County, and has by examination and excellent record as a student fully established his right to receive this honorable testimonial.

Issued in compliance with the Rules of the State Board of Education

In witness whereof we have set our hands this Sixth day of June 1935.

On FRIDAY, JUNE 7, 1935, he was "Honorably Discharged" from the safety patrol by the New Jersey State Police School Safety Patrol:

Know ye, that Charles Florig, having served as a member of the New Jersey State Police School Safety Patrol of Verga School from September 1934 until June 7, 1935 and having faithfully and loyally performed the duties of his office and having complied with the requirements and qualifications requisite thereto, is hereby Honorably Discharged from the New Jersey State Police School Safety Patrol.

Given under my hand at Trenton, N.J. this Seventh day of June, one thousand nine hundred and thirty-five.

/s/ Col. H. N. Schwarzkopf

Superintendent, New Jersey State Police

Col. H.N. Schwarzkopf was Herbert Norman Schwarzkopf, the first Superintendent of the New Jersey State Police and the father of General Norman Schwarzkopf, Jr., later the commander of coalition forces for Operation Desert Storm in Iraq and Kuwait. Col. Schwarzkopf had been the lead investigator into the kidnapping and murder of Charles Lindberg's son, and had informed the family of Baby Charlie's death.

Oddly, by the time my father finished eighth grade, his worst grades were in spelling (they had been his best in third grade) and his best were in reading, where he got straight A's. The only A+ was in music, which seems strange, since I never saw him play an instrument, don't think he knew how to play any, and rarely heard him sing except in church, but he *was* an inveterate whistler. Marge could play a little bit of piano, but Charlie never touched it.

Charlie never finished high school. He dropped out during his sophomore year. I don't know why and never asked. While working for the phone company after the war, he went to night school and got his GED, which he was justifiably proud of.

I don't remember ever hearing this story, but Charlie apparently saved his sisters, Theresa and Agnes, from drowning one day. On SATURDAY, JULY 20, 1940, the *Courier-Post* reported this story under the headline, "Brother, Nurse Save Two Drowning Girls":

> *Two sisters were saved from drowning in Almonesson Lake this afternoon by their brother, Charles Florig, 17, of Burkett Avenue, Verga, and Mrs. Charlotte Wilkins, a nurse at the Philadelphia General Hospital. Theresa Florig, 5, went in beyond her depth and screamed, attracting her sister Agnes, 14. The girls struggled in the water and both started to sink when their cries brought their brother and Mrs. Wilkins from the opposite shore of the lake. The Runnemede Emergency Squad, summoned by other bathers, gave first aid treatment and took the girls home.*

Marge was not a drinker. Maybe twice in my life did I see her have a sip of wine or some kind of sweet mixed drink, but that's about it. At one time, she was even a member of the Women's Christian Temperance Union. The Eighteenth Amendment had become law the year she was born. Charlie didn't drink when I was younger, either, that I know of. I never remember so much as a beer being in the refrigerator. I'm pretty sure that alcohol was one reason why we were estranged from Charlie's family. Unless I was too young to remember, I don't think that I went to a single birthday, baptism, wedding, funeral, party or event with his family.

Charlie and Marge were married on SATURDAY, OCTOBER 10, 1942. The *Courier-Post* had announced the engagement on TUESDAY, OCTOBER 28, 1941. The only people in the wedding party were Rose Murray (Marge's sister) and William J. McClyment, Jr., who may have served as Best Man. The Reverend William J. Herman, pastor of Grace Baptist Church in Westmont, officiated. Only eleven people signed the guestbook:

Jim, Robert and William Scott - Marge's brothers

Rose Murray - Marge's sister

John Murray - Rose's husband

John Murray, Jr. - Rose's son

Anna H. Lowden - Marge's grandmother

Lee Shute

Bill McClyment

Anne Remick

Harrison Lowden - Marge's mother's brother

Not a single guest was from Charlie's family - or at least they didn't sign the guestbook.

Their black and white wedding picture is hanging in our living room, next to wedding pictures for Nancy and I, and Nancy's parents, James and Doris. Charlie never looked happier.

On SATURDAY, AUGUST 26, 1944, while World War II was still being fought, Charlie was inducted into the United States Marines in Woodbury, New Jersey, leaving Marge, like so many other women, to take care of things at home. The next day, he was at Parris Island, South Carolina, for basic training. By October, Charlie was at Camp Lejeune, North Carolina, and by February, 1945, was stationed at Camp Pendleton in California. On MONDAY, MAY 28, 1945, Charlie arrived via ship at Pearl Harbor in the Hawaii Territory. He would be stationed there for more than a year. Of course, the attack on Pearl Harbor had happened in 1941, but the United States continued to maintain a large military presence in the Pacific throughout the war. On WEDNESDAY, AUGUST 7, 1946, Charlie was honorably discharged as a PFC at the United States Navy Training Center in Great Lakes, Illinois. His military record showed nothing but "Excellent" scores in all categories - Military Efficiency, Neatness and

Military Bearing, Intelligence, Obedience and Sobriety. His pay rate upon discharge was $80 per month and the federal government reimbursed him $.05 per mile to make his way home from Illinois to Philadelphia. He never saw combat.

At the time he joined the Marines, Charlie was working as a welder at the New York Shipbuilding Corporation in Camden. He and Marge were married and living at 20 Park Drive, Crescent Park, Bellmawr, New Jersey. Although Charlie had never finished high school, he had learned welding at the Pennsauken Trade School.

Four years before I joined the family, my brother, Dennis, had been adopted. He was less expensive than I was. The total adoption cost was $115.00, a $75.00 legal fee and $40.00 in costs. That was ten dollars less than my adoption would cost four years later. John Finnegan, Jr., Esquire, handled the adoption for my parents, as he would later handle mine, as well. At eight months old, on SUNDAY, MARCH 25, 1951 - Easter - Dennis was baptized at the Marshall Memorial Methodist Church in Woodlynne by Reverend William McClelland.

Since we still lived on Woodlynne Avenue, Dennis started elementary school at the Thomas Sharpe School in Collingswood. In first grade, he had a "Memories of School" booklet to fill out. There were two photos on the "Pals of Mine" page, Bobby Phillips and Kenny Simpkins. There used to be a picture on the "That Extra Special One" page, the one with the heart and arrow, but that picture, whoever's it was, was removed for unknown reasons at an unknown time. Under "Favorites of Mine," his favorite TV star was Annette (Funicello) of the *Mickey Mouse Club* (which boy's wasn't?), favorite food was turkey, favorite comic was *Dennis the Menace* and favorite car was a blue and white Chevrolet. There are pictures of six "Classmates of Mine" - Robert Pinto, Paul, Ronald Hales, Linda Lee Phillips, Marjorie B. and Wayne Adams. Once we moved to Haddon Township in 1957, Dennis attended Strawbridge School, like our mother had, and later Haddon Township High School.

I think that the only sport Dennis tried in high school was football. He was pretty big, but slow, so he was a lineman. I still have his *Certificate of Meritorious Award* for freshman football from 1964, signed by Albert Tanner and Donald Koehler.

Dennis was elected to the Haddon Chapter of the National Honor Society (which I was not) on FRIDAY, JANUARY 16, 1967. His advisor was John H. Davis, always known as "Jack," who would be my German teacher in high school. Membership was based on "Scholarship, Leadership, Service and Character," at least one of which I was obviously deficient in.

Along with Frances Schaevitz, Dennis was also a finalist (which, again, I was not) for the 1967-68 Merit Scholarship Program, one of 14,000 such students across the country. Academically, he was far my superior. He graduated from Haddon Township High School on THURSDAY, JUNE 13, 1968.

Dennis attended American University in Washington, D.C., starting in 1968 during the height of the anti-war movement and the counterculture revolution. I vaguely remember our whole family traveling to Washington, seeing the school, and visiting some of the Washington attractions. He graduated in 3 ½ years, on WEDNESDAY, DECEMBER 22, 1971, with a Bachelor of Arts degree in Political Science. Although his legal name was "Charles Dennis Florig," the name on his diploma was "Dennis C. Florig." So was the name in his obituary.

Dennis also had a Master's in political science from the University of Maryland and a Ph.D. from Stanford University. On TUESDAY, APRIL 27, 1982, *The Cowl*, the Providence College newspaper, contained the following announcement: "Dennis Florig, a visiting instructor in the Providence College political science department and a Ph.D. candidate at Stanford University, will present a lecture on, "The Ideology of Equal Opportunity," on MONDAY, MAY 2, 1982, at 4:00 p.m. in Aquinis Hall Lounge on the PC campus."

In 1992, Praeger Publishers in Westport, Connecticut published his book, "The Power of Presidential Ideologies." Dennis was apparently interested in "ideologies," judging from his lecture at Providence and his book. The book was dedicated, "To Bob, a friend in need." I assume that was a reference to Bob Snow, a high school friend from Collingswood, but I'm not really sure. By then, Dennis had moved to Tokyo to teach, and in 1993 to South Korea, where he was Director of the KOTESOL Conference Job Center at Wonkwang University in Iri City. For many years thereafter, he taught at the Hankuk University of Foreign Studies in Seoul. While in Seoul, he married Meyoung Lee.

I received a letter postmarked FRIDAY, JUNE 17, 2016, from South Jersey, less than a month after Nancy and I had moved to Maine:

Dear David,

I am a Meyoung Florig, Dennis's wife.

I am so sorry . . . . . .

My husband passed away last Month. (May/28)

I found your E-mail address recently.

He was sick in Korea (Cryptogenic Liver Cirrhosis)

We moved last year to America. We want to liver transplantation.

He done every tests and medical examinations, but he could not get the opportunity.

Fortunately, He didn't have the pain and he got the most peaceful death. He was cremated.

Just I am informing you.

This year, May First (May/1), Dennis said, 'Today in my brother David's birthday. He is a nice person.'

I wish you, you have good health.

I hope to peace and happiness of your family

Dennis was cremated through Foster-Warner Funeral Home in Collingswood, just like our parents were. I guess I know where I'm eventually headed. Before he died, Dennis and Meyoung had moved to Haddon Township, into the Haddonview Apartments where Charlie had also moved after leaving our house on Burrwood Avenue. Dennis spent his final days at the Abigail House for Nursing and Rehabilitation in Camden, although I never knew he was there. For reasons that I don't know or understand, he never tried to contact me, even though I lived less than 10 miles away. Families are so damn complicated, which at least partially explains why I've never pursued learning about my natural mother.

The guestbook from the funeral home has an entry from David Skidmore, which reads:

Dennis was a dear friend from our days as graduate students together at Stanford University. We spent much time together listening to music, attending concerts, playing basketball and discussing politics and philosophy. He once visited me in Iowa, where I ended up, and I discovered a previously unknown talent as he played a wonderful classical composition of his own creation on our piano. Dennis believed in the ideals of the sixties counter-culture and attempted to live those ideals in some degree in his own life even as the surrounding world moved in quite different directions. He was a deep thinker, interesting personality and a good friend. I am sorry that he passed so young.

Yoo Jin Kim submitted his Master's thesis to the Columbia Graduate School of Arts & Sciences as part of the Human Rights Studies Master of Arts Program in July, 2017. Kim's final acknowledgement read, "And to Professor Dennis Florig. Your dedication inspired me to dream bigger and reach higher. Without your encouragement, I would not be where I am today. I remain forever grateful, and you will always be remembered. Rest in peace." Not at all a bad way to be remembered.

Chapter 2

We got a puppy for Christmas - a collie which we named "Lassie." Not very creative, I know. I was in Mrs. Rod's kindergarten class at Strawbridge School, the same elementary school my mother had attended, although kindergarten for me was in an addition which had been built later. Dennis  was in fourth grade, in the older, red brick part of the school. We had had at least two dogs when I was younger and living in Woodlynne. I've seen the Woodlynne house in home movies and pictures, and I've seen the dogs, too, but I don't otherwise have any real memories of either the house or the dogs. I don't know what kind of dogs they were, but their names were Pinky and Ginger, nor do I know whether they moved with us to Haddon Township. I wasn't even three when we moved.

On Friday, September 14, 1956, my parents had entered into an Agreement of Sale with Rodman and Virginia Goode to purchase a house at the corner of Woodlawn and Burrwood Avenues, at 215 Burrwood, in the "Bluebird" section of Haddon Township. They paid $14,500, with a $1,000 down payment. I would guess that they bought it on the GI Bill. The house had passed from Earl R. Lippincott Realty Company to George Pleibel on Wednesday, December 3, 1924, then to Bruce V. Hanson "and wife" on Saturday, March 5, 1955, and then to the Rodmans. Charlie and Marge finally closed on the house on Friday, March 29, 1957. We lived in that house the entire time that I was growing up, except for one summer. My mother, like lots of people, always said that she wanted to die in that house, not in some hospital or nursing home. She got that wish. She left Burrwood Avenue for the final time on the night of Wednesday, April 12, 1995. My father didn't stay there much longer. He sold it on Wednesday, December 4, 1996, after nearly 40 years.

The one summer that I didn't spend at Burrwood Avenue was in the early or mid-1960's, when we lived in a small apartment in Asbury Park.

From as far back as I can remember, my father worked for the phone company. Western Electric, more specifically. In fact, he worked for Western Electric for more than 33 years, retiring at 59 years old on THURSDAY, MARCH 13, 1980. He was an area or regional supervisor, and Haddonfield, Woodbury, Collingswood and Laurel Springs were in his area. I'm sure that there were many other offices, as well. In the summer of 1973, my father got me a job with the phone company and I spent most of that summer traveling back and forth to Hamilton Square, near Trenton, making union money and a travel allowance. It was dirty, hard hat work, running and installing cable in a new telephone office. It was pretty sweet, though, pulling down $200 a week back then. In today's world, that would be like making $1,225 a week for a summer job. It's good to have connections.

I also had another job with the phone company one summer - long distance telephone operator, often working the graveyard shift. It was boring work, mostly handling collect and person-to-person calls. At least I got to talk to Isaac Asimov, Richie Hebner (a baseball player with the Pittsburgh Pirates, nicknamed the "Gravedigger") and Stu Nahan (a/k/a "Captain Philadelphia").

Charlie had a big project in Asbury Park that one year and commuting would have been impossible, so he got (or maybe the company provided) an apartment. I don't recall a lot about it. It wasn't a big apartment complex, and it was on the second floor. It may simply have been the upstairs of someone's house. In the spring and fall, we either went up there on weekends, or, more often, Charlie came home. But for that one summer, we all went to live in Asbury Park. Asbury Park had a boardwalk and I know that I spent a fair amount of time at the Ripley's Believe It or Not Museum there, as well as on the beach. I still have some of the oversized black and white baseball cards that I got out of a vending machine on the boardwalk. I would watch the Mets on a small black and white television when there was nothing else to do.

Lassie was a great dog and family pet. She would stay outside on her own and lay behind the bushes along the Burrwood Avenue side of the house for hours without leaving the yard, even though it wasn't fenced. The result was that she almost always had ticks. To a young boy, that was no big deal. It was fun picking ticks off of a dog, and I would pull them out with my bare fingers. It was especially fun to find the really big ones, fat and gray and gorged on dog blood. The best time to pick ticks was in the colder weather, when we would both be in front of the fireplace and I could dispose of the ticks in the fire. The fatter ones made a nice little pop. The rest of the time, I had to flush them down the toilet, which wasn't nearly as much fun.

Lassie would, however, go for a little stroll outside of the confines of her yard on occasion. One day the phone rang and my mother answered.

Elaine Welden was calling to tell my mother to look down Burrwood Avenue toward the Weldens' house. Walking up the sidewalk, carrying a full loaf of bread in her mouth, still in its wrapper, was Lassie. As near as we could tell, she had pilfered it from a delivery to a small store on Conger Avenue behind the Weldens' house and was bringing it home for the family. I would bet that it was Wonder bread.

Most of my friends' families had dogs when I was growing up. Scott Welden's family at 227 Burrwood had a dachshund named Otto, Kevin Manns' family on New Jersey Avenue had Thumper and Julius Sacchetti's family on Morgan Avenue had Snookie. Snookie was the wildest one, with a penchant for roaming the neighborhood and a special fondness for actually chasing cars. Thumper was pretty hyper, too, but no match for Snookie. Snookie lost an encounter with a bee once, resulting in a severely swollen nose.

We all lived within a block or two of each other - Scott Welden on Burrwood; Kevin Manns, Tom Genetta, Mike Clifford, Paul Bailey and Steve Ibbeken on New Jersey; Jules Sacchetti on Morgan; Ricky Divis on Guilford. For the sake of numbers, and as we got older, the circle expanded to include kids from a little farther away, like Tom Lingo from Emerald Avenue, Kevin and Colin McGrath from Bradford Avenue and Rich Gant from Stratford Avenue. We were almost always outside playing. In the fall, we would play football at Cooper River behind the old Camden County Park Police building. In the winter, we played basketball, usually in the driveway behind my cousin Duane Scott's house on Burrwood, and in the spring we played baseball at Cooper River. At one of the baseball games, Steve Ibbeken was drinking a soda from a can, unaware that a yellow jacket had crawled inside. We thought it was really funny when the bee stung him on the lip. Steve didn't think that it was all that funny. We would all ride our bikes down to the river and play until too many of us got summoned home for supper. Some kids had watches and knew when to leave, but others would hear a bell or a parent would drive by to tell them to come home.

Sometimes, when there weren't enough kids to play a team sport, we would go down to the edge of Cooper River and race bottle caps in the water. This involved, first of all, finding a metal bottle cap, which was usually pretty easy to do, and then placing it in the water upside-down so that it would float like a raft. If the river was flowing hard, the caps would move fast. If not, they just kind of sat there. Naturally, we had to compete to see whose cap went faster and farther. In the end, it almost always devolved into throwing stones to try to sink the opponents' bottle caps. We would sometimes play the same game in the gutters on Burrwood Avenue. Burrwood was good for this game, since it was slightly downhill from our house toward the higher-numbered houses. After it rained, we would find bottle caps and race them on the rainwater flowing down the street. This was a little trickier than on the river, since the turbulence would sometimes sink the cap, or the cap would get caught up in some leaves or debris. In that case, you were allowed to free your bottle cap and continue the race, like a free drop in golf.

In the fall, we would often go to Scott Welden's house to catch leaves. The Weldens had an enormous oak tree in their backyard and in the fall leaves would rain down in the wind. We would stand in the front yard and on the street and try to catch the leaves as they helicoptered down. This was not quite as easy as it sounds, since it was windy, and large oak leaves tend to behave erratically in the wind. We could amuse ourselves for hours.

If the leaves weren't falling and we couldn't round up enough kids to play tackle football at the river, we would settle for playing football in the street on Burrwood. This only required four kids, but it did have its challenges. For one thing, Burrwood was pretty narrow. For another, it had curbs, which resulted in a lot of falling down. The biggest challenge was the trees. Burrwood was lined with hundreds of trees and they all had low-hanging branches. So low, in fact, that it was hard to throw a pass more than 10 or 12 feet down the street without hitting one. Since three completions in a four-down series resulted in a first down, we resorted to throwing passes which advanced the ball a couple of feet at a time, until we finally came to a spot where there was an opening between the branches and we could finally attempt a longer pass. The "field" was about two blocks long, so it was pretty rare to actually score a touchdown by advancing the ball a couple of feet at a time. Extra points were made by kicking the ball off of a tee and over the electric and telephone wires.

The fall also meant yard work, especially raking leaves, the bane of kids' existence, exceeded only by having to "do the dishes." Raking isn't much fun and I don't remember leaf blowers back then, but the reward was sometimes worth the work. In those days, there were two options for leaves. Rake them into the gutter and wait for the leaf-sucker to come and pick them up, or do what most of the people in the neighborhood did - burn them right on the street in the gutter. We usually opted for the latter if the leaves weren't too wet. When we had a large pile of leaves in the gutter, my father would come out and light them. Fire is always captivating for kids, and I was allowed to "tend the fire" and rake more leaves and throw sticks into the conflagration. We got some pretty good fires going and would often see several piles burning up and down the street. On fall weekends, the whole neighborhood usually smelled like a forest fire. No houses were lost in our neighborhood, but I'm quite sure others elsewhere were.

While the fall meant playing football, catching leaves and yardwork, outside in the summer meant mosquito trucks. Mosquito trucks were common in our neighborhood and were a source of great excitement for the kids. The trucks could be heard from miles away as they approached our neighborhood, white smoke pouring out behind them. Once we heard the truck coming, we bolted outside to grab our bikes. It was much more fun than decorating our bikes (which took work) and riding in the Fourth of July parade. We would ride and run and dance through the sweet-smelling fog of DDT that enveloped the street. We were lucky to grow up back then, when we could inhale all the toxins in the world without worry or fear. Nowadays, you can't eat a peanut within ¼ mile of a kid without being reported to the Department of Child and Family Services.

One summer, we spent virtually every day playing a game that we had invented using a tennis racket and plastic golf balls. We also played this game at Cooper River, usually me, Kevin Manns and Scott Welden. At Cooper River, on South Park Drive at the foot of Shady Lane, was an open space with two massive trees side-by-side at one end. The object of the game was to hit the plastic golf ball into one of the trees for a home run. With three players, one would pitch, one would bat, and one would play the outfield. The pitcher and outfielder had to catch three fly balls to retire the team that was at bat. Whoever was batting chose a real major league team and, because we knew every team's entire lineup, would bat those players in order and from the correct side of the plate. Whoever chose the Phillies, for example, would bat Tony Taylor and Dick Allen right-handed; Johnny Callison, Clay Dalrymple and Wes Covington left-handed; and so on through the lineup. The highlights of the games were always when an outfielder "robbed" the batter of a home run by catching a ball as it cascaded down out of a tree, which we deemed to be a legal catch. The lowlights were when the plastic golf ball stayed in the tree and we had to throw sticks and rocks at it to try to knock it down, or, even worse, when a passing car would run over the ball.

Of course, being kids, we loved watching cartoons and all kinds of kid shows. We all watched *Captain Kangaroo*, which featured the *Tom Terrific* cartoons. Everyone, especially the boys, watched *Popeye Theater*, featuring Philadelphia legend Sally Starr, dressed up as a cowgirl and showing *Popeye* cartoons on afternoon television. Rumors of Sally appearing in some porn film didn't reach us until much later. There was *Pixanne*, a Philadelphia-based show starring a woman dressed up like a pixie who flew across the stage *a la* Peter Pan and sang to puppets. Colin McGrath and I especially liked the *8th Man* cartoons from Japan, featuring Tobor (Robot spelled backwards), the 8th Man, a Superman/Million Dollar Man kind of character who renewed his strength by smoking special cigarettes stored in his belt buckle. And we watched all of the *Looney Tunes* characters - Bugs Bunny, Daffy Duck, Elmer Fudd, Porky Pig, Tweety and Sylvester, Yosemite Sam and Foghorn Leghorn. When we got a little older, we transitioned into the Marvel Comics cartoons, with Captain America, Spiderman and the Hulk.

Of all the *Looney Tunes* characters, the Road Runner was, by far, my favorite. Everyone loved seeing Wile E. Coyote foiled in his extravagant attempts to capture and eat the Road Runner. The lengths and expense to which Wile E. Coyote went were extraordinary. It wasn't until much later that I realized that the cartoon wasn't about a canine and a bird and nature's hunter/hunted divide. It was about the utter futility of violence and the Road Runner's resistance to, and refusal to participate, in it. At least when I was a kid, the Road Runner never did anything to affirmatively harm Wile E. Coyote, but rather let the coyote's obsession with violence result only in harm to himself. I'll bet that Mahatma Gandhi would have been a fan of the Road Runner.

When we were around 10 or 11 years old, Coca Cola issued bottle caps with football players pictured on the inside. To see the player, you had to peel off the cork lining of the bottle cap, which was not entirely easy, but would pass the time. There was a Coca Cola plant at the airport circle in Pennsauken and you could stop in and pick up a large sheet of paper onto which you would glue the bottle caps in the appropriate circle. If you got a certain number, or completed an entire team, you would take the sheet in and redeem it for prizes, like rubber footballs or other trinkets. Obviously, you would have to drink a lot of Coke to complete a sheet. We came up with an alternative to drinking gallon upon gallon of Coke, which was, of course, the Coca Cola Company's hustle.

We, and I think the crew included Kevin Manns, Scott Welden, Jules Sacchetti and Steve Ibbeken at least, would hop on our bicycles and ride up and down Haddon Avenue, the main commercial thoroughfare in Collingswood and Westmont, and stop at every soda machine that sold Coke, usually at gas stations. Coke came in glass bottles and the machines had bottle cap removers built in. When the cap was removed, it would drop into a little collection bucket inside the machine. Even with our young hands, it was tough to reach down into the collection till and successfully extricate many caps. We had discovered that by using a large magnet, and I had a large red horseshoe one, we could put the magnet outside of where the collection bucket was located and slide the magnet up toward the opening, bringing the caps within reach of our fingers. It often took several swipes to get most of the caps out. The nicer gas station owners would unlock the machine and simply give us the bottle caps, the meaner ones would chase us away. By the time we completed the circuit, we usually had several dozen, if not several hundred Coke bottle caps. We would divide them up, peel the corks, make trades, and glue them to our sheets. I know that I won a couple of prizes, and I think that everyone else did, too.

Also located on Haddon Avenue was the Westmont Theatre, a classic movie theater built in 1927. It was the go-to place for high school couples and first dates. When Steven Spielberg was a kid living in Haddon

Township, he saw *The Greatest Show on Earth* at the Westmont Theatre, which he claims inspired him to become a director. Anyway, I spent a lot of time at the theater as a kid. I still remember the burgundy rug and curtains in the lobby, which always smelled of buttered popcorn. On Saturdays, the theater would sometimes have sci-fi double features, which my friends and I would go to, plunking down the nickel, dime or quarter that it would take to get in. They were mostly low-budget B movies, but we weren't there as critics, just as kids wanting a good scare. The only one I remember seeing was *The Angry Red Planet*

I also saw some real movies there, like *The Guns of Navarone*, *Thunderball* and the terrifying *Wait Until Dark*. As a complete aside, I have the same birthday as Audrey Hepburn, who received an Academy Award nomination as Best Actress for her performance in *Wait Until Dark*. In a sign of how different, and not necessarily in a good way, things are today, the old Westmont Theatre is now, sadly, a Planet Fitness. At least they kept the theater's marquee.

On Haddon Avenue, two blocks west of the Westmont Theatre, was another local treasure - the Collmont Diner. The Collmont had its rightful place in South Jersey diner culture, along with Olga's Diner in Marlton, the Oaklyn Diner, Ponzio's in Cherry Hill and dozens of others. The Collmont was a classic, complete with Formica and stainless steel siding. What set the Collmont apart was the full-sized restaurant and banquet facility which had been added on. It was in the restaurant that I became a connoisseur of two of life's childhood treats - sugar cubes and butter pats. When I was a kid, our family sometimes went to the Collmont for dinner. The Collmont, like a lot of other restaurants back then, placed butter pats (think quarter-inch thick slices from a stick of butter) on the table to go with the meal. I would take a pat from the plate, peel the little piece of waxy paper from the top, and eat the butter. Usually, after around four or five pats, my parents would make me stop. If I had reached my limit, I would turn to eating the sugar cubes, which were exactly what they sounded like - cubes of sugar. They were designed to go in coffee - not to be eaten - but that didn't matter. It's a wonder I've lived to be this old.

We used to walk past the Collmont on our way home from junior high and high school. Occasionally, if someone had a leftover nickel or dime from his lunch money, we would stop in. In the small lobby, there were bakery items as well as an ice cream freezer. On one particular day, we were walking home from school during a blackout. I'm not sure whether we were dismissed early that day, but a blackout was underway. Back in the 60's, it seemed like every time someone crashed into a telephone pole near Utica or some such place, 40 million people on the East Coast lost their power. The blackout brought us incredible good fortune. With no power, the ice cream in the freezer was going to melt, and when we went in, the woman at the counter told us to take whatever we wanted. You can't lose with free ice cream sandwiches.

Occasionally, we would do things that were organized by adults. A bunch of us joined a bowling league for kids on Saturday mornings. We would all get on our bicycles and ride up Cuthbert Boulevard to Baker Lanes, a pretty large bowling alley. No parent in their right mind would let their kid ride a bicycle on that stretch of road today. My team was called "The Little Dinkers" and Jules was my teammate. Neither of us were very good bowlers, but I was better than Jules. My average was probably around 115-120, while Jules was probably barely above 100. Although we weren't good bowlers, we were highly competitive in the league, since our low averages meant that we were always awarded a boatload of pins as a handicap, probably 40-60 pins a week, depending on who we were playing. We could beat the better teams just by bowling a little bit better than average and adding our handicap pins.

Once the bowling was over, we headed to the snack bar for a cheap burger or hot dog and soda. We always liked sitting on the red swivel stools and spinning around as fast as we could. Baker Lanes also had three or four pinball machines, and if anyone had some spare change, we would play pinball before heading home for whatever we were going to do next on a Saturday afternoon. One of the pinball machines was baseball-themed and you could hit various tabs at the top for a single, double, triple or home run. One of us hit the silver pinball with the flippers at just the right speed and it got wedged against the "double" tab, resulting in the machine registering double after double after double after double, until we had amassed dozens of free games.

All of us boys, of course, played Little League baseball starting at six or seven years old. We played at the athletic complex on Crystal Lake Avenue, which had at least four baseball fields, a football field and two softball fields at the time. In the "minors," I was a catcher and second baseman, primarily. Once, at around seven years old, I was playing second base and fielded a grounder. I managed to tag the baserunner heading for second base with my glove, which was the correct thing to do. However, I was holding the ball in my bare hand when doing so, which is the incorrect thing to do. The umpire called the runner safe, which was the right call, but still a little mean. That play haunts me 60 years later.

The "majors" were for 10-12 year-olds, and to make the majors, you had to have a tryout and get selected by a team. As a 10-year-old, I was drafted and went through preseason practice with a team, but ended up being the last person cut and sent back to the minors. I was beaten out by Ed Day. The manager said that it was because Day batted left-handed and he didn't have any lefties on the team. It was really because Ed was better. Adults think kids are stupid.

The next year, I made the majors with the Westmont Lions. When I was 11 we were OK, but when I was 12, we actually won the championship. After starting the season 4-4, we won our final seven games once our coaches discovered that Gary Rab was the best pitcher in the league and elected to have him pitch every single game. You're not allowed to do that these days, for any number of reasons, but I really don't remember Gary being any the worse for it.

For some reason, my parents never bought me a decent bike. I don't want to sound like an ungrateful brat, because I was pretty spoiled as a kid and had lots of stuff that most kids never had. I just never got a decent bike, that's all. It seemed like everyone else had a good bike, a sting ray, or at least something with inflatable tires. Mine was a hand-me-down, a monster of a bike with solid rubber tires. It probably weighed on the order of six or seven hundred pounds and required a herculean effort to peddle. It could destroy anything in its path. In a head-on between that bike and a Volkswagen bus, I'd bet on the bike. I hated that bike and never 100% forgave my parents for making me ride it, because we went almost everywhere by bicycle.

The only thing that seriously interfered with our play was work. A lot of us, me included, were introduced to the notion of working for money by the paper route. I got mine when I was 11 or 12 years old, delivering the *Courier-Post* to about 50 houses on Burrwood Avenue, Tatem Avenue and Shady Lane. The *Courier-Post* was an afternoon paper which we would rush to deliver after school or in the summer so that we could get to the important business of playing. Charlie had affixed an enormous basket to hold the newspapers to the front of my bike, adding yet more weight to its already hefty mass. Throw in the weight of 50 newspapers and it would take nearly half-a-mile to brake to a complete stop once it got moving. Not with hand brakes, either, but with an old-fashioned, counter-clockwise, back-peddle.

There were two possible strategies in delivering the papers. Pick them up and take a few minutes to fold and rubber-band all of them before starting delivery, or fold and rubber-band while riding, a much trickier maneuver and the one which I usually employed. It also helped to ride on the sidewalk with my right side nearest to the houses, so that, being right-handed, I could toss them with an across-the-body motion, like throwing a frisbee, using my right hand. Folding, rubber-banding and throwing all along the route, without stopping, required a masterful choreography and was a thing of beauty. It took some skill to get the paper to where it was supposed to land. Some of the fussier subscribers wanted the paper in a particular place, like on the porch, steps, or particular section of walkway. None wanted it in the bushes or under a car, where it occasionally came to rest.

The *Courier-Post* was published Monday through Saturday, meaning that I had a six-day work week. Collection day was Friday, when I would have to stop at each house and get paid. That made the 20-minute paper route last for a couple of hours. I had to stop, ring the doorbell, hope someone would answer and then wait until the homeowner scrounged up 42 cents, since the paper cost seven cents per day. That meant that if everyone paid me each week, I collected $21.00 for the week, plus tips. Some people gave them, some didn't. Many would give me 45 or 50 cents. The weight of so much coinage made peddling the old bike that much harder. If the average tip was 5 cents, that meant that I grossed $23.50 per week. On Saturdays, I had to pay my bill to the newspaper, which was probably around $15.00, netting me around $8.50 a week for six or so hours of work. A cool $1.41 an hour, for working in the sweltering heat, freezing cold, snow and rain. And missing out on valuable play time.

Before we had paper routes, we tried to make a little money however we could. I think that I tried a lemonade stand once, but that business quickly folded. Once in a while, our neighbor, Mr. Clegg, a shut-in who I never saw wearing anything but pajamas, would pay a nickel or dime for me to go to the store where Lassie had pilfered the Wonder bread and get him a couple of empty cardboard boxes. In the winter, if it snowed, we would spend an hour or two putting on snow gear, including the dreaded galoshes with buckles. Perhaps it was just the ones that I had to wear, but the buckles on those things were nearly impossible to snap closed and could leave a person without any flesh on a finger that was in the wrong place at the wrong time. It sometimes required several people to get me snapped into those galoshes. Once snapped in, there was a fairly good chance that there would be little to no blood flow to one's feet until, by the grace of God, the galoshes came off. It was in the snow shoveling business that we learned about capitalism and competition.

Usually, by the time that I was able to get all of my snow gear on, meet up with my friends and fellow shovelers, and get outside to go knocking on doors, there were scores of kids going up and down every street in the area trying to find someone who needed their driveway or sidewalk shoveled. If we were lucky, we would knock on the right door at the right time and find a customer. Whatever price we quoted, the homeowner would offer less, which we had to agree to, because we didn't have any other takers. So we usually shoveled an entire property, which the homeowner would invariably inspect and frown at, to make $3 or $5 dollars to split among us.

At the foot of New Jersey Avenue there was a playground. Not a nice, safe playground like the ones we have today, but one filled with death traps like the one pictured. I have no idea what these things are called, or who was sadistic enough to invent them, but the playground was full of such horrors. Monkey bars, where we watched with a mixture of

fascination and fright as a kid named Timmy Mead dropped to the ground and broke his wrist; seesaws, where the person on the low end would jump off and send the other kid crashing to the ground, resulting in many a bruised coccyx; swings on metal chains, more or less anchored into the ground; merry-go-round contraptions which, if spun fast enough, could launch a sitting kid backwards and airborne at about 3 or 4 G's; and metal sliding boards, which could easily reach temperatures of 400-500 degrees in the summer and which would cause third or fourth-degree burns to the legs of any kid stupid enough to slide down while wearing shorts. Plaintiffs' lawyers finally killed all of those wonderful things.

Plaintiffs' lawyers and helicopter parents have nearly succeeded in ruining childhood. Kids used to be able to play with things like Atomic Energy Laboratory, which contained real radioactive stuff; Snacktime Cabbage Patch Kid, whose "real chewing action" often targeted kids' fingers and hair; Lawn Darts, simply one of the best games ever, with heavy metal pointed tips perfect for lobbing toward friends' feet; Clackers, which made a great sound when the acrylic balls banged together and occasionally shattered into flying death shards; Splash-Off Water Rockets (which I had and loved), where a hose was used to build up pressure to launch a hard plastic rocket up into the air and, on occasion, directly at a playmate or into a window; and Easy-Bake Oven, the perfect childrens' toy, which could actually reach a temperature of 400 degrees, just right for that five-year-old future *James Beard Award* winner. Some folks are now going after sidewalk chalk because - SURPRISE! - it releases dust that can be breathed in. The anti-chalkers obviously never received the greatest honor an elementary school kid could receive - being asked by the teacher to erase the blackboard and clap the chalk dust out of the erasers.

We would play a game on the contraption shown above that involved three kids hanging onto the poles in the center. The rest of us would stand on the top rungs and wait, which gave us lots of time to work up good loogies. The first kid who slid down the pole to the ground would be spat upon until he was able to escape to the outside. Only the last of the three pole-huggers escaped without consequences. It was hours of disgusting, spit-soaked fun.

If it rained, we had to entertain ourselves indoors, much to the dismay of our mothers, who were almost all stay-at-homes back then. One popular indoor game involved moving all of the furniture in the living room of the host and playing card baseball. Since we all had loads of baseball cards, we could make entire major league teams from them. Once the furniture was moved out of, or at least to the side of the living room, the team playing defense would place his cards in their appropriate spots in the field. If the

Orioles were playing, we would have a Brooks Robinson card at third, a Luis Aparicio card at shortstop, Boog Powell at first, et cetera, et cetera. Whoever was batting would hold the card of the player at bat in either his right or left hand, while kneeled down, and hit a little wad of salivated, rolled-up paper, which served as the ball.

The team in the field would have to use the thumb and index finger to flick one of the fielders to where the wad of paper landed. If he hit the wad on the first flick, he was deemed to have caught the ball. Otherwise, it was in play. Then, the batter would likewise flick the batter's card toward first base, which he had to hit in order to be safe. If the fielder reached the wad of paper, he could then throw it to another card, which he had to hit, in order for that player to have the ball. If it was thrown to first base and hit the first baseman before the batter touched first, he was out. Complicated stuff. These games went on for hours.

The key to the entire game was getting the wad of paper that would serve as the ball just right. It had to be hard enough not to come apart when hit, but not so hard that it flew too far, leading to nothing but home runs, which were batted balls that landed over the row of books we had set up as the outfield wall, or that landed on the stairs, or that flew over the piano, depending on whose house we were playing at. Newspaper didn't work well, since it was too soft. We found that writing paper from a notebook served the purpose quite well, not fraying too much or flying too far. Unfortunately, balls were often lost by rolling under pianos or by occasionally going down heating registers, which most of the houses had. In that case, the game was halted so that we could chew on some more paper to make a new ball.

Not everything was fun and games, though. Sometimes we got into a little bit of mischief. Like the time that Jules and I, for reasons known but to God, decided that it would be a good idea to combine a cherry bomb with gasoline. We had secured the pyrotechnic and found an empty gable top paperboard milk carton, probably a quart. We filled it with about a cup or so of gasoline from Jules' garage. Not really thinking through exactly what might happen, we put the milk carton on the front lawn of Jules' next-door-neighbor's house, belonging to a nasty old woman who always chased us away from her property. We lit the fuse and dropped the cherry bomb into the gasoline.

The best way to describe what happened next is to imagine an explosion at an oil refinery. The milk carton went "boom," rattling neighborhood windows and sending a column of flame and thick black smoke about twenty-five feet into the air. Somewhat surprised by our success, but also a little bit shaken, we stomped out the pieces of burning milk carton scattered about the lawn and ran like hell, probably to hide behind the garage. With the wisdom that comes with age and experience, we never tried that again.

I'm not sure why, exactly, but at one time I had a "pet" pigeon named "Lillypidge." I kept it (despite the name, I have no idea about the bird's sex) in a rabbit hutch in our back yard. Why I would even want one of those filthy birds is troubling, but apparently, I did. There were always quite a few pigeons in our back yard, since Marge was constantly feeding the birds. Pigeons, being slow and lazy, were a fairly easy target. We (Charlie and I) set up a large box in the yard, upside down, propped up by a stick with a string attached. We ran the string across the yard and into a basement window, from which I could watch. The plan was that when a pigeon walked under the box to get some of the seed we had placed there, I would pull the string, the box would fall and trap the pigeon and we would grab it and take it to the rabbit hutch. It actually worked, and I now had Lillypidge for my very own.

Honestly, pigeons in rabbit hutches don't make very good pets. You can't walk them, can't play with them, can't teach them tricks. They just eat and drop guano everywhere. Not to mention that they can't fly or do anything bird-like when stuck in a rabbit hutch. But I loved Lillypidge anyway, right to the end.

Every parent lies to their kids. We all swear that we never will, but we all do. From Santa Claus (the mother of all lies) to the Easter Bunny, to telling them that carrots and lima beans taste good, we lie to them in ways both big and small. One day I came home and the rabbit hutch was empty. I asked my mother where Lillypidge was and she told me that he/she had gotten loose and flown away. I asked some probing questions, but finally accepted the fact that he/she was free. As I came to find out many years later - thanks, I think, to Jules - Lillypidge had not, in fact, flown away. He/she had gone to that big birdcage in the sky. My best guess is that Lillypidge had died from boredom. My mother, unbeknownst to me for decades, had gathered my friends together when they were all playing in my yard and advised them, in the strongest terms, *not* to tell me that my pigeon had croaked. They obeyed, and I spent the balance of my youth believing that Lillypidge was living wild and free, like all creatures should.

It was a great time and place to grow up. No helicopter parents, not too many worries, no neighborhood tragedies that I can remember. We just did stuff that kids do. Playing king of the hill on New Jersey Avenue, tackle football in my tiny backyard, swimming or playing hide-the-belt at the Ibbekens' house, kick the can or pool at the Sacchettis' house, stickball at Strawbridge School, bicycle tag all around town. It was all so simple, but so complex. Learning how to be kids, but also growing up at the same time. Learning how to be friends while learning how to be ourselves. Competing with each other, but also taking care of each other. If only I could spend one day back there.

* * *

One last thing . . . I am well-known for getting up in the middle of the night to pee. Ever since I was a little kid, but even more so now that I'm an old man. I suspect that I have an unusually small bladder. One night when I was young, I got up for my nightly walk to the bathroom. It was only a few feet from the bedroom and I knew that path well, even in the dark. Little did I know that Lassie had also needed to use the bathroom that night and I stepped, barefooted, in what she had left. Dead center. And Lassie was a big dog, if you get my drift. I felt it ooze up between each of my five toes. Now, anyone who has had the misfortune to step on such a thing knows that it immediately releases all of the aromatics. As it oozed between my toes, it also assaulted by nose. I did what any kid would do in that situation - cried out for my mommy (fathers aren't really cut out for this kind of emergency). Marge raced in, cleaned up my dirty foot, and sent me back to bed. Not before I finally peed, though.

Lassie stayed with us throughout almost my entire public school years. My parents had to put her down at 12 years old during my senior year. Every dog I've had, in the end, reminded me of what Agnes Sligh Turnbull said - "Dogs' lives are too short. Their only fault, really."

CHAPTER 3

FRIDAY, NOVEMBER 22, 1963

I was sitting in my 4th grade classroom on the second floor at Strawbridge School on Friday afternoon, excited about the end of the school week, when the classroom phone rang. That didn't happen very often. Mrs. Parker answered. The phone hung by the door to our classroom and had a long cord, and Mrs. Parker went out into the hallway to talk, which was also unusual.

I'm not sure if we were dismissed early. Walter Cronkite didn't announce the shooting until 1:40, nor Kennedy's death until 2:00. School normally ended around 3:15 or 3:30 and we did have a class discussion about what Mrs. Parker had been told on that phone call. We walked home together like normal, a straight walk of about a mile down Emerald Avenue to Burrwood, stopping only for the traffic light on Cuthbert Boulevard, comprehending something, but certainly not too much, of what had happened. When I walked into our living room, my mother was sitting in her chair, watching the television and crying.

We spent the next three days with the television on - the news about officer J.D. Tippet, Lee Harvey Oswald's arrest, Jack Ruby, Black Jack walking behind the caisson carrying Kennedy's body, the body lying in state, Jackie with the kids, JFK, Jr. saluting. It was an awful lot for a young boy to try to comprehend.

Nancy, Dylan and I went to Arlington National Cemetery once. It is a breathtaking place, almost spiritual, in its beauty and meaning. *The Tomb of the Unknown* is chilling and haunting, with the words, "Here rests in honored glory an American Soldier, known but to God." A soldier guards the tomb every minute of every day of every year. If you have never been to the changing of the guard, you really should. Having lived through the assassinations, JFK's and RFK's resting spots have a particular meaning and resonance, maybe because they represent a lot of life's "could have beens." JFK's is the more visited, with the eternal flame, but RFK's, just 50 feet away, is my favorite - a simple white cross beneath a tree, with several of his quotes inscribed nearby, including my favorite:

It is from numberless diverse acts of courage and belief that human history is shaped. Each time a man stands up for an ideal, or acts to improve the lot of others, or strikes out against injustice, he sends forth a tiny ripple of hope, and crossing each other from a million different centers of energy and daring, those ripples build a current that can sweep down the mightiest wall of oppression and resistance.

Phil Ochs may have captured the moment best in his song, "That Was the President," when he wrote:

It's not only for the leader that the sorrow hit so hard
There are greater things I'll never understand
How a man so filled with life, even death was caught off guard
That was the president and that was the man

To say that we were caught off guard doesn't do justice to the moment. Everyone watched, stunned, as the country buried its handsome young president and much of its innocence. I don't think that we have ever recovered from that day.

Most Americans, more than 60% according to some polls, believe that there was a conspiracy to kill Kennedy and that Lee Harvey Oswald did not act alone. I am not one of them. The JFK conspiracy theory is probably the mother of all conspiracy theories - topped only, perhaps, by the government's coverup of UFO sightings and Area 51. Certainly bigger than the fake moon landing, filmed on a soundstage; the AIDS virus; or the "stolen" 2020 presidential election.

The assassination was always fascinating to me, maybe because it is the first real bit of history that I remember living through. I even read a good portion of the Warren Report in the library at Penn and have watched most of the documentaries about it on the History Channel. I have seen the Zapruder film hundreds, if not thousands, of times. Nevertheless, I most certainly am not an expert on all of the ballistics and technicalities of the assassination. What I do know is that a conspiracy theory, whether implicating the CIA, LBJ, Cuba or organized crime makes little sense to me.

I understand that there are questions about Oswald's marksmanship and the "magic bullet" and the grassy knoll and the acoustics of Dealey Plaza in Dallas. In the end, though, I keep coming back to one thing. If there was a successful conspiracy to assassinate the president, and that it extended all the way through Oswald and Ruby and whatever group was behind it, right through a coverup by the Warren Commission, how could it be that not one person involved, or at least with knowledge of the conspiracy, has revealed it? Not one person, either because of their conscience, or on their death bed, has confirmed any kind of conspiracy. More importantly, perhaps, that person could have made a fortune by telling the story. And no one has.

CHAPTER 4

SUNDAY, FEBRUARY 9, 1964

By 8:00 on Sunday night, our whole family was together in the living room on Burrwood Avenue. Not that we were part of a very select group. Half of the country was doing exactly what we were doing - waiting for *The Ed Sullivan Show* to start on CBS. We still had a black and white TV, like most of the other people watching. It didn't really matter, though, since the show was only broadcast in black and white, anyway. We watched *Ed Sullivan* every week (I really liked the guy who spun all of the plates, but Topo Gigio I found disturbing), so this wasn't anything different - except that it was.

My family no doubt waited through Part 2 of the episode "The Disappearance" on *Lassie* at 7:00 and through an episode entitled "Who Am I?" on *The Martian* at 7:30, which were part of our Sunday night watch list in 1964. But we were all waiting for 8:00, Dennis and I more so than Charlie and Marge.

It has been said many times that this was exactly what the country and the world needed by February. It had only been 11 weeks since the Kennedy assassination, after all. We had narrowly escaped a nuclear war over Cuba a little over a year earlier. The cold war was always running in the background of the country's consciousness. We knew that we would have to duck and cover under our desks in the seemingly inevitable event that a nuclear war started while we were in school. Really. At 8:04 p.m., Ed Sullivan announced, "Ladies and Gentlemen . . . The Beatles!"

The Beatles were on for two segments, performing "All My Loving," "Till There was You" and "She Loves You" in the first and "I Saw Her Standing There" and "I Want to Hold Your Hand" in the second. Fifteen-year-old future First Daughter Julie Nixon was in the audience, with her seventeen-year-old sister, Tricia. Davy Jones, who a year later would be cast as one of the Monkees, Beatles made-for-TV knock-offs, was on the show playing the Artful Dodger with the cast of *Oliver*. When the show was over, my father said that in six months, nobody would remember the Beatles. He apparently wasn't very impressed, or very prescient.

All we could talk about the next day in Mrs. Parker's fourth-grade class was the Beatles. Having an older brother, I was used to listening to rock and roll on the radio, particularly WIBG 99 ("Wibbage") from Philadelphia, but I had never seen or heard anything like this. The matching black suits, what appeared to be the pure joy of making music, the screaming girls and the hair.

Wibbage had an impressive array of DJs, including Hy Lit, Frank X. Feller, Joe ("the Rockin' Bird") Niagara and Dean Tyler, although Hy Lit, who referred to himself as "Hyski O'Rooney McVoutie O'Zoot," was my favorite. I would listen to all of them on our Motorola console and on my battery-powered transistor radios. I had a larger green one and a pocket-sized brown one. I grew up with Beatles music. Every new song and album was an experience. *Sgt. Pepper*, in particular, was fascinating. I bought it as soon as it came out in May of 1967, and sat on the living room floor in front of the Motorola listening, trying to identify everyone on the album cover and following along with the lyrics printed on the back jacket. I still have that album. In 1989, Nancy and I bought a house on Abbey Road in Voorhees, New Jersey (not London). We framed and hung the *Abbey Road* album jacket by our front door. Our first wedding dance was to McCartney singing, "Till There Was You," the second song the Beatles had played on *Ed Sullivan* that night. I played "Revolution No. 9" backwards to hear, "Turn me on, dead man." Disc one of the *White Album* was far better than disc two. Ed Hutto had a stereo system that could isolate tracks, and we could listen to just the vocals or just the instruments. I knew most of the supposed clues that Paul was dead. I can't tell if John said, "I'm very bored" or "I buried Paul" during the fadeout of "Strawberry Fields Forever." "Back in the U.S.S.R." is an awesome homage to the Beach Boys.

Surprisingly, the Beatles only released a total of 213 songs, accounting for just about 10 hours of music. It's almost ridiculous to try to name a top ten of my favorites, but here's a try, not in any particular order:

A Day in the Life (John)

Revolution (John)

Across the Universe (John)

Lucy in the Sky with Diamonds (John)

Help! (John)

While My Guitar Gently Weeps (George)

Here Comes the Sun (George)

Back in the U.S.S.R. (Paul)

I Saw Her Standing There (Paul)

She Loves You (John/Paul)

That's five written primarily by John, two by George, two by Paul, and one true Lennon-McCartney song. Seems about right to me. But if you asked me to make a list tomorrow, I'm quite sure it would be different. "Don't Let Me Down," "Ticket to Ride" and "We Can Work it Out" are certainly in the running. All Lennon songs, by the way.

Patricia Parker had us for an amazing year. Kennedy, the Beatles, the space race, the civil rights movement, a new heavyweight champion named Cassius Clay - and then the strange-to-our-ears sounding Muhammad Ali. Mrs. Parker was young, tall and beautiful. She kept a cat o' nine tails in the classroom closet. We were too young to appreciate that, though. Once, we went trick-or-treating at her apartment across the street from Strawbridge School. Mrs. Parker, like everyone else, gave me my worst grades in penmanship, noted that I "was a little too talkative in class," but ultimately wrote that I "performed beautifully all year." She promoted me to fifth grade on FRIDAY, JUNE 12, 1964.

For kindergarten, my teacher was Marie Rod, who let me bring Lassie in for "show and tell." Mrs. Rod's comment on my report card was, "David, although small, has shown *fine traits of leadership and ability*" [emphasis added]. And at such a young age! The year after that was Virginia Sirolli, who started teaching us the dying art of cursive writing and commented that, "David . . . can be depended upon to do his best at all times" and that, "He soaks up new work like a sponge." I was promoted to second grade on MONDAY, JUNE 12, 1961, where my teacher was Marian Foster. Mrs. Foster was a little mean, wore black, old lady shoes, didn't much care for my penmanship, but did find me to be "cooperative and prompt." The "cooperative" part hasn't much stood the test of time, but to this day I am habitually on time. She promoted me to third grade on FRIDAY, JUNE 8, 1962. Third grade was Catherine Mack, who read *Charlotte's Web* to us and cried while reading it. Mrs. Mack gave me straight E's (for "excellent") in the final marking period (well, except for that pesky "G" (for "good") in penmanship. In her comments, she called me a "dependable boy." Mrs. Mack gave me a "Certificate of Award," which read, "This Certificate is presented to David Florig a pupil in the schools of the Township of Haddon for Excellent Work in Spelling during the school year 1962-1963." I wasn't absent once and was promoted to fourth grade on THURSDAY, JUNE 13, 1963.

After Mrs. Parker was Lynne Shindle for fifth grade. Miss Shindle came to watch the boys play Little League, as all fifth grade teachers should do.

Miss Shindle also had us write and present a play about air pollution. We were ahead of the times. I have a picture from the local newspaper, although I don't know which one, taken of us performing the play. The picture is captioned:

> *Explore Air Pollution: These Haddon Township Strawbridge School [fifth] graders have taken on a public relations campaign to educate adults, County Freeholders and President Lyndon B. Johnson on problems of air pollution through their current events class. They are (back, left to right) Linda Grote, Steven Ibbeken and Rickie Divis. In front (left to right) are David Florig as 'David Hinkley' for interview, Susan Lovitt, and Victor Oberg as 'Chet Bruntley' for man on street idea.*

On my report card, Miss Shindle commented, quite accurately, that "David has a nice personality and is an asset to the class." I was promoted to sixth grade on THURSDAY, JUNE 17, 1965. Finally came Edna Fineberg for sixth grade, who gave me my worst grades in handwriting. I would have had a damn fine GPA in elementary school if we didn't get graded on penmanship. She did note that, "David's sense of humor is most welcome. I'm trying to encourage him to do a little more than what is required." I was promoted to junior high school on FRIDAY, JUNE 17, 1966, bringing to a close seven years at Strawbridge School.

I can barely remember the names of all of my relatives, but I do remember that during elementary school, Kevin and Colin McGrath had pet hamsters named Gunther and Gomer. One day, I was allowed to go over to their house for lunch rather than walk home to mine. Kevin and Colin only lived three houses away from the school, while I lived nearly a mile away. That meant more time to play after eating and we decided to play with the hamsters after lunch. We went up to the boys' bedroom, took Gunther and Gomer out, and let them scurry around as we watched. Eventually, Mrs. McGrath called up and told us that it was time to go back to school. We scrambled to get our stuff and headed back to Strawbridge. I don't recall which teacher we had at the time, but shortly after getting back to class we were told to run back to the McGrath house. In our haste, and being boys, we had forgotten to put Gunther and Gomer back in their cage and they were now roaming free somewhere in the house. I remember Mrs. McGrath as being none too happy, but after a frantic search under beds, behind bureaus and in closets, the MIA hamsters were located unharmed and returned to their rightful home.

Right down the street from the McGraths on Bradford Avenue lived another one of our classmates and friends, Victor Oberg. I'm pretty sure that it was in Mrs. Foster's second grade class that Victor had a minor incident. Kids write with pencils, not pens, and make a lot of mistakes which require erasing. Your standard Dixon Ticonderoga #2 yellow pencil is fine and all, but its eraser is far too small for the needs of a second-grader, so most of us supplemented it with one of those larger, pink-ish ones that fit over the regular eraser. Victor, somehow, someway, managed to stick the eraser end of his pencil, with the supplemental eraser, up his nose during class. Much to his surprise, I would bet, when he removed the pencil from his nose to resume writing, the eraser was no longer on the end of his pencil, but rather lodged in one of his nostrils. I'm surmising that Victor's attempts at extricating the eraser only exacerbated the problem. Burnishing her reputation for being mean, Mrs. Foster, while extracting the eraser from Victor's nose, took the opportunity to impress upon all of us the dangers of sticking things up our noses.

Victor was the biggest kid in our elementary school class, so Colin McGrath and I decided that we would make him the star of our upcoming feature film, *Zook, the Space Monster*. I don't recall all of the plot twists and turns, and we never really finished the script, but the film would basically entail ten-year-old Victor dressed up in some kind of alien monster suit while roaming the street breaking stuff and beating people up. I don't think Zook was going to have any special powers other than being bigger than us. Due largely to a lack of major studio backing and financing, the movie never made it into production.

By the time spring rolled around during sixth grade, we were ready to move on. The weather was warm, puberty was hitting some of my classmates hard and we had been stuck in the same elementary school with basically the same group of kids since the Eisenhower administration. We had grown somewhat rambunctious by the spring.

The windows in Mrs. Fineberg's second-floor classroom were the kind where you would open the latch and tilt the window inward toward the room. Of course, there were no screens on the windows, so our classroom was constantly filled with all kinds of bees, flies and other flying insects. A bee in a sixth grade classroom was a major source of both excitement and panic. The open windows also made for an easy target for throwing things out of. I have no idea how it started, but I think that someone rolled up a wad of paper and tossed it out when Mrs. Fineberg wasn't looking. This resulted in great hilarity, so someone else did it, too. Then someone else. And someone else.

Over the course of the afternoon, we tossed paper, pencils, pens, crayons, books, items of clothing and other small and large items out of that second-floor classroom window. Someone even managed to shoot some Silly String out. Amidst all of the excitement, what we hadn't taken into account was that there was a classroom with a teacher in it right below us. Whoever that teacher was, she had apparently become alarmed either by the sheer volume of material raining down past her windows or the rapidly growing amount of debris right outside. Our classroom phone rang. We were busted, but it was great fun while it lasted.

* * *

The whole country watched the Beatles that Sunday night and again the next two Sunday nights. By the end of the decade it seemed so passé, so naive, so innocent, so far removed from the world we were living in. Music and the world didn't look or sound the same when the 60's ended. Nor did we.

CHAPTER 5

SUNDAY, JUNE 21, 1964

It was Father's Day. I was listening to the radio as John Stephenson of the Mets struck out to end the game. Suddenly, boat horns were blasting in the harbor in Maryland. Everyone in my family liked the Phillies, so it was pretty common to have their games on the radio or television in the summer. This game was special, though, since Jim Bunning had just pitched the first regular season perfect game in the major leagues since 1922. Don Larsen, of course, had pitched the most famous perfect game eight years earlier during the 1956 *World Series*.

At some point in the early 60's, my parents decided to buy a boat on the Chesapeake. When I say "my parents," I mean my father. A 22-foot cabin cruiser which they named *Dendave*. Not every boy gets to have a boat named after him. After a year or two, "my parents" traded that one in for a 30-foot Chris-Craft, which they gave the same name. My mother was never really thrilled about having a boat. That's about the nicest way of saying it. She spent quite a bit of time seasick, but was pretty stoic about it, as she was in most things. We all, including Lassie, spent most summer weekends from Friday night until late Sunday afternoon on the boat and sometimes spent an entire week there when my father was on vacation.

There are lots of things for boys to do when their parents own a boat, some good, some not as good. In the springtime, when the boat is still out of the water, there is a lot of work to do to get it ready. The worst job, by far, is scraping barnacles off the hull. Charlie and Marge would make Dennis and I help with that nasty bit of business, but we really didn't take to it that well. Not only were we made to work, but we were away from our friends for the weekend and not even on the water. It's mindless, boring, laborious, tedious work. Like my lifelong dream job - toll taker. A job you don't take home with you. Although I'm sure we complied for a little while, there were far more fun things for boys to get into at a boatyard than scraping barnacles. And most kids know that if they annoy their parents long enough, they'll eventually be released from duty. Our marina had a wooded area and a tall earthen embankment behind the main building. When we had made ourselves enough of an annoyance to Charlie and Marge, we went back there to play.

Boys, of course, like to throw things. I know that this is sexist and stereotyping and all of that bad stuff, but it's true. It's genetic. It's next to the eye color genes, OCA2 and HERC2. Dennis threw left handed, I'm a rightie. Dennis, being four years older and much bigger than I was, usually prevailed at whatever contest we got into with each other. We eventually settled into picking up clumps of dirt and hard red clay and throwing them at each other. The clumps would immediately break apart when they hit something, including either of us, although that didn't happen that often. It didn't hurt and it was fun to occasionally land one on my older brother. I had probably just finished an assault when I turned to run away and grab more clumps.

My brother had the high ground, standing on top of the embankment, when he caught me in the back of the head with one. To be honest, it must have been a pretty good toss. I should have been wearing a hat. I instinctively reached for where I had been hit, although I don't remember it hurting, more out of reflex than anything. It was pretty bloody. I started crying and wailing and went running for my parents. I was afraid of the bleeding, Dennis was afraid of the repercussions, which were sure to follow. All work on the boat stopped while I was taken to the hospital, had part of my scalp shaved, and got sewn up. It was my first, but not last, experience with getting stitches.

Stitches aren't really too bad and I probably didn't have more than three or four of them. What's bad is having part of your head shaved and having to show up at school with it like that. Kids instinctively recognize weaknesses in their peers, and having a bald spot on my head was a serious vulnerability. My teacher, Mrs. Mack perhaps, was very kind and kept my classmates from pointing and staring and making fun of my shaved head as best she could.

Dennis also broke my collarbone, although, again, quite by accident. We were playing catch with a baseball in the backyard. I was really young - six, seven, maybe eight. He threw one that I completely missed and it hit me in the collarbone. It hurt, and I ran inside to show my parents. They diagnosed the situation and decided that I was sore, but fine. I disagreed, but they prevailed for the moment. Sometime in the next day or two, I went to sit down on the toilet and heard a crack in my shoulder, and now it really hurt. This time, my parents concluded that I did, indeed, need to go to the hospital.

I had a broken collarbone, which isn't much fun in and of itself. It required wearing a sling for a few weeks and generally took me out of the neighborhood festivities with my friends. To add insult to injury, because my collarbone was broken, I could not raise my arm over my head to take off my shirt. This is one of those traumatic, life-defining moments that people remember, although there is absolutely no real reason to. When I sat down on that toilet, I was wearing my favorite tee shirt, the one with the picture of New Jersey on it. And the doctor, kindly though he surely was, took out his scissors and cut the shirt off of me. Although Charlie and Marge promised at the hospital that they would get me a new one, they never did.

I suffered some other childhood trauma, too. We took summer vacations, like most families. A few times, we went to Maine or New Hampshire and rented a house on a lake. I can remember three times specifically, different houses on different lakes, but can't say where or when it was, other than the early 1960's. At one of those rentals, I was playing with my Texaco Tanker, my favorite toy at the time. I'm thinking that it was the summer of 1962, because I remember hearing "My Daddy is President" on the radio while we were there. The Texaco Tanker was 27 inches long, battery-operated, and made of mostly metal, not the cheap plastic stuff like they use today. It actually had a rudder and you could operate it in the water. I believe you had to buy some gas and plunk down $3.98 at a Texaco gas station to get one back in 1961. Anyway, I was playing in the lake with the tanker, when, somehow, it sank. To the bottom. Over my head. Frantically, I implored Charlie to rescue it.

Because the water was so clear, I could see my beloved ship lying on the bottom, *Titanic*-like, only in about 10, not 12,000 feet of water. I don't know whether I was being punished for something or not, but Charlie waited until the last day of our vacation to raise my toy. He got into a rowboat and went out to the site of the sinking, hooked up a fishing pole, dropped his line, snared the Texaco Tanker, and slowly reeled it to the surface. I had my toy back, but not until after a lot of worry.

Around this time at Strawbridge School, we had a music teacher named Mrs. Long. There was apparently some kind of contest to select an official state song for New Jersey and she wrote one titled, "New Jersey, Our State." Leave it to New Jersey to be the only state never to have adopted an official state song. On music days, Mrs. Long would have us sing the song over and over and over and over again while she recorded it to submit. As nearly as I can remember, the lyrics, or at least some of them, were:

New Jersey, our state, all our best is addressed to you
New Jersey, our state, we'll keep abreast of the times with you
At work and at play we will lead our nation all the way
Once again we're here to tell the many ways that we excel
In New Jersey, the state that is great, great, great
In New Jersey, the Garden State

Whatever kind of contest there was, "New Jersey, Our State" didn't win. Nor did any other song. In 1972, New Jersey came *this* close to finally adopting a state song. Both houses of the state legislature voted "I'm From New Jersey" to become the official state song, but Governor William Cahill, a Republican, to his everlasting credit, vetoed the bill. "I'm From New Jersey" is a perfectly awful, insipid song, both musically and lyrically. The lyrics were:

I know of a state that's a perfect playland with white sandy beaches by the sea
With fun-filled mountains, lake and parks, and folks with hospitality
With historic towns where battles were fought, and presidents have made their home
It's called New Jersey and I toast and tout it wherever I may roam, 'cause

I'm from New Jersey and I'm proud about it, I love the Garden State
I'm from New Jersey and I want to shout it, I think it's simply great
All of the other states throughout the nation may mean a lot to some
But I wouldn't want another, Jersey is like no other, I'm glad that's where I'm from

If you want glamour, try Atlantic City or Wildwood by the
sea
Then there is Trenton, Princeton, and Fort Monmouth, they
all made history
Each little town has got that certain something, from High
Point to Cape May
And some place like Mantoloking, Phillipsburg, or Hoboken
will steal your heart away

Have you ever been to Atlantic City? "Glamour" is not a word that jumps immediately to mind.

There were many happier times on the boat, of course. We fished for catfish, caught blue-claw crabs using chicken wings on string as bait, went underneath bridges and even spent a day or two in Annapolis during one of my father's vacations. Sometimes, my father would let me sit in the captain's chair and "drive" the boat. We went swimming with Lassie, and on one or two occasions, I was allowed to have a friend come down with us for the weekend. I skipped all of the stones I wanted, learned to drink powdered milk because the icebox was too small for fresh milk, slept in the top bunk and fell out once, caught a snake in a bucket, stuck my head up through the hatch on the bow while we cruised and rowed around in an inflatable raft. I also played a game at the marina which consisted of finding a glass soda bottle (they were all made of glass back then) and throwing it out into the water so that it would stay afloat, with the neck sticking up out of the water. I would then stand on the beach and try to sink it by hitting it with a stone and breaking it. Not quite as easy to do as you might think.

In Delaware, on the route home from the boat near Wilmington, was a little roadside place that sold "foot-long hot dogs." It was too enticing to pass up. What kid can pass up on a place with a neon sign advertising foot-longs? On Sunday nights, driving home from Maryland, we would often stop there, grab some dogs, and eat them during the rest of the ride home. I'm not sure if this is related, but we did pull off to the side of the road one time so that I could get out and puke.

Fifty years later, when Dylan, who you have not really heard about yet, was playing lacrosse in college, Nancy and I went to one of his games, at Salisbury or Virginia Wesleyan. Driving back to New Jersey, we drove through Delaware and I actually, amazingly, spotted the place, still open, still advertising foot-long hot dogs. They weren't as special as only a small boy could believe, and Nancy wasn't quite as enamored of the place as I had once been, but there was no way that I was just going to drive by.

* * *

Rick Wise, an 18 year-old rookie, pitched the second game of the doubleheader against the Mets on Father's Day, following Bunning's perfect game. It was his first win in the major leagues. The Phillies, of course, went on to one of the greatest collapses in baseball history in 1964, blowing a 6 ½ game lead with 12 games left to play by losing 10 straight in September. My father took me to the first of those 10 losses, on MONDAY, SEPTEMBER 21, 1964, when Chico Ruiz stole home with Frank Robinson at bat for a 1-0 Reds win. After the game, Phillies' manager Gene Mauch was heard through the clubhouse door yelling, "Chico f---ing Ruiz! Chico f---ing Ruiz! I can't believe it. You guys just let Chico f---ing Ruiz beat you!" I didn't know that Chico Ruiz had a middle name.

The Phillies won their final game of the 1964 season, on SUNDAY, OCTOBER 4, 1964. A loss by St. Louis would mean that the Phillies would be in a playoff to go to the *World Series*. Driving home from the boat, probably eating a foot-long as we crossed over the Delaware Memorial Bridge, we heard the score on the radio - St. Louis Cardinals 11, New York Mets 5. There would be no playoff or *World Series* for the Phillies. If you mention 1964 to any Philly sports fan, they know exactly what you mean, and will immediately start spouting all of the morbid details.

By the time I was 14, my parents had sold the *Dendave* and my father had taken up golf to fill the void. It was sad, because I was beginning to dream of the time when I could get my pilot's license and driver's license and use the boat for parties with my friends. That may have factored into their decision to sell.

CHAPTER 6

I developed my interest in politics at a pretty young age. My parents weren't active in politics, but Dennis was very interested, and politics was often a dinner table topic of conversation - and we almost always ate dinner at the dining room table. Charlie and Marge at either end, and Dennis and I on either side, me to Charlie's right and Marge's left, and Dennis to Charlie's left and Marge's right. Always at the same seats and always in the dining room. The meal was always prepared by Marge. We usually ate at around 5:30, shortly after Charlie got home from work. He would generally still be wearing his suit, maybe without the jacket, when we ate. He often had a pocket protector, too. Despite the occasional ink stain on our shirt pockets, we kids wouldn't be caught dead with pocket protectors. We'd rather throw out our favorite shirt than suffer that indignity.

There were certain staples and a kind of comfort in the repetitiveness and predictability of it. We usually had steak once a week, along with a fairly consistent diet of tuna casserole (not my favorite), meat loaf, pork chops, cornish hens, liver and onions on occasion, mashed potatoes, peas and rolls. We drank either whole milk or iced tea, which Marge would steep in a pitcher on the kitchen window sill. There was often homemade cake or pudding (butterscotch being my favorite) for dessert. If not, there was usually ice cream in the fridge. On many Saturdays, I would go with Charlie to the McDonald's on Route 38 and pick up supper for the family. Hamburgers, fries and milkshakes were 15 cents each. Charlie would usually get an extra order of fries which we would eat in conspiratorial secrecy on the ride home.

On rare occasions, we would have "specials." For instance, Charlie once brought home bear steaks that someone had given him. I doubt that Marge knew how to cook bear, but she did it anyway. They were tough and gamey, and we all agreed that we didn't need to do that again. Another time, a shop in Oaklyn specializing in horse meat opened, which caused quite a local stir. Protesters picketed outside of the store, carrying signs which said things like, "Would Roy Rogers Eat Trigger?" and the like. We bought some horse steaks anyway, Marge cooked them, and we had horse for dinner. It was unlike the bear, being stringy and kind of flavorless. That was our only known experience eating horse meat. The horse meat shop was destroyed by an arsonist in 1973. "Haddon Township, Oaklyn, Haddonfield, Collingswood - they're just not horse meat-eating towns," one man opined.

A couple of times, Charlie and I went deep-sea fishing with a friend of his and ate the bluefish which we had caught. The other different meal that I remember was one Christmas, when we (Charlie, probably) decided to have goose. We bought one at a butcher shop, Marge, of course, prepared it, and we had an old-fashioned Christmas dinner with goose. As I recall, it was kind of greasy and had mostly dark meat. Certainly not as good as turkey, which we returned to in the following years.

Most of the mealtime drama when I was young revolved around my mother's insistence on making lima beans several nights a week and my enduring hatred of said beans. I was a brat about it, raising a stink every time she insisted on making them, resulting in a standoff until the issue of me eating lima beans was resolved. Reaching an armistice involved long negotiations regarding how many I had to eat, and we usually settled on seven. There was simply no way that I was going to eat lima beans straight up, so I always resorted to mixing them in with something, like mashed potatoes, and swallowing them whole. This behavior continued until I was around eighteen or twenty years old. I don't believe that I have voluntarily eaten a lima bean since then.

It was that time - the Vietnam War was escalating, students were organizing and demonstrating and sitting in, and the civil rights movement was in full throat. On THURSDAY, APRIL 4, 1968, Martin Luther King, Jr. would be assassinated in Memphis. Dennis would leave in September for American University, where he majored in political science. Later, he would publish *The Power of Presidential Ideologies* when he was teaching in South Korea. Most of my interest in politics came from talking to Dennis.

By this time, I was also consuming more news. I would read the *Philadelphia Inquirer*, the *Camden Courier-Post*, and we subscribed to *Newsweek*, which I usually read cover-to-cover. While Dennis supported Eugene McCarthy in the 1968 Democratic presidential primary, but couldn't yet vote, I was a fan of Bobby Kennedy, perhaps more because of the name and charisma than the policy, but I supported him nevertheless. When I saw that Kennedy was coming to the Camden Convention Hall on April 1st, I talked my father into taking me and Steve Ibbeken to see him. Kennedy had only announced his candidacy two weeks earlier, on SATURDAY, MARCH 16, 1968. New Jersey's primary was scheduled for TUESDAY, JUNE 4, 1968, the same day as California's.

I'm not sure how many people Convention Hall held, but the press reported that around 6,500 people attended and filled it to capacity. Not everyone there was a Kennedy supporter. There were quite a few McCarthy folks holding signs and heckling. Dennis may have been among them, but I didn't sit with him. I had never been to a political event before and it was pulsating - loudspeakers, balloons, bunting, pennants, signs. My memory of it, oddly, is in black and white, like an old photo. Lyndon Johnson had announced that he would not be running for re-election the night before, on SUNDAY, MARCH 31, 1968, which meant that Hubert Humphrey had not yet entered the race. It was Kennedy versus McCarthy. There was a palpable sense that things were changing in America.

As Kennedy spoke, he rattled off a list of perceived injustices, most involving race and poverty. After each one, he would say, "I don't think that's fair and I think we can do better!" It became a mantra of sorts. Naturally, I liked him even more after seeing him.

Three days later, on THURSDAY, APRIL 4, 1968, Kennedy was in Indianapolis under very different circumstances. He gave an improvised speech, against the advice of his staff and local law enforcement, which is considered one of the great speeches of modern American political history. Standing on a flatbed truck, in front of an almost exclusively Black audience, long before cell phones and instant news, he said:

I have bad news for you, for all of our fellow citizens, and people who love peace all over the world, and that is that Martin Luther King was shot and killed tonight. Martin Luther King dedicated his life to love and to justice for his fellow human beings, and he died because of that effort.

In this difficult day, in this difficult time for the United States, it is perhaps well to ask what kind of a nation we are and what direction we want to move in. For those of you who are black--considering the evidence there evidently is that there were white people who were responsible--you can be filled with bitterness, with hatred, and a desire for revenge. We can move in that direction as a country, in great polarization-- black people amongst black, white people amongst white, filled with hatred toward one another.

Or we can make an effort, as Martin Luther King did, to understand and to comprehend, and to replace that violence, that stain of bloodshed that has spread across our land, with an effort to understand with compassion and love.

For those of you who are Black and are tempted to be filled with hatred and distrust at the injustice of such an act, against all white people, I can only say that I feel in my own heart the same kind of feeling. I had a member of my family killed, but he was killed by a white man. But we have to make an effort in the United States, we have to make an effort to understand, to go beyond these rather difficult times.

My favorite poet was Aeschylus. He wrote: 'In our sleep, pain which cannot forget falls drop by drop upon the heart until, in our own despair, against our will, comes wisdom through the awful grace of God.'

What we need in the United States is not division; what we need in the United States is not hatred; what we need in the United States is not violence or lawlessness; but love and wisdom, and compassion toward one another, and a feeling of justice toward those who still suffer within our country, whether they be white or they be Black.

So I shall ask you tonight to return home, to say a prayer for the family of Martin Luther King, that's true, but more importantly to say a prayer for our own country, which all of us love--a prayer for understanding and that compassion of which I spoke.

We can do well in this country. We will have difficult times; we've had difficult times in the past; we will have difficult times in the future. It is not the end of violence; it is not the end of lawlessness; it is not the end of disorder. But the vast majority of white people and the vast majority of Black people in this country want to live together, want to improve the quality of our life, and want justice for all human beings who abide in our land.

Let us dedicate ourselves to what the Greeks wrote so many years ago: to tame the savageness of man and make gentle the life of this world.

Let us dedicate ourselves to that, and say a prayer for our country and for our people.

No teleprompter. No speechwriters. No script. Almost impossible to imagine today.

Indianapolis was the only major city in the United States which remained in a state of calm the night that Dr. King was assassinated. Kennedy went on to win the Indiana primary on TUESDAY, MAY 7, 1968, and, on Tuesday, June 4, lost the New Jersey primary to McCarthy, but won the California primary, giving his victory speech at the Ambassador Hotel in Los Angeles with Ethyl standing beside him. Whether he would have gotten the Democratic nomination instead of Humphrey, or defeated Nixon in the general election, we'll obviously never know. If only he had gotten the chance.

We were sitting in the music room at Haddon Township High School. The music room was different from all of the other rooms in the school because it was tiered, so that we could sing like a choir. I was in eighth grade music class with Mrs. Helen Russ and I had brought my small brown transistor radio to school with me to listen to the news.

The only song that I specifically remember singing as a class in eighth grade was "Toreador" from the opera *Carmen*. We actually kind of liked the song, but outside of class changed the lyrics to, "Toreador, be ready. Don't spit on the floor. Use the cuspidor." We found that to be pretty funny and sang our version as we walked down the hall after class.

Haddon Township still didn't have a junior high school or middle school. It didn't even have its own high school until a few years before I arrived. I would spend six years at Haddon Township High School, from seventh through twelfth grades, even crossing paths with Dennis for the first two years. Although seventh and eighth grades were technically junior high, it really didn't make much difference, since all of us, whether 12 or 18 years old, shared the same hallways, classrooms, cafeteria, gyms, lockers and bathrooms. It was more than a little intimidating the first year or two - it was sometimes frightening. During the first days of seventh grade, we sometimes had to abandon all dignity and ask an upperclassperson for directions in school, since we didn't yet know our way around, and were met with all manner of derision. On rare occasions, we got accurate directions. On others, we were directed to the non-existent elevator.

This may seem like bragging, but it really isn't. In seventh grade, I was placed in Section 701. There were also sections 702, 703, 704, 705, 706, 707 and 708. Haddon Township was pretty transparent about the hierarchy. We weren't dumb. Everyone knew that Section 701 was for the "best" students. Section 702 was for the next best, and so on down the academic chain. A few of my Strawbridge classmates were also in 701 - Kevin Manns, Steve Ibbeken, Karen Schmidt, Charlie Peffall, Rich Gant and Lee Felheimer, for sure, and maybe Gary Murza and Laurie Haines. We were thrown in together with the cream of the crop from Thomas A. Edison School, Clyde S. Jennings School, Stoy School and Van Sciver School - Ann Bogar, Ted Coyle, Larry Fink, Deborah Carey, Anne and Barbara Jacobs, Sherri May, Sandra Poots, Margie Keefe, Bob Siman, Joyce Dudley, Donna Lackman, Alvin Stern and Al Yourich, for sure, and maybe Tim McCarthy, Arlene Mayer and Ron Love.

Section 701 had Dorothy Moldoff for social studies, Kathryn Loux for English, Michael Gallagher for science and Connie Smolsky for math. My father told me that he knew Mr. Smolsky from his childhood and that Smolsky had fallen in one time when they had gone outhouse-tipping. I never brought that up to Mr. Smolsky, although it probably would have earned me some seventh-grade cred. The boys had William Rosborough for gym. Rosborough told the boys on day one that if they weren't in their proper gym clothes, they would receive a "P.U." for "partial uniform." I don't know who the girls had for gym. Our only elective was taking either Spanish or French. Being a romantic, I suppose, I chose French with Madame Phyllis Pelouze. After a semester of art, the boys moved on to shop class with G.R. Digby, while the girls took home economics. We thought that it was funny that Lee Felheimer had been assigned to shop class, apparently due to some confusion over her name.

Mary Miller taught seventh grade art. I am terrible at art - always was and certainly always will be. The worst possible game someone could suggest playing is Pictionary. I would rather play a four-hour game of Monopoly and go bankrupt than play Pictionary. I got stuck playing it once, but never again. Unlike our regular classrooms, the art room had tables, not desks. Most of the tables had either four or six kids sitting at them, which seemed like fun, especially if you were assigned to a table with some of your friends, which I wasn't. I was assigned to a table of two in the back of the room, and with a girl of all people. Nancy Sue Weil.

Nancy Weil was the first girl who ever broke my heart, although she didn't do it on purpose. It was because of her parents.

Most of the other teachers in 7th grade had us sit alphabetically by last name. That meant that I usually sat behind Larry Fink and in front of Rich Gant. It also meant that Nancy Weil was usually three rows away, so the only time I really had any interaction with her during classes was in art. At first, I don't think we talked much, but as time passed, we grew a little more comfortable with each other. I remember art being early in the day, first or second period, so there was probably plenty of seventh-grade news or gossip to catch up on. We also shared a dislike for Mary Miller. I theorized that Mrs. Miller hadn't liked my brother and was punishing me by making me sit with a girl. Her little scheme didn't work.

Note-passing was all the rage for seventh-graders - the 1966 hard copy equivalent of texting. Most news circulated through class that way. In almost any class, at some point, when the teacher turned away from the class, you could see someone surreptitiously "passing a note." Notes often came with directions, either mouthed or through hand or head gestures, to pass the note on to someone who wasn't contiguous to the note-writer, thereby putting the intermediary in jeopardy of getting caught. It wasn't good to be the intermediary for two people having an entire conversation via notes. It was also considered a breach of adolescent etiquette to unfold and read a note intended for someone else, particularly if it smacked of a budding romance. You always had to be very careful about what you wrote, since most teachers were quite proficient at sniffing out and confiscating notes. Study hall was a prime time for note-passing, since the proctor usually didn't care and there was less talking when things were being hashed-out via notes. One day in study hall, probably in late fall or early winter, I got a note from Eileen Halloran (she wasn't in 701, but was in my study hall). It said, "Nancy likes you."

"Like" is a troubling word in the boy/girl dynamic at 12 years old. I know (s)he likes me, but does (s)he *"like"* me? Does (s)he *"like like"* me? Emphasis on the first "like," How much does (s)he *"like"* me? Does (s)he just *"like me as a friend*?" The note caught me by surprise (both the notion that Nancy might "like" me and Eileen passing me a note) and it meant that I would have to decipher the note's meaning. I had never been "liked" before. It couldn't mean that she just liked me as a friend, because that wouldn't really be seventh-grade note-passing worthy. It was also very unlikely to mean that she *"like liked"* me, since we really didn't know each other all that well, just from art. The fact that Nancy had apparently disclosed this to Eileen provided a clue. After all, Nancy must have pointed me out to Eileen at some point, because Eileen and I weren't in any classes together and didn't know each other. It also meant that Nancy had apparently told Eileen that she liked me, since I doubted that Eileen would just make something as important as that up. So the meaning that I settled on was that, although the note said that Nancy "liked" me, it really meant that she *"liked"* me.

Even though I refer to her as "my seventh-grade girlfriend," she wasn't really. We never did anything together outside of school that I can remember and certainly never did anything like go on a date, or hold hands or kiss. Probably the closest we ever came to doing anything together was at a 7th and 8th grade dance, where I and some of my friends danced with her and some of her friends. No slow dancing. All of us may have gone to Green Valley Farms for ice cream after the dance, but maybe not. We saw each other at football and basketball games, too, but were always with our own group of friends. So instead of being a "girlfriend," she was more like my first real girl friend.

For reasons that I don't really know or remember, it was all pretty secretive, at least from my side. Although there were quite a few "couples" in seventh grade, I suppose I just wasn't ready to make that public of a commitment. It would have meant getting parents involved, for both transportation and financial purposes, and having to deal with whatever teasing or gossip inevitably came with being in an official relationship. The pressure would have been unbearable. So we kept it largely under wraps.

After the Eileen note and inspired by the belief that Nancy *liked* me, I decided to make the big move and call her. I doubt that I made that decision on my own, though. It seems more likely that we decided one day in art class that we would talk on the phone and she probably gave me a note with her number. Or maybe I looked it up in the phone book. I knew that she lived on Crystal Lake Avenue, so that would have made it easy to choose from the multiple "Weil" phone numbers in the Camden County phone book. Unfortunately, it was all land lines in 1966, and usually just one number per household, so that meant that parents would be involved anyway, at least at some level. Dominating the phone was a pretty serious offense in most homes, especially ones with multiple kids.

The worst part of calling any friend on the phone was the risk that a parent might answer. In that case, you would have to identify yourself and ask, "Is [friend's name] there?" It would have been far more polite to ask, "May I speak with [friend's name], please," but I usually opted for the former, as did most of my friends. Even worse than having a parent answer was the friend not being home and the parent asking, "Can I tell him (or her) what this is about?" Usually, that was fended off with a, "Could you ask him/her to call me," without any further, unnecessary, intrusive details.

Over the course of that winter, into spring, it seems like we talked on the phone for hours each night. I know that we didn't really, but we spent a lot of time on the phone, usually until a parent or sibling forced us off, or until homework called. Then, of course, we did the "You hang up first," "No, you hang up first" thing until we would finally settle on "One, two, three . . ." and hang up together. There are some universal codes of adolescent conduct, I suppose.

There must have been an awful lot to talk about, probably seventh-grade gossip, mostly. I think that we also talked about whether to go public, carefully considering the pros and cons. Those kinds of decisions have to be made with the utmost care and reflection in junior high. Usually, I would talk from my parents' bedroom, since that was where the only upstairs extension was, and where I could find a semblance of privacy. I don't know where Nancy was talking from, never having been in her house, but I'm sure she found a private place as best she could. You couldn't just stand in the kitchen and have the whole family hear. I almost always had a radio on, both for the music and to add an extra layer of privacy. We both liked, "I Think We're Alone Now," by Tommy James and the Shondells. Since our "romance" was pretty much our little secret, I think we imagined ourselves in the lyric:

Look at the way, we've gotta hide what we're doin'
'Cause what would they say if they ever knew . . .

Like anyone would have really cared. But it added to my *Romeo and Juliet* construct.

We've kept in sporadic touch over the years. I visited her one time in New York City with Becky Hutto, once in Ridgewood when we were still in high school, or maybe had just graduated, and one time in Lodi when we were both out of college, I believe. I remember those visits as being uncomfortable and conversation being difficult. Maybe it was because other people were there, or maybe we just didn't have much to talk about anymore.

Things got much better as we got older. We had some common life experiences. We both spent most of our careers as lawyers and part of them running nonprofits. We did it in reverse order though - I was a lawyer first and then in the nonprofit world, she was vice versa. We both had one child and they were close in age. I met her one time in Seattle, where she had moved years and years ago, when I was there with Kevin and Joe on a "boys' weekend" to see the Mariners, drink beer, and hike Mount Rainier. I met her one other time in Seattle in 1994 or 1995, when I had gone to see my brother, who was visiting from South Korea, to tell him that Marge was dying. I did that mostly for our mother, to tell her that I had seen him and that he was doing well.

During one of the visits to Seattle, or maybe it was on the phone, I told her something like my main regret about any of the people I had known or dated, not that there were too many, was that she and I never really had the chance to see what might have happened. I don't know what led me to say it, but it seemed right in the moment. I'm not sure that she agreed, but she did thank me for saying it. She drove me back to my hotel and I kissed her on the cheek, for the one and only time.

I still think of her sometimes when I'm reminded about something or someone from junior high or high school. It's all so sweet, so unencumbered, so uncomplicated. I guess that's because there was nothing to complicate it - no boyfriend/girlfriend drama, no jealousy, no breakup, no growing apart, not even a hug goodbye. It just ended. Not because of anything we did or decided, and certainly against our will. It was on MONDAY, MAY 1, 1967, that Nancy and her parents moved to 502 Downing Street in Ridgewood, New Jersey, about 100 miles away. To a 12 year-old boy, it might as well have been New Mexico. And my heart was broken for the first time.

We kept in pretty regular contact for a while, at least at first - letters and long-distance calls. I got in serious trouble with my parents for running up a $13 long-distance phone bill shortly after she moved. I still remember her birthday, although I'm not going to print it here. I'm pretty good about remembering birthdays. And I still remember what must have been her first letter to me after moving. She told me that on her first day at her new school she wore a yellow dress. I probably knew which one she was talking about. She also said that all of the other kids were way cool and wore sunglasses, although she was joking. I kept the letters for a few years, but eventually tossed them. Too bad - they would have been invaluable in reconstructing those days. Not to mention how much fun it would be to copy one and send it to her, just for the embarrassment factor.

* * *

Sitting in that 8th grade music class, I was listening to the news with my transistor radio to my ear. Nancy Weil had been gone for over a year and I'm pretty sure that my broken heart had mostly healed by then. I was waiting for news about Bobby Kennedy, but Mrs. Russ made me turn it off. Kennedy would die a few hours later. The world was becoming way more complicated to me.

CHAPTER 8

I listened to a lot of AM radio during high school. WIBG 99 at first, until WFIL 56 changed formats and started playing pop and rock in 1966. If I was feeling particularly adventurous or impulsive, I might listen to WDAS-FM, the first Philly station playing "progressive" rock. I think that they called it "underground radio" at the time. Until then, I mainly listened to whatever Dennis had on. Lots of British bands at first, then some of the San Francisco wave. Mostly just pop stuff, with the Who and the Doors about as heavy as I really cared for. To give you some idea, *Sherry* by the Four Seasons was the first album that I owned. Like WIBG, WFIL had a decent lineup of DJs, although not nearly as impressive as Wibbage's - George Michael, Jay Cook, Jim Nettleton, Don Cannon, Jim O'Brien.

I'm not sure how, or why, we got them - I'm pretty sure I never would have bought them. A pair of tickets to see Blind Faith at the Spectrum in Philadelphia. If I had to guess, Becky Hutto probably won them from one of the radio stations. We used to call in a lot and actually won some stuff. Usually, it wasn't a contest per se, but more of a "The first ten callers will win ..." or "When you hear me play 'Angel of the Morning,' be the ninth caller." I got my first copy of *Abbey Road* that way. Since you could only win something once every 30 days, or something like that, I resorted to using friends' names and addresses, and won copies of *Abbey Road* for them as well.

Blind Faith was one of the first "supergroups," with Eric Clapton, Ginger Baker, Steve Winwood and Ric Grech. Although I liked Cream, I was never a big Traffic fan. Nor did I really know any of the songs from Blind Faith's album, which had just been released. Regardless, the tickets were likely free, and I had never gone to a rock and roll concert before.

It was the day before Becky's 16th birthday. Becky was the oldest of the three Hutto girls - Becky, Chris and Carol, and the daughter of Mary and Ed. She was also (with apologies to Nancy Weil) my first real girlfriend, and I went with her to the Spectrum to see Blind Faith. Since neither of us had driver's licenses, one of the parents - Ed, I think - drove us and picked us up. For reasons that boggle the mind, I still remember Becky's phone number (662-1353) and her address (8 Ambler Road, Cherry Hill). And, of course, her birthday. Although her name was Rebecca Ann, she told me once that her father thought about naming her Rebel Ann.

Becky and I met at the First Baptist Church of Collingswood, where our families were members. She was 10 months older than me, lived in a different town, was smarter than me, was a year ahead of me in school and went to a different high school, Cherry Hill West. Those things made us a somewhat unlikely match. She was shorter than me, though, which helped. I guess that we met through the youth group, since we both would have been in the senior high group at the same time.

It's hard for me to pinpoint when Becky and I started and stopped going out with each other, especially since I think that we were friends before starting to date. I've resorted to searching release dates for movies that I know we saw in theaters in order to try to figure it out. The first two that I recall seeing with her were *Charly* (released MONDAY, SEPTEMBER 23, 1968) and *Romeo and Juliet* (released TUESDAY, OCTOBER 8, 1968), both of which we saw at the Cherry Hill Mall. *Romeo and Juliet* might have been our first date, but it could have been *Charly* as well. I was early in my freshman year and Becky was a sophomore. With those clues, I'm guessing the fall of 1968.

We saw a bunch of movies in 1969 - *The April Fools* (released WEDNESDAY, MAY 28, 1969), *True Grit* (released FRIDAY, JUNE 13, 1969), *Butch Cassidy & the Sundance Kid* (released WEDNESDAY, SEPTEMBER 24, 1969), *The Sterile Cuckoo* (released WEDNESDAY, OCTOBER 22, 1969), and *They Shoot Horses, Don't They?* (released WEDNESDAY, DECEMBER 10, 1969). We saw Blind Faith. And I know that we incessantly heard "Sweet Cream Ladies, Forward March," on the radio, so we clearly spent all of 1969 together. Our parents wisely passed on letting us go to Woodstock, despite our half-hearted pleadings.

On SUNDAY, AUGUST 17, 1969, the final day of Woodstock, Becky and I, along with Roy Earnest, a church friend, started camp at the New England Baptist Youth Conference in Ocean Park, Maine. You had to be entering at least tenth grade in order to attend. Becky, being a year older than me, had gone the year before, along with Doris String, another church friend, at the urging of Lorna Bixby, who was a member of our church and had gone to the camp some years earlier, along with her brother Chester. Becky had a "camp boyfriend" in 1968, who thankfully didn't return in 1969. Even though we weren't dating quite yet in 1968, I still didn't care much for hearing about him. Camp meant two whole weeks without parents, a godsend for a teenage couple. We spent as much time as we could at the beach, both day and night, and usually had to hustle back to make curfew at night.

 We were still together in early 1970, since we saw *The Boys in the Band* (released TUESDAY, MARCH 17, 1970) in New York with Nancy Weil and *Woodstock* (released THURSDAY, MARCH 26, 1970), I believe at the Regency Theater on Chestnut Street in Philadelphia. I must confess that I had no clue what *The Boys in the Band* was about in 1970. We saw Pete Seeger at the Academy of Music in Philadelphia on SUNDAY, FEBRUARY 8, 1970. The only song that I remember from that concert was "Abiyoyo," about a father, a son, a giant and a ukulele. We went to Becky's junior prom at the Ivystone Inn in Pennsauken, probably in the spring of 1970. I didn't much like the prom, since I didn't know anyone except her and all of the kids were older than me (and bigger than me, since I probably weighed around 120 pounds at that point). I was a sophomore at another school's junior prom. But it's one of those things you do for a high school girlfriend, I guess. It was also my first time wearing a tuxedo.

My best guess is that we broke up soon after her junior prom in the spring of 1970. I don't think that we ever went on a date where one of us drove and she would have gotten her license in July of 1970. Becky was growing up faster than I was. She was thinking about senior year, visiting colleges and applying (she chose Bates), graduation, having a driver's license, living away from home, all of the things that a 17 year-old kid should be thinking about. The last thing she needed was a younger boyfriend from another school who wasn't really thinking that far ahead yet.

We actually considered getting back together a couple of times during our late teens and early 20's, but that never happened. I'm sure that we each knew that it wasn't really a very good idea.

We did have fun, though, while we were together. We fancied ourselves hippies and sewed buttons along the outside seams of our jeans. We saw *Kiss Me, Kate* at Haddonfield Plays and Players on Kings HIghway, because Chris was in it. Sometimes, our parents would take us to Jimbll's on Haddon Avenue in Westmont for ice cream after Sunday evening church. We did lots of church stuff, including the church picnic at Holiday Lake in Willingboro and a youth retreat during the winter somewhere in the Poconos. We listened to music on her back porch and played pool in my basement, although that was mainly just an excuse to get out of sight of my parents. Ed took us to play tennis. We went on a picnic at Strawbridge Lake in Moorestown. And, of course, we hung out at the mall, rarely buying anything.

Ed Hutto worked for RCA and had a lot of really cool, sophisticated electronic gadgets, including the most amazing sound system I have ever heard. Ed especially liked big band music. RCA was working on a camera that could take pictures in the pitch black and Ed wanted to try it out, so he piled a bunch of us into a car one night and took us out into the Pinelands in South Jersey, away from any light. I don't know how the camera worked, nor do I remember seeing any of the pictures, but at least we weren't all disemboweled by the Jersey Devil.

The Huttos took me out to dinner at the Greenbriar Inn, according to Carol, on Route 70 for my birthday. Given the timeline which I have assumed to be true, it would have been my 15th, in 1969. A mostly gray-haired man sitting at the bar must have overheard that it was my birthday and summoned me over. I wasn't used to strange men sitting at bars asking me to come talk to them, but I went nonetheless. When I approached, the man asked me if I knew who he was. I did, I thought. It was Lorne Greene, "Pa Cartwright" himself, and one-hit wonder "singer" of the song "Ringo," which had been *Billboard's* #1 song in December of 1964, nursing what was probably his third or fourth scotch. He was in town to appear on *The Mike Douglas Show*, which taped in Philadelphia. He wished me a happy birthday, asked my name, took out his wallet, and autographed a $1 bill. I still have that bill, tucked away in a little metal box with some other old coins and bills.

Sometime in 2017, Becky emailed or texted me saying that she had a reservation for four at The Lost Kitchen, a restaurant in Freedom, Maine, and asked if Nancy and I would like to go. She and her husband, David Gottlieb, had purchased a house in New Portland, Maine years earlier, although they only used the house on occasion. Being relatively new to living in Maine, I wasn't familiar with The Lost Kitchen, nor with Erin French, its owner and chef.

The Lost Kitchen is a story unto itself, having received three *James Beard Award* nominations, and having been named one of *Time* magazine's "World's Greatest Places" and one of *Bloomberg's* "12 Restaurants Worth Traveling Across the World to Experience." It took Nancy and I about two hours to drive to Freedom, a town seemingly in the middle of nowhere, on SATURDAY, NOVEMBER 18, 2017. Eating at The Lost Kitchen is an experience more than a meal. Only 40 people or so dine each night and the evening lasts more than three hours. Guests eat whatever is being prepared that night, almost all of it local. Erin French personally explains each course, visits with all the guests, and seems to absolutely love cooking for people. Her rather amazing journey from abuse and addiction to decorated chef is chronicled in her memoir, *Finding Freedom*. The restaurant is housed in an old mill in Freedom that she has converted into a restaurant. The menu that night was:

potato leek soup

creme fraiche

bronzed fennel

trout roe

. . . .

bitter radicchio, baby kale & spinach

sweet carrots, pear & heirloom turnip

smoked ricotta & parmesan

honey, shallots & cider

. . . .

katahdin lamb chops

creamy polenta

whipped feta butter

braised brussels

cabbage, apple & thyme

spicy greens

. . . .

roasted kabocha squash semifreddo

salted nut brittle

whipped cream

warm caramel

husk cherry

The lamb chops, she explained, were from a lamb that was born, raised and died in Freedom. We have entered the lottery each year (along with 20,000 other people) to try to get another reservation, but have never gotten the call. We will certainly keep trying.

Becky, Chris and Carol's father passed away on FRIDAY, MARCH 9, 2018, at the age of 94. The family had decided to spread Ed's ashes in the woods next to Becky and David's house in New Portland. Becky asked if I would like to come. I went, not having seen Mary, Chris or Carol in decades. We chatted, reminisced, laughed and finally went outside in the cold rain to spread the ashes. Each of us took some and let them go. David played some music that Ed would have liked before we headed back inside. After a meal together, I headed for home, happy that I had been able to say goodbye to Ed and visit with Mary and the girls.

On TUESDAY, APRIL 27, 2021, I received a text message from Becky saying that her mother, Mary, had passed away at 4:00 a.m. that morning. She had entered into hospice care on Thursday, suffering from cancer. I sent my condolences to Becky and her sisters. On TUESDAY, OCTOBER 5, 2021, I again made the two-plus hour drive north to New Portland, where Becky, David, Chris and Carol had gathered to scatter Mary's ashes. We took them to the same spot where we had taken Ed, David played a couple of songs, including "Autumn Leaves," and we took turns scattering the ashes. When we were done, we watched a few slides from back in our early days at the First Baptist Church of Collingswood, had lunch, and I got ready to leave. As I was going, I said, "There's a pretty good chance that I'll never see at least two of you again," meaning Chris and Carol. We hugged, said goodbye, and I headed back home.

* * *

At my first concert ever, Delaney, Bonnie and Friends opened for Blind Faith. I actually enjoyed them more than the headliners. My first concert with my first girlfriend. And the next day, we celebrated her 16th birthday together.

CHAPTER 9

SUNDAY, JULY 20, 1969

Some memories are much clearer than others. On Sunday night, I was sitting by myself on the enclosed porch on the Burrwood Avenue side of our house. It was a long, skinny room, maybe six or seven feet wide and 25 feet long. It had long since been enclosed. Whether my parents enclosed it or bought it like that, I don't know. The room was used as a place for books, although you couldn't really call it a library, an aquarium, games and a chair or two. We referred to it as "the den." My mother had painted our fireplace red, with the mortar painted white. The porch had the back of the chimney exposed, meaning that the porch had been added after the house had been built. The actual firebox, where I popped Lassie's ticks, was in the living room.

I was watching a small black and white portable television with rabbit ears. Fortunately, it was summer, so there was no school the next day. I had seen Blind Faith four days earlier. At around 10:40 p.m., the hatch to the lunar module, the *Eagle*, opened. In grainy black and white, Neil Armstrong emerged from the module, climbed down the ladder, stepped onto the moon, and at 10:56 transmitted the famous words, "That's one small step for [a] man, one giant leap for mankind." Although the "a" was inaudible, Armstrong always insisted that he said it. Eight years earlier, on THURSDAY, MAY 25, 1961, JFK had addressed a joint session of Congress and proposed that the United States, "should commit itself to achieving the goal, before this decade is out, of landing a man on the moon and returning him safely to the Earth." Amazingly, we did it. And we did it with a computer on board Apollo 11 which had about 1/100,000th of the processing power of a smartphone.

It is hard to overestimate how important the space race was to the country in the early 1960's. Every successful mission was cause for national celebration. Russia had beaten the U.S. into space, which was a blow to both our national ego and to our belief that we were destined to be the first, and the best, at nearly everything. It was also a shock that the communists, of all people, seemed scientifically and technologically more advanced than we were. As the space race heated up, we learned the names of all of the astronauts, particularly the original *Project Mercury* seven - Scott Carpenter, Walter Shirra, Alan Shepard, Gordon Cooper, Gus Grissom, Deke Slayton and John Glenn. They seemed almost mythical. At Strawbridge School, we would have assemblies where the entire school gathered in the assembly hall to watch the Mercury launches on a black and white television. I don't know what would have happened if something had gone terribly wrong, like it later did with the *Challenger*.

The Project Mercury astronauts were American heroes in a way that we haven't had since. And heroes got parades. In 1962, two ticker-tape parades were held for astronauts in New York City, on Broadway. John Glenn had his on THURSDAY, MARCH 1, 1962, in honor of his TUESDAY, FEBRUARY 20, 1962, flight aboard *Friendship 7*, which was the first manned U.S. orbital flight, successfully orbiting Earth three times before landing in the Atlantic Ocean. Glenn was reportedly showered with nearly 3,500 tons of ticker tape. Scott Carpenter had his parade on TUESDAY, JUNE 5, 1962, in honor of his THURSDAY, MAY 24, 1962, Mercury 7 mission aboard *Aurora 7*, which repeated Glenn's three successful Earth orbits. Gordon Cooper earned his WEDNESDAY, MAY 22, 1963, parade by flying the last American solo astronaut flight, Mercury 9, aboard *Faith 7*, completing 22 Earth orbits on WEDNESDAY, MAY 15, 1963. Gus Grissom finally got his parade on MONDAY, MARCH 29, 1965, but it was for his flight with the Gemini program, not Mercury; and Alan Shepard had to wait until MONDAY, MARCH 8, 1971, for his, for the *Apollo 14* moon landing. Walter Shirra and Deke Slayton never got ticker-tape parades. Gus Grissom died less than two years after his parade, on FRIDAY, JANUARY 27, 1967, in a fire aboard the command module of *Apollo 1* on the launch pad at Cape Kennedy. It was the worst disaster in NASA history until the *Challenger* explosion.

I was working at Foley, Hoag & Eliot in Boston on TUESDAY, JANUARY 28, 1986, when the *Challenger* disaster happened. I had gone out to grab an early lunch and when I returned I learned what had happened. At 11:39 a.m., 73 seconds after it launched, an O-ring failed in the booster rocket, causing an explosion that killed the entire crew, consisting of Francis Scobee, Michael Smith, Ronald McNair, Ellison Onizuka, Judith Resnick, Gregory Jarvis and, of course, Christa McAuliffe. The country was paying special attention to the *Challenger* launch because of Christa McAuliffe, a teacher from Concord, New Hampshire, who was to be the first teacher in space. I didn't know it at the time, but Nancy MacDonald, a teacher who I would meet in a few months, was watching the launch with her class in Lowell.

CHAPTER 10

THURSDAY, OCTOBER 1, 1970

The Phillies beat the Montreal Expos 2-1 in 10 innings in the last game of the 1970 season, when Oscar Gamble singled home Tim McCarver for the winning run. I was there with Charlie and the three Hutto girls, sitting on the first base side. The Huttos all loved the Phillies, apparently so much so that Becky went with us, even though I think that she had dumped me a few months earlier. The Phillies finished the 1970 season at 73-88, good for fifth place (in a six-team division) and 15 ½ games behind the first-place Pittsburgh Pirates. Better days would come for the Phillies in the second half of the decade.

Connie Mack Stadium in Philadelphia was where we went to watch major league baseball in the 1960's. Usually, it was me and Charlie, but sometimes my mother, brother or a friend would come, too. The stadium was a marvel. As we drove down Lehigh Avenue, the first things that I could see from blocks away were the lights towering over the stadium. Then the enormous stone, brick, terra cotta and glass facade on Lehigh Avenue. There must have been some parking lots around the stadium, but I don't remember ever parking in any of them. The stadium was set in a poor, largely-residential section of Philadelphia, not in one of the affluent, downtown or industrial areas. Charlie preferred to park on the street and pay one of the local kids a dime or quarter to "watch" the car during the game. Those kids must have been good car-watchers, since we never had any problems with our car when we were leaving.

We usually entered the stadium through the main entrance at 21st and Lehigh. Actually, that might have been the only entrance. Connie Mack was like no other stadium, then or since. From the left field foul pole to the right field foul pole, circling behind the dugouts and home plate, was the grandstand, with a lower bowl and an upper deck. Obstructed views,

caused by the steel columns supporting the upper deck and roof, were
plentiful. But it was in the outfield where the stadium had most of its
character and charm.

Left field, from the foul pole to dead center, had bleachers with an
upper and lower deck. On the roof of the bleachers there were three large
billboards, one of which (I think it was the center one) seemed to always
be for Coca-Cola. The roof of the bleachers was probably 65 feet above
field level, while the tops of the billboards must have been at least 75 feet
above. By comparison, the "Green Monster" at Fenway Park in Boston is
37 feet high, meaning that the tops of the billboards were more than twice
as high as the Monster.

Right field was possibly the most
unique of any ballpark in history.
From the right field foul pole to the
scoreboard in right-center was a 34-
foot high corrugated steel wall. The
wall had been constructed in 1935,
when the owner, Jack Shibe, got tired
of people watching games from rooftops and windows across the street.
Some homeowners had even erected bleachers on the roofs of their houses
and sold tickets. Nearly 3,000 people watched *World Series* games in 1929
(involving the Athletics, not the Phillies) from across 20th Street. So
Shibe's "spite wall" went up. Left-handed hitters and right fielders hated
that wall. Left-handed hitters because the wall was high and far away and
right fielders because, when a ball would hit the corrugated wall, they had
no idea where it would go - straight down, all the way back to the infield,
or directly right or left. Balls hit hard enough against the wall would cause
it to vibrate and make a "boing" sound that echoed through the stadium.

In right-center field, about mid-way between the right field foul pole
and dead center, and attached to the "spite wall," was an enormous - 50
feet tall and probably 60 feet wide - scoreboard. Atop the length of the
scoreboard was a 10-foot high Ballantine Beer sign. The Ballantine sign was
constantly changing its slogan. One year it might be, "Enjoy that premium
flavor," and the next it might be, "Cold-brewed," "You get a smile every
time," "Hey friend, do it again," "The crisp refresher," or even "Save
Herman Ballantine." In 1964, the slogan started out as "Tote'm home
plenty," an arguably racist slogan, but no one seemed to care, since there
weren't many Native Americans in Philadelphia. As the Phillies mounted
their ill-fated pennant run, Ballantine quickly rebranded it as "Tote'm
home pennant." The "tote'm home" part of the slogan may have been
inspired by Phillies rookie Dick Allen, who hailed from the tiny borough
of Wampum, Pennsylvania.

On top of the Ballantine sign was a 15-foot by 10-foot Longines clock,
complete with hands. The scoreboard was 380 to 400 feet away from home

plate and 60 feet high, not counting the clock. A batted ball which hit the clock would count as a home run. No one ever managed that feat. Dick Allen, however, did manage to do something no other right-handed hitter ever did - hit one completely over the massive scoreboard and Ballantine sign. Allen also hit 18 home runs completely over the left field bleachers, including one that traveled 529 feet over the Coke sign on the roof of the bleachers, on SATURDAY, MAY 29, 1965.

The late, great Dick Allen is probably the greatest baseball player who is not in the Hall of Fame. His feats are all the more amazing considering the outright racism he had to endure, especially in Philadelphia, which was the last National League team to integrate, in 1957, a full decade after Jackie Robinson joined the Brooklyn Dodgers. He had to wear a helmet in the field because fans threw things at him, like pennies, fruit, bolts and bottles. He was blamed for a fight between he and Frank Thomas, a white player, even though Thomas had been directing racial slurs at Black teammates. The Phillies and the media referred to him as "Richie," even though he preferred "Dick" and had been called that in the minor leagues. Fans dumped trash in his front yard. The Phillies had even sent him to play at their minor league affiliate in Little Rock, Arkansas in 1963, making him the first Black player there, where he watched segregationist governor Orval Faubus throw out the first pitch one night. While at Little Rock, someone painted, "Nigger, go home" on his car windshield. Despite the treatment, Allen hit .289 with 33 home runs and 97 runs batted in as a 21-year-old at Little Rock. As a 22-year-old major league rookie in 1964, Allen won the National League *Rookie of the Year* award, playing in every game and batting .318 with 29 home runs and 91 runs batted in. But whatever he did, it was never enough for Philadelphia fans.

I went to some memorable games at Connie Mack Stadium, in addition to the "Chico f***ing Ruiz" game. On SUNDAY, OCTOBER 2, 1966, I went to the final two games of the season with Charlie, an afternoon doubleheader against the Dodgers. We sat on the third base side. Game 1 featured Don Drysdale of the Dodgers against Larry Jackson of the Phillies. The Phillies won that game 4-3. Game 2 featured Sandy Koufax of the Dodgers against Jim Bunning of the Phillies. Pitching on just two days' rest and needing a victory for the Dodgers to go to the *World Series*, Koufax threw a complete game, and the Dodgers won 6-3 to clinch the National League Pennant. It was the last regular season game that he ever pitched. That season, Sandy Koufax went 27-9 with a 1.73 ERA and 317 strikeouts. He was the unanimous choice for the *Cy Young Award*. Two months later, at the age of 30, he retired due to arthritis in his elbow. Koufax, Drysdale and Bunning all ended up in the Hall of Fame in Cooperstown. And I saw them all pitch on one October day.

On SUNDAY, JUNE 26, 1966, I went to a game against the Pirates featuring a left-handed rookie pitcher named Woody Fryman. Fryman pitched a 3-hit shutout against the Phillies. The only highlight for the Phils was Dick Allen boinging a line drive off of the right field wall for a triple.

I saw Jim Bunning win his 18th game of the season, a 5-4 victory over the St. Louis Cardinals, on SATURDAY, SEPTEMBER 24, 1966, from the upper deck in the left field bleachers with my father and Kevin Manns. I got my one and only souvenir baseball at that game. Unfortunately, it wasn't from the game itself, but from batting practice. Someone had hit one into the upper deck near us and I picked it up. I'm sure that I held it tight the rest of the night. I still have that baseball, which I inexplicably had autographed by a journeyman left-handed pitcher named Darold Knowles, who spent just one year in Philadelphia.

My favorite player as a kid was Johnny Callison, a left-handed hitting right fielder from Bakersfield, California. I think that I wore his Number 6 in Little League. I don't know how or why I chose him as my favorite, but all of us had a favorite player. Jules had Bob Skinner, Kevin had Dick Stuart and Stan Musial, and Scott had Callison, like I did. I used to know all of Callison's stats, but only remember a few now. I know that he hit 31 home runs in 1964 and 32 in 1965. He came in second in the MVP voting in 1964 and would have won except for the Phillies' epic, legendary collapse at the end of that season, fueled by Chico Ruiz. I was watching on television on TUESDAY, JULY 7, 1964, when he hit a three-run home run off of Dick ("the Monster") Radatz of the Boston Red Sox in the bottom of the ninth inning to win the All-Star Game at Shea Stadium for the National League. He won the MVP trophy for that game, if not for that season. All-Star games were played during the daytime back then, so I hurried outside to play with my friends when it was over.

It was a challenge getting autographs from players at Connie Mack Stadium, although I had some autograph-seeking experience from my days visiting the Eagles' training camp at the Cherry Hill Inn. Callison, especially, was said to be not very keen on signing. The only place to really try to get autographs after the game was in a concourse at the bottom of the stadium. To get to the locker room, the players had to take a tunnel from the dugout under the stands and then walk about 15 feet across the concourse to the locker room, their metal spikes clattering on the concrete. My father sometimes took me down there after games, and I was specifically looking to get my favorite player's autograph. For whatever reason, he stopped and signed my book one day. I think that it was my father, 6'4", standing behind me in a business suit, who caught his attention. Most men wore suits and ties to games in the 1960's. I still have that autograph in a little notepad full of autographs from the 1960's, along with Tony Taylor, Ruben Amaro, Johnny Klippstein, Tony Gonzalez, Paul Brown, Chris Short, Al Widmar, Bob Oldis and Cal McLish, whose full name was Calvin Coolidge Julius Caesar Tuskahoma McLish. He signed with the short version. Years later, I got Callison's autograph the easy way - I paid for it. I went to a card show with my 1964 Phillies yearbook and got his signature on the cover.

Over the ensuing years, I got a few more Phillies' autographs for my collection. I got Jim Fregosi, the Phillies manager when they went to the *World Series* in 1993, to sign a MONDAY, MAY 3, 1971 *Sports Illustrated* with his picture on the cover, although he was playing for the Angels in 1971. I got Pete Rose to sign a MONDAY, MAY 28, 1979 *Sports Illustrated* with him in a Phillies uniform, although that's nothing special - Rose would sign anything, any time, if you paid him. Also on *Sports Illustrated*, from MONDAY, JUNE 8, 1981, I have Greg Luzinski's autograph from when he was with the White Sox. The last *Sports Illustrated* with a Phillie autograph is the MONDAY, MARCH 14, 1983, edition signed by Joe Morgan. I also have autographs from three Hall of Famers - Willie Mays on a MONDAY, MAY 22, 1972 *Sports Illustrated*, Ozzie Smith on a MONDAY, SEPTEMBER 23, 1985 *Sports Illustrated* and Ron Santo on a MONDAY, JUNE 30, 1969 *Sports Illustated*. I put all of the autographed magazines in frames and hung them in my home office - when I used to have a home office.

I once found $6.00 lying on the sidewalk while walking to our car after a game at Connie Mack Stadium. I thought that I had found a dollar, which would have been great, noticed another bill inside, and thought that I had found two dollars. The inside bill was a five. Given inflation, that would be like finding $49.00 in 2022. I was rich.

* * *

As the last game ever played at Connie Mack Stadium got into the sixth or seventh inning, the crowd was nearly rioting. It sounded like a construction site, with a non-stop, almost rhythmic banging echoing through the stadium. It seemed as though everyone wanted a piece of the place as a souvenir. Foolishly, the Phillies had given out 5,000 red wooden slats that were to be used as replacements whenever a seat slat would break. With the stadium about to be closed, the Phillies would no longer need them, so they decided to just give them away.. They apparently didn't consider that the slats would be used as tools to help dismantle the place. I still have my red wooden souvenir slat from that night.

Fans took anything and everything that they could from the stadium - entire rows of chairs, lightbulbs from scoreboards, urinals, toilet seats, boards from the left field wall, signs, handfuls of dirt from the infield and chunks of grass. With no real stadium security in those days, the more well-prepared fans brought screwdrivers, wrenches, hammers, crowbars, jackhammers and backhoes into the stadium to secure their pieces of Philly history. I may be mistaken about the jackhammers and backhoes. The sounds of the slats banging went on for at least the final hour of the game. The team had plans for an elaborate post-game ceremony, complete with a helicopter landing on the field and taking home plate to Veterans Stadium, the Phillies soon-to-be new home. All of those plans were cancelled because of the riot going on inside of Connie Mack Stadium.

Although I still have that red slat, I helped myself to another reminder of the final night at Connie Mack. One way to exit the stadium was through a large overhead gate in the right field wall. Fans would file down the aisles and walk along the cinders which made up the warning track that circled the field. That was how the five of us made our way out that night. As we were walking along the warning track, I spotted a small, probably 10" x 12" iron  drainage grate in the warning track. It wasn't attached to anything, so I grabbed it and kept walking. A security guard yelled at me, but I don't think that he really cared all that much, certainly not enough to stop me. Nobody would know what it is without my telling, but that drainage grate is sitting in my shed, waiting to be brought out and shown off on special occasions.

I've gone to a lot of baseball games at a lot of venues through the years, but Connie Mack Stadium was the best, probably because it was my first and because I usually went with my father. The others that I have gone to, some even with the dates I went, were:

<u>Veterans Stadium</u> in Philadelphia. Between 1971 and 2003, I went to literally dozens of Phillies games at the Vet. It was quintessential 1970's - circular design, used for multiple sports, artificial turf - everything antithetical to baseball. But multi-purpose stadiums were the rage back then and Philly got stuck with one of the worst. In addition to going to Game 6 of the 1980 *World Series* at the Vet (<u>see</u> October 21, 1980), I was also there on TUESDAY, OCTOBER 5, 1978, when the Los Angeles Dodgers won 4-0 behind a 4-hit shutout by Tommy John to take a 2-0 lead in the best-of-five National League Championship series. That year would be the third consecutive year that the Phillies lost in the championship series, losing to the Dodgers in 1977 and 1978 and to the Cincinnati Reds in 1976.

I was also there on SATURDAY, SEPTEMBER 27, 1980, when the Phillies lost 5-4 to the Montreal Expos and saw their division lead cut to ½ game over the Expos. Exactly one week later, the Phillies would clinch the division title in Montreal.

I was there on FRIDAY, APRIL 9, 1993, when the Phils lost their home opener to the Chicago Cubs, 11-7, and again five days later on WEDNESDAY, APRIL 14, 1993, when the Phils beat the Reds 9-2. That same year, on SUNDAY, JULY 11, 1993, I saw the Phillies get crushed by Barry Bonds and the San Francisco Giants, 10-2. Nonetheless, that 1993 Phillies team made it all the way to Game 6 of the *World Series*, although that game ended poorly.

In the high school and college years, when I had little spare cash, I would park on the street down among the warehouses in order to avoid paying to park in one of the stadium lots. I know that I saw Dwight Gooden of the Mets one night and remember Gary Carter turning around from the on-deck circle after I called him a "fish head," for no reason except that he was Gary Carter.

I actually got to play at the Vet once. In 1978, there was a professional slow-pitch softball team in Philadelphia called the Philadelphia Athletics, in honor of the former major league baseball franchise which had abandoned Philadelphia for Kansas City in 1954. The softball Athletics played their games at the Vet, and had convinced my favorite childhood player, Johnny Callison, to serve as player/coach. He didn't last long, resigning after starting the season 10-25. The A's were having tryouts for the team at the Vet, so I decided to go, fancying myself a pretty good player. To my surprise, there were hundreds of guys there to try out (or at least to play on the turf at the Vet). Everyone got five swings or so in. The team was looking for hitters with lots and lots of power.

We batted from between the pitcher's mound and the baseball home plate. I don't remember a single person hitting one over the outfield fence. Until Lawrence "Boom Boom" Hutcherson was asked to take a few swings. He was already on the team and the A's wanted to show us what they were looking for. "Boom Boom" was a huge man and proceeded to hit ball after ball over the left field fence. *That's* what the team was looking for. I don't think that any of us were invited to join the team.

Nancy and I went to "Fireworks Night" at the Vet with Cindy and Dave Cunningham, Nancy's sister and brother-in-law, sometime around the Fourth of July in 1990 or so. They let people who were sitting in parts of the stadium with bad views of the fireworks go down onto the field to watch, so we did, sitting down on the Astroturf in right field.

Citizens Bank Park in Philadelphia. After Veterans Stadium was demolished in 2004, the Phillies moved into Citizens Bank Park for the 2004 season. I went to a game that year on WEDNESDAY, JUNE 30, 2004, mainly to see the new park. The park was beautiful, but the Phils lost 6-3 to the Montreal Expos. Dylan and I did, at least, get to see Jim Thome's 27th home run of the season.

Dylan was home from college in the summer, and he, Nancy and I decided to take in a Phillies game on TUESDAY, JULY 24, 2012. It was the last gasp for the Phillies core which had won the *World Series* four years earlier - Jimmy Rollins, Chase Utley, Ryan Howard, Shane Victorino and Carlos Ruiz. It was a miserable, hot, humid night, still sitting at 95 degrees at 7:00 at night, as we sweltered in Section 106 in right field. There was not a whiff of a breeze the entire night. The Phillies won a wildly entertaining game by a score of 7-6, but it was just nasty hot.

Wrigley Field in Chicago. I've probably gone to five or six games at Wrigley, including a 7-3 Cubs victory over the Phillies on SUNDAY, JUNE 10, 1990, when I sat in Section 115 with Roger Roble and Kevin Schildt. Roger lived in Chicago and had secured the seats. Future Hall of Famers Andre ("the Hawk") Dawson and Ryne Sandberg played for the Cubs. Dawson homered. Before one of the games that weekend, we had some beers across the street from Wrigley at Murphy's Bleachers, which was probably the most crowded bar I have ever been in, and very probably had the most disgusting Porta Potties ever.

Kevin and I again went to Chicago to see the Cubs two years later. On SATURDAY, JUNE 27, 1992, we again sat in Section 115 as the Phils won 5-4. For the SUNDAY, JUNE 28, 1992, game, we again had the box seats, but we didn't want to sit in them. We wanted to sit with the real people, the Bleacher Bums, in the left field bleachers. It's the place to be at a Cubs game. So we waited outside of Wrigley, found someone who would trade us bleacher seats, and took our place amongst the people. At this game, an enterprising young man, a true Bleacher Bum, in exchange for $1.00, took my empty plastic beer cup and got it refilled (a couple of times) by the guy he knew at the concession stand. Everybody won. By the way, the Cubs beat the Phils 5-2.

Fenway Park in Boston. I've been to Fenway Park lots of times, more times than I've been to Citizens Bank Park in Philly. The first year that I was dating Nancy, I got us tickets for a Red Sox game. It was a red-themed Christmas, and I tried to get her as many red items as I could, including Red Sox tickets and what were then very stylish red high-top Reeboks. Since Nancy has always been a huge Red Sox fan, tickets to a game seemed natural. I don't know which game it was, but it was during the 1987 season, before we got married. We sat down the right field foul line, right by the Pesky Pole.

I took three or four trips to Boston for boys' weekends with Kevin and Joe. We went to the game on FRIDAY, JUNE 25, 2004, sitting in the right field bleachers. The Red Sox crushed the Phils 12-1, behind Pedro Martinez, who pitched two-hit ball for seven innings, and home runs by Manny Ramirez and David Ortiz. We hung out at Boston Beer Works before and after the games that weekend and saw a man in a Smarty Jones horsehead walking on Yawkey Way, Smarty Jones being a Philadelphia hero, since he was from Chester County and had just won the Kentucky Derby on SATURDAY, MAY 1, 2004. Smarty almost won the Triple Crown that year, winning the Kentucky Derby and Preakness Stakes, but on SATURDAY, JUNE 5, 2004, he was passed in a race for the only time in his career, finishing second. It was the only time Smarty lost and he never raced again.

Little did we know that 2004 would be an historic year for the Red Sox. Trailing three games to none to the hated Yankees in the playoffs, and trailing in the ninth inning of game four, the Red Sox rallied to win that game on SUNDAY, OCTOBER 17, 2004, and the next three, to advance to the *World Series*. Nancy, Dylan and I watched all of the games from our living room on Abbey Road. The Sox then swept the St. Louis Cardinals in the *World Series*, winning their first world championship since 1918 on WEDNESDAY, OCTOBER 27, 2004, and breaking the Curse of the Bambino.

Usually, when going to Boston, I would hit up my friend from softball and basketball, Tony Fazzie, for tickets. His company had season tickets to the Red Sox and he always came through when I asked. In 2003, I had asked him for tickets and he called a few days later to say that he had gotten them. Not to be ungrateful, but he said that he could have gotten us either seats behind the third base dugout or on the Green Monster, atop of which the Sox had put a few seats beginning that season. Not knowing which we would prefer, he opted for the third base seats. We all make poor decisions. Since Faz always got me four tickets, and there were only three of us making the trip, I often invited one of my Massachusetts friends to come with us. We took in games with Bob Thomas, Martine Taylor, Carole Bennett and Katie Bedard. Scoring good Sox tickets and inviting someone to go along for free can make one popular in Boston.

Mile High Stadium in Denver. Kevin, Joe and I spent the weekend in Colorado watching baseball and scaling a waterfall near Winter Park. Even though it was June, there was still snow in the Rocky Mountains. We stopped at the base of a waterfall and began climbing up alongside it. Wearing shorts, and sometimes sinking into snow up to our hips, we nevertheless scaled a couple hundred feet along the waterfall. We came to an opening among the trees and Joe decided to keep going. With uncertain footing, and with nothing for support, he ended up flat on his stomach on a steep incline. Trying to be helpful, I threw him a stick, but it didn't help much. After a lot of consternation and swearing, he managed to scrabble back down to safety. Displaying an unusual degree of foresight, we had bought a six-pack of O'Doul's (non-alcoholic beer) and placed it in the frigid water at the base of the waterfall for when we were done climbing.

One of the games in Denver was on SATURDAY, JUNE 12, 1993, between the Rockies and the Astros, which the Rockies won 14-11. Hall of Famers Jeff Bagwell and Craig Biggio played for the Astros and Biggio homered. We also went to Rock Bottom Brewery, which may have been the first craft brewery, among hundreds of others, that I have visited.

Municipal Stadium in Baltimore. See June 17, 1990.

Camden Yards in Baltimore. See June 17, 1990.

Busch Stadium II in St. Louis. I was in town for work and decided to take in a Cardinals game at Busch, since it was right across the street from my hotel, where most visiting players also stayed. There have been three stadiums in St. Louis named Busch Stadium. This was the middle of the three, an unfortunate multi-purpose stadium with little to no charm, like most of the 1960's and 1970's stadiums, although it was definitely nicer than the Vet in Philly. When Yogi Berra was asked what he thought of the new stadium, he reportedly said, "Well, it holds the heat well." I was lucky enough to see Hall of Fame shortstops Barry Larkin of the Reds and Ozzie Smith of the Cardinals, along with Hall of Fame closer Lee Smith recording a save, in a TUESDAY, MAY 12, 1992, game won by the Cardinals 6-4.

Kingdome in Seattle. On FRIDAY, MAY 13, 1994, Kevin, Joe and I watched the Angels demolish the Mariners 11-1. The Kingdome was an absolutely dreadful place, just a small notch better than Olympic Stadium in Montreal. It was cold, damp and depressing. The following year, seven fans were injured when wooden tiles fell on them from the upper deck. At least we got to see Bo Jackson, Ken Griffey, Jr. and Edgar Martinez play, and we hiked a little on Mount Rainier and saw one of the glaciers, which was very cool.

PNC Park in Pittsburgh. Absolutely nothing of note happened, and we didn't see any Hall of Famers, as the Pirates defeated the Royals 2-0 to improve their pitiful record to 34-54 on THURSDAY, JULY 12, 2001. It was the first year that PNC Park was open, and the stadium is fantastic, overlooking the Allegheny River and the Pittsburgh skyline. The way baseball should be.

Olympic Stadium in Montreal. The only stadium worse than the Kingdome in Seattle was Olympic Stadium in Montreal. Dank, musty and utterly devoid of any charm, it feels like a concrete crypt more than anything else. I went there many times and enjoyed every visit, simply because it was in Montreal, one of my very favorite cities. Montreal also allowed 2-for-1 drinks during Happy Hour, which we often took advantage of at Carlos and Pepe's.

Exhibition Stadium in Toronto. I don't really remember a thing about the stadium or the games I went to with Kevin at Exhibition Stadium. I do remember going up to the top of the CN Tower, which was a little scary. I also remember being a smart-ass at a bar one night. We had been drinking mostly Labatt's Blue that weekend, a great beer, with the occasional Molson thrown in. At one point I decided to get cute and ask for an imported beer, I wound up with a can of Stroh's, far inferior to "Bleu," and paid an extra Canadian dollar for the privilege. Sometimes, I would be wise to just keep my mouth shut.

Daniel S. Frawley Stadium in Wilmington, Delaware. I went with a bunch of people from my fantasy baseball league to see the Wilmington Blue Rocks play the Durham Bulls, of movie fame, on FRIDAY JULY 9, 1993. Minor league baseball is fun, but I didn't really know any of the players. I think that I spent the entire evening trying to make trades to improve my fantasy team. I used to be guilty of this when I played fantasy sports, but didn't realize it until I stopped playing - there is absolutely nothing more boring than listening to fantasy players prattle on about their make-believe teams.

Campbell's Field in Camden, New Jersey. We took Dylan and a few of his Little League friends to see the Camden Riversharks, an independent minor league team. It was in 2003 or 2004 and I think that the game was against the Nashua Pride, because I vaguely recall former major league outfielder Dante Bichette trying to reinvent himself as a knuckleball pitcher with the Pride. In any event, the stadium was awesome, set at the foot of the Ben Franklin Bridge beside the Delaware River, with a magnificent view of the Philadelphia skyline.

Hadlock Field in Portland, Maine. Our friends from trivia night, Rob and Lisa, asked us if we wanted to go with them to see the Portland Sea Dogs play the Reading Phillies on SATURDAY, JUNE 22, 2019. We accepted, and spent a beautiful summer evening watching the Red Sox and Phillies minor leaguers and enjoying a couple of exquisite Maine craft beers.

I went to see the Sea Dogs again on TUESDAY, MAY 25, 2021, when the pandemic seemed to be waning, with Kevin and Joe, who were up visiting. The Sea Dogs suffered an 8-5 loss to the Hartford Yard Goats (one of the best things about minor league baseball is the team names) in a game which featured no fewer than five home runs.

* * *

On FRIDAY, AUGUST 20, 1971, less than a year after I went to that final game at Connie Mack Stadium, two brothers snuck into the stadium and started a fire that destroyed most of the upper deck. In 1976, Philadelphia hosted lots of events in celebration of the bicentennial. The NBA and NHL held their All-Star games in Philadelphia, as did major league baseball. On TUESDAY, JULY 13, 1976, while the baseball All-Star Game was being played at Veterans Stadium in South Philly, the last remaining part of Connie Mack Stadium, its famed tower and copula at the corner of 21st and Lehigh, became the final part of the stadium to be demolished. A megachurch now stands on that sacred ground.

CHAPTER 11

TUESDAY, MAY 4, 1971

M y 17th birthday. But there were more important things to worry about than some birthday. It was election day for student council officers (president, vice president, secretary and treasurer) at Haddon Township High School. No one, especially me, thought that I could possibly win.

I basically became president of the student council on a dare. Student council elections were coming up in the spring of 1971 for the following school year, when I would be a senior. We were sitting around before class - trigonometry, I think - talking about how useless student council was, when someone came up with the idea that somebody should run on a platform of abolishing student council. It might have been Steve Ibbeken who first suggested it.

Steve had been a friend going all the way back to kindergarten at Strawbridge School. At some point in my junior high/senior high years, maybe around 8th or 9th grade, I was sitting in class with Steve sitting to my immediate left in the next row. For some inexplicable reason, I decided to take my Ticonderoga #2 yellow pencil, freshly sharpened, and stick it through Steve's brown-bag lunch which was sitting on his desk. It had some kind of sandwich inside. This was not a gentle or subtle move, but a full-on assault on the brown bag and its contents, which left the pencil standing straight up out of the bag. I did it not out of malice, but for fun. I never had time to enjoy my triumph. Steve immediately grabbed my pencil and returned the favor, only not into my lunch. With one swift motion, he raised the pencil and stabbed it into my left thigh, leaving the pencil standing straight up, just like it had been in his sandwich. I still have the bluish-gray pencil tip, or at least some graphite, embedded in my thigh.

Of course, running on a platform of abolishing student council sounded like a fun, devious and subversive thing to do. The only issue was, was anyone willing to risk being branded a fool and actually run on that platform? For some reason, it was decided that I would do it. My friend,

Ted Coyle, volunteered to be my campaign manager and deliver the nominating speech. As it turned out, my candidacy would gain unexpected traction.

I certainly started out as a long-shot, at best, and the route to actually being elected was circuitous. Running for student council president involved, as I vaguely recall, filling out some kind of nominating form, probably with signatures of the requisite number of students and the signature of the student council advisor, who at that time was Susan Donahue, a science teacher I had never had. I filled out the form and submitted it. I was officially a candidate for student council president, albeit an illegal one, since I had never served in student government before. At the time, no one seemed to notice or to care. The other candidates were Larry Fink, a classmate from way back in Section 701 and Jeff Kowalczyk, a very good player on the basketball team, and certainly the people's choice heading into the election.

Part of the election process involved making a speech to the entire student body in the school auditorium. Public speaking never bothered me, so the speech was actually the most fun part of the process, although still a little nerve-wracking, not knowing how my proposal would be received. Speeches were scheduled for my 17th birthday. Jeff ran as the Red (or White) Party candidate, who knows, Larry as the White (or Red) Party candidate (our school colors were red and white), while I was an Independent, without the benefit of a party affiliation or color designation. There had never been more than two candidates before. Jeff and Larry wore ties. I wore a flannel shirt and was given a seat on the stage farthest away from the podium. I got to speak last.

What happened next was captured in the WEDNESDAY, JUNE 9, 1971, issue of *The Hawker*, our school newspaper. I think that a good friend of mine, Tom Lichtman, co-editor of the paper, wrote the article under the headline, "Florig, Meyer Victorious in Second Council Election."

On May 4, the veil of apathy was lifted from the student body at Haddon Township High School. This miraculous deed was accomplished by student council elections, the likes of which Haddon Township has never seen. For a starter, when was the last time a candidate had to win three times before being declared the winner? When was the last time an election was run with three students vying for the presidential office? How many times have we had the right to vote without registration? And finally, when was the last time the students were really interested in the processes?

The single response that answers these questions is - Never. David Florig, a dark horse to say the least, caused these misoccurrences and by the end of the fiasco, he had the whole school in the pocket of his flannel shirt.

On the morning of the speeches it appeared that Jeff Kowalczyk, an amiable basketball player had the election in the bag. Some people thought that Larry Fink might give him some competition because he was 'more intelligent and had a more definite platform.' On the Monday before the speeches, David himself didn't think he had a prayer.

The Tuesday morning speeches changed all that. Jeff spoke first and told the students not to expect "champagne in the water fountains" and that he would try to change the detention system and abolish exams for B-students and above. Larry Fink's platform was somewhat similar . . . Florig's speech was completely different; as Ted Coyle, David's campaign manager stated, "In the past, the voters had only Red and White, but this year you have a choice, David Florig." In his speech, David made a proposal to abolish student council until such time that council is given the right to legislate instead of simply making suggestions to the administration. He talked of having doors on the toilet stalls, lavatory passes, intellectual freedom and power to the people. There was a pulsating applause throughout his speech. The spirited response reached its height as David ended his speech quoting Eldridge Cleaver's statement, "If you are not part of

the solution, you are part of the problem." He fielded the
questions sloppily and won the election the next day by a
strong plurality.

I'm not sure that I agree with the "sloppily" part. I recall "smoothly" and "seamlessly." I also recall Jeff's younger sister, Vanessa Kowalczyk, asking a rather nasty question during the Q&A, which I found rather unseemly. In one morning I had transformed from fairly anonymous high school kid to rock star. Nonetheless, by the end of the day on Wednesday, after the results were announced, it looked like I was the student council's president-elect. It wasn't going to be nearly that simple.

There were apparently some problems with my candidacy and electoral victory. For starters, neither Susan Donahue nor William Wolf, an assistant principal, were particularly fond of my speech. I heard through the grapevine that Al Tanner, one of the great teachers among a whole slew of them at Haddon Township, had referred to me as a "demagogue." Now, if you look up the definition of "demagogue," there are at least two distinct meanings, one flattering and one not quite so: (1) a leader who makes use of popular prejudices and false claims and promises in order to gain power; or (2) a leader championing the cause of the common people. I've never asked Al which he meant, but I suspect that I know.

The administration informed the sitting student council that the election was "unconstitutional," which, quite frankly, it was. An emergency council meeting was called by council president Sandy Schmidt and council ruled that the election results were void, citing constitutional provisions about the number of candidates and qualifications for office. Apparently, there could only be two candidates, which there were not, and the council president had to have previously served in student government, which I had not. According to *The Hawker*, "After fierce bickering between Mrs. Donahue, the executive board, the council members and the administration, a decision was arrived at. The first election was void, but because the council was a mirror of student opinion they would have to amend the constitution to admit David." Imagine - "fierce bickering" over me. The constitution was amended to remove all prerequisites for the offices of president and vice president.

Of course, all of this meant that there would have to be another election, limited to two candidates. Sensing an opening, a fourth candidate, Mike LeFever, co-captain of the wrestling team, entered the race. Since there were now four candidates and only two could constitutionally be on the ballot for president, a primary was held to narrow the field. Mike's scheme blew up when he and Jeff split the jock/school spirit vote. Larry Fink and I survived the primary and faced off for the third time, which I again won, although I suspect by a smaller margin than the first time.

The Hawker summed things up:

> *In retrospect, Larry Fink had a fine platform and made a fine showing of himself. But it was David who caught the pulse of the students. Some of his sayings had an original ring to them, and there were a few inconsistencies in the talk. All things considered though, David has done something no one has ever accomplished; he has made the individuals of our school an actual student body.*

Again, I must take issue with "inconsistencies," and don't know that I had "sayings," but, mercifully, it was finally over. After an election, a primary, and another election, I was officially the next president of the student council. Larry Fink wrote in my yearbook, "To the darkest horse I ever knew, good luck next year with Student Council or whatever you want to make of it." In the true spirit of patronage, I put my friend Larry in charge of re-writing the council's constitution.

As you may have guessed, I didn't abolish student council, my major campaign plank. There were simply too many perks to being president. I learned that I could call council meetings during whichever period I chose, which I used to avoid my least favorite classes, and that I could walk the halls without a hall pass. I was a high school celebrity, of sorts. I doubt that anyone else on council wanted to do away with it, either. With college applications on the horizon, it was nice filler to note that you were an officer or member of the student council, demonstrating your outstanding leadership skills and the high esteem in which your schoolmates held you. We, especially I, had been corrupted by power. The saddest part is, I don't really regret any of it.

It was a lot like Newt Gingrich's "Contract with America" in the 1990's. Promising term limits seemed like a really good idea until the Republicans actually won and took control of Congress. Suddenly term limits didn't seem so important, and limiting one's own power and standing was just foolish. So that idea was quickly forgotten, just like I quickly forgot about my pledge to do away with student council.

I honestly don't know if council accomplished anything meaningful that year, although I do seem to remember a boycott in the cafeteria leading to an upgraded menu, a constitutional convention to rewrite council's constitution, and maybe we were finally allowed to wear jeans to school. And I learned that the saying, "Power corrupts; absolute power corrupts absolutely," is true.

* * *

That birthday was special for a much, much more important reason. I got out of school early to go with Marge to Berlin, New Jersey, where I would pass my driving test and get my license.

CHAPTER 12

MONDAY, NOVEMBER 8, 1971

Elvis was alive and well at the end of 1971. His final #1 single, "Suspicious Minds," had reached the top of the Billboard chart in November of 1969. This wasn't "fat Elvis," but Elvis still in the midst of a resurgence of sorts. He had some other hits in the late 60's and early 70's - "In the Ghetto," "If I Can Dream" and "Kentucky Rain." It was nothing like in his prime, but a respectable presence on the charts nonetheless, given all that had happened to rock and roll - Motown, the British invasion, the Summer of Love, Woodstock and metal - since it had arrived, courtesy of Chuck Berry, Buddy Holly, Jerry Lee Lewis, Little Richard and Elvis himself in the mid-1950's.

On Monday night, Elvis wore a white jumpsuit called either "Snowflake" or the "Spectrum Suit," so-called because on this night, at the Spectrum in Philadelphia, he wore it onstage for the first time. It was white, with a black-lined white cape, bell bottoms and white boots. No suit is complete without a cape.

The next day, the *Philadelphia Inquirer* reported:

> *The most ballyhooed entertainment to hit*
> *Philadelphia in years came and went Monday night, Elvis*
> *Presley struck and now everything is back to normal in the*
> *South Philadelphia neighborhood surrounding the Spectrum.*

A capacity crowd filled the sports arena for the splashy Vegas-type show. Most of them - 16,601 paid - screamed and shouted and oohed and aahed. And it was just like the good old days of rock 'n' roll. Back when Elvis brought the new sound and his nervous hips out of Memphis to establish a whole new direction for pop music.

Certainly, it cannot be said that Elvis failed to give the customers their money's worth. He gave them an hour of what they came to see and hear, Elvis Presley.

There was a chatter of disenchantment from many in the audience when it became evident that they would have to endure an hour of unexpected entertainment before being greeted by Elvis. The Sweet Inspirations opened the show with a 20-minute set of soul-oriented music. Then came comedian Jackie Kahane, who had a rough time winning over the Elvis fans with his club-based act. Kahane was scheduled for 35 minutes, but he gave up ahead of schedule. Small wonder. The crowd didn't come to giggle. They came to rip it up with Elvis.

But they had to rip it up with restraint as a result of stern warnings that no one was to leave their seat during the performance. The penalty for disobedience was not made clear by the announcer, but the man seemed to mean business.

Elvis pounced on stage in a dazzling white outfit and blinked at the explosion of flash bulbs that greeted his arrival. There wasn't much chatter with the audience. Just that splashy

brand of Elvis showmanship and most of the big songs that
one associates with Elvis, spanning the past 15 years - "That's
All Right, Mama," "I Got a Woman," "Love Me Tender,"
"You've Lost That Loving Feeling," "Johnny B. Goode,"
"Heartbreak Hotel," "Blue Suede Shoes," "Suspicious Minds"
and all the others.

Elvis obviously will never be what he once was. A country boy
who sang the life out of a blues song. It's all too slick now. But
he is a showman. Maybe that's the trouble. It's all so well-
planned and choreographed.

I've gone to far better concerts than the one Elvis gave, but he was *the*
King, and not many of my friends can claim to have seen him (except
maybe in Vegas, which doesn't really count). Here is the list of everyone
else I've seen in concert, as best as I can remember, in more or less
chronological order. Rock and Roll Hall of Fame members are in **bold**:

Blind Faith - (see July 16, 1969)

Pete Seeger - Becky and I saw Pete Seeger in Philadelphia in 1970. This
was the same Pete Seeger, who just a few years earlier, on SUNDAY, JULY 25,
1965, outraged by Bob Dylan playing an electric set featuring "Maggie's
Farm" at the Newport Folk Festival, allegedly threatened to cut the
electric chord with a hatchet.

Leon Russell/Freddie King - WIBG was hosting a free concert starring
Leon Russell. The only problem was, they weren't announcing where the
concert would be held. Wibbage had around a half a million listeners in
1971 and they were afraid that the venue would be overwhelmed with
concert-goers if they announced the location. Instead, they gave out clues
to the location over the air. By the day of the concert, we had figured out
where it was. On MONDAY, AUGUST 9, 1971, I drove to Conshohocken
with some of my high school friends - I think Kevin Manns, Scott Welden
and Bob Siman went - for the show. A week earlier, Leon Russell had been
at Madison Square Garden as part of the Concert for Bangladesh put on
by George Harrison. Russell was a musician's musician, recording and
producing with the Beach Boys, Bob Dylan, Frank Sinatra and the Rolling
Stones. Freddie King was one of the "Three Kings of the Blues Guitar,"
along with B.B. King and Albert King (none of whom are related). The
long-defunct *Philadelphia Evening Bulletin* headlined, "Rock Show by

Leon Russell Attracts 30,000 to Stadium in Conshohocken." To this day, it remains the largest single gathering in Conshohocken history.

*Joe Cocker and **Dave Mason*** - I saw Cocker and Mason together at the Spectrum on WEDNESDAY, MARCH 22, 1972. I most likely went with Leona, although I don't specifically remember that. I listened to a lot of both Cocker and Mason in high school, and seeing them together would be a bonus. It was Cocker's first U.S. concert in two years. Although I enjoyed it, critic Steve Amadio did not:

> *Cocker should go back to England. To all outward appearances, the performer with the big red heart on his tee shirt was Joe Cocker, but he couldn't communicate his identity to the audience. Cocker still sounds as if he needs someone to apply a plunger to his throat to extract whatever he has lodged down there, and he still moves about like an epileptic chicken in its death throes. His backup band . . . played well together, but Joe and the band seemed miles apart. And the audience sensed this. They reacted to Cocker's contortions with the enthusiasm usually reserved for a funeral.*

Dave Mason opened, Cocker came next, and they closed together with "Feelin' Alright."

*Badfinger/**Faces*** - (see July 2, 1972)

Bob Dylan/The Band - Dylan had not toured in eight years, but returned to the road in 1974. On SUNDAY, JANUARY 6, 1974, he performed two shows at the Spectrum. I went to the first one with Bob Bowdoin. Dylan was touring with The Band, who also did a solo set in addition to backing Dylan. I don't remember Dylan speaking a word during the show. He rarely does. His setlist went:

Ballad of Hollis Brown
Lay, Lady, Lay
Just Like Tom Thumb's Blues
It Ain't Me, Babe
Tough Mama
Ballad of a Thin Man

All Along the Watchtower

Leopard-Skin Pill-Box Hat

Knockin' on Heaven's Door

To Ramona

Mama, You Been on My Mind

The Lonesome Death of Hattie Carroll

Nobody 'Cept You

It's Alright Ma, I'm Only Bleeding

I Don't Believe You

Forever Young

Something There is About You

Like a Rolling Stone

Dylan, of course, is my favorite artist of all time. I know he can't sing and I don't care. The music is genius.

Picking a Top 10 of favorite Dylan songs is a much more difficult undertaking than picking a Beatles Top 10. For one thing, Dylan has written more than twice as many songs as the Beatles did. For another, Beatles songs encompass a very short time frame - 6 or 7 years, whereas Dylan has been writing and recording for six decades. And Dylan songs span a much wider range of styles. Nevertheless, here's a try, in no special order:

Desolation Row

Highway 61 Revisited

Hurricane

Positively 4th Street

Sad Eyed Lady of the Lowlands

Just Like a Woman

Mississippi

Queen Jane Approximately

Like a Rolling Stone

I Shall be Released

Things Have Changed

For those reading closely, that's II not 10. I just couldn't cut any of them. And for those who think that Dylan was simply a product of the 60's and 70's, you really should listen to the stuff he's released this century.

John Denver - OK, I'm not overly proud of this one. On FRIDAY, APRIL 18, 1975, I took Barbara Boenning to the Spectrum to see Denver. We had upstairs seats for the grossly overly-produced show, featuring a 25-piece orchestra, fake stained-glass windows and three projection screens. Don't get me wrong, some of the songs are pretty good, but the music should be the star, not the production. And the sad part is, he was a pretty good songwriter and performer, but they turned him into a ("far out, man") caricature of himself.

Billy Joel (see December 5, 1977)

Rick Nelson - This one gave me fits trying to remember. I (almost) definitely saw Rick Nelson three times. I clearly remember two of them - SATURDAY, NOVEMBER 10, 1979, at the Broadway Theater in Pitman, New Jersey and another time in the mid-1980's in Massachusetts - Marblehead, maybe. I went to the Massachusetts concert alone at some outdoor venue. I still have one ticket stub (remember those?) from a show in Pitman, but torn in half by the usher. Unfortunately, I don't have the half that gives the date. What I do know is that I went with Mary Erhard, who ran down to the stage and kissed him, in a very *Ozzie and Harriet* kind of way, at the November show. I think that I had also seen him in Pitman earlier that year, on SATURDAY, APRIL 21, 1979, with some friends, but that's not a guarantee. Rick Nelson doesn't get nearly the credit he deserves for bringing rock and roll into the mainstream of America. While Chuck Berry, Little Richard and Elvis may have been a little scary to white, middle-class America, Ricky Nelson most certainly was not.

Rick Nelson is sometimes credited with creating the first music video. On WEDNESDAY, APRIL 5, 1961, Nelson, known then as "Ricky," sang "Travelin' Man" at the end of one episode of *Ozzie and Harriet*. Superimposed behind him while he sang was some Nelson family vacation movie footage. The family had discovered that record sales soared whenever Ricky closed the show with a song, so they often used the last couple of minutes to promote one of his records.

Tom Paxton - Tom Paxton played at the Bijou Cafe in Philadelphia around 1980, give or take a year. The Bijou Cafe was a cozy little 275-seat venue on Lombard Street. The first United States performance by U2 was at the Bijou Cafe. The only song I remember from Paxton's concert is "Boney Fingers" ("Work your fingers to the bone and what do you get? Boney fingers.") What I remember the most about the evening was the warm-up act, a little-known comedian named David Letterman.

Steve Goodman - Sadly, I only saw Steve Goodman one time, most likely in the very early 1980's, somewhere in a small venue in Philadelphia near the Penn campus. He had been diagnosed with leukemia in 1969, but survived much longer than expected, given the lack of real treatments back then. He was an amazing talent and had given himself the nickname "Cool Hand Leuk." His most famous composition was "City of New Orleans," with which Arlo Guthrie had his biggest hit. He also wrote "A Dying Cub Fan's Last Request," which featured the chorus:

> *Do they still play the blues in Chicago when baseball season rolls around*
>
> *When the snow melts away do the Cubbies still play in their ivy-covered burial ground*
>
> *When I was a boy, they were my pride and joy, but now they only bring fatigue*
>
> *To the home of the brave, the land of the free, and the doormat of the National League*

Goodman was a life-long Chicago Cubs fan and had been invited to sing the national anthem before their first playoff game since 1945, a TUESDAY, OCTOBER 2, 1984 game against the San Diego Padres. While the Cubs' management was reportedly not too keen on "A Dying Cub Fan's Last Request," Goodman had gotten back into their good graces by writing "Go, Cubs, Go," a rah-rah song. The Cubs had never made it to the postseason during Goodman's lifetime. Unfortunately, by 1984, his leukemia had returned and he died on THURSDAY, SEPTEMBER 20, 1984, at the age of 36, just twelve days before he was scheduled to sing the national anthem. Jimmy Buffet filled in and dedicated the anthem to Goodman. Four years later, a few of Goodman's friends snuck into Wrigley Field and scattered some of his ashes there.

Goodman's show in Philadelphia oozed with joy and laughter and was pure fun. His songs were funny, sweet, satirical and poignant, much like those of his good friend, John Prine, another of my absolute favorite singer-songwriters, who, after recovering from cancer in both his neck and lung, passed away on TUESDAY, APRIL 7, 2020, one of the early victims of COVID-19.

John Fogerty (see September 14, 1986)

Bonnie Raitt (see September 14, 1986)

Patty Larkin - Nancy and I saw Patty Larkin in a church basement somewhere in Massachusetts, most likely in November or December of 1986. I'm pretty sure of the year because it was maybe the third or fourth date that we went on. Patty Larkin was very funny and entertaining, donning wigs and such, although I couldn't name a single song of hers without looking it up.

Lee Andrews & the Hearts - Nancy and I went to some kind of summer festival at Penn's Landing in Philadelphia, probably around 1988 or 1989. It was one of those events where everyone just kind of mills around looking at the various food and craft booths. There were two or three stages set up. Lee Andrews & the Hearts were on one of them. The group was a very popular Philadelphia doo-wop group who had a Billboard No. 45 hit with "Long, Lonely Nights" in 1957, and two other hits, "Teardrops" and "Try the Impossible." We watched part of their set and then wandered off.

Jimmy Buffett - Talk about someone who's apparently got it made. Seemingly every summer, Buffett hits the road for three months, rakes in about $30 million or so, and goes home to Florida or wherever. No wonder he's worth $500 million. Anyway, around 1991 or so, Nancy and I went to see him at the Mann Music Center and sat on the lawn. Among the 14,000 or so "Parrotheads," roughly 13,975, including me, were wearing Hawaiian shirts. A friend of mine from high school who has actually met Buffett tells me that, to phrase it politely, he's not exactly the carefree, happy-go-lucky, beach bum character that he cultivates.

All Buffett has to do is play the Big 8 songs - "Margaritaville," "Volcano," "Changes in Latitudes, Changes in Attitudes," "Come Monday," "Fins," "A Pirate Looks at Forty," "Cheeseburger in Paradise" and "Why Don't We Get Drunk (and Screw)" - throw in a few others, and call it a night. While a Buffett concert is great fun, it also has this underlying feel of simply being a money grab.

The Mavericks (see Saturday, November 5, 1994)

Reba McEntire - It was a Saturday, sometime in the 1990's, and Nancy was at a school fair at Edison School in Haddon Township, where she was a teacher. WXTU 92.5, Philly's largest country music station, had a van there at the fair. They were giving out tickets for some kind of country music festival at the outdoor amphitheater in Camden. It's been through quite a few name changes, so I have no idea what it was called then. Reba was the headliner. The only problem was that the concert was that night. Nancy took some tickets and we decided to go. I have no recollection whatsoever of who else was on the ticket, but it was free and it was fun. Even Dylan liked it, although I doubt that he even remembers.

Mary Chapin Carpenter - (see Saturday, November 5, 1994)

Bruce Springsteen & the E Street Band - Had it not been for Hurricane Floyd, I never would have seen Springsteen. He had been scheduled to play on September 16th, but the show was postponed because of the hurricane. It was to be the first of six consecutive shows in Philly. Instead, it was rescheduled for FRIDAY, SEPTEMBER 24, 1999, at the Spectrum, even though the other shows were held at the Wachovia Center. For some reason, Kevin Schildt and Brian Adams had an extra ticket and asked me on short notice (I probably wasn't their first choice) if I wanted to go. Without great enthusiasm, I said yes.

I simply was not a huge Springsteen fan, although I'm not sure why. He is exactly the kind of musician I like - a storyteller, songwriter, - not a "singer." And I certainly didn't dislike him, I just never went all in on Springsteen like I did for Bob Dylan, or John Fogerty or John Prine, for example. I have to say, though, that the concert was amazing. It was Springsteen's first concert after turning 50. When he was younger, Springsteen would run across the stage and jump up onto the piano during a song. At 50, he sorta climbed up onto the piano. Springsteen and the E Street Band are legendary for putting in an honest night's work at their concerts and they played for three hours with no break. The setlist was:

Growin' Up

No Surrender

Prove it All Night

Two Hearts

The Promised Land

Spirit in the Night

Does This Bus Stop at 82nd Street?

Mansion on the Hill

Independence Day

Youngstown

Murder Incorporated

Badlands

Out in the Street

Tenth Avenue Freeze-Out

Working on the Highway

The Fever

Backstreets

Light of Day

Bobby Jean

Born to Run

Thunder Road

If I Should Fall Behind
Land of Hopes and Dreams
Blinded by the Light

Our seats weren't very good for how the stage was set up. We had some kind of obstruction or light shining in our eyes or something, so we went and stood in a little area in front of one of the press boxes or luxury boxes. An usher came and told us that we had to move, and we explained the problem. *Nevertheless, she persisted*, as Mitch McConnell might say, until Brian palmed her a $20 bill and she left us alone for the rest of the concert.

John Mellencamp - (see September 14, 1986)

Dar Williams - By far, the worst concert I ever went to was Dar Williams. All three of us - Nancy, Dylan and I - went, and we are all in agreement. I don't have anything against Dar Williams. In fact, she had released an album, *End of the Summer*, in 1997, which I bought and listened to a lot. There were a couple of really good songs on it, like "Are You Out There" and "Better Things." After seeing her open for Chapin and listening to the album, I got tickets for us to see her at the Scottish Rites Auditorium in Collingswood, I believe on FRIDAY, NOVEMBER 21, 2003.

It was a disaster. She didn't sound great, didn't perform a single song that I knew, rambled and had a local high school girl wearing saddle shoes as the opener. Plus, the auditorium smelled really, really musty.

Joe Scarborough - Nancy and I went to see Joe Scarborough (*Morning Joe* on MSNBC) at Vinegar Hill Music Theater in the summer of 2016, our first summer living in Maine. Scarborough served six years in the United States House of Representatives, then went on to a television career as a political pundit. Although he made his name as a political talking head, his first love is music. He and his band have performed at *South by Southwest*, the huge music and arts festival in Austin.

At Vinegar Hill, Scarborough did a show which consisted first of just some talking and answering questions, along with some of his morning show regulars at the time, Mica Brzezinski, John Meacham and Nicolle Wallace. For the second act, Joe and his band played. They were really, really good, although they were also really, really loud. They were all staying at the Bush compound in Kennebunkport, occupying, as one might expect, a spectacular peninsula on the southern coast of Maine. You can always tell when "W" is there, because a Texas flag is flying, or when Jeb is there, because a Florida flag is flying, in addition to the United States and Maine flags.

ZZ Top (see September 14, 1986)

John Sebastian - On SUNDAY, AUGUST 5, 2018, Nancy and I took a short detour down memory lane and went to Jonathan's in Ogunquit, Maine to see John Sebastian. We sat about 25 feet from the stage in a room that seats maybe 200 people. Sebastian was the frontman for the hippie/jugband group the Lovin' Spoonful in the 1960's and famously forgot the words to his own song, "I Had a Dream" while performing at Woodstock. He didn't have a band, just himself and a guitar, couldn't sing a lick anymore, but was very personable and played a bunch of Spoonful songs, so everyone went home happy.

The Quebe Sisters - We had tickets to see the Quebe Sisters for more than a year-and-a-half. I got them as a Christmas present for Nancy in 2019, for a show scheduled for the summer of 2020. Obviously, not many concerts were happening in 2020, so the show was postponed until FRIDAY, JULY 16, 2021. Nancy had seen the Quebe Sisters a few years earlier at the Lowell Folk Festival and had always said she would like to go see them again. I had never heard of the Quebe Sisters, who actually are sisters who each play fiddle and sing. The tickets were for Stone Mountain, where we had seen Mary Chapin Carpenter twice before.

This time, we were even luckier in getting our seats than the times before. As soon as we arrived, we were ushered into the hall and started walking toward the front. I kept expecting to be stopped and seated, but we kept walking all the way down to the stage, where we got a table for two right up against the stage. When the Quebe Sisters started playing their Texas swing music, we were no more than five feet away from where they stood.

Taste in music is subjective. I get it. I like jazz, you like rap; I like Motown, you like disco. Everyone's entitled to their opinion, but do they really have to broadcast it? One particular moron, Ethan Reynolds, desperately begging for "likes" or "clicks," I suppose, posted his list of "The Most Overrated Rock Bands of All Time." Included in his list were (and I'm not making this up) The Rolling Stones, Creedence Clearwater Revival, Fleetwood Mac, Bruce Springsteen & The E Street Band, The Doors, The Eagles, Bon Jovi, Nirvana, The Jimi Hendrix Experience and Janis Joplin. Here is probably all that you need to know about Mr. Ethan Reynolds: He describes himself this way - "Ethan grew up in sunny Los Angeles, where he learned the 27 uses of the word 'chill' . . . [H]e's convinced that he was a wine-loving, harp-playing wood elf in a past life." He no doubt was.

The brilliant folks at onee website put The Beatles, Bob Dylan, Nirvana, Queen, Beyoncé, The Rolling Stones and Bob Marley on their list of most overrated bands. Their insightful comments included this about Bob Dylan - "Bob Dylan sucks, and most people know it . . . His lyrics are actually 100 percent shallow . . ." (Kirk Adams). About Queen - "The top 10 worst songs of all time are Queen songs." (Maggie Ellery).

About The Beatles - "[N]o band that's not overrated would've recorded 'Revolution 9.' No way." (Marion Eddy). About Nirvana - "[Kurt Cobain] didn't have any talent or original ideas." (Heather Gorham). About the Rolling Stones - "Rock and roll is a young person's game. Nobody proves that better than these wrinkled potatoes." (Julie K. Bressler). Nothing says "I'm a serious music critic" like saying someone sucks or calling people "wrinkled potatoes." As an aside, I've seen Ms. Bressler and I have a bit of unsolicited advice - you probably shouldn't be commenting on other people's appearance.

To save these savvy social commentators the trouble, here's my best guess of who they might deem "overrated" in a few other categories:

Tennis Player - Serena Williams

Civil Rights Leader - Martin Luther King, Jr.

Golfer - Jack Nicklaus

Sculptor - Michelangelo

President - Abraham Lincoln

Writer - Fyodor Dostoevsky

Poet - Emily Dickinson

Sprinter - Usain Bolt

Painter - Leonardo da Vinci

Hockey Player - Wayne Gretzky

Tickets to see Elvis that night in 1971 were $5.00, $7.50 and $10.00. I certainly didn't spring for the $10.00 tickets. I might have splurged for the $7.50 ones, since our seats weren't bad. Poor Jackie Kahane, trying to get some laughs when all we wanted was to see Elvis. Imagine how Jimi Hendrix felt opening for the Monkees. He lasted only seven dates as the Monkees' opening act in 1967, not really playing the kind of music the mostly-teenage girls came to hear and see. My date for Elvis was Leona Miller.

I first recall meeting Leona on a church trip to Haiti in August of 1971, although I had likely met her before. Around 25 of us went, adults and high school kids. My parents went, along with Carl and Georgia Glover, Pastor Floyd Brown, Jim Schmidt, Sr., Bernice Bisbing, Bob Van Osten and some other adults I don't really remember. As for the kids, Bob Bowdoin, Bob Hunsberger, Barbara Bisbing, Sue Holcombe, Diane Lewis, Barbara Ilgenfritz, Rich Johnson, Betty Siner, Bonnie Glaser, Chris Hutto, Jim Schmidt, Jr., Doris String, Phyllis String and John Moser went for sure, as well as Leona. She was a year younger than me, went to Collingswood High School, just like my mother had, and wasn't nearly as active in the church as the other kids and their families.

To get to Haiti (Ouanaminthe, Haiti, to be more precise), we took the church bus from Collingswood, leaving at 4:30 a.m. on THURSDAY, AUGUST 26, 1971, for JFK Airport in New York. At 8:30 a.m., we took off for Port-Au-Prince, Haiti's capital, arriving at 10:55 a.m. From Port-Au-Prince, we embarked on an 80-mile bus ride over mostly dirt, and mud, roads to Cap Haitian. It took us 10 ½ hours. A good ultramarathoner could have run there in that amount of time. There were times when we had to get off of the bus and walk so that the bus could get through the mud. Haiti was, and still is, the poorest country in the Western Hemisphere.

My first specific recollection of Leona is from one of those bus rides. She was sitting in front of me with Chris Hutto and we all began talking, Leona and I taking a particular interest in each other. Chris I knew well, since she was Becky's sister. Over the course of the bus ride, I was reminded several times by some of her classmates that Leona had a boyfriend. I think his name was Kenny. By the time we headed home twelve days later, she and I were a couple and Kenny was about to get some unwelcome news.

On TUESDAY, SEPTEMBER 6, 1971, we began the trip home. We divided into two groups and mercifully took two separate planes, not a bus, to Port Au Prince. On Tuesday night, we stayed in a nice hotel downtown, although the power went off for a few hours. There were troops with serious faces and serious-looking weapons all over, with Jean-Claude ("Baby Doc") Duvalier's presidential palace not far from our hotel. Baby Doc was the 19-year-old president of Haiti, having inherited the position from his father, François "Papa Doc" Duvalier, much like Don, Jr. was hoping to do with his father. On WEDNESDAY, SEPTEMBER 7, 1971, at 11:15 a.m., we flew from Port Au Prince to Miami, then on Eastern Airlines at 4:00 p.m. to New York. By 11:00 p.m., we were back home on Burrwood Avenue.

When we finally returned to Collingswood, Leona faced the chore of breaking up with her boyfriend, which she did with great dispatch, if not great relish. It didn't seem to bother her too much, though. We were together for the next 2 ½ years.

Leona was starting her junior year, I was starting my senior year. By this time I had both a driver's license and a car, so dating was a lot easier than with Becky. It also provided much-needed privacy for a couple of teenagers.

I'm not really a car person. For me, a car is a way to get from here to there. Utilitarian, as Elaine Benes would say. Shortly after I had gotten my driver's license, I somehow convinced my parents to get me my own car. They finally agreed, probably for their own benefit as much as for mine,

and we found a 1959 Opel Rekord for sale in the *Courier Post* classified ads. Stick shift, clutch, choke, push-button radio, crankable windows, the works. Charlie took me to Laurel Springs to see it and we ultimately paid the owner $50 cash and headed home.

We almost made it, too. But at the intersection of Lawnside and Emerald Avenues, three blocks from home, the Opel died. I'm not exactly sure what went wrong, but Charlie ended up pushing it the final three blocks with the family car while I sat in the Opel and steered. Whatever had gone wrong, Charlie was ultimately able to fix it and that car took me through my senior year. I even put "DSF" decals on the driver's side door and "LAM" decals, for Leona Ann Miller, on the passenger's side.

I don't think that I can list all of my cars, in order, but it goes roughly like this:

1959 Opel Rekord (Light green) [used]

1972 Honda 600 Coupe (Orange) [new for $1,625]

Ford Pinto (Light Blue) [used]

Chrysler (White, I think) [used]

Volvo 164E (Dark Blue) [used]

Mazda Coupe (White) [new]

Toyota Camry (Dark Blue) [hand-me-down from Nancy]

Lexus ES250 (Black) [new]

Lexus 300 (Maroon) [used]

2003 Jeep Liberty (White) [used]

2013 Kia Soul (White) [new]

The orange '72 Honda Coupe was, by far, my favorite, not only because it was my first new car, but because it was way cool. It was roughly the size and shape of a size 13 roller skate, with a stick shift and a 2-cylinder, air-cooled engine. Basically a motorcycle engine under a hood. It cost no more than $1.50 to fill with gas if the gauge was below "E," which it often was. I once managed to cram seven people inside. The roof was barely as high as my belt buckle.

Leona had long blonde hair, blue eyes and, not surprisingly, was a cheerleader. She was bubbly, smiled and laughed easily, and was enthusiastic about almost everything. She and my mother dieted together, eating cheese, melba toast, and drinking Tab.

Leona and I went to my junior/senior prom on FRIDAY, MAY 12, 1972, at the Sheraton Poste Inn on Route 70 in Cherry Hill, across Route 70 from the Garden State Racetrack, before the track burned down.. We also went to her junior prom that spring, probably just a week or two apart. *The Hawker* described my prom this way, under the headline, "'Tapestry' Unfolds Memorable Evening":

On Friday, May 12, the Haddon Township High School juniors and seniors held the attractive, spring prom, 'Tapestry' at the Sheraton Poste Inn.

The prom began at 8:00 p.m. with all of the guests at the prom passing through the traditional receiving line. The line was a little awkward due to a few late members, however, the line was the start of an exciting and memorable evening.

Once all the guests were settled inside the large, beautiful banquet room, a delicious dinner of a variety of foods was served in a buffet fashion. The dinner consumed a great length of time due to the large crowd but was very much worth the time. Pictures were being taken outside by the Inn's pool and fountain during dinner and continuing for the rest of the evening.

Dancing followed dining and everyone glided along the dance floor displaying their handsome tuxedoes and gowns to the enjoyable music of T.K.'s. The excellent band performed a variety of many songs along with a few Carole King numbers which brought forth the theme of 'Tapestry.'

Group table pictures interrupted the dancing for a time as the photographers went from table to table, then followed the grand march of the seniors. The senior couples paraded around the dance floor in elegant fashion while the juniors watched in disappointment, for not being asked to march also. As the grand march continued the faculty guests carefully eyed each girl and her gown to decide on the prom queen.

Then came the moment everyone was waiting for. The faculty discussed among each other for a few exciting minutes and Karen Schmidt was chosen as prom queen with Robin Kaigh, Nancy Justice and Debbie Gizelbach in her court. Flowers were given to the girls and the dancing continued for the remainder of the evening.

At 12 midnight everyone left the Inn and rode to Baker Lanes for an enjoyable bowling party, with refreshments supplied by the PTA, which ended a pleasurable and memorable evening.

Honestly, I don't remember any of that. Proms just weren't my thing, even though I went to at least four of them, an unfortunate by-product of dating girls either slightly older or slightly younger than me.

Like with Becky, it's hard to remember all of the specific things that Leona and I did together. I do remember going to the harness races at Liberty Bell Park and losing a contact lens in the parking lot. We also went to the Army-Navy football game on SATURDAY, NOVEMBER 27, 1971, at JFK Stadium in Philadelphia, along with 97,045 other people. By all accounts, it was one of the best Army-Navy games ever, with Army prevailing 24-23 after stopping Navy on fourth down in the final minute. All I remember is that it got cold, rainy and windy during the game and we spent a good deal of the game under cover in a concourse. Like with Becky, we did go to camp together in August of 1972. Someone took one of my favorite pictures, Leona and I standing outside of the Temple on Temple Avenue in Ocean Park that year.

Leona's father, Ray, was intimidating, although I don't think that he necessarily tried to be. He was ex-military, had short, dark, Brylcreemed hair ("a little dab'll do ya," for those old enough), smoked and made me terrified to deliver his daughter home past curfew. Nevertheless, Ray and I got along great and I discovered that he was a very good softball player, so I recruited him to play for my team. He was a lefty with good power, good speed, great instincts and a very good arm. He apparently was a bit of a South Jersey softball legend.

By 1973 or 1974, I was feeling a little smothered. I was at Penn, Leona was at Eastern College, and it was time. After a couple of failed attempts, I was finally able to pull the plug on it, as gently as I could. The last time that I saw Leona, Ray, and her younger sister, Sally, was sometime around the early 2000's. I got a call from Leona saying that she was visiting her family at Sally's home in Medford and asking if I wanted to stop by. I did, and it was great to see the three of them and laugh and reminisce.

A few years later, I got an email from Sally, telling me that Leona had passed away from colon cancer on THURSDAY, SEPTEMBER 4, 2008, at the age of 53, leaving two sons, two daughters and two stepchildren. Her mother, Sara Miller, died on FRIDAY, AUGUST 30, 2013. Her father, Ray Miller, Sr., died on WEDNESDAY, MAY 14, 2014. Her brother, Ray Miller, Jr., died on TUESDAY, MAY 19, 2015, at age 56. In the span of 6 ½ years, Sally had lost her mother, father, sister, and brother.

CHAPTER 13

THURSDAY, JUNE 15, 1972

Commencement exercises for the Haddon Township High School Class of 1972 began at 6:30 p.m. at Centennial Field behind the school. It was pretty hot to be in a cap and gown - 82 degrees. There were 250 or so kids in my class and we sat on bleachers on the football field facing the stands and our proud guests. As student council president, I sat front and center next to Tom Genetta, the senior class president and a classmate since way back in kindergarten at Strawbridge School. After "Pomp and Circumstance," the first order of business was the Pledge of Allegiance, which, as president of the student council, I was charged with leading. My last official act.

I'm not one of those people who absolutely hated high school, but I know a lot of people who did. Not that they were the best days of my life, either, or that I spend much time reliving the glory, but I generally had fun. I went to almost all of the football and basketball games, as well as the wrestling matches, and many of the plays, talent shows and musicals. It was what we did, and it was all the more fun because we always had friends who either were participating or who went with us. Occasionally, we would go to Green Valley Farms afterwards for ice cream, or maybe to Carvel's on Haddon Avenue, but not often, since we usually had to go home to finish our homework.

During my freshman year, I was active in two sports - one at school and one outside of school. I played what was then called "midget football" with the Westmont Tigers since seventh grade, starting out on the 95-pound team my first year, wearing No. 70, then moving up to the 120-pound division, where I wore No. 56. A bunch of my friends played, too - Julius Sacchetti, Kevin Manns, Jim Reed - plus some kids from Collingswood, since Collingswood didn't have its own midget football team. We played at the athletic complex on Crystal Lake Avenue, straight across the street from Green Valley Farms.

I was thrown out of a game my first year. It was very near the end of the game and I was playing tackle. The kid playing across from me grabbed my facemask and pulled me down. As we lay on the field, I said, "Let go of my facemask, asshole." That, of course, led to some pushing and shoving and general misbehavior. The referee didn't make too big a deal out of it, but did inform both of us that we were out of the game. I'm not sure if I was tossed for fighting or for calling the other kid an asshole.

By my third year of playing, I was one of the bigger kids. The weight limit was 120 pounds and I was about 115 or 116. I looked bigger because they gave me "animal pads," which were enormous shoulder pads, nearly as big as Linda Evans and Joan Collins wore on *Dynasty*. On offense, I played center and on defense, nose guard. Julius Sacchetti's dad, Pete, was our coach and I usually rode to and from practice with them. Sometimes, though, we would ride our bikes to and from practice. On occasion, we would stop into Green Valley on the way home, walk sheepishly up to the counter where they had buckets of pretzel sticks, which were complementary for the paying customers, and fill our helmets with them. During the bike ride home, we would actually eat them out of the helmets hanging from our handlebars.

At the end of my final season, the league had arranged for all of the teams to play a game at the Atlantic City Convention Hall - the one where they used to hold the Miss America pageant. Real grass had been brought inside of Convention Hall and an actual, regulation football field laid out. This was all pretty exciting stuff for kids. We were limited by time, so each game was only 30 minutes long. I can't be completely sure, but I think that we played Oaklyn. During our regular season game with Oaklyn, one of their kids, who they called "Stash," was abusing me pretty badly at the start of the game. On fourth down, I hiked the ball straight up in the air, thinking our quarterback was directly behind me taking the snap. He wasn't. We were punting, but I was too preoccupied wondering what to do about Stash. When I got to the sideline, Mr. Sacchetti simply said, "What the hell was that?"

For the game in Convention Hall, I painted my cleats gold. Toward the end of the regular season, I had painted them white, but too many kids copied me, and we had half the team with white cleats. So I decided to go with gold. The game went quickly and neither team had scored. With time running out, we had the ball, but we were out of time outs. So, on what would be the penultimate play of the game, and my last in organized football, I hiked the ball, put a quick block on somebody, and fell to the turf holding my knee and writhing in apparent agony. I wasn't in any pain, though. When our coaches were huddled over me and asking what was wrong, I looked up and said, "Call another play." Because the referees had stopped the clock so that I could be attended to, I had to leave the game for at least one play, doing my best fake limp as I left. We did run one more play, an incomplete pass, and that was the game. My three-year career playing midget football ended with me standing on the sidelines.

The fake injury is a time-honored tactic in sports, used to stop the action for a while as the "injured" player's team takes a moment to regroup. Soccer and football are notorious for the fake injury ploy. It was especially prevalent in professional football when Chip Kelly was coaching the Eagles. Kelly's teams ran a "no huddle" offense which played at an almost manic pace. It was designed to not let the defense line up in time or in the correct formation. After eight or nine plays at that pace, defensive players would often pretend to be injured so that the referees would be forced to call timeout. In doing so, the entire defense got the chance to catch their breath and get organized. I'm proud to have brought the tactic to midget football.

I made the league all-star team my final year and there was some kind of banquet for the all-stars that fall. It was in a restaurant/banquet facility on the White Horse Pike, but the name has long-since escaped me. I still have my "W" letter for Westmont midget football 1968, never sewn onto a jacket. I used to have an all-star trophy, but I think that I finally tossed it. Maybe not, though. I'll look in the attic.

I tried my hand at wrestling my freshman year. I had never wrestled before in my life, until they taught us how during gym. The fact that I had never wrestled before showed, and I was really, really bad at it. Not to say that I lost every match, because I didn't, but I doubt that I won that many, either. Like with midget football, I still have my freshman wrestling letter and certificate, but that letter, too, was never sewn onto anything. I think you had to be a serious high school athlete to actually wear your letter. Or be like Richie, Potsie and Ralph from *Happy Days*.

During my sophomore year, I had Mrs. (Dale) Payne for English. My goodness. I had about as serious a crush on a teacher as a fifteen-year-old boy could have. She was tall, slim, athletic, smart, stunning and irreverent. I'm sure that I wasn't the only boy crushing on her at HTHS. She came from the Longstreth family in Philadelphia. Philadelphia bluebloods, although she was way more down-to-earth than you would expect. Some of us went to her house on Crystal Lake Avenue a couple of times to visit, which I'm sure she was thrilled about. I remember that she had a dog, an Irish Setter, I think, that was bounce-off-the-walls crazy. Anyway, she was one of my favorite teachers ever, probably because she let me know when I was just cruising and not doing my best work. The best teachers make you *want* to do your best work.

Mrs. Payne was obviously pregnant by the spring of 1970. The class chipped in and bought her a baby gift - some kind of swing set or such - and gave it to her in class. We arranged for someone in the office to detain her for a few minutes before class so that we could set it up. Lin Foley, I believe, spearheaded the gift drive. Lin was a pretty close friend of mine, although I don't know that I have seen her since the day that we graduated.

Lin was a pretty classic high school overachiever. Or at least achiever. She started at Haddon Township in tenth grade. I don't know where she went to school before then. She was a joiner and a doer, but also warm, friendly, approachable and absolutely adorable in every possible way. Despite starting at Haddon Township in tenth grade, or maybe because of it, she made the most of her time there. Her entry, compared to mine, in our senior yearbook is as follows:

Linda Foley

National Honor Society 3-4

Spanish Honor Society 3-4

Varsity Club 3-4

Debate 2-4 (captain 3)

Spanish Club 2-4

Talent Show 3

Student Council 2-4

Class Secretary 3

Anvil (Yearbook) 3, Editor-in-Chief 4

Hawker 2-4

Girl's State 4

Senior Play 4

Basketball 2-4

David Florig

One Act Play 2

Hawker 3-4

Literary Club 3

Student Council President 4

Wrestling 1

Debate 3-4 (co-captain 4)

Golf 3-4

I don't think I was ever actually on *The Hawker* staff, although the yearbook claims that I was. But I *was* in the senior play, which for some reason is not listed. Other than student council during our senior year, we weren't in many of the same activities or clubs during high school except for two - debate and the senior class play, "The Man Who Came to Dinner." Lin and I were in homeroom together (she sat, alphabetically, behind me), Mrs. Payne's English class together, speech, and probably algebra and chemistry, too.

Why I ended up in the senior play, I don't really know. I had no interest in acting and was always uncomfortable when I had to do it. Nonetheless, I auditioned and got a small part as Dr. Bradley, who tends to the lead character, celebrity Sheridan Whiteside, after Whiteside injures himself in a fall. Lin played the part of Maggie Cutler, Whiteside's secretary, who falls in love with Bert, played by my student council election foe, Larry Fink.

The play opened on FRIDAY, DECEMBER 10, 1971, and went relatively smoothly, except that one of us, I won't say who, knocked over a Christmas tree which was part of the set, causing a little bit of ad-libbing and laughter. A few of us decided to spice up the SATURDAY, DECEMBER 11, 1971, performance a little bit. Ed Pfeifer, a kid that we picked on a lot, had the lead role as Whiteside. For most of the play, Whiteside is confined to a wheelchair. At one point, Whiteside is supposed to pull his x-rays out of a large envelope and look at them. On Friday night, he did just that, without incident. But on Saturday night, unbeknownst to Ed, we had replaced the x-rays with a *Playboy* centerfold. According to *The Hawker*, "Playboy photos were slipped in without some cast members' knowledge, creating near hysterics on stage. The cast and crew who knew about the plot were in hysterics, but they were hidden by flats." Ed, though flustered, managed to stay composed enough to get through the scene. He was really good in the play.

I have this vague recollection that I may have given Lin rides home a few times after play practice. She lived on Oneida Avenue and I know that I drove to her house a few times, but I think that I only went inside once, briefly. I'm surmising that it was after play practice, because I had my Opel during senior year.

Lin had been on the high school debate team during our sophomore year, but I had not. Elissa Plasky, who coached the debate team, was a second-year teacher at Haddon Township in 1970. Haddon Township had developed a pretty progressive curriculum by 1970. In the Social Studies Department, for example, rather than just *History I, II, III* and *IV*, we could also take *Contemporary Issues, Sociology, Human Relations, Contemporary Ideologies* or *Independent Study*. In the English Department, we could take, in addition to *English I, II, III* and *IV, Journalism, Public Speaking* or *Independent Study*. By 1971, Social Studies had added *Contemporary Civilizations* and *Humanities*, while English had added *Business Communications, Linguistics, Creative Writing, Theater and Cinema, Short Story and Novel, Poetry and Drama, Poetry in*

Contemporary Music, American Philosophy, Russian Literature, Discussion and Debate and *20th Century Literature*. I know that I took at least *Contemporary Issues, Public Speaking, Creative Writing, Theater and Cinema* and *Russian Literature*. How many high school kids back then got to read Fyoder Dostoevsky, Ivan Turgenev and Aleksandr Solzhenitsyn for credit?

I was in Miss Plasky's Public Speaking class my sophomore year. Lin was in that class, too. She wrote in *The Anvil*, our yearbook:

> *Dear Dave,*
>
> *To the _funniest_ and _greatest_ Fig-Newton I know. We've had the greatest times together, especially in English, Speech, Rutgers and Glassboro. I'll never forget those days. Always remain the terrific friend you are! Have a grrrr . . . eat summer, o.k., tiger! Never forget our sophomore year.*
>
> *Love always,*
>
> *Lin (Toes, Froggy, and also Lima Bean)*

The Rutgers piece is eluding me - it was certainly some kind of speech competition - but I do remember Glassboro. Lin and I went with Miss Plasky on a Saturday to Glassboro State College, now Rowan University. Less than four years prior, beginning on FRIDAY, JUNE 23, 1967, President Lyndon Johnson and Soviet Premier Alexei Kosygin held their "Hollybush Summit" at Glassboro State, because it was midway between Washington, D.C. and New York City, where Kosygin was addressing the United Nations.

It may have been during Glassboro's spring break, or maybe winter break, because I don't remember very many college kids being around. Maybe that's because Glassboro was largely a commuter school, I believe. I remember absolutely nothing about the contest - where it was on campus, how many kids were there, what the format was, or what kind of competition either Lin or I were entered in. Nor do I remember winning any awards.

We had an extended break at some point during the day, because I know that Lin and I ended up walking around the campus by ourselves, just talking. I doubt that we had ever been alone together, since I think we mainly saw each other during class. We ended up sitting on some bleachers near a football or soccer field. We were the only ones there. Looking back, it was *Love Story*-esque, the part where Ryan O'Neal and Ali McGraw were the only ones sitting in the stands at Harvard Stadium. What we might have talked about, I have no idea, nor does it matter to me. I had a new friend.

Anyway, Lin, at some point, convinced me to join the debate team during my junior year. High school debate teams had four members back then - 1st Affirmative, 2nd Affirmative, 1st Negative and 2nd Negative. For the entire year, teams debated a single topic, which began, *Resolved, . . .* I don't know what the resolution was that year, but it had something to do with governmental regulation of pollution. There was one senior - Jeffrey Packer, one sophomore - Debbie Ott, and a bunch of us juniors - Ann and Barbara Jacobs, Arlene Mayer, Lin, Robin Kaigh and Rita Stabler - on the team. Elissa Plasky was our coach. We must have had two teams, since there were eight of us. Lin was my partner, which made debate fun. We were 1st and 2nd Affirmative and made a pretty good team, as I remember. Not great, but good. Most importantly, we had become real friends. In my junior yearbook in 1971, Lin wrote,

> *My dear Dave,*
>
> *To my greatest friend (believe it or not). I'll never forget our great times together. We've gone through an awful lot, but it was all fun. Well, Pres., next year is our year &miss you terribly this summer, so you better come & see me, OK.*
>
> *Love always, Lin.*

I'm not sure that I was really her greatest friend, but it was one of the sweetest things that anyone ever wrote to me. Lin wasn't on the debate team during senior year, which the yearbook claims went undefeated, but she was involved in lots of other things. She had a boyfriend, Tom Fitzgerald. I had a girlfriend, Leona, and we just seemed to be mostly moving in different orbits, except for that senior class play. We graduated together and then just lost touch. She didn't sign my 1972 yearbook. I don't remember her being at any of our class reunions, although she claims that she was.

In that brief moment, just a couple of years, she made my life more fun . . . better . . . richer. And she did it, I think, without even trying. I believe that there are those people who spend some time in your life, who are there for some reason, leave their mark, and then they're gone . . . too quickly, without goodbyes, and without you even knowing that they're gone until much later. People who make you smile when, by chance, you think of them. That was Lin. I want to thank her one day.

Our school was horrible at football, although we were good, and even great, in some other sports, like cross-country, track and wrestling. When the yearbook sums up the football season by writing, "Although the team record was not the best in HTHS [history], it is not the worst!," that about says it all. Most of my friends played on at least one of the school's interscholastic sports teams over the four years, with quite a few playing football. During my sophomore and junior years, the football team won a total of three games, but I went to just about all of them, anyway, even the away games. It's what we all did on Saturdays, before Friday night football became the rage.

Probably the most memorable game in school history took place on SATURDAY, NOVEMBER 1, 1969, against Haddon Heights High School. Our team was already 0-3-2, having been outscored 99-18 on the season and coming off consecutive shutout losses to Haddonfield (23-0) and Sterling (38-0). Next up was Haddon Heights, which was undefeated and which ended the season ranked No. 2 in South Jersey. Under the best of circumstances, it was not going to be a pretty game for the Hawks.

What happened the week before the game ensured that the game would be the worst loss in Haddon Township football history, and there have been a lot of bad ones. It seems that a good number, maybe most, of the varsity players had been at a party where, surprisingly, alcohol was not only present, but abundant. Coach John McCarthy was an old-school disciplinarian of the highest order and suspended all of the partygoers for the game. It was the talk of the school leading up to the game. The result was that a bunch of undersized, young, terrified and inexperienced kids from an already bad team had to play one of the best teams around. At least we had home field advantage for the game.

The result was predictable, hysterical and tragic. If I recall correctly, Haddon Heights scored touchdowns on its first four plays and was winning 29-0 before the first quarter ended and 43-0 at halftime. Haddon Heights scored touchdowns on runs of 1, 2, 5, 10, 11, 30, 33, 44, 61 and 69 yards. Many of my friends were victims of the massacre, Charlie Peffall most of all. Charlie was the JV quarterback and could throw the ball pretty well, but he wasn't very fast or very big. He got pounded, as did almost everyone. We watched in horror and amusement, feeling sorry for our friends who were playing, but thoroughly enjoying the spectacle.

In the end, the Haddon Heights coach took some pity and stopped trying to score once it was 71-0. Over the course of 15 days, the varsity football team had lost three games by a combined score of 132-0.

We decided to have a touch football game on the Friday during Thanksgiving break, while in 10th or 11th grade, which we dubbed "Jews versus Gentiles" because of our rosters. Andy Gelman, Bob Siman, Tom Lichtman and Ron Love on one side and me, Kevin Manns, Rich Gant and Mark ("Goose") Grussenmeyer on the other. It was decided that the game would be played on the street, and Bewley Court, in our opponents' neighborhood, was chosen as the site, since it was fairly wide and didn't see too much traffic. After serious and nuanced discussion about the rules, and a whole lot of trash-talking, we played. It was during this game, or maybe the second one, that Tom Lichtman had a small emergency and needed to use a bathroom badly. To our surprise, he knocked on a complete stranger's door and actually talked his way in. Tom was a really good friend of mine during high school. He always told us that his father was a pig farmer, whether true or not. Through a quirk of scheduling, he and I were the only seniors with a study hall in the morning and gym with some underclassmen. During study hall, we would go to the student lounge, which we had to ourselves, and watch *Sesame Street*, always hoping to see Snuffleupagus, our favorite character, who was Big Bird's mammoth-like friend. Sadly, Tom was one of my first friends and classmates to pass away, just a few years after graduation.

The Gentiles won that first game, thereby earning bragging rights until the next year, when we played again. Once again, we won, retaining bragging rights for yet another year. We played a third and final game the next Thanksgiving break. Our opponents had made a roster change and added Rich Toll for either Love or Lichtman, very much an upgrade. This time, rather than playing at Bewley Court, we decided to play on one of the practice fields at the high school. Facing a revamped roster, we lost that final game. Two out of three ain't bad, as Meat Loaf would say.

The biggest sporting event in the spring of our junior year was not a school event at all. It was the first fight between Joe Frazier and Muhammad Ali, on MONDAY, MARCH 8, 1971, at Madison Square Garden, for the heavyweight championship of the world, a title held by Frazier during Ali's forced exile from boxing. Both men were undefeated at the time. Emotions ran hot as we debated who would win for months leading up to the fight. I think that we were split about 50/50 and largely along political lines. There was never a question that I would root for Ali. On the day of the fight, we all wrote our predictions on the blackboard before trigonometry class. The only person who called it correctly, a judges' decision for Frazier, was Bruce Pellnitz, our teacher, a wonderful man and one of the people who interviewed Nancy for her teaching job in Haddon Township many, many years later.

Inspired by Ali-Frazier, a few of us decided to stage our own boxing matches. These weren't high school fights, just fun "I can whoop you" matches. We bought some boxing gloves and scheduled the matches for somebody's backyard one day after school. At least I think it was after school, because there were quite a few spectators. There were two matches that I recall. I fought my friend Tom Lichtman, who proved to be a not-so-good opponent. I whipped him pretty good. Kevin Manns fought someone, but I have forgotten who. I even had the matches filmed with my parents' movie camera, but have no idea what became of the film. I wish that I had it. Jim Doherty claims to have photos.

Ali would have to wait three years to get his revenge, defeating Frazier in a 12-round unanimous decision, also at Madison Square Garden, on MONDAY, JANUARY 28, 1974. The win earned Ali a fight with George Foreman, the new heavyweight champion, for the crown. A heavy underdog, Ali knocked Foreman out in the 8th round of the "Rumble in the Jungle" to claim the world heavyweight championship, introducing us to "Rope-a-Dope," seven years after his title had been stripped for refusing induction into the military because of his opposition to the Vietnam War. A third Ali-Frazier fight - widely considered one of the greatest boxing matches ever - was held on WEDNESDAY, OCTOBER 1, 1975, in the Philippines. The "Thrilla in Manila" was won by Ali when Frazier's trainer asked the referee to stop the fight after Round 14. Boxing was a really big deal back then. I couldn't name the heavyweight champion today.

The highlight of my high school athletic career came during the spring of my senior year. When I was a sophomore, Haddon Township had a golf team, but I wasn't on it. Ron Love, Steve Rosenberg, Tom Lichtman, Brad Lindberg, Andy Gelman and Bob Siman comprised the team. Miller Preston, a South Jersey Athletic Hall of Fame member as the long-time wrestling coach at Haddon Township, was also the golf coach, although I think he just liked to play golf after school in the spring, once wrestling season was over. He knew me from my brief high school wrestling career. During our junior year. Kevin Manns, Gary Murza and I decided to join the team and Tom Lichtman dropped off.

Haddon Township was a member of the Colonial Conference, which consisted of Audubon, Collingswood, Haddon Heights, Haddon Township, Haddonfield, Paulsboro, Sterling and Woodbury high schools. All but Collingswood and Sterling had golf teams. Our home course was not that close to our school, but was in West Deptford, at the Westwood Country Club. The course at Westwood was not all that great, but I guess the price was right for the athletic department. While the other teams played mostly at tonier country clubs, we played on a public course. There were certainly closer courses that we could have played on - Merchantville Country Club was only three or four miles away. I don't remember that much about the golf team from my junior year and I definitely don't remember Steve Rosenberg being on the team, but he's in all of the pictures, so I guess he was. We weren't horrible, but we weren't in contention for a championship, either.

I have saved a few newspaper clippings from our matches and seen some other results online from our junior year:

Wednesday, April 21, 1971: *Audubon 4 - Haddon Township 2 (Bob Gordon, A def. Dave Florig 1-up at Medford Village Resort CC)*

Thursday, April 22, 1971: *Haddon Heights 4 - Haddon Township 2 (Dave Florig, H, def. Pat Trainer, 2 and 1 at Tavistock CC)*

Monday, April 26, 1971: *Haddonfield 3 1/2 - Haddon Township 2 1/2 (Geoffrey Wolf halved Dave Florig, HT at Tavistock CC)*

Tuesday, May 11, 1971: *Haddon Township 3 1/2 - Paulsboro 2 1/2 (Dave Floig (sic), H. def. Wayne Bikuiel 4 and 3 at Westwood CC)*

Friday, May 14, 1971: *Haddon Township 3 - Eastern 3 (Ron Lemanowicz, E. def. Dave Florig 2 and 1 at Westwood CC)*

Unknown Date: *Haddon Township 6 - Camden Tech (B) 0 (Dave Florig, H def. Dave Brownlow 5 & 3 at Westwood CC)*

-During our senior year, we convinced Rich Toll, a good athlete and a very good golfer (and the roster addition that led to the Gentiles' only loss in the touch football games) to join the team. Rosenberg had graduated and Murza wasn't interested in playing again, having just finished a sensational wrestling season. Rich Toll was so good that he immediately assumed the number one spot on our team. High school golf, at least back then, consisted of six matches. Each school's top player played against the other, the number twos against each other, number threes, and so on through six players per team. I started out the season as the sixth man. It was match play, meaning that each hole was a different game, and we played up to nine holes per match. It didn't matter if you won a hole by five shots or one shot, you simply were credited with winning that hole. Once it became impossible for the losing player to catch up the match was over, after as few as five holes. Winning "5 and 4" meant that you were five holes up with four to play, winning "4 and 3" meant that you were four holes up with three to play, and so on.

There were seven of us - Toll, Lindberg, Gelman, Manns, Love, Siman and I - competing for six spots. The first two spots unquestionably belonged to Toll and Lindberg, and that never changed the whole season. They were easily our two best players. Ron Love started the season in the number three spot, but he was playing terribly, slowly dropping down in the lineup until, finally, Siman replaced him as sixth man. That meant that I moved up from sixth to fifth man, which also meant playing a slightly better opponent - the other team's fifth-best (or second-worst, depending on how you want to view it.) We started the season slowly, winning only two of our first five matches.

By the end of the regular season, though, the lineup was Toll, Lindberg, Gelman, Manns, Florig and Siman, and we rallied to beat Woodbury and Paulsboro in the last two matches of the season to tie for first in the Colonial Conference. We tied for first with Haddonfield, which had won every previous conference championship in golf. Haddonfield was much-despised, since it was the wealthiest and snobbiest of the towns, and they played their home matches at the private and exclusive Tavistock Country Club, while the rest of us were relegated to lesser courses. To Tavistock members, every course was a lesser course. During the season, we had split two matches with Haddonfield, each team winning by a 4-2 score. That meant a playoff match against Haddonfield at a neutral site, and Laurel Oak Country Club was chosen by the schools' athletic departments. My father and I happened to be members at Laurel Oak, although that would not end up helping me in the championship match.

In the playoff on TUESDAY, MAY 30, 1972, No. 1 Rich Toll lost on the final hole; No. 2 Lindberg won on the sixth hole; I played as fifth man and lost to a kid named Ed Ferrin; Bob Siman played at No. 6 and won on the seventh hole. So the score was tied 2-2, with Kevin Manns and Andy Gelman still playing their matches. Manns and Gelman were notoriously the slowest players on the team, so the four of us who had finished watched from the tee as they played the eighth hole at Laurel Oak, a par four. We weren't allowed to walk along with them as they played. As we watched from 300 yards away, we saw Gelman putt and then he and Manns raise their arms over their heads in victory. Manns had won and Gelman had made his putt to assure at least halving (tying) his match, and we succeeded, by the narrowest 3 ½ - 2 ½ score, to become the first team other than Haddonfield to win the Colonial Conference. We finished the year 10-4-1. The *Courier-Post* reported the match the next day under the headline, "Colonial Golf Championship to Haddon Twp.":

Haddon Township High School won its first Colonial Conference golf championship yesterday when it defeated defending kingpin Haddonfield, 3 1/2 - 2 1/2 at Laurel Oak Country Club. Brad Lindberg, Kevin Manns and Bob Siman won matches and Andy Galmin (sic) halved his opponent to [give] Haddon Township its points.

I don't know everyone's record from that season, but I know these:

Kevin Manns 10-3-2
David Florig 9-3-3
Andy Gelman 7-3-5
Brad Lindberg 9-4-2

The 1972 season played out like this, according to the *Courier-Post*:

WEDNESDAY, APRIL 12, 1972: *Haddon Township 6 - Haddon Heights 0 (Dave Florig, H def. Wayne Rudolph 4 and 3 at Westwood CC)*

MONDAY, APRIL 17, 1972: *Paulsboro 4 - Haddon Township 2 (Frank Scherer, P def. Dave Florig 1 up at Swedesboro CC)*

FRIDAY, APRIL 21, 1972: *Haddon Township 3 ½ - Audubon 2 ½ (Dave Florig, H def. George Geist 4 & 3) at Medford Village Resort CC)*

MONDAY, APRIL 24, 1972: *Haddonfield 4 - Haddon Township 2 (Dave Florig, HT halved Bob Grabiak at Westwood CC)*

TUESDAY, MAY 2, 1972: *Haddon Township 4 ½ - Gloucester*

Catholic 1 ½ (Dave Florig, H def. Bill McGinn 5 and 4 at Westwood CC)

FRIDAY, MAY 5, 1972: *Lenape 4 1/2 - Haddon Township 1 1/2 (Dave Florig, H. halved Joe Perrone at Westwood CC)*

MONDAY, MAY 8, 1972: *Haddon Township 3 1/2 - Haddon Heights 2 1/2 (Dave Floric (sic), HT def. Wayne Rudolph 4 and 3 at Tavistock CC)*

FRIDAY, MAY 12, 1972: *Haddon Township 4, Haddonfield 2 (Dave Florig, HT def. Bob Grabiak 2 and 1 at Tavistock CC)*

WEDNESDAY, MAY 17, 1972: *Haddon Township 3 1/2 - Gloucester Catholic 2 1/2 (Dave Florz (sic), H won by forfeit at Wedgwood CC)*

MONDAY MAY 22, 1972: *Woodbury 4 - Haddon Township 2 (Joe Simkins, W def. Dave Florig 2 and 1 at Westwood CC)*

TUESDAY, MAY 23, 1972: *Haddon Township 3 ½ - Paulsboro 2 ½ (Dave Florig H def. Wayne Dilugi 2 and 1 at Westwood CC)*

FRIDAY, MAY 26, 1972: *Haddon Township 4, Audubon 2 (Dave Florig, H def. Jay Taraschi 3 and 2 at Westwood CC)*

TUESDAY, MAY 30, 1972: *Haddon Township 3 1/2 - Haddonfield 2 1/2 (Ed Ferren H def. Dave Florig 2 and 1 at Laurel Oak CC)*

We all received red school "HT" letters for playing varsity golf. As conference champions, the athletic department also gave us very nice red and white Haddon Township High School jackets, much like Archie sported for Riverdale High, which Leona proceeded to lose. That was tough to forgive.

* * *

We walked across the stage on that hot June night in 1972, accepted our diplomas and graduated together, promising to do things together over the summer and to keep in touch forever. And then we headed off for summer jobs, the shore, college and the rest of our lives. Many of those people I have never seen again.

CHAPTER 14

SUNDAY, JULY 2, 1972

I got tickets to the double bill of Badfinger and Faces at the Spectrum for 8:00 on Sunday night. I'm not sure which band I wanted to hear more, but if I were pressed, I would probably say Badfinger, even though Faces was the headliner. Badfinger was on the Apple label at that time and sounded remarkably like the pre-*Sgt. Pepper* Beatles, which is probably why I liked them. The resemblance was no coincidence, either, since George and Paul were both involved in writing and producing for them. Badfinger had had a string of hits leading up to the concert, including "Come and Get It," written and produced by McCartney; "No Matter What" and "Day After Day," produced by Harrison; and "Baby Blue."

"Baby Blue" was played in the final scene of the final episode ("Felina," an acronym of "finale") of what I think was the greatest television show ever made, *Breaking Bad*. I watched the show every Sunday night when it aired, knowing that the series was ending on SUNDAY, SEPTEMBER 29, 2013. How quaint - watching shows when they aired. Not only was the entire series brilliantly written, filmed and acted, but they nailed the ending, which most great series are unable to do (although *The Americans* did a great job and *Homeland* was pretty good, too). *The Sopranos* and *House of Cards*, not so much. No less an actor than Anthony Hopkins sent a letter to Bryan Cranston after binging *Breaking Bad*, writing, "Your performance as Walter White was the best acting I have seen - ever." And Hopkins had performed with Laurence Olivier, Judi Dench, Omar Sharif and Emma Thompson.

Some of Badfinger's members played on George's remarkable *All Things Must Pass* album, including on "My Sweet Lord," "Isn't It a Pity" and "What is Life." Pete Ham played acoustic guitar with George on "Here Comes the Sun" at the *Concert for Bangladesh* on SUNDAY, AUGUST 1, 1971. at Madison Square Garden, the largest rock and roll benefit concert at the time, and a forerunner for shows like *Live Aid* and *Farm Aid*. Some members of Badfinger played on Ringo's "It Don't Come Easy" and recorded with John on his *Imagine* album.

Faces, of course, was fronted by Rod Stewart, and consisted of Kenney Jones, Ian McLagan, Ronnie Lane and Ronnie Wood, who later went on to join the Rolling Stones. Rod Stewart went on to a most unfortunate post-Faces life of disco and singing old standards, but this was Rod at his rock and roll best.

The show remains something of a blur, although not for any illicit reasons. I don't remember where we sat, or even who I went with, but I was in the middle of dating Leona, so I'll assume it was her. I had just graduated from high school a couple of weeks earlier, was working a summer job with the phone company, courtesy of Charlie, and was looking forward to starting college at the University of Pennsylvania in two months. I didn't feel like a snotty little high school kid anymore. It almost felt like being grown up.

CHAPTER 15

TUESDAY, NOVEMBER 7, 1972

It was the first time that I could vote. The 26th Amendment had become law on MONDAY, JULY 5, 1971, after President Richard Nixon signed it, granting 18 year-olds the constitutional right to vote. I voted for George McGovern and Sargent Shriver in the presidential election, but, of course, Richard Nixon and Spiro Agnew won 49 states and re-election. Neither of them would finish his term, both resigning amidst their own individual scandals. Massachusetts was the only state that McGovern carried (although he did win the District of Columbia. as well), resulting in Nixon's 520-17 Electoral College victory and spawning the famous, "Don't Blame Me, I'm From Massachusetts" bumper stickers. I would have to wait four years to vote for a winning presidential candidate, Jimmy Carter. Although his presidency wasn't great, Jimmy Carter is the best former president that this country has ever had.

I had seen McGovern speak at a large rally on Broad Street in Philadelphia on WEDNESDAY, SEPTEMBER 13, 1972, along with Ted Kennedy and Pennsylvania Governor Milton Shapp. I had also, coincidentally, seen Richard Nixon at a campaign stop at the Cherry Hill Mall before the 1968 election. on SATURDAY, SEPTEMBER 21, 1968. I was a 14 year-old heckler. Carol Hutto, Becky's youngest sister, went with me, and was mortified, mainly because she lived in Cherry Hill and was at high risk of being spotted with me by someone she knew.

I've crossed paths with a few politicians over the years, in addition to Nixon, McGovern and the two Kennedys. I met John Kerry, running for the United States Senate for the first time, and Evelyn Murphy, who would become Lieutenant Governor of Massachusetts, at a breakfast at Foley, Hoag & Eliot in Boston where I was working. Later, former Senator Paul Tsongas went to work at the firm while I was there, but I don't think that he did any lawyering - just schmoozing.

While working at Manta and Welge in Philadelphia and taking Amtrak to Washington, D.C. one day, I said hello to Senator Joe Biden. I shook hands with Michael Dukakis during one of his campaign stops at Cooper

River in Pennsauken in 1987 or 1988. I asked a question of Philadelphia Mayor Michael Nutter at an event in West Philly. Dylan did an unpaid internship with United States Representative Robert Andrews one summer and we met Congressman Andrews at a reception he held for students he had provided small scholarships for, including Dylan. Nothing against any of those people personally, but I've always thought that anyone that ambitious by definition can't be trusted. Like they say, every representative looks in the mirror and sees a senator and every senator looks in the mirror and sees a president.

I have voted in every presidential election since 1972 - for George McGovern [D-SD] (1972), Jimmy Carter [D-GA] (TUESDAY, NOVEMBER 2, 1976), John Anderson [I-OH] (TUESDAY, NOVEMBER 4, 1980), Walter Mondale [D-MN] (TUESDAY, NOVEMBER 6, 1984), Michael Dukakis [D-MA] (TUESDAY, NOVEMBER 8, 1988), Bill Clinton [D-AR] (TUESDAY, NOVEMBER 3, 1992 and TUESDAY, NOVEMBER 5, 1996), Al Gore [D-TN] (TUESDAY, NOVEMBER 7, 2000), John Kerry [D-MA] (TUESDAY, NOVEMBER 2, 2004), Barack Obama [D-IL] (TUESDAY, NOVEMBER 4, 2008 and TUESDAY, NOVEMBER 6, 2012), Hillary Clinton [D-NY] (TUESDAY, NOVEMBER 8, 2016) and Joe Biden [D-DE] (TUESDAY, NOVEMBER 3, 2020). Six winners, seven losers. Twelve votes for the Democrat, one for the Independent, and none for the Republican. I was both physically and emotionally ill following the 2016 election and basically remained so for the four years before WEDNESDAY, JANUARY 20, 2021. No vote ever felt better than the one for Biden in 2020.

There was another election three months after I first voted. I was one of seven candidates for three seats on the Haddon Township Board of Education. Coming off of my stunning student council victory the year prior, and making no pledge to abolish the Board of Education, I may have overestimated my electoral appeal. As the *Courier-Post* previewed the upcoming election on FRIDAY, JANUARY 5, 1973:

An 18 year old University of Pennsylvania freshman is the youngest of four challengers who will vie with three incumbents for three three-year terms on the board.

David S. Florig of 215 Burrwood Avenue, a June graduate of Haddon Township High School is the youngest challenger. While a student he was captain of the debate team and member of student council.

Incumbents seeking re-election are Joseph Bretschneider of 775 Mt. Vernon Avenue, Mrs. Elizabeth Krayer of 118 Hampton Road and Mrs. Adele Walton of 100 Mt. Vernon Avenue.

Newcomers in addition to Florig are Anthony Bezich of 1149 Lake Shore Drive, Charles DiPietropolo of 14 East Greenwood Avenue and R. James Tredinnick of 20 East Holly Avenue.

In the election on TUESDAY, FEBRUARY 13, 1973, all of the incumbents won and I came in seventh out of seven, ending my only foray into politics. DePietropolo came in fourth, with 521 votes; Bezich came in fifth with 515 votes; and Tredinnick came in sixth with 430 votes. I received 208. I'm not even 100% sure that my parents voted for me.

CHAPTER 16

The first Ronald McDonald house in the world opened in Philadelphia on TUESDAY, OCTOBER 15, 1974. There are now more than 350 Ronald McDonald Houses in more than 60 countries around the globe. I played the tiniest, tiniest role in that - so tiny and insignificant, in fact, that it's almost too embarrassing to write about. Almost.

Ronald McDonald Houses provide a place for families to stay when a child is hospitalized for an extended period. They are an outgrowth of the Philadelphia Eagles' "Eagles Fly for Leukemia" charity, founded in 1973 after Eagles player Fred Hill learned that his three-year-old daughter, Kim, had leukemia. In the fall of 1973, during the Eagles season, they held their first fundraising telethon. Someone arranged for a group of us, mostly from the church, to help answer the telephones and take pledges. We all gathered in a room at Veterans Stadium to answer the phones.

Many of the players were around for the evening, and I'm pretty sure that I spent more time trying to get autographs than actually answering phones. I had done some preparation in advance (for getting autographs, not answering phones) by finding my football cards for Eagles players and by cutting out pictures from my *Sports Illustrated* collection. Once we arrived, we were also given copies of the media guide, which contained pictures and bios for all of the players.

This Eagles team was the epitome of mediocre, finishing the season at 7-7. But they were tall. Their passing game featured the "Fire High Gang," named for the quarterback, Roman Gabriel, who stood 6'4"; tight end Charlie Young, who was also 6'4"; and wide receivers Harold Carmichael (6'8") and Don Zimmerman (6'3"). I secured Gabriel's autograph on a *Sports Illustrated* picture and the other three in the media guide. In addition to the "Fire High Gang," I got Marlin McKeever and Kermit Alexander on football cards; Norm Bulaich and John Reaves on *Sports Illustrated* pictures; and Lee Bouggess, Al Coleman, Tom Dempsey, Richard Harris, Mark Nordquist, Steve Smith, John Sodaski, Richard

Stevens, Tom Sullivan, Steve Zabel, Bill Dunstan, Jim Maxwell, Greg Oliver, Rex Putnal and Joe Lavender in the media guide.

All of those autographs were in addition to the ones I had secured at Eagles training camp nine years earlier. We had fun answering the phones and seeing the players. I have no idea how much money was raised that night - but the Philadelphia Eagles' Fly for Leukemia charity still exists nearly 50 years later.

Kim Hill, the girl whose leukemia diagnosis at the age of three ultimately led to the creation of that first Ronald McDonald House, died in 2011 at the age of 44, 40 years older than her doctors thought she would ever be.

Chapter 17

B illy Joel was in the middle of his "The Stranger" tour in 1977. The album of that name had been released in September, and the tour was making a stop at the Spectrum in Philadelphia. For reasons that I can't recall, Dorothy Schroeder asked me if I wanted to go with her. Of course I said yes, because I liked both her and Billy Joel.

Dorothy, who I knew as Dottie, and who would later be known as Eloise (which I'm still not used to), was two years younger than me and had also attended Strawbridge School and Haddon Township High School. I have no idea when, or why, she became Eloise, but she did. She lived at 315 Fern Avenue, I believe. We were also both Tauruses, sharing May birthdays. I'm not sure exactly how we met, being different ages and in different grades. She was two years behind me in school. We might have met in one of Al Tanner's social studies classes when I was a junior. However it happened, we became friends.

She was smart, funny, a little sarcastic, and had wonderful pale blue eyes. Occasionally, usually after a literary magazine meeting (the *Jellybean*, with faculty advisor Karenellen Cechvala), we would end up walking home from school together, even though we didn't live that close to one another. I had to go a little bit out of my way to do it. To head home, we walked down a path from the high school that passed the softball and baseball fields to Cuthbert Boulevard. Turning right onto Cuthbert, it was a straight walk of a mile or so to Fern Avenue, where Dottie would turn right to get to her house a block away, while I had to turn left, cross Cuthbert, and walk the six or seven blocks to my house. Although we never actually planned to walk home together, I think that we both kind of hoped that we would.

One of those walks was in the winter, when it was getting dark and snowing pretty hard. Not a blizzard, but a good snow for South Jersey. When leaving the path onto Cuthbert, the first place we passed was the Acme supermarket, where most of the people in Haddon Township, including my mother, did their grocery shopping. Apparently, her mother shopped there, too. As we were walking, Dottie's mother was just leaving the Acme parking lot. Seeing her daughter, she cranked down the window and asked if we wanted a ride home. I don't know that I had ever seen or met her mother before. Fully expecting to hop in the car and get out of the snow, I was surprised when Dottie said, "No, thanks." It seemed a little strange at the time, but I certainly didn't mind all that much. I would have done the same thing had it been my mother. After all, we really didn't get to spend much time together, and I always looked forward to spending time with her. And a parent would have ruined the vibe. I teased her over the years about being forced to walk home in a snowstorm. It wasn't until many years later that I asked why she didn't accept the ride. "Because I had a crush on you," she said. I had suspected as much, but wasn't really sure. I certainly had one on her.

Dottie's father, Ken, passed away while we were still in high school, leaving behind a wife, a son and two daughters. I don't remember ever talking to her about it. What was there to say, except that I was sorry? I surely wouldn't have brought it up. Death was something that I didn't have much experience with at that time, although learning to cope with it is an inevitable part of growing older, as I would later learn. As adults, Dottie told me that I had been nice to her after her father had died. I hope that is true.

There was never really anything romantic about our relationship, although maybe there could have been. We did a few things together over the high school and college years, but not too many. She had inexplicably bought a Volkswagen Rabbit with a stick shift. The problem was that her mother had to drive her to pick it up, and Dottie didn't know how to drive with a stick shift. I did, so she recruited me to go with them to pick up the car. Apparently we made it home without incident. I don't remember who drove.

In the 1970's, there was a terrible hockey arena on Brace Road in Cherry Hill known as the Cherry Hill Arena. It went by a few names over the years, including the Ice House, Delaware Valley Gardens and the Centrum. The arena held around 4,000 people and was home to a couple of minor league hockey teams over the years. *Sports Illustrated* dubbed it the worst facility in the World Hockey Association. The visiting team's locker room didn't even have showers, so players routinely rode the bus back to their hotel in full uniform after games to shower and change. The ice was sloped, so that the visiting team was forced to skate uphill for two out of three periods in order to score. The Jersey Aces of the Northeastern Hockey League began the 1978-79 season at the arena, but relocated to Hampton, Virginia, after a few games because the arena had to close after its liability and fire insurance were abruptly cancelled. It was mercifully torn down to make way for a suburban shopping center soon thereafter.

The arena also occasionally hosted concerts and other events. Sly and the Family Stone, Leon Russell, Santana, the Chambers Brothers, Rare Earth, the Doobie Brothers, John Sebastian, the Four Seasons and Jay and the Americans all played there. One night, there was some kind of charity tennis match involving Billie Jean King, Martina Navratilova and some local athletes. One of them was either Mike Schmidt from the Phillies or Doug Collins from the 76ers. Maybe both. Again, I think that it was Dottie who asked me if I wanted to go with her. We went, along with Ken Ecklund and Sandy Campbell, friends of mine from college. I don't think that they were married just yet. Ken's recollection is that I went with Barbara Boenning, but I think it was Dottie.

I also (but this is only the vaguest of memories) recall being at my parents house on Burrwood Avenue one time with *Saturday Night Live* on TV. *SNL* debuted on SATURDAY, OCTOBER 11, 1975, so the timing makes sense. I also have this recollection that she wasn't too crazy about our dog(s). But honestly, I have no idea why we would have been together at 11:30 on a Saturday night in 1975 - unless it was after the tennis match that we may or may not have gone to together.

I did, one time, actually ask Dottie out on a "date" myself. I remember her saying that her boyfriend was "ensconced" in England, so it was OK for us to do something together. I don't know whether she said it to make clear that she had a boyfriend or to make clear that he was out of the country. I should have asked her. Whatever, we went out to dinner, albeit not quite what you would expect for a date. Centerton Country Club had a buffet on Sunday afternoons, which I had been to a couple of times with my parents - lots of food, but pretty short on atmosphere. I don't know that a buffet in the afternoon with a couple of hundred people could ever be romantic. It might have been on SUNDAY, NOVEMBER 19, 1978, because it sticks in my mind that it was on the day of the "Miracle at the Meadowlands," when the New York Giants, rather than simply running out the clock, inexplicably tried to hand off the ball, resulting in a fumble recovery by Herman Edwards, which he ran in for a touchdown and an Eagles victory with just seconds remaining. I missed that game because of my "date" with Dottie.

Years later, I also missed another of the most famous games in NFL history - the "Fog Bowl" playoff game between the Eagles and the Chicago Bears on SATURDAY, DECEMBER 31, 1988. Chris Mooney, a friend from the Appellate Department at Marshall, Dennehey, Warner, Coleman & Goggin, and David Brenner got married that day in Philadelphia, at the same time as the game. There are tax benefits to getting married on December 31st. Lots of other people missed much of the Fog Bowl, too, even those who attended and those who were watching on television.

During the second quarter of the Fog Bowl, a dense fog rolled over Soldier Field, limiting visibility to about 10-20 yards for the rest of the game. The fog was said to cover only a tiny fraction of Chicago - about 15 blocks - but it managed to settle into Soldier Field. When halftime arrived, the Bears were leading 17-9. With both teams barely able to see, only two field goals were kicked the rest of the game, despite the teams combining for 771 yards of offense, and the Eagles lost 20-12. Both quarterbacks (Randall Cunningham for the Eagles, Mike Tomczak for the Bears) threw three interceptions. *NFL.com* ranks the "Fog Bowl" as the 50th best NFL game ever and *Bleacher Report* ranks it at No. 49.

I rarely miss an Eagles game. My schedule revolves around them in the fall. As soon as the NFL schedule comes out in May, I put the games on my calendar so that I can avoid anything that might conflict with an Eagles game. Even since moving to Maine, I manage to watch almost every game through a little internet trickery. But I managed to miss both the "Miracle at the Meadowlands" and the "Fog Bowl."

Marshall, Dennehey, Warner, Coleman & Goggin held black-tie Christmas parties each year. I only went to two, since I didn't stay at the firm for that long, but one was very memorable for all of the wrong reasons. Nancy and I went and were having a perfectly fine evening until the wife of one of the more senior attorneys confronted Nancy as Nancy was getting something out of her purse, and accused her of going through *her* purse. In fairness, Nancy's purse and the other woman's looked quite similar. Nancy assured her that this wasn't so by showing the woman the contents. Nonetheless, the other woman became more and more animated and threatened to "clock you in the face." Nancy made a beeline for the ladies room, we quietly gathered our things, and headed for the exit. You don't want your wife getting clocked in the face under any circumstances, much less at a work Christmas party. It's just not a great career move. And I certainly wasn't looking forward to going to work on Monday.

One day, I got a letter in the mail. It was from Dottie. She was in England for some reason, perhaps a college semester abroad, and I guess she was a little homesick or lonely. I don't remember anything about what the letter said, and being rather thoughtless, and, frankly, unkind, don't think that I ever wrote back to her. What I do remember is that she enclosed a lock of hair with the letter.

* * *

The concert was great. Billy Joel played for about two-and-a-half hours without a warmup act or a break. His band, especially the sax player, was awesome. It was Joel's first time as a headliner at the Spectrum and the first of 28 times that he had a sellout crowd there. I think that we went straight home after the concert.

I haven't seen her in at least 30, maybe 40 years, but some people just stay with you for a lifetime. They're a part of who you are. Dottie is one of those people. One of those hundreds, or thousands, of people that are part of your life for a while, and then they're not. If I'm lucky, I'll see her again someday.

CHAPTER 18

FRIDAY, JUNE 15, 1979

Rocky II was released on FRIDAY, JUNE 15, 1979. *Rocky*, set in Philadelphia and released three years earlier, starred Sylvester Stallone, won Best Picture and Best Director Oscars at the 49th *Academy Awards*, and earned acting nominations for all of the main actors - Stallone for Best Actor, Talia Shire for Best Actress and both Burgess Meredith and Burt Young for Best Supporting Actor. Rocky Balboa had lost the heavyweight championship fight to Carl Weathers' Apollo Creed in the 1976 movie, but had launched a franchise that has included, so far, *Rocky, Rocky II, Rocky III, Rocky IV, Rocky V, Rocky Balboa, Creed* and *Creed II*. *Creed III* is scheduled for a 2022 release. Made for a little over $1 million, *Rocky* grossed more than $225 million at the box office. There was no doubt that there would be a sequel. This time, Rocky would defeat Apollo Creed.

The most iconic scenes in the first two *Rocky* movies involve Rocky Balboa running up the steps of the Philadelphia Museum of Art in his sweatpants and hoodie. In *Rocky II*, Rocky runs up the steps after seemingly running through every single neighborhood and tourist stop in the city. Now a celebrity, Rocky is followed and surrounded by a group of kids at the top of the steps. But in the original *Rocky*, no one knew who he was and he ran in solitude, ending at the top of the Art Museum steps in the early morning. Once at the top, he turns and looks down the Benjamin Franklin Parkway toward Philadelphia City Hall to the east. No other people are around, just some passing cars. It is now required, by law, that each and every Philadelphia tourist run up those steps, imitating Rocky Balboa. They even put a statue of Rocky at the top of the steps for a while. There was quite a bit of consternation amongst the well-bred about whether the statue belonged at the Art Museum. so it shuffled back and forth between the museum and the now-gone Spectrum. It finally settled into its current home at the foot of the famous steps.

I was in Philly the morning they were shooting that scene in *Rocky*. I'm not sure why I was there so early, but I was. Driving by, I noticed the activity at the Art Museum and drove past to investigate. I saw that there were barricades to the sides of the steps so that no pedestrians would be in the scene and I saw Stallone in his trademark gray sweats. There were camera crews in several different locations, including at the top of the steps, so that they could shoot as Rocky ascended and could use the parkway and City Hall as background.

There was no apparent way to insinuate myself into the scene, but I knew that I had to try. At the base of the steps, directly across the street, is Eakins Oval, a small park with some fountains and statues. People gather in the park for events held in front of the Art Museum, like concerts, fireworks, speeches and one notable *Super Bowl* parade. Eakins Oval gets its name, obviously, from its shape. Around the park is what amounts to a very large traffic rotary, treacherous to navigate when there's a lot of traffic, but easy when there isn't. On this weekend morning, there wasn't much traffic, so I settled on driving around in a circle, hoping that I would pass the base of the steps while they were shooting a scene that would make it into the movie.

It worked. As Rocky stands atop the steps, looking out over his beloved Philadelphia in the early morning light, a light blue Ford, headlights on, drives past. It's me, an uncredited extra in an *Academy Award* winning film, one of the greatest sports movies ever made.

CHAPTER 19

TUESDAY, OCTOBER 21, 1980

I was sitting maybe three rows from the top of Veterans Stadium, in centerfield in the 700 section, when Tug McGraw struck out Willie Wilson of the Kansas City Royals to end the *World Series*. It was the Phillies' first world championship ever.

I had waited in line at the Vet for three or four hours to get *World Series* tickets. There was no ordering online, because there *was* no online, nor could you get tickets at any other ticket outlets. I knew better than to ask Biz to let us in for free. I had to go to the Vet and get in line. When I finally got to the ticket window, I was told that the only tickets left were to either Game 6 or Game 7. Although a *World Series* Game 7 would have been the most dramatic, I figured that there was a much better chance of there being a Game 6 than a Game 7, so I opted for the former.

The Phillies had reached the playoffs by winning the National League East in the penultimate game of the season. With a one game lead over the Expos, playing in Olympic Stadium in Montreal, Mike Schmidt hit an extra-inning home run, resulting in a 5-4 Phillies win and the NL East title. Houston, on the other hand, had tied for first place in the National League West by entering the final weekend with a three-game lead over the Los Angeles Dodgers and proceeding to lose three straight games to the Dodgers, forcing a one-game playoff. The Astros easily defeated the Dodgers, 7-1, on MONDAY, OCTOBER 6, 1980, to clinch the NL West, but then had to fly across the country to Philadelphia for the League Championship Series beginning on Tuesday.

On TUESDAY, OCTOBER 7, 1980, the Phillies and Astros began what many consider to be the most exciting playoff series in baseball history. MLB playoffs were five games back then, not seven, and four of the five games between the Phillies and Astros went extra innings. The first game was the only one that didn't, with Steve Carlton defeating Ken Forsch 3-1. Greg ("the Bull") Luzinski, the Phillies' left fielder, hit what would be the series' only home run in the sixth inning.

The Astros tied the series by winning the second game 7-4 in 10 innings. With the game tied at four in the bottom of the ninth in Philadelphia, the Phillies loaded the bases with only one out, but series MVP Manny Trillo struck out and Garry Maddox fouled out to end the inning. Houston proceeded to score three runs in the top of the 10th for the win. Game 3 went nine innings with neither team scoring a single run. Then, in the bottom of the tenth, Joe Morgan of the Astros led off the inning with a triple, and scored on Denny Walling's sacrifice fly to put the Phillies on the cusp of being eliminated from the playoffs, down two games to one.

By the end of the seventh inning of Game 4 on SATURDAY, OCTOBER 11, 1980, it looked like the Phillies would be eliminated from the playoffs for the fourth time in five years. The Astros had a 2-0 lead. In the top of the eighth, the Phillies scored three runs on singles by Greg Gross, Lonnie Smith, Pete Rose, Mike Schmidt and Manny Trillo. In the bottom of the ninth, the Astros tied the game and the third straight game went to extra innings. Pete Rose singled, Greg Luzinski doubled and Manny Trillo singled as the Phils scored two runs in the top of the tenth and won, 5-3.

The deciding game, on SUNDAY, OCTOBER 12, 1980, looked like a disaster for the Phillies. After seven innings, they trailed 5-2, with Hall of Famer Nolan Ryan pitching for Houston. As I watched on TV, the Phillies amazingly rallied for five runs in the top of the eighth inning against Ryan, an inning that featured an unlikely infield hit by catcher Bob Boone and a bunt single by Greg Gross. It was looking promising, with a 2-run lead heading into the bottom of the eighth, but the Astros tied it with two runs. Eventually, the Phils scored a single run in the top of the tenth, brought in a starting pitcher, Dick Ruthven, as a reliever, and retired the Astros 1-2-3 to reach the *World Series* for the first time in my lifetime.

And so I sat in the upper deck in centerfield as the Phillies tried to clinch what would be, up until then, their only *World Series* championship. They held a three games to two lead over Kansas City in the series and Hall of Fame pitcher Steve Carlton was on the mound. The Vet was packed with more than 65,000 people. The Phillies, for a while, looked like they might make it uncharacteristically easy on themselves. They built a 4-0 lead after seven innings, but quickly made the finish interesting. They gave up one run in the eighth and headed to the top of the ninth inning with a three-run lead. Tug McGraw retired the first batter, but quickly loaded the bases by giving up a walk and two singles. There was a palpable unease in the stadium, fueled by years of Philadelphia sports failures. On the first pitch to Frank White, he hit a foul pop-up between home plate and first base. Catcher Bob Boone attempted to catch it, the ball popped out of his mitt, and first baseman Pete Rose reached out and plucked it out of the air for the second out. For a moment, those of us in the cheapest seats had no idea what had happened, but we heard the roar. With the bases still loaded, Willie Wilson struck out for the twelfth time in the series, Tug McGraw leaped into the air and the celebration was on, at the Vet and in the streets of Philly.

I have the autographs of a few of the players involved in the 1980 championship - Greg Luzinski on a *Sports Illustrated* magazine, although he was with the White Sox at the time; Pete Rose on a *Sports Illustrated*; and Joe Morgan on another *Sports Illustrated*. They're in the attic in boxes now, along with dozens of other old magazines, yearbooks, pictures, and thousands and thousands of baseball and football cards.

I saved the *Philadelphia Inquirer* from the next day, WEDNESDAY, OCTOBER 22, 1980, along with my ticket stub. Some years later, Steve Carlton was signing autographs at the Moorestown Mall and he signed the front page of the newspaper. I had the paper and tickets framed, but after 42 years, they have faded. There's no place to hang it in our little house anyway. But I was there.

CHAPTER 20

SUNDAY, JANUARY 25, 1981

The Eagles finally made it to the *Super Bowl - Super Bowl XV* to be precise. It was a heady time for Philadelphia sports fans, of which I am obviously one. The Phillies had won the *World Series* in October, 1980, with me sitting in the 700 level; the Sixers had reached the NBA finals in May, 1980, but lost the series four games to two to the Lakers on FRIDAY, MAY 16, 1980, with rookie Magic Johnson scoring 42 points, with 15 rebounds and 7 assists; and the Flyers had reached the Stanley Cup finals in May as well, also losing their series four games to two, on SATURDAY, MAY 24, 1980, to the New York Islanders. A word about that Flyers' loss. In the deciding Game 6, referee Leon Stickle egregiously blew an offside call (Clark Gillies, who passed away as I was writing this, was at least 1-2 feet offsides) resulting in an Islanders goal and eventual overtime win. Had there been coach's challenges back then, the Flyers may have won their third Stanley Cup. Leon Stickle went down with Chico f***ing Ruiz, John ("Havlicek stole the ball!") Havlicek, Joe Carter, Mitch Williams and the Cheatin' Patriots in Philadelphia sports infamy. I watched all of those.

By the time the Eagles reached *Super Bowl XV*, we had already been through three championship series in eight months. Although Philadelphia had lost two of the three championships, it was a whole lot better than, say 1973, when the Phillies had finished 71-91, good for last place in their division; the Eagles had finished 5-8-1; and the Sixers had finished 9-73, including losing their first 15 games of the season and later losing 20 in a row. During one stretch, they lost 34 of 35 games, and are always in the discussion about the worst teams of all time.

I watched *Super Bowl XV* with some college friends at Ken and Sandy (*nee* Campbell) Ecklund's apartment in the Norwayne Apartments in Wayne, Pennsylvania. I believe that Kevin Schildt, Reed Smith and Dave Stewart ("Stew") were also there, either with wives or girlfriends. Maybe Bob Bowdoin, a college roommate, was there, too. But Ken and Sandy, at least, were definitely married by then. I went to Reed and Joyce's wedding and Dave and Sarah's wedding, as well as to Ken and Sandy's. The only things I remember about Dave and Sarah's wedding are that it was dry and that Joyce was drinking wine out of the bottle in the back seat of my car in the parking lot. All I remember about Ken and Sandy's wedding was dancing with Kim Forsyth. Reed and Joyce's wedding is a blank, other than the fact that I played guitar and sang "Sunrise, Sunset" during the service.

For the first few years after we graduated, we would often meet at the Eastern College gym on Friday or Saturday night and play basketball. Nobody else ever seemed to use the gym and no one ever bothered us for using it, either. Basketball was invariably followed by beers at a local bar, Connus's or something like that, where the bartender, Todd, poured us free beer in exchange for a healthy tip. It was a win-win for everyone. We usually didn't leave until they turned the lights on around 2:00 a.m.

We all thought that we were better athletes than the others, although none of us were really anything special. The most accomplished was probably Reed, who at least played some basketball and baseball in college. I decided at one point to find out who really was the best athlete in the group and came up with the idea of us holding our own decathlon, albeit not by official decathlon rules. We weren't really going to pole vault and throw the javelin, or even run hurdles. So, for three straight years, Ken, Reed, Stew, Kevin and I held our own version of a decathlon. The events, as near as I can recall, were:

100 yard dash

Long jump

Soccer

Bowling

¼ mile

Basketball

Mile

Baseball throw

Bench press

Shot put

Home run derby

Discus

Field goal kicking

Tennis

I know that that is 14, not 10, events, but all of those were events at some point. Shot put and discus were dropped after one year, since none of us had any earthly idea how to throw them. Which events were for which particular year, who knows. We had to do a fair amount of driving around to complete all of the events, looking for soccer nets, long jump pits, tracks, softball fields and goal posts. We would hold the decathlon over the course of two days, since it wasn't possible to do all ten events in one day. Some results were givens - Ken would win the bench press, Reed would win basketball, Kevin would win the mile and I would win the 100 yard dash and bowling. It was also a given that I would finish last in the baseball throw, with my pathetic arm. Fortunately, points were also awarded for finishing second, third, fourth or fifth. Bowling was always the last event, since it was the least taxing and could be done indoors at night. Kevin won the first two decathlons, but I managed to win the third. After the third, we stopped holding them, maybe because I had moved to Massachusetts, or, more likely, because we didn't want to deal with the pain that always followed.

After I moved back to New Jersey, we tried to organize one more, but no one other than Kevin, the most competitive of the group, was too interested. So Kevin and I asked Joe Strong if he was up for it, which he was. We held several events on day one, drank lots of beer that night, and finished up the next day. I think that I won that one, too, but barely. Joe gave me a run for my money in the 100 yard dash, although I managed to edge him out.

We did some strange stuff while living in the dorms at college, like all college kids do. Being stupid college kids, we invented a game that we called "Flying Rupture," which involved two people lying flat on their backs on dorm beds, which were against opposite walls, maybe six feet apart. The object of the game was to bounce a tennis ball off of the wall next to your bed so that it would land on the other player's most private of parts. The opposing player was not allowed to flinch, moan, scream or react in any way, if the tennis ball found its target. Flinching, moving or crying out in pain meant disqualification and the player lost. We would play for what seemed like hours.

I got into a debate one time with a woman at work about which pain was worse - labor pains or getting hit in the nuts with a frozen Snickers bar. After some time, I asked her if she would go through labor again, and she said she would. I replied, "Well, I never want to get hit in the nuts with a frozen Snickers bar again." That ended the debate. I won.

At the behest of Stew, and against my better judgment, I went with my girlfriend at the time, Barbara Boenning, Ken and Sandy, and Reed to a dance to benefit the Young Republicans Club in Radnor or Wayne, Pennsylvania. Reed wasn't yet dating Joyce and he went with a date who didn't approve of drinking, so the rest of us spent part of the night distracting her, so that Reed could enjoy a little beer. Although I am admittedly a horrible dancer, Barb and I managed a second-place finish in a "Bump" contest, probably more for her dancing than mine. I'm a little embarrassed to admit that I contributed money to a Republican cause, but it wasn't much money, and I swear that I have never done it again.

Ken and Sandy went on a couple of double-dates with me and whoever I might be able to scare up. One night, in November or December 1979, we got tickets to see the Philadelphia Fox, Philadelphia's entry in the Women's Professional Basketball League. It had to be one of those two months, because the Fox only survived for a month, playing their first game on SATURDAY, NOVEMBER 17, 1979, and their last on TUESDAY, DECEMBER 18, 1979. According to the scorecard I have, they played the St. Louis Streak. The Streak played the Fox on FRIDAY, NOVEMBER 23, 1979, in Philly, so it was most likely that night. The Fox played before tiny crowds of fewer than 1,000 fans in the Philadelphia Civic Center and lost eight of the ten games that they played. Sandy apparently kept my scorebook at the game, since it contains what look like her doodles in the margin.

During college, naturally, we had little money to spend on luxuries like baseball games. Fortunately, I had an acquaintance from church in Collingswood, Willard Bisbing, known simply as "Biz," who worked at the courtesy gate for Phillies games. He was my parents' age, went to high school with my mother, where he was a local legend as a football player, and had a daughter, Barbara, who was my age. The courtesy gate was mostly for players' families and friends. I would occasionally show up with Ken and Reed and others at a game, with no tickets, and stop at the gate and ask for Biz. He didn't always seem too happy to see me and my friends, but he would look around (presumably to see if his supervisor was nearby) and let us in, usually saying something like, "Go upstairs and get lost." We would climb the ramp to the 700 level, find some unoccupied seats, and take in a game courtesy of Biz.

For one particular game in 1978, after we were out of college, we actually had tickets and didn't have to rely on Biz. It was Photo Night at the Phillies game and fans were allowed onto the field before the game to snap pictures of the players as they walked down a roped-off aisle. This, of course, was before picture-taking became too easy using cellphones. You had to purchase the correct kind of film, bring an actual camera to the game and wait to get the film developed before you could see your pictures. You also had to be judicious in taking shots, since rolls of film only had so many exposures on them. I had my father's pretty hefty camera and managed some good shots. Sandy, in particular, was good at photo night since many of the players didn't seem to mind stopping and having their photo taken with a young blonde woman. The slides from that night are in a box in my attic.

Sandy was a very good athlete. She played softball, basketball and field hockey in college. She was a much better athlete than Ken, although he was OK in some sports, like basketball. She played on the field hockey team with Barbara Boenning, my girlfriend at the time, as well as Kathy Wiley, Debbie Darling and Kim Forsyth. She also loved dogs. She and Ken met in college, started dating, and were married not too long after graduation.

The field hockey team featured some very good-looking women - Sandy, Barb, Kathy and Kim. [*Sitting, left to right - Barb, Kim, Sandy; front - Kathy*]. To this day, I swear that Kim Forsyth was the best-looking college kid I ever knew. And it's not even too close. Anyway, there was a tournament of some kind one weekend, and I went with Ken to watch since Barb and Sandy were both playing. I also took Sheba, my Alaskan Malamute. Sheba was an absolutely beautiful dog. Between games, I talked to Barb and Sandy and Kim and some of the other players, who stopped by to pet Sheba. Kim liked Sheba, and Sheba was on her back getting a belly rub from Kim. I said something like, "She likes that," and I heard a young guy, maybe whispering to Ken, say, "So would I."

Ken and Sandy ultimately got divorced several years later. They each got remarried, Ken to Marie and Sandy to some guy I never met, Joseph Dixon. I'm sure that it was Ken who either called or emailed one day to tell me that Sandy, not even 50 years old, had passed away from cancer on MONDAY, SEPTEMBER 29, 2003. I didn't even know that she was ill.

* * *

The Eagles team in 1980 had talent, but was certainly not amongst the most talented teams ever. There were only two players who made it to the Hall of Fame - Claude Humphrey, a defensive end, and Harold Carmichael, a wide receiver. Humphrey's best days were behind him and they had been spent with the Atlanta Falcons. During the regular season, the Eagles went 12-4. They started out 11-1, then proceeded to lose three of their last four to end up tied with the Dallas Cowboys. The Eagles won the tiebreaker and defeated the Minnesota Vikings 31-16 on SATURDAY, JANUARY 3, 1981, in the first round of the playoffs. Despite trailing 14-7 at halftime, the Eagles forced eight turnovers, seven of them in the second half, to win the game. The day before, the Dallas Cowboys had routed the Los Angeles Rams 34-13, to set up the NFC championship game.

At 1:00 p.m. on SUNDAY, JANUARY 11, 1981, it was 12 degrees in Philadelphia and the wind was blowing 13 m.p.h., resulting in a wind chill of -3 degrees. The Dallas Cowboys were in Philly for the NFC Championship Game at the Vet. The Cowboys themselves are rightfully despised in Philadelphia, as they are in most places. Even more despised are the people who have no connection to Dallas or the Cowboys, yet become Cowboys fans just to get a rise out of everyone else. They think the Cowboys' stars on their helmets are really pretty, I guess, because what other earthly reason is there to root for them? And yes, Philadelphia fans did boo Michael Irvin as he lay injured on the Veterans Stadium turf. Just like they would have done in New York, or Washington or Green Bay.

Every national announcer who broadcasts an Eagles game is required, at least once per season, to mention that Philadelphia fans once booed Santa Claus and pelted him with snowballs. This is done solely to demonstrate how mean and horrible Philadelphia fans are. Yes . . . they did boo Santa, but a little context would be helpful. On SUNDAY, DECEMBER 15, 1968, the Eagles record was 2-11 heading into their game with the Minnesota Vikings at Franklin Field in Philadelphia - the final game of a miserable season. The Eagles had started the season by losing their first 11 games. Had they just lost their next two, they would have had the number one draft pick in the upcoming draft and would have drafted a fellow named O.J. Simpson. Instead, they won those two games and had to settle for the third pick. So, by that Sunday afternoon, Eagles fans were already in a foul mood.

The Eagles had planned a Christmas celebration at halftime. The only problem was that their Santa Claus didn't show up. So they plucked a skinny guy who stood about 5'6" out of the stands to fill in. They picked him because he was already in a Santa suit that he had worn to the game - apparently not all that great a suit, either. As the would-be Santa paraded around the field, fans booed and threw snowballs. Boo-hoo. But it gets mentioned every . . . single . . . year, despite the fact that it happened MORE THAN 50 YEARS AGO, PEOPLE! Yet we don't constantly hear about the death threats from St. Louis Cardinals fans directed at an umpire who blew a call; or about Red Sox fans screaming racial epithets at minority players; or about Los Angeles Dodgers fans actually murdering a visiting San Francisco Giants fan. And how often do you hear about Kansas City Chiefs fans throwing snowballs at the Colts while the game was going on, or about New York Giants fans throwing snowballs for an entire game in 1995, resulting in 14 arrests, 175 ejections from the stadium and three security guards being hospitalized? So can we just get over booing and throwing snowballs at a scrawny fill-in Santa when Lyndon Johnson was president?

Despite the NFC championship game being in Philadelphia, the Cowboys were favored to win. The Eagles always wore their Kelly green jerseys at home that year, but they had the choice about what color they would wear against the Cowboys, since they were the home team. For the championship game, they elected to wear their white jerseys, forcing the

Cowboys to wear their blue jerseys, which the Cowboys believed were jinxed. On just their second offensive play of the game, the Eagles' Wilbert Montgomery ran for a 55-yard touchdown, giving the Eagles a 7-0 lead early in the game. The Eagles would go on to win 20-7 and reach their first *Super Bowl*.

The *Super Bowl* was a disaster. Rod Martin, who would win the game's MVP award, intercepted Ron Jaworski's first pass of the game and returned it 17 yards to the Eagles' 30-yard line. Oakland scored a touchdown and then another later in the first quarter on an 80-yard touchdown pass, to take a 14-0 lead after one quarter. The Eagles did manage to score three points in the second quarter on a field goal by barefoot kicker Tony Franklin, but Oakland scored a touchdown to open the third quarter, Jaworski threw a second interception to Martin, and the game was essentially over at 24-3 after three quarters.

The Eagles finally scored a touchdown in the fourth, but Jaworski also lost a fumble and threw a third interception to Martin and the Raiders won in a rout, 27-10, becoming the first wild card team to win a *Super Bowl*. While heartbroken, we were sure that the Eagles would soon be back in the *Super Bowl* and that they would win this time. We were wrong. It took more than two decades for them to play in another, and more than three decades before they would actually win one.

CHAPTER 21

MONDAY, NOVEMBER 11, 1985

I found out about Pelle Lindbergh's car accident while sitting in Logan Airport in Boston, I believe, with Kevin and Ken. Maybe we were riding on the T, but I think it was at the airport as they were getting ready to fly back to Philadelphia. We saw someone reading a newspaper with a headline something like, "Flyers' Goalie Brain Dead."

Pelle Lindbergh was the 26 year-old goalie for the Philadelphia Flyers and had won the Vezina Trophy as the league's best goaltender in the spring after leading the Flyers to the Stanley Cup finals against the Edmonton Oilers. That Oilers team was one of the greatest NHL teams ever, boasting Hockey Hall of Famers Wayne Gretzky, Paul Coffey, Glenn Anderson, Mark Messier, Jari Kurri and Grant Fuhr. Not many teams have six Hall of Famers on the same roster. They crushed the Flyers four games to one in the Stanley Cup finals, clinching the Cup with an 8-3 win on Thursday, May 30, 1985. In his final game four days before his death, on Thursday, November 7, 1985, Lindbergh made 18 saves in a 6-2 Flyers win over the Chicago Blackhawks.

I also learned of another death by reading someone else's newspaper. I was riding on the T in Boston one morning when I saw a story on the front page of the *Boston Globe* or *Boston Herald* that Jessica Savitch, the first woman to host *NBC Nightly News*, had been killed in a car accident in New Hope, Pennsylvania the day before, on SUNDAY, OCTOBER 23, 1983. Like almost everyone who lived in the Philadelphia area in the 1970's, I knew who Savitch was from her days as a *KYW Eyewitness News* anchor. For a time, she may have been the most recognized person in the city. They said that the camera loved her. Women wanted to be like her and men wanted to be with her. I guess that's whey they called her the "Golden Girl." Things aren't always what they seem, though.

In the very early morning of November 10th, Lindbergh drove his Porsche 930 Turbo into a concrete wall at the intersection of Somerdale Road and Ogg Avenue in Somerdale, New Jersey, about a mile or so from what would later be our home on Abbey Road in Voorhees. Sadly,

Lindbergh had a blood-alcohol reading of .24 and was speeding after leaving a party at the Coliseum, where the Flyers practiced. I've driven by that wall hundreds of times, and think of the accident every time. In one careless and reckless moment, the fates of a family and of an entire hockey franchise were changed forever. The Flyers have been searching for a goalie ever since.

Kevin and Ken happened to be visiting that weekend while I was living at 78 Baker Street in Beverly, Massachusetts. We picked that weekend because the Celtics and Patriots were both playing at home and we could get tickets to each game, which sounded like a fun boys' weekend. Don't hold me to this, but I think that we went to the Celtics-Pistons game on FRIDAY, NOVEMBER 8, 1985, at the old Boston Garden.

We definitely went to the Patriots-Colts game on SUNDAY, NOVEMBER 10, 1985, at the old Sullivan Stadium in Foxboro. Although the attendance was officially listed as 54,176 and the temperature was 61 degrees, I don't remember half that many people being there. We had had a couple of drinks at some club in Beverly the night before and none of us were feeling totally chipper, especially Ken. The drive to the stadium was a good hour-and-a-half and Ken spent most of it lying down on the back seat of my Volvo, complaining that he didn't feel good and was hungry. We finally stopped and got him some doughnuts.

Kevin and I threw a football around the parking lot at the stadium, ate some leftover fried chicken, and then we finally headed inside for the game. Sullivan stadium had benches for seating and no one was sitting next to us, so Ken laid down and slept through most of the game, a 34-16 Patriots win over the Indianapolis Colts. The Patriots went on to defeat the Jets, Raiders and Dolphins in the playoffs that year, only to face off against the Chicago Bears in *Super Bowl XX*. The Bears absolutely mauled the Patriots in that game, 46-10.

* * *

Although Pelle Lindbergh was declared brain-dead shortly after the accident, he was kept on life support until his father arrived from Sweden and gave permission to remove the life support on MONDAY, NOVEMBER 11, 1985. The things that people are capable of never ceases to amaze me. How, as a parent, do you endure that 10-hour flight, knowing what awaits at the other end?

During the 1985-86 hockey season, fans posthumously elected Lindbergh to the NHL All-Star team. It was the first time in North American sports that a player was elected to an All-Star team after his death. To this day, no Flyer has ever worn Lindbergh's #31.

CHAPTER 22

SUNDAY, SEPTEMBER 14, 1986

John Fogerty, the frontman for Creedence Clearwater Revival, was born the day that my father arrived at Pearl Harbor during World War II - MONDAY, MAY 28, 1945. I have always thought that Creedence was the best American rock and roll band, but that, of course, is completely subjective. Deadheads would surely disagree, as would fans of the Doors, Metallica, Aerosmith, Nirvana, the Allman Brothers, Lynyrd Skynyrd, the Beach Boys, the Eagles and KISS. Fill in your personal favorite. Those insightful critics who think that all of these bands are overrated probably prefer the Ohio Express or Spin Doctors. On Sunday night, alone, I drove to what was then called Great Woods, an open-air pavilion in Mansfield, Massachusetts to see Fogerty on his "Rockin' All Over the World" tour. It was his first real post-CCR tour. Bonnie Raitt opened.

It was the first time that I saw Fogerty live and it was, honestly, disappointing. He had released four solo albums of varying quality - *The Blue Ridge Rangers* (on which he played all of the instruments himself), *John Fogerty, Centerfield* and *Eye of the Zombie* - since Creedence's breakup. His solo career certainly hadn't lived up to his CCR work - nor was it as prolific, with the band releasing a total of five studio albums in 1969 and 1970 - although the *Centerfield* album had reached number one in 1985, with Fogerty again playing all of the instruments. *Centerfield* and *Eye of the Zombie* had also received *Grammy* nominations. The problem with the Great Woods show was that Fogerty was still involved in litigation over rights to the songs he had written while with CCR. He had sold the rights long ago, as a very young man, and refused to play the songs publicly because the royalty went to the people he thought had "stolen" his music. So, at Great Woods, we ended up with a setlist that looked like this:

Mr. Greed

Vanz Kant Danz

Knockin' on Your Door

Headlines

The Old Man Down the Road

Centerfield

Wasn't That a Woman

Violence is Golden

Eye of the Zombie

Sail Away

Soothe Me

Mary Don't You Weep

Goin' Back Home

Big Train (From Memphis)

Soda Pop

Change in the Weather

Rock and Roll Girls

Knock on Wood

Rockin' All Over the World

Not horrible, but not overly impressive, either. It would be nearly 20 years before I went to another Fogerty concert, and then I became something of a groupie.

By July of 2005, Dylan was 13, as was his best friend, Patrick Carlin, who lived two doors from us on Abbey Road. Nancy and I decided to take them to see Fogerty and John Mellencamp at the Tweeter Center in Camden, a nice outdoor venue, on FRIDAY, JULY 15, 2005. Parents always want their kids to like the same music as they do. We got lawn seats. I went mainly to see Fogerty, but Mellencamp was an acceptable act as well. Little did I know that Mellencamp would steal the show.

By this time, Fogerty had ended the litigation over the rights to his Creedence songs and was performing them publicly again. Fogerty took the stage first. The setlists for the two that night were:

Fogerty

Travelin' Band

Born on the Bayou

Who'll Stop the Rain

It Came Out of the Sky

Lookin' Out My Back Door

Midnight Special

Bootleg

Deja Vu (All Over Again)

I Heard It Through the Grapevine

Have You Ever Seen the Rain

Keep on Chooglin'

Sweet Hitchhiker

Hey Tonight

Down on the Corner

Centerfield

Up Around the Bend

The Old Man Down the Road

Fortunate Son

Bad Moon Rising

Proud Mary

Mellencamp

Small Town

Love and Happiness

Lonely Ol' Night

Green River (with Fogerty)

Rain on the Scarecrow (with Fogerty)

Walk Tall

Paper in Fire

I Need a Lover

Authority Song

Jack & Diane

Crumblin' Down

R.O.C.K. in the U.S.A.

Hurts So Good

Pink Houses

Ain't Even Done with the Night

Check It Out

Cherry Bomb

With the addition of the Creedence material, the 2005 setlist was a lot more impressive than the one from 1986. By 2005, Fogerty had gone through a creative resurgence, having released two albums, *Blue Moon Swamp* in 1997 and *Deja Vu All Over Again* in 2004. *Blue Moon Swamp* won the *Grammy Award* for Best Rock Album, beating out albums from Aerosmith, the Foo Fighters, U2 and the Rolling Stones.

By October, 2007, Fogerty had released another album, *Revival*, which was again nominated for a *Grammy Award* for Best Rock Album. This time, the Foo Fighters won. Dylan and I listened to *Revival* a lot, particularly "Gunslinger." The album is teeming with references to CCR, including the album title, and "Creedence Song" ("She said, 'You can't go wrong if you play a little bit of that Creedence song.'") The Revival Tour was stopping at the Tower Theater in Upper Darby on SATURDAY, NOVEMBER 3, 2007, so Nancy and I asked Dylan and Patrick if they wanted to go again. Of course they did.

The show opened with a recreation of the album cover as Fogerty stood on a platform which rose from under the stage, in silhouette, leaning on a guitar, and standing in a wheat field. He opened with "The River is Waiting." In my opinion, it was the best concert of the six of his that I've been to.

We next saw him on SATURDAY, JUNE 27, 2015, at the Mann Music Center in Philly. The Mann was just like Great Woods in Massachusetts and the Tweeter Center in Camden - an open-air pavilion. We tailgated a little bit before going in, with Dylan now being of legal age. Thankfully, we were under cover and seated toward the center, because a pretty good storm with lots of wind and rain passed through during the show. In addition to Dylan, who was home from North Carolina visiting, we met up with Kevin Schildt there.

The Mann show was a little bit different in one respect, although it was heavy, as usual, with Creedence material. Forgerty's son, Shane, had joined his father's band on guitar. Fogerty, as a father should do, bragged on his son when introducing the band. Fogerty himself is a fabulous guitar player, ranked the 40th best ever in one *Rolling Stone* list. Shane is very good, too, and at one point they jammed together for about ten minutes. Nancy got a little misty-eyed sitting there watching father and son.

Nancy and I were now going to see Fogerty whenever he came close to wherever we were living. On FRIDAY, JUNE 22, 2018, he was playing with ZZ Top on their "Blues and Bayous Tour" at the Bank of New Hampshire Pavilion in Gilford, New Hampshire, near Lake Winnipesaukee, and we went with Nancy's sister, Donna Cochrane. Donna's husband, Roy, was supposed to come but bailed for some reason. ZZ Top went first. The setlists were as follows:

ZZ Top

Got Me Under Pressure

I Thank You

Waitin' for the Bus

Jesus Just Left Chicago

Gimme All Your Lovin'

Pearl Necklace

I'm Bad, I'm Nationwide

I Gotsta Get Paid

Sixteen Tons

Beer Drinkers & Hell Raisers

Just Got Paid

Sharp Dressed Man

Legs

La Grange

Tush

Fogerty

Travelin' Band

Hey Tonight

Rock and Roll Girls

Who'll Stop the Rain

Good Golly Miss Molly

Psycho

Up Around the Bend

Holy Grail (with Billy Gibbons of ZZ Top)

Green River (with Billy Gibbons)

Love and War

Have You Ever Seen the Rain?

I Heard It Through the Grapevine

Long as I Can See the Light

Keep on Chooglin'

Born on the Bayou

My Toot Toot

Jambalaya (On the Bayou)

New Orleans

Down on the Corner

Centerfield

The Old Man Down the Road

Fortunate Son

Bad Moon Rising

Proud Mary

I didn't realize what a great guitarist Billy Gibbons is until seeing him. ZZ Top still sported their famous beards, gray now, except for Frank Beard, the drummer, who, ironically, was clean-shaven.

The last time that we saw Fogerty was on SUNDAY, AUGUST 11, 2019, during his "My 50-Year Trip" tour at Rock Row in Westbrook, Maine. This time, we went with Donna, her daughter Christine Bell, and Nancy's sister Cindy and her husband, Dave. That makes five states over the span of 33 years in which I've seen a Fogerty concert, which must officially qualify me as a groupie. The only other artist I have seen as often is Mary Chapin Carpenter, who Nancy and I have also seen six times (but only in three states). Chapin would have moved into first place by herself, since we had tickets to see her in Portland on WEDNESDAY, SEPTEMBER 29, 2021, but the show was cancelled.

I won't bore you with a Top 10 list of my favorite Creedence/Fogerty songs.

CHAPTER 23

SATURDAY, OCTOBER 24, 1987

B oarding for the *M/V Fort Warren* began at 4:30 p.m. on Northern
Avenue, Pier 7 in Boston. Eighty guests were expected on board. It
had snowed on the previous weekend, but on this day it was 65 degrees,
sunny and clear. The weather was almost too perfect for late October in
Boston, but so perfect for our wedding.

Nancy Theresa MacDonald and I met on "Singles Night" at Mr. Tipps,
a decent-sized bar in Billerica, Massachusetts, on SATURDAY, OCTOBER 4,
1986. For our first date, we decided on a sunset dinner cruise on Boston
Harbor on FRIDAY, OCTOBER 24, 1986. A few months later, while on a ski
lift at Gunstock Mountain in Gilford, New Hampshire, I turned to Nancy
and said, "October 24th falls on a Saturday. If we got married then, it
would be exactly one year since our first date. We could get married on a
boat in Boston." It wasn't a planned proposal. It wasn't even a proposal in
the traditional sense. It's hard to get down on your knees on a ski lift and I
didn't have a ring. We were talking, and it just happened. So, on the one
year anniversary of our first date, we got married aboard the *Fort Warren*.
The Reverend Milt Ryder, a friend of mine from camp, officiated.

Milt, who I had known since I was in high school, passed away on
SATURDAY, MARCH 30, 2019, at the age of 81. On SATURDAY, MAY 18, 2019,
Nancy and I drove to Portland for Milt's "Celebration of Birth and Life"
service at the Williston-Immanuel United Church. Although it was
obviously a sad occasion, it was also full of warmth and fondness
remembering a good friend and wonderful man.

I should probably give you a quick bio on Nancy. She was born on
TUESDAY, FEBRUARY 26, 1952, at St. Joseph's Hospital in Lowell,
Massachusetts, to James and Doris MacDonald, who at that time were
living at 225 Cheever Avenue in Lowell. Had Doris held out for three more
days, Nancy would have been a "Leap Day" baby. But she didn't. At eight
days old, on WEDNESDAY, MARCH 5, 1952, Nancy was baptized at St. John
the Baptist Parish in Lowell. She is the eldest of six siblings - five girls and
one boy.

Nancy graduated from Dracut High School in 1970 and from Fitchburg
State College in 1974. On SATURDAY, JUNE 8, 1974, the Commonwealth of
Massachusetts Department of Education issued her Teachers Certificate.
She taught in the public schools of Lowell until 1987, when we moved to
New Jersey. After moving to New Jersey, she taught at the Jennings,
Edison, and Strawbridge elementary schools in Haddon Township until
retiring after the 2014-15 school year. On THURSDAY, MAY 21, 2015, the
Haddon Township Board of Education adopted the following Resolution:

> *WHEREAS, Mrs. Nancy Florig has for the past twenty-
> seven years dedicated her teaching career to the students of
> Haddon Township and has served as a dedicated
> professional educator endeavoring to provide the best possible
> education for our students, and*
>
> *WHEREAS, the said Mrs. Florig has ably represented the
> Haddon Township Board of Education in her role as teacher
> since 1988, now therefore*
>
> *BE IT RESOLVED, that the Haddon Township Board of
> Education recognizes the excellent service that Nancy Florig
> has rendered the said Township of Haddon and the said
> Board of Education, as well as the service rendered to the
> many students over the past twenty-seven years in the field of
> education, and that the Board of Education does sincerely
> appreciate her efforts in their behalf and also in behalf of all
> the students in Haddon Township, and therefore*
>
> *BE IT FURTHER RESOLVED, that a copy of this
> resolution be spread upon the minutes of this meeting and a
> copy be presented to Mrs. Florig.*

Our romance and wedding very nearly didn't happen. At Mr. Tipps, we
had danced a couple of times. Nancy was there with her friend Mary
("Manya") Matyka, and they were much more interested in a couple of
guys they had met there than they were in me. I only learned a little about
Nancy, like that she taught first grade in Lowell and had previously taught
special education. Other than that, not much, and we all left Mr. Tipps
without further conversation. But I was thinking about her. On

WEDNESDAY, OCTOBER 8, 1986, after a few days of cogitating, I decided to take a chance and see if I could contact her. I wrote the following letter:

Dear Nancy,

This must seem really weird, but I had no other way of reaching you. We met briefly at Mr. Tipps on Saturday and danced a couple of times. I didn't think of it at the time, but I thought you might like to go out sometime. If you would, you can reach me at (W) 1-482-1390 ext. 4176 or at (H) 1-438-1867. Yours,

Dave

P.S. Ever been asked out by letter before?

Smooth. I wrote the letter on Foley, Hoag & Eliot law firm letterhead, placed it in a law firm envelope, sealed it, and stamped it "Personal and Confidential" in red. On the outside of that envelope, I put a Post-It note with the message:

Dear Madam or Sir:

I need to get this letter to one of your first grade teachers. Her name is Nancy, she is about 5 feet tall with shoulder-length brown hair. Unfortunately, I do not know her last name. I would appreciate it if you would forward this.

Thanks

I placed that sealed envelope with the Post-It note attached inside of a larger law firm envelope and sent it off to the Lowell Board of Education.

Amazingly, it worked. Even though Lowell was a large school district, the administration managed to track her down and get the letter to her, and a few days later I got a phone call at my apartment in Stoneham. I'm sure that Nancy consulted with Manya first to see if either of them could even remember who I was. We finally settled on a dinner cruise in Boston. Nancy drove her Camry to my apartment and we went to Boston in my Mazda Coupe, which Nancy later derisively referred to as the "Flintstone car." It probably would have been easier if I had just asked her out while we were at Mr. Tipps.

Our second date was at a little neighborhood sports bar called "Johnny's Bench" three days later on TUESDAY, OCTOBER 27, 1986. Normally, a second date wouldn't be on a Tuesday, but we had decided to meet and watch Game 7 of the *World Series* between the Red Sox and Mets. Nancy was, and remains, a huge Sox fan, and the fact that she decided to watch Game 7 with me could only mean that she was falling hard. Through 5 ½ innings, it looked like the Red Sox would win the *World Series*, holding a 3-0 lead. But things fell apart, with the Mets taking a 6-3 lead after seven innings, and holding on for an 8-5 win. It was disappointing, more for her than for me. Little did we know on that night that a year later we would be married.

Although I wore a tux and Nancy wore a wedding gown, the wedding was pretty casual. No big rehearsal dinner, no break between the ceremony and the reception, no photographer or videographer. The ceremony itself lasted about 15 minutes. Nancy read from *The Giving Tree* by Shel Silverstein, and I read from *The Little Prince* by Antoine de Saint-Exupery, and we exchanged vows. The bar couldn't begin serving until the ship left port, so it was important to get out on the water quickly. This was, after all, a boat full of thirsty friends and family. And there was a beautiful sunset to enjoy. I wasn't feeling especially great for the wedding. Apparently, I had eaten something that gave me food poisoning when we went out to dinner with Charlie and Marge the night before. Stuffed peppers were the likely culprit. Somehow, I soldiered through the night without serious incident, although I was pretty green in our hotel room afterwards.

When you get married on a boat, you have a captive audience. No one can leave until it's over. Our 80 guests, like it or not, stayed for the entire time while we sailed the harbor, past the *USS Constitution* ("*Old Ironsides*"), a United States Navy frigate first launched in 1797 and the oldest naval vessel still afloat, and past Logan Airport, where we watched the planes taking off and coming in to land directly overhead. We all sang "Viva L'Amour" for the French-Canadian side of the family when we docked.

Among our guests were Bob Thomas and his girlfriend, Wendy Lincoln, who also joined us at the Boston Harbor Hotel for the after-party.

They gave us a card, in Wendy's handwriting but most definitely in Bob's voice:

Oh Nancy, oh Dave (sob-sob)

We're so happy for you little love kittens. We hope you will follow your dreams always (sob-sob) and send each other books of poems when you're apart.

Oh God, we love you!

Bob & Wendy

Thirty years after our wedding, we decided to re-create the event, but this time in Portland, Maine, not Boston.

CHAPTER 24

Christmas Eve was spent with the extended MacDonald family at Linda (*nee* MacDonald) and Billy Tierney's house on Coral Drive in Dracut, Massachusetts. MacDonald Christmas Eves were mandatory if one were to maintain one's standing within the family. Roughly 2,000 - 3,000 extended family members attended each year. Nancy and I had been married for exactly two months and were living in my old apartment in Stoneham. I received my best Christmas present ever that night - a puppy.

It wasn't only Christmas when the entire clan would gather. Thanksgiving was also a massive MacDonald event, although not on the scale of Christmas Eve. Nancy, Dylan and I would pick one holiday or the other to attend and would spend the other one at home in New Jersey. When Dylan was very young, we usually opted to stay home on Christmas so that Santa could visit, so we usually made the trip to Dracut on Thanksgiving. For a few years, Thanksgiving was also held at Linda and Billy's house. It was at one of those meals that Jim, Nancy's father, when presented with the spiral ham that was being passed, committed a minor social gaffe. As the patriarch, Jim was presented with the ham first. He took the large serving fork, jammed it into the ham, and took what most estimates place at around two pounds of ham and set it on his plate. We watched in feigned amazement, because it didn't surprise us all that much. Jim didn't seem aware of his *faux pas*.

By the time that the Thanksgiving meal was over and everyone had headed home, we were all pretty-well overstimulated. Knowing that the madness would continue on Black Friday, Dylan and I had to find alternative activities which would give us a good excuse to get away. For a couple of years, we settled on college hockey, while Nancy opted for shopping with her mother and sisters.

The Tsongas Arena in Lowell was the home ice for the University of Massachusetts-Lowell River Hawks. They held college hockey doubleheaders there on the Friday after Thanksgiving. UMass-Lowell would play somebody in one game and two other college teams would play in the other. That gave Dylan and I a good six hours of bonding time and respite from the MacDonald madness. Although the arena held a few thousand people, there were usually no more than 75-100 people there, so we pretty much could do whatever and sit wherever we wanted. We liked to be close to the action, so we usually sat behind one of the goals in the first or second row. If a puck happened into the stands near us, Dylan would grab it. Another time, one of the referees tossed Dylan a puck during warm-ups.

One of the games that we saw involved the University of Vermont Catamounts. Vermont wore head-to-toe green uniforms, while UMass-Lowell wore red, white and blue. In any event, that caused some heckling directed at a small Vermont player, with taunts such as, "Use the force, Yoda." The little guy got his revenge by scoring the game-winning goal. In hindsight, we think that it was 5'8" Martin St. Louis, who played at Vermont from 1995 to 1997, and who ended up in the Hockey Hall of Fame.

We would leave New Jersey very early on Thanksgiving morning, usually around 5:00 a.m. or so, in order to "beat the traffic." It worked, too, and we never arrived late for the Thanksgiving feast. It was a long ride of around 330 miles and took six or seven hours to complete. That meant that we would have to keep ourselves amused and awake, so we usually ended up putting the radio on at some point. It was on one of those car rides that I introduced Nancy and Dylan to "Dr. Laura."

"Dr." Laura Schlessinger is not a medical doctor, but rather has a Ph.D. in physiology. She gives personal and relationship advice to callers on her talk radio show. You might wonder why she is qualified to do that and what kind of advice she might give. Let's take a quick peek at what qualifies the good doctor to "offer no-nonsense advice infused with a strong sense of ethics, accountability, and personal responsibility," and to lecture and belittle people for what she is convinced are their moral and personal failings. Her "traditional family values" apparently don't exactly apply to her, since she was estranged from both her mother (they hadn't spoken for 20 years before her mother's death) and her sister. Her estrangement from her mother was, of course, her mother's fault, and she has said that she did not mourn her mother's death. How's *that* for accountability?

Her decades-long rants against unmarried couples "shacking up" likewise don't apply to her. She met and moved in with a married man, living with him for four years before he got divorced and another six before she married him.

Dr. Laura has called homosexuals "biological errors" and "mistakes," based on her biblical literalism. Those comments led to one of the funniest internet takedowns ever, a letter to Dr. Laura from Professor

James. M. Kauffman, Ed.D. (is he Dr. Kauffman?), presented below in abbreviated form:

Dear Dr. Laura:

Thank you for doing so much to educate people regarding God's Law. I have learned a great deal from your show, and try to share that knowledge with as many people as I can. When someone tries to defend the homosexual lifestyle, for example, I simply remind them that Leviticus 18:22 clearly states it to be an abomination . . . end of debate.

I do need some advice from you, however, regarding some other elements of God's Laws and how to follow them.

Leviticus 25:44 states that I may possess slaves, both male and female, provided they are purchased from neighbouring nations. A friend of mine claims that this applies to Mexicans, but not Canadians. Can you clarify? Why can't I own Canadians?

I would like to sell my daughter into slavery, as sanctioned in Exodus 21:7. In this day and age, what do you think would be a fair price for her?

I know that I am allowed no contact with a woman while she is in her period of menstrual unseemliness - Lev. 15:19-24. The problem is how do I tell? I have tried asking, but most women take offense.

I have a neighbor who insists on working on the Sabbath. Exodus 35:2 clearly states he should be put to death. Am I morally obligated to kill him myself, or should I ask the police to do it?

Lev. 21:20 states that I may not approach the altar of God if I have a defect in my sight. I have to admit that I wear reading glasses. Does my vision have to be 20/20, or is there some wiggle-room here?

Most of my male friends get their hair trimmed, including the hair around their temples, even though this is expressly forbidden by Lev. 19:27. How should they die?

I know from Lev. 11:6-8 that touching the skin of a dead pig makes me unclean, but may I still play football if I wear gloves?

My uncle has a farm. He violates Lev. 19:19 by planting two different crops in the same field, as does his wife by wearing garments made of two different kinds of thread (cotton/polyester blend). He also tends to curse and blaspheme a lot. Is it really necessary that we go to all the trouble of getting the whole town together to stone them? Lev. 24:10-16. Couldn't we just burn them to death at a private family affair, like we do with people who sleep with their in-laws? (Lev. 20:14)

I know you have studied these things extensively and thus enjoy considerable expertise in such matters, so I am confident you can help.

Your adoring fan,

James M. Kauffman, Ed.D.

A nuanced discussion about race is also a Dr. Laura specialty. On TUESDAY, AUGUST 10, 2010, a Black woman who was married to a white man called for advice on how to deal with her husband, who apparently didn't care when she was the subject of racist comments. Dr. Laura's wise advice was that "some people are hypersensitive," and that the caller had "a chip on her shoulder." She went on to explain the 2008 presidential election by stating, "a lot of Blacks only voted for Obama because he was half Black. Didn't matter what he was going to do in office, it was a Black thing; you gotta know that." As the caller tried to respond, Dr. Laura admonished her, "Don't NAACP me."

The caller explained that she had been called the "n-word." Dr. Laura proceeded to go on a rant about about how it is OK for Blacks to use that word, but not whites, in the process saying the full "n-word" 11 times. After the enlightening call ended, Dr. Laura concluded the discussion by saying, "If you're that hypersensitive about color and don't have a sense of humor, don't marry out of your race."

Tragically, a few days later, Dr. Laura announced that she was leaving radio so that she could regain her First Amendment rights. Not only did "Dr." Laura not go to medical school, she clearly did not go to law school, either. But don't worry, fans. Sirius picked her up.

If I were ever having trouble with my family or with a relationship, I can't think of anyone better to turn to. So, if you need to talk through any problems you may be having, you can reach her at 1-800-DRLAURA. Really.

There were better things to listen to on the radio on those trips. It was on one of the early morning Thanksgiving Day drives to Massachusetts that I introduced Dylan to "Alice's Restaurant Massacree," Arlo Guthrie's classic about being arrested for littering on Thanksgiving Day and how that possibly meant that he "wasn't moral enough to join the army, burn women, kids, houses, and villages." Surfing around the radio, I found the song, which is pretty commonly played on the radio on Thanksgiving. Due to the song's length, listening to it provided entertainment and killed 20 minutes of the car ride.

When Dylan and I couldn't find a college hockey game in Lowell one year, we decided instead to go to a Bruins game to get away from the craziness. By good fortune, the Flyers were in Boston on FRIDAY, NOVEMBER 25, 2005, the day after Thanksgiving, at the TD Bank Garden for an afternoon game. I got some tickets and Dylan and I took the train from Lowell to Boston for the game. In a really fun game, the Flyers beat the Bruins 5-3 to improve their record to 13-5-3 behind goals from Simon Gagne, Eric Desjardins, Michael Handzus and two by Peter Forsberg. It was Gagne's 21st goal in just 21 games, and he would go on to a career-best 47 goals that year. Forsberg never again would have such a good year, beset by injuries, but eventually he made his way into the Hall of Fame.

As good as the Flyers game was, something even better happened *after* the game. Dylan and I went out to eat at The Fours, a little bar/restaurant on Canal Street right outside of the Garden. On MONDAY, FEBRUARY 7, 2005, *Sports Illustrated* had named The Fours "the best sports bar in America." The place was teeming with sports memorabilia, mostly from Boston sports. Autographed jerseys, pictures and trophies filled the place. It was at The Fours that Dylan and I first discovered the joys of buffalo chicken nachos. They were, simply put, the best nachos ever. Over the years, we went to The Fours as many times as we could, always ordering one, and sometimes two, giant plates of them. They were awesome every single time. One final time, just before Christmas in 2019, Dylan and Elizabeth flew into Logan Airport and Nancy and I drove to Boston to pick them up. Of course, we stopped at The Fours, not knowing that it would be the last time that we would ever savor our favorite food there. The pandemic forced The Fours to close its doors on MONDAY, AUGUST 31, 2020, after 44 years, another in a long, long list of victims of the pandemic.

Back to the 1987 Christmas Eve. Jesse Jackson, who always went by simply "Jesse" or "the Jester" was a husky-collie mix. The Reverend Jesse Jackson had run for president in 1984, although I didn't support him - I had voted for Walter Mondale. Nevertheless, I liked Jesse Jackson (the person) and decided that the least I could do was honor him by naming my new, best Christmas present ever, puppy after him. So we settled on Jesse Jackson as his name.

When Jesse made his appearance at the Christmas Eve party, I didn't know who he was for. Nancy said he was for me, but I didn't believe her at first. Finally, she convinced me. Of course, everyone, mainly me, wanted to play with the puppy and the puppy was happy to play, so Jesse was the hit of the party. Since puppies don't really know how to self-regulate, he was going pretty hard the entire night, besieged by dozens of MacDonalds. Finally, exhausted, he collapsed on the floor in front of the fireplace. He curled up in a circle and passed out.

Jesse knew how to talk, or so we thought. He was very vocal, smarter than some people I know, and we think that he really did at least try to talk. If you told Jesse to say a word or phrase, he could repeat it, usually with at least the right number of syllables. Sometimes, it sounded like he was actually trying to repeat our words. He sounded a little bit like Scooby-Doo.

Our apartment in Stoneham didn't allow pets, although we did clandestinely keep Jesse there for a week or so while Nancy was home on school vacation. By this time, we had entered into an Agreement of Sale for a house at 211 East Palmer Avenue in Collingswood, New Jersey. Nancy, I believe, was the first MacDonald to ever leave Massachusetts. Since Charlie and Marge (especially Marge) loved dogs, they agreed to take Jesse for a couple of weeks until we moved down from Massachusetts. So, on a snowy, treacherous day for driving, I put Jesse in a crate and drove him to Logan Airport for his solo flight to Philadelphia, where Charlie and Marge picked him up. By the time Nancy and I moved down in January, we were greeted by a well-trained and growing Jesse.

Jesse liked to jump up onto the bed, like most dogs. One morning while we were probably watching *Pee-Wee's Playhouse*, he jumped up, stood over me, and, without warning, puked. I didn't have a shirt on and was lying face down. He puked a perfect puddle into the small of my back. Moving, of course, would mean that I would spill the warm, soupy puddle all over the bed. Nancy, once she stopped laughing and regained her composure, reluctantly managed to clean me up. Jesse seemed pleased with himself.

We lived only a couple of houses up from Cooper River, and Nancy and Charlie would take Jesse for walks at the park. There were usually hundreds of geese down there and geese are prodigious poopers. That suited Jesse just fine, since he could bark at them, roll around in what they deposited, and occasionally scarf down one of the Tootsie-Roll shaped treats they left behind.

Those goose droppings were not the only exotic treat that Jesse ate. One time, in our kitchen on Abbey Road, Dylan was still a toddler and walking around naked, which was obviously no big deal. What was a big deal was that he somehow managed, while standing, to drop a little turd onto the kitchen floor. Before either Nancy or I could clean it up, Jesse swooped in, and, with one quick gulp, downed the little brown nugget. Jesse, like Erin later on, would instinctively grab anything that fell on the kitchen floor, without sniffing or thinking. I don't know whether Jesse regretted this particular decision or not.

Jesse lived with us in Collingswood and after we moved to Voorhees. He was there when we first brought Dylan home from the hospital in 1991. Dylan loved Jesse, and Jesse loved Dylan. It was heartbreaking when Jesse got old and was in failing health. For a couple of years, he had some disorder that left his head slightly cocked, but that was more charming than anything. We had made the decision that we would have to put him down. Those decisions take time to come to grips with. We are, after all, deciding that the pet must die. But the decision had been made that I would be taking Jesse to the veterinarian the next day.

On Jesse's last night, we were upstairs in bed and Jesse was downstairs, no longer able to climb the steps. We heard him moaning and crying, so I went downstairs to stay with him and sleep on the couch. I lay on the couch with my arm hanging over and my hand resting on Jesse. When I woke up that morning, he was dead. In one final act of kindness, Jesse had spared me the awful car ride that day. I like to think that he knew and decided not to make me do it.

I went upstairs and told Nancy that Jesse was gone. We told Dylan that Jesse had died and asked if he wanted to go down and say goodbye. He did. Jesse was still warm and lying on the floor next to the couch. Dylan petted him, talked to him, and said goodbye.

The problem, of course, was that we now had a dead 70-pound dog lying on the living room floor. Nancy and I had to go to work and Dylan had to go to school. So I called Rothman Animal Hospital, our veterinarians, for advise. They told me that I could bring him right over and make arrangements. I found an old sheet and slid it underneath Jesse, so that Nancy and I could carry him out to the trunk of my car.

On the count of three, we each picked up one end of the sheet and began carrying Jesse to the laundry room, then through the garage, and finally out to my car. Nancy, being short and certainly not a weight-lifter, told me that he was heavy and we had to put him down. And so we did. When Jesse hit the floor, he let out a sound that I can best describe as a low-pitched "hoomph!" Nancy jumped at least a foot back and said, "He's alive!" I assured her that he very much was not and that the sound was simply the air rushing out of his lungs when he hit the floor. We finally got him into the trunk of my car, I wrapped the sheet around him, and he took his last car ride to the vet.

The only remaining question was what to do with him. The vet suggested three options. First, we could bury him in a pet cemetery. I've always thought that was a little weird, although pet cemeteries are interesting places to visit. People bury all kinds of pets there and write some really odd things on the gravestones, like the Keval family who buried "Cat #1 and Cat #2" in Aspin Hill Memorial Park. On the other hand, there are some really nice places where people honor their pets. On MONDAY, AUGUST 16, 2021, Nancy and I took a walk around Mackworth Island State Park in Falmouth, Maine. In the park, off of the trail, is the Percival Baxter Pet Cemetery. Baxter was the governor of Maine in the 1920's and was instrumental in helping to create its many state parks. Inside of a circular stone wall are the graves of Baxter's many, many Irish Setters, as well as his horse, Jerry. The inscription on the large stone in the center of the cemetery reads:

The State of Maine by Legislative Act, Chapter 1, Laws of
1943, accepted the gift of Mackworth Island and covenanted
to maintain forever this burial place of my dogs with the stone
wall and the boulder with the bronze marker thereon erected
to their memory. Percival P. Baxter.

The second option for what to do with Jesse was to have him buried in a "mass grave," which basically means tossing the pet into a big hole and bulldozing it over. That just didn't seem right. The third option, and the one which I chose, was to have him cremated.

A few days later, the Rothman Animal Hospital called to say that Jesse's remains were ready. They were in a nice burgundy-colored metal box, with a tassel. It was far nicer than the cardboard shoe boxes that Marge and Charlie came back in.

Dylan, in third grade at the time, wrote a poem, "The Band in the Box," about us putting Jesse's collar in the box with his ashes:

The band in the box has meaning to me
With its silvery hook, and red, slick background
With its yellow stars, and white Saturn silhouettes

The band in the box has meaning to me
Every time Jesse scratched
And his license would jingle
The collar was there
Something I always remember

The band in the box has meaning to me
A reminder of Jesse's personality
A beggar for food
Lovable, not pettable
Acting dumb, but always smart

The band in the box has meaning to me
I still remember that October morning
When I got the news
I went down to see him
He looked fast asleep
When I went to school that day
I tried not to weep

The band in the box has meaning to me
Fenway's a good dog
But not quite the same
Fenway's a dog who loves to be petted
Much unlike Jesse
These dogs are so different
In their own unique ways
So that collar's still Jesse's
Never to be Fenway's

After all these years, Jesse's ashes are still in that box, along with his collar and tags. I have never found the right time nor place to let them go. Nor do I really want to.

We purchased 211 East Palmer Avenue, an 1,100 square foot, three-bedroom, one-and-a-half bathroom, two-story home in Collingswood for $100,000 from the Estate of Lora Riester. The deed was prepared by David L. Finnegan, Esquire, the son of John Finnegan. The same John Finnegan, coincidentally, who had arranged my adoption by Charlie and Marge 34 years before and who had unsuccessfully argued against mandatory polio vaccination for schoolchildren.

We chose Collingswood largely because I had begun working in Philadelphia at Marshall, Dennehey, Warner, Coleman & Goggin at 16th and Locust, and there were PATCO High-Speed Line stops in Collingswood and right outside of my office. Nancy was able to get substitute teaching jobs, as well, in Collingswood and Haddon Township. The house had a small backyard and roses along the side of the house. Once, while we were living there, a biathlon, consisting of a 2.5 mile run, followed by a 20 mile bicycle ride, followed by another 2.5 mile run, was held at Cooper River Park. Fancying myself a pretty good athlete, and without any real training, I entered. At least by now I had a real bike. Somehow, I managed to finish, although way, way at the back of the pack, and I vowed never to do such a stupid thing again. I haven't, but I've done plenty of other stupid things.

Jesse, of course, was also living with us on East Palmer. Jesse was used to staying in his crate during the day when Nancy and I were working. We had gotten a crate for Jesse after he tried to escape from the kitchen, where we confined him during the day, by chewing his way through the wooden kitchen door. He liked his crate, as many dogs do, and probably felt safe and secure there. One day, while both of us were working, Jesse got a case of diarrhea. Dogs get sick just like people do. However, people are generally not confined to a 10 cubic foot space with no escape. When we arrived home and opened the door, the smell hit us with a full frontal blow, just like opening the door to a burning building creates a backdraft. I have never smelled anything like it, before or since, nor do I want to. It was the most vile thing ever to assault my olfactory nerve, and I've boiled cabbage indoors.

There is actually a science behind bad smells, which I won't get into here. Some people think that something called "Stench Soup" is the worst smell ever. According to the *Chicago Tribune*:

> *In 1998, Pamela Dalton, a cognitive psychologist at the Monell Chemical Senses Center, was tasked with developing a stink bomb for the Defense Department. Her experiments found that people from different backgrounds and different parts of the world, who grew up smelling and eating different things, often completely disagreed about which smells were good or bad.*

> *The best candidate she found for a universally distasteful smell was something called "U.S. Government Standard Bathroom Malodor," a substance that was designed to mimic the scent of military field latrines in order to test cleaning products. She chose the aromatic liquid as the base of her stink-bomb recipe. The resulting formula, which she called Stench Soup, may well be the worst smell ever created.*

> *Mary Roach, a science writer, is one of the few humans who tried inhaling Stench Soup. In her 2016 book "Grunt: The Curious Science of Humans at War," she described the aroma as "Satan on a throne of rotting onions."*

First, a few observations:

• Leave it to the government to fund research into a stink bomb.

• Naturally, a woman was in charge, since women can detect smells far beyond what men can detect. Nancy, for example, could smell a fly fart in a barn.

• Mimicking the smell of a military field latrine as "the base" for a stink bomb seems like overkill. Does anything really need to be added?

Anyway, I am fairly confident that Jesse gave Stench Soup a run for its money that day. The cleanup was extensive, took hours, and was the most disgusting thing I ever experienced. I suspect that there are still remnants of that odor at 211 East Palmer.

A couple of weeks after moving into our home on East Palmer, we received a letter dated SUNDAY, JANUARY 24, 1988, from Dr. Albert E. Riester of San Antonio, which read:

Dear Mr. and Mrs. Florig,

Our family is pleased that you are the new occupants of our childhood home. You will enjoy the porch and garden this spring and the security that a well built home will offer. The neighborhood is very unique and you will enjoy meeting them in the future.

As you will hear, my mother was loved and respected by everyone. She loved her home and the family has many memories of 211 E. Palmer. We wish you the same enjoyment that we had over the years in the best built home in Collingswood. Many people say that it is built like a "bunker" which would make my proud father smile.

I know that you will update the home and restore it to its original beauty. My mom refused to have interior work done, but we were able to keep up the outside.

I look forward to meeting you someday when I go to Philadelphia to visit my 19 year old son at Penn. I can give you some of the history of the house and tell you about a few of the parties that I had when I was a teenager.

Good luck with 211 East Palmer.

Sincerely,

Al Riester

I don't think we ever got to meet Dr. Riester or hear about the parties, nor did we stay in Collingswood for very long, but it was a lovely, warm home in which to begin our married life.

CHAPTER 26

TUESDAY, FEBRUARY 23, 1988

The bar exam is pretty stressful and exhausting, but not nearly as much as waiting for the results. I was working at Marshall, Dennehey, Warner, Coleman & Goggin in Philadelphia, in the Appellate Department, when I took the exam. It is normal for aspiring lawyers to start work before taking the bar exam, although they can't sign anything or actually represent clients. I was scheduled to sit for the Pennsylvania exam and the New Jersey exam beginning on Tuesday. The Pennsylvania portion consisted of Pennsylvania-specific essay questions on Tuesday and the multistate exam on WEDNESDAY, FEBRUARY 24, 1988, with the New Jersey portion consisting of New Jersey-specific essay questions on THURSDAY, FEBRUARY 25, 1988. It is also common to take the exam for multiple states at one time, as I was doing. No sense sitting for another exam later if you moved or took a job in another state.

The Pennsylvania exam site was in King of Prussia in a hotel ballroom. I had gotten a cheap hotel room nearby for Monday and Tuesday nights in which to do some last-minute cramming. Cramming for the bar exam is pretty much useless, but everyone does it anyway. Coffee is *de rigueur*. A bag or two of Doritos is helpful, too. Brain food.

I don't know how it is administered now, but in 1988 the essay questions were answered in blue books using pencils. Security was tight, but not nearly as tight as I understand that it is now. On Day 1, there were three hours of writing answers to Pennsylvania essay questions in the morning and three more in the afternoon. During lunch break, it is absolutely crucial not to talk to anyone else who is taking the exam, lest your brain be turned into a "skull full of mush," as Professor Kingsfield referred to it in *The Paper Chase*, by fellow examinees, wittingly or unwittingly mentioning everything you had messed up during the morning session. I made sure to eat alone. Bar exam essay questions usually involve complicated fact patterns and the examinee is expected to recognize and analyze every possible issue implicated by those facts under the law of the particular state. Coming to conclusions is far less important than spotting all of the possible legal issues. It was tiring and draining, but I got through it without any problems, not even writing cramps.

Just to show you that I'm serious, the following is an actual question which has been used in the Pennsylvania bar exam:

Susan and Doug are a married couple who reside in Steel Town, Pennsylvania. They have been married for 25 years and have one child together, Sophia, age 21. Sophia is an undergraduate student at nearby Steel Town University. For the past 20 years, Doug has worked for Big Cable Co. in Quaker City, Pennsylvania, 300 miles from his home. Doug primarily worked from home, but he also traveled to Quaker City for a few days each month. In 2002, during business trips to Quaker City, Doug had an extramarital relationship with Maria, a single coworker. Maria became pregnant. She resigned from her job and moved out of state. Maria later gave birth to a son, Max. She believed that Doug was Max's father but never told Doug.

In March 2019, Doug's mother Dottie died. Dottie's will included a gift of $500,000 to a "Grandchildren's Trust," providing as follows:

My trustee shall make distributions from the trust for the undergraduate education of my grandchildren, including payment of tuition, room and board and other expenses as each grandchild shall require. For purposes of this trust, "grandchildren" shall mean the children of my son, Doug. I name Doug as trustee and, if Doug is unable to serve for any reason, I name Susan as successor trustee.

In August 2019, Max, now 17 years old, enrolled at Quaker City College to begin undergraduate studies in art history. At the same time, Max contacted Doug and explained that he was Doug's son. After an initial shock, Doug agreed to take a genetic test, which was administered by a physician and proved that Doug was Max's father. Doug promptly brought Max back to Steel Town, and introduced Max to Susan, Sophia, and other family and friends as his long-lost son. He also told Max about the trust that Dottie had established. For the next few months, Doug maintained contact with Max and saw him regularly.

In October 2019, Max purchased a painting at an antique store for $100. He suspected that it was actually an original work by a famous artist and had it appraised. The appraiser confirmed that Max was correct and valued the painting at $25,000. A few weeks later, Max was scheduled to travel to Steel Town with Doug. He brought the painting with him, planning to leave it with Doug for safekeeping. On the trip, Doug's vehicle was involved in an accident with a semi-tractor-trailer truck. Max sustained serious injuries and Doug was killed.

The painting was destroyed in the crash, and on December 1, 2019, Max received $25,000 from Doug's insurance company for the loss of the painting. Max used the insurance funds to finish paying his tuition for the fall 2019 semester.

Soon after Doug's death, Susan received, in her capacity as trustee, $500,000 from Dottie's estate and established a bank account in the name of Grandchildren's Trust. Susan *promptly paid Sophia's 2020 tuition using trust funds. A few weeks later, Max asked Susan for trust money to help with his college expenses for the spring 2020 semester. Susan refused.*

1. Assume that Doug died without a will and had a substantial estate and that Susan will not seek an elective share. Under the Pennsylvania Probate, Estates and Fiduciaries Code, to whom will Doug's estate be distributed and in what proportions?

2. Assume that Max is a valid beneficiary of the Grandchildren's Trust and that he files a procedurally proper action seeking to compel Susan to pay his college expenses from the trust. What arguments should Max make in support of that action and what is his likelihood of success?

3. What, if any, are the 2019 federal income tax consequences to Max on the receipt of insurance proceeds? Assume that Max is a cash-basis, calendar-year taxpayer.

Meanwhile, Allen, a Quaker City attorney, learned about the accident. Despite having no prior contact with Max, he called Max, suggesting that Max retain him for a contingent fee to sue the truck's owner for his personal injuries, and said, "Hire me and if we win, I'll get us both a lot of money." Max replied, "I am not interested, don't contact me again." Later, Allen sent a follow up letter, stating, "You should reconsider hiring me, you have a great case!"

4. Did Allen's communications with Max about the accident violate the Pennsylvania Rules of Professional Conduct?

Day 2 was the multistate, in the same hotel ballroom. The multistate consisted of 200 multiple choice questions, which were answered in the familiar "fill in the oval" format for machine grading. The exam took six hours, again, three in the morning and three in the afternoon. By the time the multistate was over, I was pretty beat and ready to head home to my own bed. Late Wednesday afternoon, I headed east on the Schuylkill Expressway toward Collingswood.

The third day was the New Jersey essay portion. It was held at the long-since-demolished Cherry Hill Inn on Route 38 across from the Cherry Hill Mall, where I had heckled Richard Nixon 20 years earlier. When I was in elementary school, the Eagles held their training camp at the Cherry Hill Inn in 1964. The NFL was not quite the behemoth that it is today, and training camp was much less formal, at least for fans. There wasn't even an admission charge. We could watch practice on the field behind the inn and autographs were easy to get. We went when we could, watched practice, and got autographs from players as they walked from the field to the hotel. No designated autograph signers, no rope lines, no fences to keep us away from the players. Just kids trying to get close to their favorite players. I managed to get Bill "Red" Mack, Gary Mansfield, Ulysses Kendall, John Meyers, Bobby Walston, V. Randall, Will Scott, Tom Woodeshick (twice), Pete Retzlaff, Ray Poage, Bobby Richards, Jim Schrader, Norm Snead, Dave Lloyd, Mike Morgan, Don Burroughs, Riley Gunnels, Roger Gill, Izzy Lang, Dave Graham, Pete Case, Dick Evans, Howard Keys and Gary somebody. Not a bad haul for a little kid. I did not, however, manage to get Tommy McDonald.

Tommy McDonald was my favorite Eagle when I was growing up. Although I didn't get his autograph during training camp at the Cherry Hill Inn, I did get something even better a little later - a signed black and white 8 x 10 photo of McDonald in his Eagles #25 uniform. McDonald had made an appearance at the Ellisburg Shopping Center in Cherry Hill and they gave out photos and let us ask questions. I asked a lot - so much so that the emcee started ignoring me after a little while. Later in life, after collecting Eagles autographs at the Cherry Hill Inn and at the Fly for Leukemia, I snagged a couple more - Bill Bergey on a poster that used to hang on my wall and Sheldon Brown on an 8 x 10 photo that the Eagles donated to a *WePAC* fundraiser.

I completed the six hours of New Jersey essay writing, again in blue books, and headed home for the two-month wait for results. This is a terrible time for any would-be lawyer. Failing the bar exam meant not only having to go through the entire ordeal again, with confidence shattered, in hopes of passing, but also telling the firm, or wherever you were working, that you had failed. On top of that, the legal publications in each state printed the names of those who passed the exam. Mercifully, at least, they did not publish the names of those who did not, but the omissions from the "passing" list were glaring.

I must have found out about Pennsylvania first, because I got a notice from the Pennsylvania Board of Law Examiners dated FRIDAY, APRIL 29, 1988, which began, "We are pleased to inform you . . ." As anyone applying to college, for a job, or awaiting some kind of results knows, those are good words to read. I was also informed that my scaled multistate score was 153. I knew what that meant at the time, but have no idea now. At a minimum, it was a passing score.

The Legal Intelligencer, "The Oldest Law Journal in the United States," is read by virtually the entire Pennsylvania legal profession. The THURSDAY, MAY 5, 1988, edition contained the names of the 678 candidates who had passed the February bar exam. It did not list the names of the 367 who did not. There, between Shirley J. Fletcher of Youngstown, Ohio and John Walsh Folcarelli of New York, New York, was "David Scott Florig, Collingswood, NJ." On MONDAY, MAY 9, 1988, the *Pennsylvania Law Journal-Reporter* published the same list. Finally, on FRIDAY, JUNE 3, 1988, on motion of Audrey Jacobsen, Esquire, a friend and fellow appellate lawyer from Marshall, Dennehey, the Supreme Court of Pennsylvania admitted me to the Pennsylvania bar.

My time at Marshall, Dennehey, Warner, Coleman & Goggin was pretty uneventful, and I only stayed there for a couple of years, mostly working on appeals and writing briefs, but I welcomed the experience. I did manage to write the brief in a case, *Town & Country Fine Furniture v. Workmen's Compensation Appeal Board*, 523 Pa. 424, 567 A.2d 1042 (Pa. 1990), which we won in the Pennsylvania Supreme Court on FRIDAY, JANUARY 5, 1990. Mostly, however, it was win some, lose some.

On THURSDAY, MAY 19, 1988, the *New Jersey Law Journal* published the names of the 631 candidates who had passed the New Jersey bar exam, but not the 438 who did not. Apparently, the Pennsylvania exam was easier, since 64.9% passed, while only 59% passed the New Jersey exam. In New Jersey, my name was between Isabel Bogorad Fleiss of Wayne, New Jersey and C. Maria Flynn of Chatham. On THURSDAY, JUNE 2, 1988, I attended the admission ceremony for new attorneys at the War Memorial Theater in Trenton. I was admitted to the Bar of the Supreme Court of New Jersey that day by Chief Justice Robert N. Wilentz, reciting the oath, "*I solemnly promise and swear to support the Constitution of the State of New Jersey and of the United States and to perform the duties of an attorney at law faithfully, impartially and justly, to the best of my ability. So help me God.*" I was also admitted to the Bar of the United States District Court for the District of New Jersey by Chief Judge John F. Gerry, reciting the oath, "*I do solemnly swear or affirm that, to the best of my knowledge and ability, I will support and defend the Constitution of the United States against all enemies, foreign and domestic, and that I will bear true faith and allegiance to the same; that I take this obligation freely, without any mental reservation or purpose of evasion, and that I will demean myself as an attorney of this Court, uprightly and according to law. So help me God."*

And so, as I swore to do in my oath, I began demeaning myself as an attorney-at-law.

CHAPTER 27

WEDNESDAY, DECEMBER 21, 1988

The *Clipper Maid of the Seas* took off from Heathrow Airport at 6:25 p.m. local time bound for JFK Airport in New York, carrying 243 passengers and 16 crew members. At 7:02, radio contact was lost, and no one on the plane was ever heard from again. The first section of the plane hit the ground a minute later. Most of Pan Am Flight 103 came down near Lockerbie, Scotland, where 11 people on the ground were killed.

Nancy and I watched the nonstop news coverage at home on East Palmer Avenue. What footage there was showed parts of the plane, luggage, seats and papers strewn everywhere. The debris field covered nearly 850 square miles. Terrorism was almost immediately suspected as the cause. The coverage mentioned that among the passengers were a group of students, 35 of them it turned out, spending a semester abroad with Syracuse University's Division of International Programs Abroad in London. Some of the students were returning home for Christmas.

I finally worked up the nerve to call Bob Thomas in Massachusetts. I remember nervously asking how he was doing, not really believing that the inconceivable could actually be true. "Wendy was on that plane," he said. Other than those words, I don't remember any of the conversation.

The *Lowell Sun* ran a piece by Joseph Day entitled, "A Strange Kinship with a Victim" a couple of days later, just before Christmas. I only saw it because Nancy and I were in Dracut for Christmas with her family. He wrote:

> *Her photo came spewing out of the AP Laserphoto machines along with all the rest. She was blonde and beautiful in a soft, gentle way.*

She was . . . presumably a happy college student heading home for the Christmas holidays from study in Britain. She was headed to my hometown.

I didn't know her, but I had heard of the family. Like me, the Lincolns come from North Adams, a mill city surprisingly like a little Lowell, set in the spectacular landscape of the Berkshires . . . She was graduated from Drury High School, old "mother on the hill," in 1985, so Wendy and I came from different eras. Yet she was from home, from the mountains - and I immediately felt a kinship with her.

But even as I felt the connection, I recognized the separation. Before I had even heard of Wendy Lincoln, the girl with the sweet face from Syracuse University, she was gone, snatched up in the brutality of an instant.

As I gather with my family and friends at home, we will celebrate, of course, but we will know of the tears in one particular North Adams house. This year, as I head home to the mountains, I shall think of Wendy Lincoln. I expect I'll hear the bells down in the city on Christmas morning. And I shall remember the words of John Donne's poem.

Nancy and I continued watching the news coverage over the next hours and days. Once daylight arrived in Scotland, there was extensive footage of the site in Lockerbie. One piece of tape, played over and over again, showed an open passport lying in the wreckage, with a photo of a young blonde woman. To this day, we think that it was Wendy's passport. Just a year earlier, she had been celebrating our wedding with us aboard the *Fort Warren* on Boston Harbor, smiling, laughing and dancing with a whole life before her. Wendy Anne Lincoln was 23 years old.

I fully intended to go to Wendy's memorial service in Massachusetts, but there was a snowstorm that made it impractical for us to make the trip up from New Jersey. I did, however, receive a memorial card from the Flynn & Dagnoli-Montagna Funeral Home. On the back was printed this poem:

Angel

When God calls a loved one to dwell with Him above
We mortals sometime question the wisdom of His love
For no heartache compares with the death of a Daughter, a
Sister, a Grandchild, a Friend
Who does so much to make our world seem wonderful and
mild
Perhaps God tires of calling the aged to His fold
So He picks a rosebud before it can grow old
God knows how much we need them and so He takes but few
To make the land of Heaven more beautiful to view
Believing this is difficult, still somehow we must try
The saddest word mankind knows will always be "Goodbye"
So when a young lady departs, we who are left behind
Must realize God loves everyone, but Angels are hard to find

CHAPTER 28

FRIDAY, SEPTEMBER 29, 1989

We had been looking for a bigger house for a little while. Our house in Collingswood was only 1,100 square feet. One Sunday, I went to an open house for a larger property at 131 Abbey Road in Voorhees. I liked it, so I made arrangements for Nancy and I to look at it with Jules Sacchetti, now a realtor, who had played midget football with me and who had been my co-conspirator on the cherry bomb/milk carton/gasoline detonation.

Abbey Road was 2,659 square feet with four bedrooms and 2 ½ baths, much better for two working adults, dogs, and what we hoped would be an addition one day. It had a far more modern kitchen than the house on East Palmer, a two-car garage, a full basement and attic and a built-in pool. After a few years, I vowed never again to buy a house with a pool. I was constantly threatening to fill it in. Roughly 100 hours of work is required for each hour of actual pool time. Not to mention the annual outlay of several hundred thousand dollars for chlorine, DE, pH stabilizer, water testing kits, hoses, vacuum bags, water, electricity and pool toys. Or the occasional major expense, such as we incurred on FRIDAY, MAY 11, 2007, when we hired Del Val Pool Maintenance to:

Empty pool and clean with chemical solution hook-up equipment
Pressure test lines (any leaks billed separately)
Remove existing tile, cope and bad sections of bond beam
Remove debris and sandblast interior surface of pool
Rebuild bond beam and install red brick coping with safety edge
Install acid and frost free 6" border

Install expansion and poured rubber caulk the perimeter of pool

Replaster interior surface of pool and plug pool and leave filling

Return to start system and review plaster care letter

And for only $14,900!

The house also had the benefit of not being on a through street, so there wasn't a lot of traffic. And, I must confess, I liked the thought of living on Abbey Road. Nancy, Dylan, Fenway and I had a Christmas card made which roughly  recreated the *Abbey Road* album cover. If I could have located a VW Beetle, I would have.

We made an offer to Herbert and Diane Kerr and settled on a price well below what they were asking. We settled on September 29th, and began moving in.

The other thing about the Abbey Road neighborhood that Nancy noticed first was that it was very diverse - definitely a selling point for us. We had old neighbors, young neighbors, Black neighbors, white neighbors, and neighbors of both Asian and Middle Eastern descent. We also had a neighbor at #129 who we dubbed "Basketball Man," because he wore a white tank top undershirt and walked the neighborhood carrying a basketball. There was also a neighbor who creeped me out when he asked if he could take a picture of Dylan, Patrick and Sean when they came to his house trick-or-treating.

I got myself into some situations at Abbey Road. There was a fair amount of yard work to do at the house and it was mostly me who did it. I was raking under a huge pine tree in the front yard, trying to get rid of the fallen brown needles which were everywhere. My rake kept getting caught on some thin roots, or vines, or something, and I dropped the rake and began pulling them out. They were long and came up pretty easily. To Nancy's dismay, I rarely wear gloves while doing yard work. When I had pulled as many as I could, the raking was much easier and I completed that job. It was probably a Sunday, maybe Saturday, sometime around 2005 or 2006.

What makes some people allergic to poison ivy is an oily resin called urushiol found in its leaves, stems and roots. People who are allergic to poison ivy may develop a rash, redness, itching, swelling, blisters, and even difficulty breathing if smoke from burning poison ivy is inhaled. I had had poison ivy a couple of times before and the itching is, in fact, almost unbearable. No matter what they tell you, the only way to deal with it is to scratch the hell out of it. If you look online, there are a number of helpful, friendly suggestions for how to stop the itching. Here are my assessments of the efficacy of each - wet compresses (no), cool water (no), hot water (no), lukewarm water (no), calamine lotion (no), over-the-counter topical corticosteroids (no), zinc acetate (no), zinc carbonate (no), zinc oxide (no), calamine (no), baking soda (no), oatmeal (no), aluminum acetate (no), mentholated cream (no), antihistamines (no), rubbing alcohol (no), apple cider vinegar (no), chilled black tea (no), aloe vera gel (no), bentonite clay (no), cucumber slices (no), cucumber paste (no), banana peel (no), lemon juice (no), witch hazel (no), urine (can't say). Nothing short of general anesthesia can stop the itching.

At work on Monday, I felt a little off and suspected that I may have had a touch of poison ivy, since I had a couple of itchy spots on my arm that morning and I recognized the little straight line of bumps that it makes on the skin when getting started. By noon, I could actually feel my head swelling around the ears and forehead. I asked Christine Parsells and Susan Albino to come into my office and take a look at my head. Their faces reflected an odd mixture of concern and horror. Their strong advice was that I immediately head home and get medical attention. I did the former, but not the latter, which is my usual *modus operandi*, much to Nancy's chagrin.

As I drove, I could feel my head continuing to puff up and could feel the swelling migrating down toward my eyes and neck. It continued to move south throughout the day and night, and when I woke up the next morning, I thought that I had gone blind. I initially tried to open my eyes, but couldn't, as they were swollen completely shut, although I was eventually able to squint and at least know that I hadn't, indeed, gone blind. I probably looked a little bit like Mr. Magoo. Nancy and Dylan were both justifiably concerned and annoyed, and suggested that I go to the doctor and get a steroid shot, which I, of course, elected not to do. I continued to feel the poison migrating downward through my body as the day went on, but at least I could see. Fortunately, it stopped before reaching any really, really sensitive areas. I eventually recovered and have learned not to mess with poison ivy again, which I have managed to do, for the most part. There is, however, a growing expanse of the stuff in our side yard and I'm fighting the compulsion to do something about it.

We had an entrance to the house off of our driveway. At the top of the driveway was an attached two-car garage with a laundry room alongside. Two steps led up to the laundry room door, which was how we usually entered the house. Next to the door was a holly tree which was probably 15-18 feet tall with an 8-10 foot wingspan. [*Pictured are the offending holly tree and roof*]. It grew quickly and incessantly, and I had to trim it a couple of times each year to keep its branches and leaves from getting under the

eaves, into the wall light, under the shingles, and from laying on the laundry room roof. Most of this work could be done from a six-foot A-frame ladder by using clippers and a telescoping tree pruner. The worst part was usually picking up the fallen branches and leaves, since the holly leaves were extremely spinescent, capable of piercing any gloves or sleeves that I might be wearing, including Kevlar.

Occasionally, I would have to use the ladder to climb onto the roof of the laundry room and cut some of the bigger branches. On these occasions, since I could never be dissuaded, Nancy nearly always had some urgent errand to run so that she wouldn't be around in the unlikely event that I had some kind of mishap. Usually, I didn't have any, and I pretty easily managed to cut the branches and get down off of the roof. Usually.

On this particular occasion, Nancy had found some reason to vacate the premises, but I was happy to be on the roof and pruning. Anyone who has worked on a shingled roof knows that asphalt shingles do not provide the best footing and that they are like coarse sandpaper on steroids. Naturally, I lost my footing at one point and was on my chest and stomach, sliding down the roof in slow motion, feet first and flailing for something to grab onto, which of course there wasn't. Had I not cut the holly branches, I could have maybe grabbed ahold of one of them to stop my slide. But there was nothing, and my slide down the roof was resulting in all three layers of skin - epidermis, dermis and hypodermis - being shredded along the way. Finally, while sliding off the roof into the back yard, I was able to grab onto a gutter, which, FYI, is not designed to hold the weight of a human being.

My feet were probably five or six feet above the ground when I looked down, suspended. A four or five foot drop was doable, I supposed. The only issue was that directly below me was an evergreen shrub, arborvitae, I think. Shimmying along the gutter was not really an option at that point, since the gutter was bending and about to give. So I chose the only available option and let go. Now, shrubs don't do quite as much damage to the human body as asphalt shingles, but they are formidable in their own right, so in addition to my raw torso and arms, I now took the fury of the evergreen on my arms and legs as I landed in the bush. Nancy, of course, did not witness any of this.

After we sold Abbey Road, the new owners wisely decided that, rather than continue to maintain the holly tree, they would just cut it down. I probably should have thought of that.

A wiser man would have been forever dissuaded from working on the roof, but I have that genetic flaw, found mainly in men, that causes the occasional lapse in judgment. I had a 32-foot ladder for reaching high parts of the house, including the main roof, which also had asphalt shingles. We had a couple of vent pipes on the roof which I decided needed some sealing, so I got out my ladder and went up on the roof. It was tricky, but I managed to get up there and successfully apply the sealant. I inched my way back toward the ladder. Now, a younger man (I was probably in my late-50's at this point) could have gotten back onto the ladder without much difficulty, but I was no longer a younger man. The ladder was pretty steep and its feet rested on the concrete patio around the pool below.

Luckily, Nancy hadn't found an immediate and urgent errand to run, and I managed to call her. I calmly told her that I was momentarily stuck and that she needed to stand at the base of the ladder, angle it a little bit, and put her feet behind the ladder's feet so that they didn't slip. Her confidence level in doing that was not very high and she decided, against my wishes, to summon help, so I sat there on the edge of the roof and waited. She eventually returned with Tom Fanelli, our neighbor from across the street. After much discussion and consternation, we were able to manipulate the ladder a bit and stabilize it so that finally, and sheepishly, I made my way down. Luckily, we were in the back of the house, so at least I didn't provide entertainment for the whole neighborhood.

I sometimes referred to our back yard as Wild Kingdom, since all manner of wildlife found their way back there. An in-ground pool is a death trap for all kinds of animals, and I would annually have to remove dead squirrels, rabbits, mice, chipmunks and/or baby possums which had fallen in and been unable to escape. At least they floated. It also makes a nice place for ducks to take a little swim. One pair, a male and female, we named Frank and Murphy, after characters on the TV show *Murphy Brown*. In the early 90's, *Murphy Brown* was a hit show which had become embroiled in the culture war going on in the United States. In the final episode of Season 4, the fictional Murphy Brown, a single woman who was an investigative journalist and news anchor, had given birth to a baby boy.

Dan Quayle, then the vice president of the United States and running for re-election with president George H.W. Bush, gave a speech on TUESDAY, MAY 19, 1992, in San Francisco, during which he criticized the fictional Murphy Brown for, "mocking the importance of fathers, by bearing a child alone, and calling it just another lifestyle choice." The show retaliated in the first episode of the next season, entitled, "You Say Potatoe, I Say Potato," a reference to the vice president's famous misspelling of the word during a campaign stop at an elementary school in New Jersey. Candace Bergen, who portrayed Murphy Brown, won an *Emmy Award* that year. During her acceptance speech, she said, "I'd like to thank the vice president," and then thanked her writers for "not only writing these great words, but spelling them correctly."

Frank and Murphy (the ducks) built their nest in the same spot for a couple of years underneath the bush that I had fallen into while pruning the holly tree. Murphy tended to the eggs and had a number of ducklings, who also swam in the pool. Eventually, having raised the family, Murphy and the ducklings left.

We somehow avoided disaster one night, when our dogs, Erin and Molly, were in the backyard. The yard was completely fenced in, so they were out back one night, unattended, when I heard quite a commotion. There was barking and howling. I went out back in the dark to find that they had managed to corner a skunk against the fence in the corner by the dreaded holly tree. It was a small skunk, possibly a baby, which may explain why it didn't unload. With great difficulty, and in much too close proximity to the skunk, I managed to grab Erin and Molly's collars and avert a really messy, smelly problem.

Shortly after Christmas in 1991, Nancy's mother and father, Doris and Jim, came to visit us and to see Dylan, who was not even three months old. We had purchased a live Christmas tree, intending to plant it in the front yard at the end of the holiday season as a reminder of Dylan's first Christmas. One morning, Jim, Charlie and I went outside, dug the hole, and planted it. At the time, the tree was probably about six feet tall. The last time I was on Abbey Road, in 2019, the tree was still there, probably 35 feet high.

There were some lighter times in that house, too. It is well-known that Nancy hates cooking and hates baking even more. This doesn't seem to be hereditary, since the majority of her five siblings seem to enjoy working in the kitchen. But not Nancy. And I don't really like it any better than she does. Once in a great while I will be inspired to actually make something, but those instances are rare. However, one night at Abbey Road I decided to make chocolate chip cookies from scratch. Not the kind that comes in a tube. From scratch.

The first thing that a serious baker needs to do is to make sure that (s)he has all of the necessary ingredients on hand. Eggs - check; butter - check; vanilla - check; sugar - check. In order to keep some of the things which we didn't use that often from going bad, and to keep insects and such out, we put staples like sugar, flour, baking soda and brown sugar into airtight containers. No one wants worms and weevils in their cookies. I retrieved the sugar, baking soda and flour from the kitchen cupboard. This particular recipe called for bleached white flour, so I grabbed the tupperware container with white flour, measured out the required amount, and mixed it into the dough. The oven was preheating as I scooped the dough out of the bowl and placed little doughnut hole sized balls onto the greased cookie sheet. There's nothing like fresh, out-of-the-oven, gooey chocolate chip cookies. The dough seemed a little sticky, but, then again, I didn't really know what it was supposed to be like.

I placed the cookie sheet into the oven and waited for the 10 minutes or so that they took to bake. They smelled so good. Cookies baking in the oven always make an entire house smell good. I was stunned when I pulled out the cookie sheet. The entire sheet was covered, about ⅛ or ¼ inch thick with what was the color and consistency of peanut brittle, only with chocolate chips. It was as hard as a rock and had affixed itself to the sheet such that I needed a mortise chisel and hammer to eventually remove it. I couldn't imagine what had happened. I had followed the recipe very precisely, since I don't really know what I'm doing in the kitchen and wanted the cookies to be just like in the recipe and picture. I showed the result to Nancy, who eventually diagnosed the problem, but not until after laughing hysterically.

  It seems that instead of using white flour, I had grabbed the storage container which held confectioner's sugar and used that instead. In my defense, an understandable mistake, since I think that bleached flour and confectioner's sugar are virtually indistinguishable. Can you tell which is which from the pictures? My cookies were ruined. I thought that it was a reasonable mistake and vowed to clearly label all of our containers from then on. I still haven't done so.

* * *

We spent 27 years of our lives living on Abbey Road before we moved to Maine, longer than either of us lived anywhere else. It was the only childhood home Dylan ever knew.

CHAPTER 29

SUNDAY, JUNE 17, 1990

Nancy and I decided to go away for the weekend to see the Red Sox play the Orioles at the old Memorial Stadium in Baltimore. Nancy mainly wanted to see her favorite player, Dwight Evans, who was in his 19th and final season with the Sox. The Sunday game started at 1:35 p.m. Evans went 0-3 in a 6-5 Sox win.

The game on SATURDAY, JUNE 16, 1990, started at 3:25 p.m. The Sox won this game, too, 6-3, with Dwight Evans going 1-2 with a sacrifice fly and a walk. While we were watching the game, Nancy started thinking about how to get Red Sox players' autographs and asked one of the ushers about it. The usher told her that it was difficult to do at the stadium and that she would likely have more success at the team hotel. He willingly told her which hotel the Red Sox were staying in.

We found the hotel and sat in the lobby waiting. Since we weren't kids and weren't professional autograph hunters, the hotel staff didn't bother us. As a lifelong Red Sox fan, Nancy recognized most of the players as they happened through the lobby. Most were nice and cooperative in signing. We hadn't planned on doing this, so we didn't have a notebook or scrapbook for the autographs, but we did have a 1990 All-Star ballot from the stadium, so Nancy took to getting it signed. By the end of the night, she had the signatures of Joe Morgan (the manager, not the player), Ellis Burks, Mike Boddicker, Randy Kutcher, Danny Heep, Wade Boggs, John Marzano, Luis Rivera, Marty Barrett, Jeff Reardon, Greg Harris, Tom Brunansky, Wes Gardner and Roger Clemens. Nancy had herself a ball. Naturally, the autographed All-Star ballot is in the box of memorabilia, with nowhere to hang in our little house. Dylan's going to inherit quite a bit of memorabilia.

We decided to go to Baltimore again the next summer, again to see a Red Sox series. By this time, Nancy was quite visibly pregnant, entering her seventh month. The game on FRIDAY, JUNE 28, 1991, was a night game, but the gametime temperature was 95 degrees, just perfect for a pregnant woman to be sitting outside in hard wooden seats, not even able to have a beer. At least the Sox won, 9-3.

Unfortunately, the SATURDAY, JUNE 29, 1991, game started in the afternoon, when the temperature was 97 degrees. There was no breeze whatsoever and we were baking. At one point during the game, a local news crew came down our aisle filming the mass of sweaty, miserable people at the game. I've been to Haiti in August and Houston in the dead of summer, but every time I've been to Baltimore in the summer, it's been worse. We went back to the hotel after the game to watch Nancy, in pregnant, perspiration-soaked glory, on the local news. To top it off, the Sox got crushed, 7-3.

At least we were going to head home after the SUNDAY, JUNE 30, 1991, game. It was another balmy day in Baltimore, with the temperature once again at 97 degrees for the first pitch. Full sun, no wind. It took 3 hours and 8 minutes for the game to play out, with the Sox losing again, 6-4. We headed to the car, me walking and Nancy waddling, turned the AC up as high as we could, and headed north up I-95 for home.

There is hot, and there is Maryland hot. When Dylan was in junior high and high school, summer weekends were booked with lacrosse tournaments. Unfortunately, many of those tournaments were in Maryland. It was invariably hot and humid, but never so bad as one ugly weekend when there was a tournament at the Timonium Race Track. Multiple lacrosse fields were set up on the infield of the race track, inside of the racing oval, which consisted of hot sand and dust. It had to be over 100 degrees, with no shade anywhere. Everyone, even the kids who were playing, seemed miserable. Even between games, there was no place to cool off.

It was so bad in the sun that Nancy, Dylan and I actually went back to the stables where the horses were kept to find some relief. At least it wasn't racing season, there were no horses around, and the stalls were empty and, luckily, clean. In our desperation to find any kind of relief from the sun and heat, we went and stood inside of a stable for shade. Eventually, it was time for another game and we dragged ourselves out of the horse stall and back into the inferno.

Nancy and I went to yet another Red Sox - Orioles game in Baltimore a couple of years later, this time at Camden Yards. Camden Yards had just opened the year before. The park was magnificent and beautiful, setting the standard for the new wave of downtown stadiums, and we got tickets for the TUESDAY, MAY 11, 1993, game from Larry Drexler, a lawyer friend from Wilmington. We saw a gem that night. Roger Clemens pitched for the Sox. He pitched a complete-game shutout, allowing only five hits while striking out 11 Orioles. One of the hits was a double by Hall-of-Famer Cal Ripken, Jr. It was the 1,766th consecutive game played by

Ripken, on the way to his all-time record of 2,632 consecutive games played.

CHAPTER 30

TUESDAY, OCTOBER 8, 1991

D ylan decided that he preferred the breech position in Nancy's uterus, so he was born by C-section at 8:15 p.m. I don't recommend fathers being present for C-sections. First of all, the doctors and nurses basically tell you that if you pass out, pee your pants, and/or die during the procedure, they're going to ignore you until they're done with the mother, and they make you sign a 15-page waiver of liability to that effect. Second, seeing the better part of the mother's intestinal cavity piled on her abdomen is off-putting. Third, yuck. Nonetheless, I was there.

Dylan was diagnosed with meconium aspiration, a pretty serious condition for a newborn. It occurs mainly in babies who are born after their due date, and Dylan was 10 days past due. Meconium aspiration is caused by the baby breathing in amniotic fluid containing meconium, the baby's first stools. He spent his first couple of days in the ICU getting extra oxygen. Not being allowed in the ICU, I went golfing with Charlie at Iron Rock Country Club the next morning, on WEDNESDAY, OCTOBER 9, 1991, before heading to the hospital.

Conception had not been an easy process. We were having no success in making a baby and finally went to some specialists to see what the problem was. At one such specialist, I learned for the first time about sperm morphology (or teratozoospermia), having to do with the size and shape of sperm. I thought sperm were just sperm and that they all looked and acted alike, like microscopic tadpoles. According to the doctor who looked at my sperm, it seemed that I had two-headers, which are notoriously bad at swimming and penetrating eggs, which are their only two jobs. Not all were two-headers, though, so the doctor advised patience and determination, which finally paid off. By the way, it really is true about the private little room and paper cup when providing sperm.

We even looked into adoption at one point. At work, Nancy had learned about a baby girl in Ireland named Emma who might be available. We actually investigated that, but it never worked out.

Bob Thomas, Jo Tedesco and I decided to head out for a drink and went to a bar on the strip in Old Orchard Beach, Maine, in August, a few weeks before Dylan was due. At least Bob and I decided, since Jo doesn't drink. Dylan was due on SATURDAY, SEPTEMBER 28, 1991, and Nancy and I already knew the sex and name of the baby. I had learned the baby's gender first. When we went for prenatal counseling, the counselor asked if we wanted to know the baby's sex. I said that I did, and Nancy said that she didn't. Not unusual for us. A couple of days later, the counselor called and I answered the phone. In addition to saying that all of the prenatal tests looked good, she asked if I still wanted to know the sex. I repeated that I did, and she told me that it was a boy.

Thank God there were no such things as "gender reveal" parties back then, where self-obsessed, insufferable parents-to-be devise ever more elaborate and asinine ways to tell a breathlessly awaiting world the sex of their gestating child. Most such events end in unmitigated disaster, such as the wildfire caused by a gender reveal explosion that burned 47,000 acres and put the father-to-be on the hook for $8 million in restitution, or the crop duster which dropped pink water and then proceeded to crash. Those pictures will look nice on your Instagram feed.

Not content with starting wildfires, crashing planes or otherwise contributing to the public health crisis fueled by the flood of injuries (and even deaths) caused by gender reveal celebrations, some Tennessee father-to-be, in 2021, overcome with joy at the news that his child would be a boy, decided to celebrate by going outside and firing his gun into the air. Fortunately, no one was injured by the projectiles. Three nearby schools did have to go into lockdown, though, after reports of an active shooter. Does anything say "I'm going to be an awesome father" better than sending your local schools into lockdown?

When I got off the phone with the prenatal counselor, I told Nancy that the counselor said that everything looked great and that things were progressing as they should. Then she asked if the counselor had told me the sex and I said that she had. Since I now knew, Nancy decided that she had to know as well. I gently reminded her that she had told the counselor that she didn't want to know, so I didn't tell her. That didn't make me all that popular, but I stood firm. Nancy was getting rather agitated that I wasn't telling her, but I reminded her that I was only doing what she had wanted, as I always do. Finally, after what I suppose was an hour or two, I broke down and told her, "It's a boy."

Next came the "name the baby" period. I think that Nancy had secured a baby names book. Over the ensuing days we tried on lots of different names, finally settling on "Dylan." We sometimes told people that it was after the Welsh god of the sea, but everyone knows it was really after Bob.

So, by the time Bob, Jo and I got to that long-forgotten bar in Old Orchard Beach, I already knew the name and sex of our child. Nancy and I had decided that we weren't going to tell anyone before the birth, and we hadn't. Dylan was a pretty uncommon name at that time. In 1989, it was not even in the top 100 most popular boys' names, and in 1990 it was only 83rd. By 1991 however, it had climbed to 46, and by 1992 it had become the 28th most popular boys name. It peaked at number 23 in 1999. What had happened to take this relatively uncommon name, not even in the top 100 names in the 1980's, to one of the top 30 names in the 1990's? *Beverly Hills 90210,* airing from October 1990 through 2000, starring Luke Perry as heartthrob Dylan McKay. Nowadays, there are lots of 20 and 30-year-old Dylans, although some use the extremely unfortunate "Dillon" variation.

Bob and Jo were bugging me to tell them the name and sex, so I made them a deal. They would each get one guess - sex and name - and I would only tell them if they were right or wrong. One of them, I don't know which, guessed something like, "Boy, Jason," and I told them that was wrong. The other guessed something like, "Girl, Emily," and I said that was wrong, too. No hints, no more guesses.

I thought that the game was over, but it wasn't. The woman tending bar, who wasn't really offered a guess, said, "Boy, Dylan." Not a word of a lie. Mathematically, there was about a 0.21% chance of that happening.

Dylan, as best we know, was conceived during a ski vacation in Winter Park, Colorado. We had gone there in December 1990 during Christmas vacation. The timing is pretty simple - Christmas vacation to September 28th. After the two-headers and the waiting, we were thrilled. It was probably the clean, crisp Rocky Mountain air. In hindsight, maybe we should have named him "Rocky." The bartendress never would have guessed that.

On SUNDAY, OCTOBER 13, 1991, there was a rosebud on the pulpit of the First Baptist Church of Collingswood. The church bulletin said, "The rosebud on the pulpit today is in celebration of the birth of Dylan MacDonald Florig who was born on October 8. The proud parents are David & Nancy Florig. Proud grandparents are Charles & Marjorie Florig." Dylan's birth was also announced in the MONDAY, NOVEMBER 11, 1991, *Courier-Post.*

When you have a young child, sometimes you improvise in order to entertain yourself and the kid. At some point when we were together, I made up a song which I think I should have shopped around as a children's book. It involved matching up animals with a rhyming kind of clothing and had a definite, albeit simple tune. Over the years, I have continued to add to it on occasion, usually during long car rides. It's working title was, "Pigs Wearing Digs," and went like this:

Pigs wearing digs - I like it, I like it!

Bats wearing hats - I like it, I like it!

Goats wearing coats - I like it, I like it!

Hogs wearing clogs - I like it, I like it!

Ants wearing pants - I like it, I like it!

Rabbits wearing habits - I like it, I like it!

Skunks wearing trunks - I like it, I like it!

Smelts wearing belts - I like it, I like it!

Squirrels wearing pearls - I like it, I like it!

Gophers wearing loafers - I like it, I like it!

Lambs wearing tams - I like it, I like it!

Gnus wearing shoes - I like it, I like it!

Apes wearing capes - I like it, I like it!

Mules wearing jewels - I like it, I like it!

Yaks wearing slacks - I like it, I like it!

Doves wearing gloves - I like it, I like it!

Turtles wearing girdles - I like it, I like it!

Fox wearing socks - I like it, I like it!

Owls wearing towels - I like it, I like it!

Squids wearing lids - I like it, I like it!

Ducks wearing chucks - I like it, I like it!

Schnauzers wearing trousers - I like it, I like it!

Geese wearing fleece - I like it, I like it!

Llamas wearing pajamas - I like it, I like it!

Fleas wearing tees - I like it, I like it!

Cocks wearing frocks - I like it, I like it!

Seals wearing heels - I like it, I like it!

Flies wearing ties - I like it, I like it!

Pugs wearing uggs - I like it, I like it!

Kittens wearing mittens - I like it, I like it!

Cooties wearing booties - I like it, I like it!

Feel free to add your own.

Not to be outdone, Dylan invented an entirely new animal and made up a song about it. The animal was a "combat bear," and the song went something like, "A combat bear is a traveling bear and he likes to eat squirrels and fences - but he don't like coffee." Come to think of it, he was a little feverish that day.

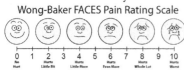

Dylan and Nancy were always trying to think of new and creative ways to injure me. Walking barefoot in our house was extremely dangerous and never advisable. There were always Legos on the floor in virtually every room of the house. For anyone who has ever stepped on a Lego with bare feet, they know that the universal "Comparative Pain Scale Chart" is wholly inadequate. Even a "10" only describes "Unspeakable, Unimaginable" pain. That little face would be doing more than frowning and crying had it stepped barefoot on a Lego, which I did many times.

One time, as I managed to successfully navigate the virtual minefield of Legos in our living room, I was blissfully unaware that Nancy and Dylan had been building an igloo out of marshmallows and toothpicks on the floor for a school project. I'm sure that they tried their best to pick everything up when they were finished, but they managed to miss one toothpick, and it remained in the rug, pointy end out, at a 45 degree angle, like an anti-aircraft gun on a battleship. My eyes were fixed on avoiding any Legos, so they missed the stealth toothpick, which lodged itself like a harpoon between my big toe and my second little piggy. The language that I deployed was strikingly similar to the language used by the cast of *Veep*.

Monster trucks were another of the many ways Nancy and Dylan chose to torture me. Dylan was always obsessed with trucks and construction vehicles, so when the Monster Truck Jam was scheduled to come to the Spectrum, I was elected to take him. Charlie volunteered to come, too. If you have never been to a Monster Truck Jam, count your blessings. If you have been to one, there's a good chance that you now wear hearing aids.

Monster trucks are basically pickup trucks with elaborate paint jobs and enormous wheels, and their sole functions seem to be to make as much noise and emit the most exhaust possible. The monster trucks race each other around a dirt track, indoors mind you, and perform tricks like jumping off of ramps and riding over junked cars. And no Monster Truck Jam was complete without an appearance by Robosaurus, a transforming, fire-breathing, car-eating robotic dinosaur. An appearance by Robosaurus is actually the best part of the whole show, because Robosaurus doesn't make much noise.

Although the very first thing that you notice with monster trucks is the noise, you quickly get a little swimmy from the fumes. By the time the first couple of races are over, the arena air is thick with blue-grey exhaust. But really, it's all about the noise.

I was simply unprepared for it. No earplugs, nothing to keep the sound waves from assaulting my head. Imagine being at an AC/DC concert with a jackhammer to your left and chainsaw to your right. Not to mention a leaf blower behind you. That will give you some idea of the volume. I have no doubt that the noise from the monster trucks has had a permanent impact on my health and well-being. Some of the known effects of exposure to loud noise are, obviously, hearing loss, but they also include inflammation of the brain, darkened mood, a weakened immune system, difficulty focusing and sleeping, and infertility. While my hearing is still quite good, I have no doubt that my brain is inflamed, my mood is often dark, at least according to Nancy, and I do sometimes lack focus. Fortunately, I don't have to worry about my fertility any more.

Despite all of my complaints, we went to see the monster trucks again the next year. Charlie passed on going again, but I strong-armed Nancy into sharing the joy with me.

Nancy and Dylan were always very good about giving cards for birthdays, holidays, anniversaries and such. I'm not as good with cards as they are. The only problem is that many of their thoughtful cards make reference to farting, which I guess that I am occasionally prone to doing. For example, Dylan gave me a hand-made card for Father's Day, which started, "Happy Father's (Farter's) Day." Nancy gave me a card which read on the front, "Happy Anniversary to My Husband - A Man with a Really Cute Butt!" On the inside it read, "Well . . . Except When It 'Talks.'" To one of my birthday cards, Dylan had added, "Remember - Hold It In and We All Win!" I don't really think that I fart all that much, but I suppose that depends on your perspective. It's the thought that counts, though. Charlie was pretty good with cards, too, even when he occasionally forgot when my birthday was. He sent me an April 4th card once. But another time, after Dylan was born, Charlie gave me a birthday card and wrote, "You are finding out from Dylan the joy you gave to your Mom and I. Every day you make me proud of you. Love, Dad."

It's really, really hard to believe how fast the time has gone. They say that time speeds up as you get older, and that is absolutely true. On FRIDAY, OCTOBER 8, 2021, Dylan turned 30. On SATURDAY, NOVEMBER 6, 2021, he got married.

CHAPTER 31

SATURDAY, OCTOBER 24, 1992

Not only was it my fifth wedding anniversary, but it was also my twentieth high school reunion. I had gone to all of the others - fifth, tenth, fifteenth - but this was the first and only one that Nancy went to. It was held at The Mansion on Main Street in Voorhees. The *In Memoriam* page of the program listed four classmates we had lost - Susan Boettcher, John Durst, Douglas Edwards and Charles Epley. There were more than that, though. I know that Stephanie Cowans and Tom Lichtman had passed away by then as well.

There have been far, far too many more in the ensuing 30 years - Arlene Bednarczyk, Phil Boyle, Sue Comeforo, Linda Cooper, John Courtney, Steve Ibbeken, Patricia Justice, Jim Kelley, Peggy Klang, John Kuswara, Bob Landry, Kevin McGrath, Kevin Meier, Jack Meyer, Michael Penney, Donna Polidora, Willard Richman, Linda Saun, Clifton Saxton, Clifford Stetler, Rich Toll, Rich Townsend, Joyce Turkelson, Richard Wesolowski - and those are just the ones that I know about. I'm pretty sure that there are more. At least 30 out of 250.

Most of them I saw nearly every day at school. A few, I knew very well, like Kevin McGrath, whose hamsters, Gunther and Gomer, we forgot to put back in the cage one lunchtime during our time at Strawbridge School; Steve Ibbeken, who inspired my student council candidacy and who stuck his pencil into my thigh; Tom Lichtman, who I had the boxing match with and who watched *Sesame Street* with me in the student lounge during our senior year; Peggy Klang, who I would see in church sometimes; Jack Meyer, student council vice president; and Rich Toll, the top player on our conference championship golf team.

Our 50th high school reunion is coming up this year. Our 50th. There will be far fewer people there than there should be.

CHAPTER 32

SUNDAY, NOVEMBER 1, 1992

B oth Secretariat and Citation raced at the Garden State Park Racetrack in Cherry Hill, before a massive fire destroyed the grandstand on THURSDAY, APRIL 14, 1977. Somehow, I heard about the fire while it was happening, went down to Cooper River, and watched from a couple of miles away. It took eight years for the track to be rebuilt and host thoroughbred racing again. By that time, thoroughbred racing was nowhere near as popular as it had been earlier in the 20th Century, and on THURSDAY, MAY 3, 2001, the rebuilt park held its final race. The site now houses a high-end, mixed-use complex, kind of a "town center" for Cherry Hill.

Some of my friends used to play hookey and go bet on the races during high school. Jules Sacchetti and Frank Baneker, for sure. Probably Dave Clark and Colin McGrath, too. Tony Black, who was two years ahead of me at Haddon Township High School, used to go to the track before school to exercise the horses. I knew Tony just a little bit from the wrestling team. Tony wrestled at 98 pounds, the lowest weight class. Nancy taught his son at Strawbridge School one year. Tony went on to become a jockey and rode Classic Go Go in the Kentucky Derby. He missed his high school graduation on MONDAY, JUNE 15, 1970, to ride a 52-1 longshot named Stand By Me in his first race. He won. Tony went on to win 5,200 races in his career, including a North American record nine straight over two days, winning his final three at Atlantic City Racetrack, followed by his only two at Philadelphia Park the next day, and his first four at Atlantic City that evening.

Tony also won the last race held at Garden State Park before the fire and was still wearing his silks when he watched it burn from across Route 70.

By the Sunday night before the 1992 election, November 1, 1992, it was pretty clear that Bill Clinton was going to be elected president of the United States. Ross Perot was becoming increasingly less relevant and incumbent George H.W. Bush had said, "Read my lips - no new taxes." Since Marge was more than happy to babysit Dylan, and since Charlie was always up for an adventure, Nancy, Charlie and I headed to Garden State Park for one of Clinton's final campaign stops. We found a spot upstairs inside of the rebuilt grandstand with a view of the stage.

Running very late, the campaign buses were headed south down the New Jersey Turnpike. The public address announcer made sure that we all knew where the buses were and that they would arrive soon, not wanting anyone in the crowd to leave. We thought about leaving, but Bill had that charisma back then and everyone wants to see a winner. It was getting close to midnight when he arrived.

Bill had no voice left and could barely talk. What he could do, though, was play the sax, and he joined the band for some classic rock less than 48 hours before he would become the president-elect. Hillary was more than happy to step in and say a few words in Bill's stead before heading to the rope line. Charlie, at 6'4" and not shy about using it, decided that he was going to shake hands with her. Nancy and I knew that dissuasion wasn't a viable option, so we waited as Charlie made his way downstairs through the crowd toward the rope line. Success seemed unlikely, given the size of the crowd, the campaign's hurry to get going, and Charlie's late decision. But Charlie was persistent if nothing else and worked his way to the front. Nancy and I watched him from upstairs, not all that surprised.

As far as I know, Charlie is the only person in my family to ever shake hands with a First Lady, or a Secretary of State, for that matter.

CHAPTER 33

I spent Friday night at the Indianapolis Airport Holiday Inn. It was quite by accident, but I did it anyway. And with only a briefcase. I know the date because I was in Jonesboro, Arkansas, on WEDNESDAY, JANUARY 20, 1993, when Bill Clinton was inaugurated for his first term as president. My sense, from my brief stay in Arkansas, was that a lot of Arkansans were glad that he was going to Washington, some because they were proud that one of their own had been elected president and some because they were just glad he was leaving Arkansas. With the Clintons, there is always drama.

Jonesboro would later become famous as the site of one of the early mass school shootings in the United States. On TUESDAY, MARCH 24, 1998, two boys, ages 13 and 11, shot and killed four students and one teacher, and wounded ten others at the Westside Middle School. There have been many, many other school shootings, both before and since:

> *University of Texas*, Austin, Texas (SATURDAY, AUGUST 1, 1966 - 18 dead)
>
> *California State University - Fullerton*, Fullerton, California (MONDAY, JULY 12, 1976 - 7 dead)
>
> *49th Street Elementary School*, Los Angeles, California (FRIDAY, FEBRUARY 24, 1984 - 3 dead)
>
> *Spanaway Junior High School*, Spanaway, Washington (TUESDAY, NOVEMBER 26, 1985 - 3 dead)
>
> *Cleveland Elementary School*, Stockton, California (TUESDAY, JANUARY 17, 1989 - 6 dead)
>
> *University of Iowa*, Iowa City, Iowa (FRIDAY, NOVEMBER 1,

1991 - 5 dead)

Lindhurst High School, Olivehurst, California (FRIDAY, MAY 1, 1992 - 4 dead)

Frontier Middle School, Moses Lake, Washington (FRIDAY, FEBRUARY 2, 1996 - 3 dead)

San Diego State University, San Diego, California (THURSDAY, AUGUST 15, 1996 - 3 dead)

Heath High School, West Paducah, Kentucky (MONDAY, DECEMBER 1, 1997 - 3 dead)

Thurston High School, Springfield, Oregon (THURSDAY, MAY 21, 1998 - 4 dead)

Columbine High School, Columbine, Colorado (TUESDAY, APRIL 20, 1999 - 15 dead)

Appalachian School of Law, Grundy, Virginia, (WEDNESDAY, JANUARY 16, 2002 - 3 dead)

University of Arizona School of Nursing, Tucson, Arizona (MONDAY, OCTOBER 28, 2002 - 4 dead)

Red Lake Senior High School, Red Lake, Minnesota (MONDAY, MARCH 21, 2005 - 10 dead)

West Nickel Mines School, Nickel Mines, Pennsylvania (MONDAY, OCTOBER 2, 2006 - 6 dead)

Virginia Tech, Blacksburg, Virginia (MONDAY, APRIL 16, 2007 - 33 dead)

Louisiana Technical College, Baton Rouge, Louisiana (FRIDAY, FEBRUARY 8, 2008 - 3 dead)

Northern Illinois University, DeKalb, Illinois (THURSDAY, FEBRUARY 14, 2008 - 6 dead)

Chardon High School, Chardon, Ohio (MONDAY, FEBRUARY 27, 2012 - 3 dead)

Oikos University, Oakland, California (MONDAY, APRIL 2, 2012 - 7 dead)

Sandy Hook Elementary School, Newtown, Connecticut

(FRIDAY, DECEMBER 14, 2012 - 28 dead)

Hazard Community and Technical College, Hazard, Kentucky (TUESDAY, JANUARY 15, 2013 - 3 dead)

Santa Monica College, Santa Monica, California (FRIDAY, JUNE 7, 2013 - 6 dead)

Marysville Pilchuck High School, Marysville, Washington (FRIDAY, OCTOBER 24, 2014 - 5 dead)

Umpqua Community College, Roseburg, Oregon (THURSDAY, OCTOBER 1, 2015 - 10 dead)

Rancho Tehama Elementary School, Rancho Tehama, California (TUESDAY, NOVEMBER 14, 2017 - 6 dead)

Aztec High School, Aztec, New Mexico (THURSDAY, DECEMBER 7, 2017 - 3 dead)

Marjory Stoneman Douglas High School, Parkland, Florida (WEDNESDAY, FEBRUARY 14, 2018 - 17 dead)

Santa Fe High School, Santa Fe, Texas (FRIDAY, MAY 18, 2018 - 10 dead)

Saugus High School, Santa Clarita, California (THURSDAY, NOVEMBER 14, 2019 - 3 dead)

Oxford High School, Oxford Township, Michigan (TUESDAY, NOVEMBER 30, 2021 - 4 dead)

Those are only the ones involving at least three deaths and don't count bombings or vehicular attacks. Just guns. A couple of kids get hurt playing lawn darts and they're banned for all eternity. Nearly 40,000 people are shot to death each year in this country and . . . ?

To get to Jonesboro, Arkansas from Philadelphia, I had to take a flight from Philly to Memphis, rent a car and drive about 70 miles west into Arkansas. I was there to take the deposition of a former employee of Monsanto. Monsanto had sued 30 or 40 of its insurance companies to cover the cost of its various environmental liabilities, of which there were an awful lot, which had arisen over the years, and I was one of a team of lawyers from Manta and Welge representing Liberty Mutual. Name a pollutant and Monsanto had dumped or leaked or spilled it somewhere. Arsenic, lead, styrene, benzene, chlorobenzene, tar, PCB, PCP, agent orange, dioxin, cadmium, vinyl chloride, asbestos . . . if it was toxic,

Monsanto made it, used it or sold it. The case was enormous, and a few of us were running around the country conducting discovery - reviewing millions of documents and taking hundreds of depositions. "A few of us" meant lawyers from Philadelphia, New York, Wilmington, Washington, D.C., Chicago and San Francisco. At one point, I was probably spending at least parts of 25 or 26 weeks a year on the road. At Manta and Welge, people had taken to calling me "Monsanto Man."

A lot of my time was spent in Texas, unfortunately. Monsanto had a couple of facilities in Texas at the time, one in Texas City and one in Chocolate Bayou. The Chocolate Bayou facility was part of Monsanto's Chemical Division and naturally wound up as a Superfund site, as did two other plots, the "North 80" and "South 20" in Texas City. I think I was only in Chocolate Bayou once or twice, but I did manage to get a Monsanto "Safety First" decal, which I affixed to a clipboard that I carried around. The theory back then was to just dump all of the waste wherever you could and hope that no one would notice or care. Monsanto used to put some of the really nasty stuff in barrels, take the barrels out somewhere, and have sharpshooters with rifles shoot holes in them so that the stuff would leak out.

I spent more time at the Texas City plant, reviewing documents, along with the other, mostly younger, lawyers. We usually stayed in a nice little hotel in Galveston. Near the Texas City plant there is a large iron anchor, dating back to 1947. On WEDNESDAY, APRIL 16, 1947, the SS Grandcamp was docked in Texas City, near the Monsanto plant on Galveston Bay. At around 8:00 a.m., a fire broke out on the ship. The Grandcamp was carrying 2,300 tons (4.6 million pounds) of ammonium nitrate, used in fertilizer and explosives. As the fire grew, the captain had his crew fight the fire by pumping steam into the cargo hold. Spectators reported that the ship had gotten so hot that the water in the bay near the ship had begun to boil and that the cargo hold and deck were bulging under the pressure of the steam and fire. At 9:12 a.m., the Grandcamp exploded.

Nearly 600 people died in the explosion and fire. The entire Monsanto plant was destroyed. Two-hundred and thirty-four of the 574 employees at the plant were killed. The explosion registered on a seismograph in Denver, Colorado, more than 1,070 miles away. Nearly 1,000 buildings were leveled. Two sightseeing planes were blown out of the sky by the blast. In Galveston, 10 miles away, half of the windows in the city were broken. The explosion was heard 150 miles away. Twenty-seven of the 28 members of the Texas City Fire Department were killed. A two ton anchor was blown from the Grandcamp into the air and landed 1.62 miles away. Another anchor, weighing five tons, flew ½ mile. Those anchors now stand as monuments in Texas City, commemorating the lives lost.

Near the rebuilt Monsanto plant in Texas City was a hazardous waste site which Monsanto had contaminated over the years, known as the

North 80. I had decided that I would make a videotape of what the area looked like, so I drove out to the North 80, an open area next to Galveston Bay which had a dike that you could drive on. There were various holding ponds and groundwater testing wells. As I was taping, I noticed some storm clouds inland, but Texas is big and flat, so I guessed that they were 40 or 50 miles away. Apparently, they weren't. I heard a very loud and very nearby clap of thunder and I felt the hair on my arms, neck and head stand up. It seems that lightning had touched the ground somewhere not too far from where I was and the ground I was standing on was quite wet. Lightning safety experts advise one of two things if you are caught in an open area during a lightning storm - either get down as low as you can by crouching (do *not* lay on the ground!) so that as little of you is touching the ground as possible, or run as fast as you can and get your ass into a car. I chose the latter.

I also spent a lot of time in Missouri, which is not quite as awful as Texas, mostly around St. Louis. Again, I was usually there with a group of younger lawyers pouring through old Monsanto documents at some storage facility. We would go to lunch together. At a little place called the Bicycle Club, one of them actually swore that Chinese food tastes better when eaten with chopsticks. I'm sure that there is a scientific reason why that *is not* true, as well as a psychological reason why it *is*.

When I was in St. Louis, I stayed at the Adam's Mark Hotel, right near the Gateway Arch on the Mississippi River. When I would see the arch on television, usually watching a baseball or football game, I just assumed that it spanned the river, which would have been really cool, although it would have required a much, much larger arch. It doesn't. It just stands there on the Missouri side of the river. I actually went up in the arch once, a harrowing, claustrophobic little ride in a tram.

There was a fairly large and popular bar at the Adam's Mark Hotel. One night, I was in the bar after work and dinner, nursing a beer and relaxing. The San Diego Padres were in town to play the Cardinals, and many of the visiting teams stayed at the Adam's Mark, since it was very close to the stadium. It was late and quite a few of the Padres players found their way to the bar. I was amazed by the number of women encircling most of the players, whether they were good players, bad players, famous players or unknowns. It didn't appear to matter whether the player was good-looking or not, as long as he was a major league baseball player. In 1992, which is around the time that I was sitting at the bar, the average major league player salary was $1,028,667 a year. It seemed that money could compensate, at least to some extent, for whatever a player might be lacking appearance-wise. I wonder what kind of audience, if any, I would have drawn if I were a twenty-something-year-old major league baseball player making north of $1 million a year. Probably a small one.

After watching for a while, it was time to go to bed. I got on the elevator and took it up to my floor. As I left the elevator and started down the hallway to my room, I saw what appeared to be Fred McGriff of the Padres walking toward me with two somewhat unsteady blondes, one on either arm, apparently living up to his nickname, "The Crime Dog."

Although I spent a lot of time on the road while at Manta and Welge, I also spent a lot of time in my office on the 37th floor of One Commerce Square on Market Street in Philly. My windows faced south, looking down toward the stadiums and the airport. A block or two over, maybe on Ludlow Street or Sansom Street, there were row houses, mostly three stories. Many people had set up tables and chairs on the rooftops for cocktails or sunbathing. One rooftop in particular caught my attention. On some hot, sunny, summer days, a woman had taken to sunbathing, topless, on a lounge chair. My office was 34 stories above that rooftop, and a block or two removed, so there really wasn't a whole lot to ogle at. I did, however, have a small telescope at home, so I decided to bring it to work, ostensibly to look down toward the stadiums or the Delaware River.

My office became fairly popular that summer, especially on those bright, sunny days that were good for working on one's tan. Although the telescope made my office a fairly popular destination, I like to think that people also stopped by just to chat or to pull the arm on my M&M dispenser and get a handful of chocolate. Nowadays, HR would probably have to be brought in and all kinds of paperwork filled out.

* * *

I finished the three-day deposition in Jonesboro, Arkansas on Friday afternoon, and I was running late. I still had to drive back to Memphis, return the rental car, take the shuttle bus to the terminal, check in and board my evening flight home to Philadelphia. I left my suitcase with the skycap, and made a beeline to the gate, which was actually physically closing when I got there. At least I hadn't missed my flight.

Of course, in 1993, air travel was far less complicated. There wasn't nearly as much security. You could wait right by the gate to meet arrivals rather than wait outside of the TSA security checkpoint, there were no tickets on your phone and there were no scanners for the tickets. Tickets were all paper, perforated, and they would be torn off by the gate attendant. I presented mine as the gate was closing, the attendant tore it off, and I hustled aboard and found my seat. There were surprisingly few passengers. It was only a minute or two before we pulled away from the gate. It would be good to get back to Philadelphia and home to Voorhees after three days of grilling a Monsanto retiree in Arkansas about how, when, where and why they had disposed of all that crap in Texas decades earlier.

Perhaps I had missed some earlier announcements from the cockpit, since I had barely boarded on time. It wasn't until after we took off that the captain came on and announced, "Ladies and gentlemen, welcome aboard our flight to Indianapolis." Yes, I had gotten on the wrong plane.

CHAPTER 34

SATURDAY, NOVEMBER 5, 1994

The only artist that I have seen as often as John Fogerty is Mary Chapin Carpenter ("Chapin"). Nancy and I first went to see Chapin and John Gorka at the Tower Theater in Upper Darby, Pennsylvania on SATURDAY, NOVEMBER 5, 1994. She played most of the songs of hers that I liked back then, like "Shut Up and Kiss Me," "Girls with Guitars," "Passionate Kisses," "He Thinks He'll Keep Her" and "I Feel Lucky." Sam Wood's review in *The Philadelphia Inquirer* was spot on:

> *Carpenter will always deliver a live show brimming with warmth and tenderness, and bound together with a gentle sense of self-deprecating humor . . . At the Tower, with only the accompaniment of longtime collaborator John Jennings and Jon Carroll on piano, it is easy to understand why she has become a phenomenon. Carpenter's marriage of blue-collar heart with Ivy League smarts places her at the intersection where Patsy Cline meets Joni Mitchell.*

That's a pretty good intersection.

I'm not sure how we stumbled upon her, but it was probably in the early 1990's when Garth Brooks melded country, pop and rock, particularly with "Friends in Low Places," bringing country music into the popular music mainstream. A wave of other "country" artists achieved mainstream success at that time, including Clint Black, Alan Jackson, Tim McGraw, and a raft of women including Shania Twain, Reba McEntire, Faith Hill, LeAnn Rimes, Martina McBride and Chapin. Nancy, Dylan and I used to watch the *Top 20 Countdown* on CMT most nights. Chapin quickly became one of our favorites.

We saw her again the next year at the Mann Music Center in Philadelphia, with the Mavericks opening, on THURSDAY, AUGUST 3, 1995. The set was a lot like the one we had seen at the Tower, although she had a slightly larger band backing her this time. The biggest surprise was the Mavericks, who were fabulous, with their blend of Tex-Mex, Latin, country and rockabilly music. The Mavericks' frontman, Raul Malo, sounds remarkably like Roy Orbison at times, and that's a good thing.

Not too much later, although I don't know exactly when, we saw her at a casino show in Atlantic City. Nancy won the tickets on a call-in contest at the country music radio station in Philly. It was a short, rather lifeless performance, in a dreary auditorium, at some casino which has probably since been torn down or abandoned. I haven't gone to another casino concert since.

The next show was much, much better when we saw her again a few years later at the Keswick Theater in Glenside Pennsylvania. Venue matters. The 1,300-seat theater has that old, single-screen movie theater charm, and she played her pretty standard set, although with a few of her newer songs incorporated. I like the older, livelier stuff better, and don't care as much for what she has written in her later career - a lot of earnest ballads, whispered lyrics, and soft, slow stuff. I much prefer her kick-ass, up-tempo, "Down at the Twist and Shout" kind of music.

It wasn't until we moved to Maine that we went to another Chapin concert. On SUNDAY, AUGUST 6, 2017, we went to see her again at the Stone Mountain Arts Center in Brownfield, Maine. Stone Mountain is easily the nicest music venue I have ever been to, located in an old barn in the foothills of the White Mountains in rural Maine, a mile or two from the New Hampshire border. It is warm, intimate, beautiful, and an absolute joy to visit. Seating is kind of random, with dinner tables in the center of the old barn, where you can have a meal before the show. Nancy and I had gotten tickets for just the concert, not dinner, but we were told that seating for concert-goers was on a first-come, first-seated basis. It was our lucky night.

We arrived nearly two hours early to secure good seats, not knowing that there really aren't any bad ones, since the place probably holds no more than 300 people or so. We were apparently the first, so we checked in and went to the bar for a drink. After a while, one of the hostesses came and got us, told us that it was our lucky day, and led us inside. She said that two of their "angels" had cancelled and that we would be getting their seats, at a high-top no more than 15-20 feet from the stage. Chapin opened the show with a cover of Dylan's "The Times They are A-Changin'." Chapin engages with the audience a little bit, and at one point someone asked her what the song was that she had opened the show with. "Oh, honey, you're so young," Chapin said.

We saw her again the next year, again at Stone Mountain, on SUNDAY, JULY 22, 2018, but this time we went with Nancy's sister, Donna, and her husband, Roy. We sat upstairs at a table in the front of the balcony. Nancy, Donna and I loved the show. Roy, not so much.

CHAPTER 35

I was driving alone on Haddon Avenue in Haddonfield, and was at the traffic light just past Haddonfield Friends School and the public library, right in front of the Hinski-Tomlinson Funeral Home, when there was a large flash of lightning, followed by thunder. I was about ten minutes away from my parents' house on Burrwood Avenue. My mother had been very sick for about six months, and by this time was confined to a hospital bed which had been brought to the house and set up on the first floor in Marge's old painting studio. The hospital bed was adjustable so that the patient could be made more comfortable. She was receiving hospice care, including morphine.

The room where we had set up the hospital bed was an addition my parents had put onto the house. On SUNDAY, APRIL 26, 1964, Charlie and Marge signed for a $2,000 loan from Inter-Boro Savings and Loan Association to put the addition on the back of the house. My mother was a very good painter, mostly oils, and the studio had large bay windows that let in lots of sunlight. We have three of her paintings hanging in our home - a large painting of a sailboat on a stormy sea over our fireplace, a red barn in a snowscape by our front door and a vase of flowers in the bedroom.

Nancy and I were trying to balance work, raising 3 1/2 year-old Dylan, and being with Charlie and Marge during Marge's final days. Charlie was pretty much a complete wreck. I had been there early in the day on Wednesday, when the hospice nurse was there. After she had checked Marge's vitals, she told Charlie and I that it was probably going to be that day. I'm not sure, but I suspect that I went into work in Philly for a few hours just to get away for a bit, then headed home to change and eat before going back to be with my parents that night. Nancy visited Charlie and Marge during her lunch break from school.

Charlie and Marge were always great with Dylan. For the first three years after he was born, he would spend Friday nights at their house, and Nancy and I could go out to dinner or on some kind of date. They would have been happy if Dylan had stayed the entire weekend. Eventually, Marge got too sick to babysit, which meant that she was *really* sick.

When he was young, Dylan was fascinated by machines, trucks, trains and the like, which eventually led us to the Monster Truck Jam experiences. He knew the names of all of the construction machines - grader, excavator, front loader, bulldozer, backhoe, conveyor - and would point them out whenever we drove through a construction zone, reeling off their names like Harlan Pepper naming nuts in *Best in Show*. He liked watching the hospital bed being adjusted and probably even pressed the controls himself sometimes. At 3 ½ years old, he certainly didn't really understand what was going on with my mother, just that she was sick and was in the cool bed that moved. He noticed the plastic bag with yellow fluid attached to the bed - the catheter bag - and asked what it was. Charlie, in perhaps his finest moment, told Dylan, "That's the gasoline that runs the engine for the bed." Sheer brilliance.

Marge's memorial service was held at 11:00 a.m. on MONDAY, APRIL 17, 1995, at the First Baptist Church of Collingswood, at the corner of Maple and Frazier Avenues. Her brief obituary ran in the *Courier-Post* on FRIDAY, APRIL 14, 1995, and SATURDAY, APRIL 15, 1995. She and Charlie had been members at First Baptist for more than 25 years and both had been very active there the whole time, serving as deacon, deaconess, trustee and on pastoral search committees. Reverend George Hawthorne, who was the pastor of the church, conducted the service. It felt good to be back in the church where I had spent so much time when I was younger and to see so many people that I still recognized. The guest book was signed by 174 people. Even one of Charlie's brothers, Thomas, and his sister, Elizabeth, came.

I gave the eulogy, at least partly because there was no way Charlie could have done it.

Although my parents had purchased cemetery plots years earlier at Harleigh Cemetery in Camden, they had long since sold them. They wisely decided to be cremated instead. So on FRIDAY, APRIL 14, 1995, my mother was cremated at the Harleigh Cemetery crematory - cremation No. 13740. I was surprised that the cremains came back in what was basically an oversized cardboard shoebox with a plastic bag full of ashes inside. I had pictured something a little more dignified. Although the cremation certificate states that, "The law requires that this certificate accompany the Cremated Remains to the final place of Interment," I'm not sure that we complied with that requirement. And there was no interment.

We now had Marge's ashes, wondering what to do with them, when Charlie decided that he would like to scatter them at the Brigantine National Wildlife Refuge on the Jersey Shore. The refuge is in the tidal wetlands of the Atlantic Flyway and is an important habitat for migratory birds. Marge was a bird-lover, always stocking her bird feeders outside of the kitchen window and waging a constant, futile battle to keep the squirrels away. The Wildlife Refuge was one of her favorite places to go bird-watching.

Sometime after the memorial service, maybe a week or two, Charlie, Nancy, Dylan and I drove down to the refuge in Nancy's red Jeep Cherokee to scatter the ashes. Charlie would be the one to release them. There is a road that winds through the refuge, with pullovers to stop and watch the wildlife, but that wasn't what we were there for. We were there to release the ashes at a place that Marge loved. Our efforts were made more difficult by the number of cars and people. Every time we found what felt like a good spot, it seemed that a car would pull up right behind us, so we kept driving.

Eventually, Charlie found a spot that he liked, and no one was nearby. We wanted to make it quick, not being certain about the legality of what we were doing and not wanting a car to pull up behind us and catch us in *flagrante delicto*. Charlie would never fit into the back seat of the Jeep, so he sat in the front passenger seat while I drove and Nancy and Dylan sat in the back. Having found his spot, Charlie opened the passenger-side door and stepped out. Since it was springtime, and we were by the water, it was windy. Charlie either didn't notice or didn't care. Probably both. He left the door open, didn't wait for anyone else to get out, and quickly dumped the ashes from their plastic bag. He didn't place them, didn't gently pour them out, didn't carefully spread them, he just opened the bag and shook it out.

Most of my mother's remains stayed at the refuge. The rest, however, blew back onto Charlie, into the Jeep, and onto us. So now, when anyone asks what became of Marge, I tell them that most of her came to her final rest at the Brigantine National Wildlife Refuge, some of her went through the washing machine, and some ended up in the vacuum cleaner at the car wash. It was a quintessential Charlie moment, and we really shouldn't have expected anything less.

The hospice nurse was right - Marge passed away at 10:30 that night, 13 months after being diagnosed with metastatic carcinoma. I wasn't there when it happened, but almost. I was on my way. When I got there, my father told me that she had died about ten minutes earlier - right when I was in Haddonfield and saw the lightning and heard the thunder. Coincidental? Of course. Or at least I think it was.

In yet another odd coincidence, Nancy was also in a car heading to visit her sick mother, but she, too, missed her mother's passing by a few minutes.

I had played softball at the field on Route 130 in Pennsauken dozens of times. It was almost always against Martin Luther Chapel, in the old South Jersey Fellowship Church League. I've played men's softball every year since I was 15 or 16 years old, starting in fast-pitch, then in slow-pitch, often in multiple leagues, in New Jersey, Pennsylvania, Massachusetts and Maine. Martin Luther Chapel was one of the better teams, but usually not as good as YMBC or Saint Gregory's, who I played for back then.

It was a pretty lousy field, really. It occupied an entire block across the street from the church, and was a softball field in only the most general sense, although it did at least have a backstop and benches to sit on. Right field was too short, so they built a high chain link fence, maybe 20 feet or so, which kept some balls in the park, although its main purpose was to protect cars on Baker Avenue and in the parking lot of the church. It only helped a little. Left field and center field had a pretty severe slope toward the infield. Grass, if it could be called that, was mostly clumps of weeds. How anyone could field a grounder in the infield is beyond me. Softball fields weren't that easy to come by, though, with probably 200-300 teams playing in South Jersey at the time, and I think the church owned the property, so Martin Luther played its home games there for years, except for one year, when they got a permit for a field at the airport circle in Pennsauken - a field so riddled with gulleys, holes, rocks, broken glass and trash - that even Martin Luther abandoned it after a year.

Most of my life I have played in the outfield, from Little League right on up through today, when I play old-man (some call it "senior") softball. Mainly I've played left field, but I've played all of the other spots as well. I think I was an outfielder because I was pretty fast, fearless about fences and diving for balls, never had the arm to play short or third, and had no interest in pitching. And second base was where lots of coaches tried to hide guys who weren't really very good at any position. So on Wednesday evening, I found myself in the outfield at the Martin Luther field, which no longer exists, having long ago been used for an apartment building, or senior housing, or something for which it was much better suited.

Nancy and Charlie came to watch me play a lot. Uncle Bob, one of Marge's brothers, lived a couple of blocks from the Martin Luther field, so he often came when I played there. Charlie sometimes brought his golf buddy and friend from the phone company, Dave Swisher. Charlie was pretty open with his opinions about what was happening on the field and about the relative merits of the various players, so Nancy and I frequently had to ask him to keep those opinions unspoken. Charlie didn't have that filter that mediated between what to keep in or speak aloud. For some unfortunate reason, not a one of them was there on August 31st.

I had never really injured myself playing softball - lots of bruises and sore arms and jammed fingers, but nothing that really made me miss any playing time. That was about to change.

Somebody hit one to my left and over my head. I turned and began running back. The field had a chain link fence in left and center fields, but it was pretty deep and not many people ever reached it, although occasionally someone would clear the fence and the ball would end up bouncing along Route 130. As I was running back, I fell. My left knee hurt, but it wasn't as painful as one might think, at least not yet. My first thought was that maybe I had actually run into the fence and banged my knee, but when I looked, the fence was at least 30 or 40 feet away.

Instinctively, I reached for my knee. By now I was beginning to realize that it might be more than just a minor injury. When I grabbed for my knee, there was something hard under the skin just above the joint and below the quadriceps muscle. It was about the size of a Girl Scout Thin Mint cookie, and I could move it from side to side. As the x-ray would soon show, it was the better part of my kneecap, which had been dislodged and split in two when the patellar tendon, which connects the kneecap to both the quadriceps muscle and the tibia, ruptured. Snapped - like a stretched rubber band breaking. That was the only time that I had to be helped off of a softball field. There must have been two people helping me, but I only remember John Franciotti. It hadn't yet dawned on me just how serious this injury might be, but judging from some faces, it apparently had dawned on others.

Why, or even how, I drove myself from Pennsauken to the hospital in Voorhees is a mystery. It certainly wasn't very smart, but I did it anyway. I put the seat as far back as I could while still being able to reach the brake and gas pedals, because I couldn't bend my left leg at all. The only position I could hold it in was perfectly straight. So I got into the car butt first, picked up my left leg with my hands, and swung it into the car. I somehow managed to drive the 12 miles or so to the hospital parking lot. By this time, someone had called Nancy and told her that she should meet me at the emergency room outside of West Jersey Hospital. Dylan also came.

I found that I could "walk" relatively painlessly by keeping my left leg perfectly straight, stepping with my right, and kind of dragging my left, like a cartoon pirate with a wooden leg. I started across the hospital parking lot like that, until Nancy saw me and summoned a nurse, who came out with a wheelchair. After figuring out how to do it without bending what was left of my knee, I plopped into the seat and was wheeled inside, with my leg extended straight out and my heel on the raised footrest. Not being a true emergency, we waited for some time after filling out the paperwork.

It had now been a few hours since I had used a bathroom, and it was time to pee. With my leg still extended straight out and resting on the wheelchair's footrest, it would be impossible for me to wheel myself through the door and into the men's restroom on my own. Very reluctantly, Nancy agreed to wheel me in. Being inexperienced with pushing a wheelchair, and more inexperienced with the layout of a men's restroom, she tried to maneuver the chair as close to a urinal as possible. In doing so, she apparently hadn't factored in my leg being stretched out in front, and ran it into the wall. That was the first time that it really, really, *really* hurt - enough so that I let out a scream - more of a yelp, really, like when you step on a dog's tail.

Peeing into a urinal while sitting in a wheelchair with one leg straight out is doable. The only real issue, which I hadn't completely thought through, was the starting and stopping process, which necessitated a little "cleanup on aisle five" afterwards.

When the x-rays came back and the doctor explained the injury and the necessity for surgery, I asked if it would be arthroscopic. The doctor looked at me, smiled slightly, and said, "No."

Dr. Robert Bachman performed the surgery two days later, on FRIDAY, AUGUST 2, 1996. Everything went well - the kneecap was stitched back together, the tendon was sewn up, and the six-inch incision was stapled shut. I had to wear an ankle-to-hip brace for nine or 10 weeks. At first, it was just a rigid foam cast, while I was waiting to get the more serious Bledsoe brace. The Bledsoe brace was black, with straps to hold it in place and had adjustable knobs. At first, the knee was kept straight for the initial recovery from surgery. As time went on, the brace could be adjusted so that I could start exercising and strengthening the joint. At first it was adjusted so that the knee could be bent 10 degrees, which I did multiple times a day, then 20 degrees, then 30, and so on until the knee was strong enough that the brace could come off. To this day, because of the atrophy, my left thigh is smaller than the right one, although no one would really notice. And I have a nice half-moon scar to show off.

Recovery for me was relatively uneventful. I was determined to get back to softball for opening day the next spring, eight months later. As soon as the brace came off, I began walking on our treadmill, thinking that it would be safer than taking walks outside and would help with developing an even stride without a limp. I was so proud of myself after my first walk on the treadmill. I had covered ¼ mile in 10 minutes, a not-too-impressive 1.5 m.p.h. clip.

Dylan, at five years old, wrote a story about the incident, entitled, "Dad Broke His Knee - A True Story." It went like this:

Dad was playing baseball. He fell and broke his knee.

The guys saw dad fall. Then they picked him up.

The guys saw dad fall. Then they picked him up.

Dad drove himself to the hospital!

Dad stayed in the hospital for two days to get his knee fixed.

Dad came home on crutches with Dylan and Mom.

That pretty much sums it up, and in a much more concise way than in my telling.

Recovery was not without its missteps. For one thing, both I and my brace stank. After the brace came off, I really wanted a hot bath, which I hadn't had for a couple of months. I like my baths to be as hot as I can possibly stand. So, with some difficulty, I managed to climb into the tub and lay down. It felt really good. Apparently, a bit too good. I fell asleep for a few minutes, I guess, because the water wasn't as hot when I came to as it had been when I climbed in. Still being a little unsure of myself, and having to climb out of the tub, I called for Nancy to help.

I only know what happened next because Nancy has reminded me several times about it. It seems that the combination of having just woken up, being somewhat unsteady on my leg anyway, and having an elevated body temperature from the hot water had made me just a little lightheaded. Nancy, sensing that things could be heading in a bad direction, summoned Dylan, who wasn't quite five years old, for help. It was too late. I passed out, and, being 50 pounds heavier than Nancy, not to mention slippery when wet, collapsed onto the cold bathroom floor tile, banging my head on the floor and blacking out for a few seconds. At least she was there to ease the fall, lest I would have added head damage to my already compromised condition by bouncing my head off of the sink, counter, toilet, towel rack and/or bathtub before hitting the floor.

I have this theory, which has not yet been confirmed by science, that men have a gene that makes it difficult, if not nearly impossible - roughly the odds of being hit by a piece of falling space debris on your birthday while going to cash your winning Powerball ticket - to foresee the possible ramifications of their actions. This genetic failing most often manifests itself around ladders, snowblowers, nail guns, firecrackers and any kind of do-it-yourself plumbing project. I think that that genetic flaw may have led to my unfortunate hot bath experience. I did, however, play on opening day the next season.

Old man softball, which I am now relegated to, has so many injuries, it's surprising that teams and leagues survive. In my Haverhill, Massachusetts, league, we didn't make it through the second inning of the first game of the year before we lost one of our players to a hamstring. Once mighty athletes reduced to this. Most of the injuries are relatively minor. Most. Usually, sore elbows, shoulders and knees, lots of pulled hamstrings and Achilles tendons, and assorted other aches and pains. Except for one time. We were losing a game by a big score, something like 14 or 15 to nothing. It was the last inning and I came up to bat. I hit a good one to left center field, right between the left and left-center fielders. Both of them decided to try to catch it and neither one ever slowed down. They collided - not a glancing collision, but a full-on crash. I circled the bases for a home run while they were both still on the ground. One of them got up pretty quickly. The other didn't. He stayed down until the ambulance arrived about 20 minutes later. After some work, they put him on a stretcher and loaded him in. I heard a week or two later that he had completely broken his humerus, the big bone in the upper arm. That had to hurt a lot. We called off the rest of the game and went home. My only question is whether that qualifies as a "walk off home run," since the game did end on my homer.

I play softball mainly because I still can, I like being on a team, enjoy the camaraderie, and generally enjoy competing. For others, though, it is something that defines their manhood and the very essence of their being. It is not played for fun, but rather for blood. They (and I'm thinking primarily of "Joe Doe" and "Tom Doe") show up at the field ready to fight and argue. They will argue and rant about absolutely anything and everything - who is the home team, how far apart the bases are, which bats are legal, what softballs to use, where the pitching mound should be, who is allowed to pinch run. Absolutely anything. And that is before the game even starts. Once the game begins, there are even more things to argue about - balls and strikes, was a foul ball in or out of play, was the runner safe or out, did the fielder catch the ball.

"Joe Doe," in particular, was a miserable prick of a man. He was one of those guys who was always trying to skirt the rules, get any kind of perceived advantage, bring illegal players to games and tell his weaker players to stay home during playoffs. Eventually, so many old men got sick of his act that they kicked him out of the league. One time, he was mad at someone on my team for some perceived slight, so instead of pitching to him, he rolled pitches to the plate to intentionally walk him. Not only did that hurt Doe's team, but it meant that the guy who was walked had hustled home from work, changed into softball clothes, and driven to the field, only to have this guy not even let him have a chance to hit. Very classy.

"Tom Doe," on the other hand, never matured emotionally beyond third grade. He just jabbered incessantly, heard every word that everyone at the field said, and went off when something happened that he didn't like or when someone said something that he didn't like. Once he started arguing, he simply would not shut up. Almost every argument ended with Tom Doe threatening to sue or call the police. It was exhausting. A miserable time was guaranteed for everyone when a Joe Doe team played a Tom Doe team. Thank God I only got stuck on a team with Tom Doe one time, which made for a long summer.

I learned recently that Tom Doe had passed away. I'm pretty sure that he was younger than I am. Obviously, I didn't much care for the guy, but that doesn't make his passing any less sad. "Any man's death diminishes me."

Softball has its lighter moments, too, regardless of the constant stream of injuries being suffered by once proud athletes. I had a teammate named Joe Milo, who was an inveterate talker under the best of circumstances and even more so when agitated. Joe was a good player and pitched for our team. He held a special contempt for umpires. During a game at Centennial Field in Haddonfield, Joe got into an argument with the umpire. The exchange went something like this:

Joe Milo: "Blah, blah, blah, blah"

Umpire: "Blah, blah, blah, blah"

Joe Milo: "Blah, blah, blah"

Umpire: "One more word, and you're gone."

Joe Milo: "You can't throw me out for what I'm thinking, can you?"

Umpire: "No."

Joe Milo: "Well, I'm thinking you're an asshole."

If that was improvised, it was simply awesome. If it was planned, it was still awesome. Needless to say, Joe was tossed.

For a number of years, I played for St. Gregory's and we played our home games at Sterling High School. One night, while standing in left field, I looked up at the sky. There, to my amazement, formed by some clouds, was a perfect Richard Nixon. I mean a *perfect* Richard Nixon. Usually, when someone sees some supposed shape in the clouds, they have to explain it and carefully point it out. Not this time. I yelled for timeout, which the umpire granted, pointed and screamed, "It's Nixon!" There, for everyone to see, was Richard Milhous Nixon, 37th president of the United States, in cumulonimbus glory for all to see. Unfortunately, those were the days before cell phone cameras, and Nixon slowly dissolved and drifted away. Joe Strong can confirm every word.

While playing old man softball at Kirkwood Park in Voorhees, I was again in left field, when the batter hit a high pop up in the infield. Our second baseman, whose name I have long forgotten, staggered under it, raised his glove, and completely whiffed. The softball - which isn't really very soft - landed directly on top of his head. As he dropped to his knees and clutched the top of his head, the first baseman, ever vigilant, spotted the ball, which had bounced about 30 feet straight up, reached over, and caught it for the out. The rest of us probably should have immediately come to the aid of our stricken teammate, but we were too busy laughing, respectfully placing our gloves over our mouths.

I, likewise, was not immune to the occasional blooper. One night, while playing at Knight's Park in Collingswood, I took one off the head, too. I was playing second base when the batter scorched a line drive right at me. It was coming straight at my face, but it was a knuckleball. I put my glove up just in time, and the ball glanced off the tip of my glove and hit the crown of my forehead. Had I not ticked it, it probably would have caught me right between the eyes. The impact spun me around and I spotted the ball arcing out toward right field, which was manned by Mike ("The Thrill") Grossman, a person of moderate size and softball ability. He was running in to try to catch it on the carom and I, having been spun around and now facing the outfield, decided to try to catch it, too. I did, and then proceeded to run over Mike. My teammates, once we got to the bench, enjoyed taking turns looking at the indentations the softball's stitches had left on my forehead.

Jay Gunn was a long-time teammate and a serious power hitter. In the Sunday old man league, we were on the same team, but on weeknights we were rivals. We were playing under the lights at Metropolitan Park in West Deptford and Jay was on the other team. I was in left when Jay hit a bomb to left-center. I was faster in those days, and, knowing that it was going way over my head, simply turned and ran as fast as I could, hoping to pick the ball up after it landed and maybe hold him to a triple. Either I was faster than I thought or misjudged how far it was going - almost certainly the latter - because rather than the ball landing beyond me, it hit me right smack in the ass and fell to the ground. Rightfully embarrassed, I turned, picked it up, threw it back to the infield, and slinked back to my position.

Jay Gunn played on my first old-man team, Parker's Lawn Maintenance, as did Dick Parker, Dick Lillich, Harry Giberson, John Franciotti and Carl Carlson in the 49ers Senior Softball League. Parker's was easily the best senior team I played for, and we won three consecutive championships in 2004, 2005 and 2006; matching the three straight I had won with St. Gregory's more than two decades earlier and the three more from 1990-1992. St. Gregory's won in 1998, as well. All told, in the nine seasons from 1980 through 1992 that I played with St. Gregory's, we won seven league championships. That's even better than the Cheatin' Patriots. After the 1994 season, age and life had caught up with us. We finished the season a little bit above .500, lost in the semi-finals of the playoffs, and folded.

Back in the 1970's and 1980's, the *Courier-Post* reported on the results of softball games. There must have been around 20 leagues, and the coverage sometimes took half a page in the sports section. I saved some of the clippings, usually the ones that my name appeared in, but others as well. They can also be found in the *Courier-Post* archives.

I started my softball career with a church league team named YMBC in the Fellowship League in the 1970's. Just about every softball player I know started out in a church league. Charlie, too, had played softball in the Fellowship League, but he played in the 1940's, for Westmont Baptist. At least I think it may have been the same league. On TUESDAY, JULY 22, 1947, Westmont Baptist defeated Audubon Lutheran 11-2, with Charlie playing centerfield and going 3 for 5. His team was apparently pretty good, since they were 10-1 at the time.

YMBC was pretty good, but I never won a championship with them. I was dating Barbara Boenning back then, and recruited her sister Sue's husband, Barry Bruner, and her sister Debbie's boyfriend, Al Ferrari, to play. Al, in turn, recruited his twin brother, Vince. Those additions made us even better. The first *Courier-Post* clipping that I have found is from 1977. My last name is variously listed as Florig, Fidrig, Floris or Florio [dates are game dates]:

WEDNESDAY, JULY 27, 1977: *YMBC scored an 8-3 win over Christ the King behind homers from Dave Florig and Vince Ferrari in a Fellowship Church League test.*

WEDNESDAY, MAY 9, 1979: *YMBC topped Audubon Mormon, 20-4, as Dave Florig belted a grand slam in a Fellowship Church League game.*

FRIDAY, MAY 25, 1979: *Dave Florio's (sic) bases-loaded triple lifted YMBC over Westmont Methodist, 13-8, in the Fellowship Church League as Barry Bruner retired the last 10 hitters in relief.*

FRIDAY, JUNE 8, 1979: *Rich Young belted two doubles and a three-run homer to lead YMBC to a 19-8 laugher over Emanuel Methodist in the Fellowship Church loop. Dave Florig also homered for YMBC.*

FRIDAY, JUNE 22, 1979: *YMBC edged St. Gregory's 11-10, with a two-run homer by Dave Floris (sic) to highlight Fellowship Church League competition.*

WEDNESDAY, JULY 11, 1979: *Dave Fidrig (sic) and Barry Bruner combined to knock in 13 runs to lead YMBC to a 27-3 decision over Haddonfield Baptist in a Fellowship Church League contest.*

Final 1979 Standings: National: YMBC 14-4, Westmont Methodist 11-7, St. Gregory's 11-7, Martin Luther 11-7, Haddonfield Presbyterian 9-9; American: Audubon Mormon 10-8, Christ the King 8-10, Oaklyn Emanuel 8-10, Gibbsboro Methodist 5-13, Haddonfield Baptist 3-15

The church league had an all-star game in 1978, which we played in Gibbsboro. I was one of YMBC's all-star representatives. I don't remember what I did that night, but I won the MVP award for the game. Thinking back, I believe that it's the only MVP that I won in any sport at any age. In 1980, I switched teams from YMBC to St. Gregory's. There was a little bit too much drama going on with YMBC for my taste, so I asked Fran Catando, who ran St. Gregory's, if I could join them. It proved to be a wise decision, as we went on to win the league championship three straight years from 1980-82. That St. Gregory's team was the best team I ever played for and Fran was my favorite manager. It's not easy, and it takes a special breed to be a good manager.

TUESDAY, MAY 6, 1980: *Headline: "Torrillo's bat powers St. Gregory." Tom Torrillo laced four hits, including two home runs, and knocked in six runs to lead St. Gregory's to a 22-6 win over Christ the King in independent softball action last night.*

MONDAY, MAY 19, 1980: *John Stelmach delivered four hits, including two home runs, and had five RBIs as St. Gregory's defeated Martin Luther, 16-5. John Murray and Dave Florig added three hits apiece for St. Gregory's.*

MONDAY, JUNE 23, 1980: *Dave Florig homered and tripled, knocking in four runs, as St. Gregory's defeated YMBC 13-4.*

THURSDAY, JULY 31, 1980: *St. Gregory's scored two runs in the seventh to squeeze by Haddonfield Presbyterian, 7-6, in semifinal playoff action. Fran Catando drove in the winning run with a sacrifice fly. Dave Florig paced the victors with three hits, including a single which launched the last inning rally.*

FRIDAY, AUGUST 1, 1980: *Saint Gregory's locked up their 9-2 victory over Haddonfield Presbyterian with five runs in the sixth inning, winning its second consecutive game in a best-of-three playoff. Dave Florig and Fran Catando each connected for three hits, while pitcher Joe Catando helped his own cause by smacking in a two-run double for the winners.*

THURSDAY, AUGUST 7, 1980: *St. Gregory's took a 1-0 lead in the best-of-three finals as it blanked St. John's, 3-0. Pitcher Joe*

*Catando gave up only three hits as Dave Florig and Tom
Torillo led the offense with two hits each.*

FRIDAY, AUGUST 8, 1980: St. Gregory's clinched the
championship series, two games to none, whipping St.
John's, 14-2. Pitcher Joe Catando had three hits, including a
solo homer, and John Murray added three hits, one being a
grand slam.

TUESDAY, MAY 5, 1981: *Dave Florig and John Murray had
four hits apiece as St. Gregory's beat Gibbsboro Methodist 16-
3.*

FRIDAY, MAY 22, 1981: *Dave Florig had three hits in St.
Gregory's 9-2 win over St. Andrew's.*

WEDNESDAY, JUNE 17, 1981: *St. Gregory's bested Westmont
Methodist, 18-1, as Dave Florig and John Murray accounted
for four hits and two RBIs each.*

THURSDAY, JULY 16, 1981: *St. Gregory's swept a doubleheader
from Haddonfield Baptist, winning 7-2 and 5-4. John
Stelmach batted 6-6 for the night, while Joe Catando and
Dave Florig had two hits each in the first game and Stan
Golas contributed two hits in the second.*

FRIDAY, AUGUST 14, 1981: *Joe Catando pitched a three-hitter
to lead St. Gregory's to a 9-0 victory over YMBC and the
league championship. The win was the 21st in the last 22
games for St. Gregory's, which finished the season 25-3. Dave
Diano and Dave Florig contributed three hits apiece.*

FRIDAY, MAY 14, 1982: *St. Gregory's raised its record to 5-0 with a 9-3 win over Martin Luther. Dave Florig blasted a two-run homer and Sal Nicosia drove in two runs.*

FRIDAY, MAY 21, 1982: *Dave Florig boomed a home run in St. Gregory's 21-2 pasting of Temple Lutheran.*

TUESDAY, MAY 25, 1982: *Dave Florig and John Stelmach hit homers to pace St. Gregory's past St. Andrew's 17-8.*

THURSDAY, JUNE 24, 1982: *Dave Florig and Tom Torillo each slammed five hits as St. Gregory's remained undefeated, beating Haddonfield Baptist 18-9.*

FRIDAY, JULY 9, 1982: *Headline: "Presbyterian sweeps unbeaten St. Gregory's." Haddonfield Presbyterian men's softball team doubled its pleasure last evening when it defeated previously unbeaten St. Gregory's, 11-5, not once, but twice. St. Gregory's, which has led the Fellowship Church League throughout the season, fell victim to a potent Haddonfield Presbyterian offense. Mike DeLuca broke the first game open with a three-run triple. The winners completed the sweep behind Carl and Alex Tarbell and George Gehring. Carl hit two homers in the second game, while Alex was 4-for-6 for the night and Gehring was 5-for-6. The winners are in second place in the National Division.*

FRIDAY, JULY 16, 1982: *Jim Hudson, Dave Florig and Stan Golas drilled three hits each to lead St. Gregory's over Gibbsboro Methodist 16-5.*

MONDAY, JULY 19, 1982: *Rob Boenning homered in the*

game-winning run and Gary Bruno (sic) homered and pitched the win as St. John's nipped St. Gregory's 4-2.

TUESDAY, JULY 27, 1982: *John Stelmach's sacrifice fly in the sixth inning handed St. Gregory's a 13-12 squeaker over Haddonfield Presbyterian.*

FRIDAY, JULY 30, 1982: *St. Gregory's earned the national division crown in the Fellowship Church League by downing Haddonfield Presbyterian 5-3. John Stelmach belted a two-run homer in the sixth for the victory.*

WEDNESDAY, AUGUST 4, 1982: *Jim Hudson singled in the game-winner in the fifth inning as St. Gregory's edged YMBC, 9-8, in the first game of a five-game championship series. Dave Florig, Tom Torillo and Stan Golas all had three hits to pace the winners.*

THURSDAY, AUGUST 5, 1982: *Tom Wisely hammered a two-run double and Greg Murphy homered to help YMBC over St. Gregory's, 7-4, to knot their championship series at 1-1.*

FRIDAY, AUGUST 6, 1982: *YMBC moved to within one game of capturing the playoff crown against defending champion St. Gregory's by posting a 10-8 victory. Bob Ilgenfritz slugged a two-run double in a six-run fifth inning for YMBC, which leads the series 2-1.*

TUESDAY, AUGUST 10, 1982: *St. Gregory's evened the championship series at two games apiece by whipping YMBC 9-3, as Bob Porter laced four hits and drove in two runs for the winners.*

WEDNESDAY, AUGUST 11, 1982: *Joe Catando tossed a two-hitter and Bob Porter and Jack Gwillam totalled five hits as St. Gregory's crushed YMBC 9-0.*

THURSDAY, JULY 21, 1983: *Dave Florig homered and Dave Diano slapped three hits as St. Gregory's edged Haddonfield, 5-3.*

MONDAY, JULY 25, 1983: *St. Gregory's demolished Haddonfield Baptist, 17-5, behind home runs by Stan Golas, John Stelmach, Dave Florig and John Murray.*

During my last three or four years playing in the church league, before moving to Massachusetts for a few years, our biggest rival was Haddonfield Presbyterian, who finally ended our three-year run of championships in 1983. I was a lot more competitive about softball back then and used to go at it pretty good with some of their players, exchanging unpleasantries with a few of them during games. After moving back to New Jersey from Massachusetts in the late 1980's, I started playing basketball on Tuesday and Thursday nights with a bunch of my old St. Gregory's teammates in Runnemede. To my dismay, a few guys from Haddonfield Presbyterian who I hadn't really cared for - Carl Tarbell, Lee Federline, Doug Schmitt and George Gehring - played, too.

Much to my surprise, it turned out that they weren't bad guys at all. In fact, I kinda liked them. I learned that the competition isn't necessarily the enemy, they're just an opponent for an hour or two. And the people on the other team are people just like the ones on your own team.

I also returned to playing softball in the Fellowship League after four years in Massachusetts. The *Courier-Post* continued to report on men's softball, so I know some of the games I played in:

THURSDAY, MAY 12, 1988: *David Florig had five hits and five RBIs as St. Gregory's defeated Haddonfield Baptist 17-7.*

TUESDAY, JULY 19, 1988: *Joe Cielia blasted two home runs and knocked in five runs as St. Gregory outscored Martin*

Luther 15-12. Dave Florig's three-run homer also aided St. Gregory.

THURSDAY, AUGUST 11, 1988: *Dave Florig knocked in the game-winning run in the sixth as St. Gregory's edged Haddonfield Presbyterian, 4-3, to advance to the league finals.*

TUESDAY, AUGUST 16, 1988: *Joe Milo tripled home the winning run in the eighth inning and Dave Florig added three hits as St. Gregory's topped St. John's, 8-7, to take a 2-0 lead in the best-of-five championship series.*

THURSDAY, AUGUST 18, 1988: *Max Ruiz slammed four hits, including a third-inning grand slam, to give St. Gregory's a 19-2 win and a three-game sweep over St. John's in the league championship series.*

WEDNESDAY, JUNE 6, 1990: *John Eberle knocked in Dave Florig with the winning run in the bottom of the seventh inning.*

WEDNESDAY, JULY 25, 1990: *David Florig's triple drove in the tying run and Mike Dominick's single plated the winning run for St. Gregory's.*

FRIDAY, AUGUST 24, 1990: *St. Gregory's defeated Martin Luther 9-4 for the league championship.*

WEDNESDAY, MAY 29, 1991: *Jeff Adams, Dave Florig and Mike Grossman combined for nine hits for St. Gregory's.*

MONDAY, AUGUST 19, 1991: *St. Gregory's defeated Martin Luther 11-9 for the league championship.*

TUESDAY, JUNE 23, 1992: *Barry Bruner was the winning pitcher, and Dave Florig, Ken Brown and Jim Cilento combined for nine hits.*

WEDNESDAY, JULY 1, 1992: *Winning pitcher Barry Bruner, Dave Florig, Dave Diano and Fran Catando combined for 12 hits.*

THURSDAY, JULY 9, 1992: *Dave Florig's two-out single in the bottom of 10th scored Joe Denote for the winning run. Denote had three hits in the game.*

THURSDAY, AUGUST 13, 1992: *Dave Florig went 3-for-3 with two runs scored to help St. Gregory's advance to the finals.*

When I was younger, I used to keep track of my stats each year. The better part of four years' worth have survived, some pretty good and others not so good. Here are what remains:

1978 Stats: Record 12-6   BA: .529/HR: 2/3B: 4/2B: 14
Playoffs - BA: .571/HR: 0/3B: 0/2B: 2

1979 Stats: Record 14-4 BA: .557/HR: 4/3B: 4/2B: 9

1980 Stats: Record 20-2   BA: .549/HR: 1/3B: 5/2B : 12
Playoffs - BA: .727/HR: 0/3B: 0/2B: 1

1981 Stats: Record 10-2 BA: .400/HR: 0/3B: 1/2B: 2

After moving to Maine, I joined the Greater Portland Senior Men's Softball League, playing for the Memories of Maine team, which later changed to Branchy's Brood. In 2021, we won the "B" division championship on WEDNESDAY, AUGUST 11, 2021. I kept my stats for the entire season, and ended up with this line:

2021 Stats: Record 13-4 BA: .544/HR: 0/3B: 5/2B: 6 Playoffs - BA: .700/HR: 0/3B: 0/2B: 0

After 12 games in 2021, I was batting .711 and leading the team in batting average. Although it is nearly impossible to do in old man slow pitch softball, I proceeded to go into a 1 for 15 slump, dropping my average nearly 200 points, before going 3-4 in the final game to rebound to .544 for the season.

Since my knee surgery, I have played 25 more years of softball, often in multiple leagues, sometimes with, and sometimes without, a brace. At 67, I still play in leagues in Portland, Maine and Haverhill, Massachusetts. I told Nancy that I wasn't quitting because of one injury. A second one, and I just might.

CHAPTER 37

The Supreme Court of New Jersey issued its opinion in *Princeton Insurance Co. v. Chunmuang*, 151 N.J. 80, 698 A.2d 9 (1997) on August 8th. I had seen my name on court opinions and orders any number of times, so it wasn't generally that big of a deal to me. When I had seen my name, though, it was always as one of the attorneys representing a party to a lawsuit. The *Chunmuang* opinion was different.

To me, the most interesting part of practicing law was the research and the writing. The worst part was always haggling with the other side about money - I sometimes referred to myself an "asset allocator" rather than an attorney, since I was mainly moving money from one pocket (the insurance company's) to another (the plaintiff's). The object of the game is to bill enough time representing the insurance company to make taking the case worthwhile, and then to settle it as the trial approached. That way, defense lawyers make money and plaintiffs wait a few years, but eventually get paid. Everybody wins. Almost all cases, nearly 99%, settle before trial. Only parties, not lawyers and certainly not judges, want to have a trial. Judges employ all kinds of tricks to get the lawyers to settle and avoid trial. Nobody ever really knows what a jury might do.

In law school, there had been a writing competition to get onto the Law Review, and I had somehow managed to win. Of all the things that you can do in law school, probably the best for resumé purposes is being on Law Review. Every law school has one. Law reviews publish articles by students, faculty, lawyers and scholars, generally on individual cases or new developments in the law. The writings often serve as fodder for Senators trying to derail Supreme Court nominees, who may have made an unfortunate comment in a law review article 30 years prior. *See, e.g.,* Robert Bork. Professors, in particular, are expected to be published.

For the writing competition, I was assigned a case commentary on a Massachusetts family law case, *Gottsegen v. Gottsegen*. The commentary was given a title that only lawyers could like: *Family Law - Merged Cohabitation Clause Unenforceable As Beyond Probate Court's Jurisdiction -*

Gottsegen v. Gottsegen, 397 Mass. 617, 492 N.E.2d 1133 (1986), 21 Suffolk U. Law Rev. 317 (Spring 1987). Other than in *The Jellybean* in high school, it was the first time that anything I wrote was actually published. The commentary may have been read by two or three family law attorneys in Massachusetts, but I suspect that that's it. As far as I can tell, no court has ever referred to it.

The next year, while a Technical Editor on the Law Review, I had a second article published, this time about a Rhode Island case, again with an unfortunate title: *Employee Successfully Challenging Commission's Jurisdiction to Amend Agreement Not Entitled to Counsel Fees,* 21 Suffolk U. Law Rev. 561 (R.I. Survey 1987). Again, there's no proof I can find that anyone actually read this one, either.

Upon embarking on my legal career, writing, other than in the normal course of filing motions and briefs, was put to the side until I decided to give it another try while working at Manta and Welge. Over the course of two years, in a prolific outburst akin to CCR recording five studio albums in two years, I had the following published:

Contra Proferentem and the Sophisticated Policyholder: The Continuing Decline of Strict Construction of Insurance Policies Against the Insurer, Mealey's Litigation Reports (Insurance), Vol. 8, No. 34 (TUESDAY, JULY 12, 1994)

Reason Versus Results: Modern Day Revisions of Past Bargains to Defend Suits, Mealey's Litigation Reports (Insurance), Vol. 8, No. 43 (TUESDAY, SEPTEMBER 20, 1994) (with Fernando Santiago, Esq.)

Insurance Coverage Under Surgical and Non-Surgical Professional Liability Policies in Pennsylvania, Counterpoint (January 1995)

Insurance Coverage for Sexual Abuse and Molestation, 30 Tort & Insurance Law Journal 699 (Spring 1995)

Insurance Coverage Under Pennsylvania Law for Allegations of Sexual Abuse or Molestation, Counterpoint (January

1996)

Sexual Discrimination and Harassment in the Workplace: Is It Covered by Insurance Under Pennsylvania Law?, Counterpoint (April 1996)

Partly as a result of doing so much research and writing, I taught some classes at the Philadelphia Bar Education Center, the Insurance Society of Philadelphia, the Nonprofit Risk Management Institutes and the Pennsylvania Association of Nonprofit Organizations, and became fairly well-versed on insurance issues related to abuse, molestation, discrimination and harassment. Most of the lawyers were there simply to get their mandatory Continuing Legal Education credits. A few were actually interested. All of it was in pursuit of clients - making it rain - which is the fastest and surest way of advancing a legal career.

One object of legal writing is persuading courts to a particular point of view or toward a particular outcome. Brief writing is on behalf of a particular client in a particular case, while "scholarly" writing is free of those constraints. Having courts, particularly higher courts, acknowledge a piece of scholarly writing as persuasive or authoritative is recognition of the value of the work. Almost all of what I had published was ignored, or at least I haven't seen any of it cited anywhere. One of the articles, though, *Insurance Coverage for Sexual Abuse and Molestation*, published in the *Tort & Insurance Law Journal*, was fairly well-read and cited. In fact, the Supreme Courts of at least six states (Iowa, Nebraska, New Jersey, Ohio, Pennsylvania, and South Dakota) have cited it as authoritative:

Gearing v. Nationwide Insurance Co., 76 Ohio St. 3d 34, 665 N.E.2d 1115 (WEDNESDAY, JULY 3, 1996)

Princeton Insurance Co. v. Chunmuang, 151 N.J. 80, 698 A.2d 9 (FRIDAY, AUGUST 8, 1997)

Physicians Insurance Co. v. Pistone, 555 Pa. 616, 726 A.2d 339 (FRIDAY, FEBRUARY 26, 1999)

St. Paul Fire and Marine Insurance Co. v. Engelmann, 2002

S.D. 8, 639 N.W.2d 192 (WEDNESDAY, JANUARY 16, 2002)

United Fire & Casualty Co. v. Shelly Funeral Home, 642 N.W.2d 648 (Iowa, WEDNESDAY, APRIL 3, 2002)

One of the courts actually quoted from it. On FRIDAY, NOVEMBER 1, 2002, the Supreme Court of Nebraska issued its opinion in *R.W. v. Schrein*, 264 Neb. 818, 652 N.W.2d 574 (2002). The Court wrote:

Furthermore, the minority rule erodes the concept of legal causation until the requirement of proximate cause is essentially meaningless. As stated by one commentator:

The decisions that find coverage for allegations of sexual abuse or molestation against physicians and dentists do so only through flawed reasoning. They appear to apply what amounts to a simple 'but for' test: Because the assault occurred during an otherwise proper and necessary medical procedure, the injury arose out of the performance of that professional service. Of course, the 'but for' test is virtually boundless, as almost no subsequent event would take place were it not for some antecedent event, and as all events are, at some level, interrelated. It is simply unreasonable to conclude that conduct such as sexual molestation of a patient, which must be known to be only harmful and not beneficial, and which also must be known by the doctor to further no preventive or corrective interest of the patient, is part of a professional medical procedure. It cannot, therefore, be part of the professional service that the doctor contracts with the patient to provide.

David S. Florig, Insurance Coverage for Sexual Abuse or Molestation, *30 Tort & Insurance L.J. 699, 727 (1995). This analysis, with which we agree, echoes some of the most basic and familiar concepts of tort causation.*

The article was also cited by several lower state courts, the United States District Court for the Western District of Virginia in *Horace Mann Ins. Co. v. Barney* on TUESDAY, APRIL 10, 2018; and even by the Supreme Court of Canada on WEDNESDAY, MAY 3, 2000.

Practicing law exposes you to some of the more interesting decisions that people make, as well as to some of the absolutely absurd lawsuits filed in this country. I once represented the homeowners in a lawsuit filed by a 19-year-old friend ("the plaintiff") of the homeowners' son. The plaintiff was visiting with the homeowners' son one day, when he found some firecrackers and various other small explosives in the son's bedroom. Being a 19-year-old male, the plaintiff did something so incredibly stupid, so mind-boggling, that it defies belief.

The plaintiff took one of the explosives, something larger than a firecracker but probably smaller than a stick of dynamite, and started messing around, while still in the bedroom. Harmlessly, he took a lighter and started waving it back and forth under the fuse, not intending to light it, just for fun and giggles. There was never going to be any outcome other than the fuse becoming lit, and the plaintiff now had an unanticipated issue to deal with.

Not exactly sure what to do, and needing to make a quick decision, the plaintiff decided that he would run with the now-ignited ordnance and douse it in the kitchen sink. He almost made it, too. As fate would have it, the lit fuse reached the powder before the plaintiff reached the sink. The resulting explosion cost the plaintiff a couple of his fingers. Fortunately, at least, the plaintiff didn't qualify himself for a *Darwin Award*, which is given only to those who "significantly improve the gene pool by eliminating themselves from the human race in an obviously stupid way." To win a Darwin, the individual must be out of the gene pool, either by death or sterilization, and the individual must have caused their own demise through "an astounding misapplication of judgment." So at least our plaintiff didn't die or sterilize himself.

This being America, none of what happened was in any way the plaintiff's fault. It was all the fault of those *reckless and negligent* homeowners for having fireworks in the house. The insurance company, terrified of what a jury might do, settled with the plaintiff for a couple hundred grand. I would be fascinated to know what a jury would have done with that one.

I also once represented an elderly gentleman who struck and injured (but, fortunately, didn't kill) a bicyclist in the early morning hours, while it was still dark out. The bicyclist had turned left from the shoulder of the road directly in front of my client's car. The police ultimately issued a ticket to the bicyclist for operating a bicycle at night without lights. The bicyclist went to court, pleaded guilty, under oath, to the charge, and paid his fine. A mere detail like that isn't going to discourage any plaintiff's lawyer worth his or her salt. The bicyclist then sued the car driver over the injuries he sustained.

I served some interrogatories, which are written questions to be answered under oath. The bicyclist answered that *he did, in fact, have the lights on his bike turned on* and that they were working at the time of the accident. I never got to ask him whether he was lying under oath in court when he pled guilty or lying under oath in answering the interrogatories.

I learned an important lesson one time in night court in Pennsauken about how the legal system views the "little people." I was doing a favor for a friend of my father. It seems that Charlie's friend had passed a stopped school bus and had been ticketed. He didn't mind paying the fine, but didn't want the points on his insurance, which would skyrocket his rates. So I went to night court to represent him and see if we could plead down to something with fewer insurance ramifications than passing a stopped school bus. There were probably 250 people there waiting to have their cases heard.

In night court, very few people are represented by lawyers. The cost of a lawyer usually far exceeds whatever fine you might receive for a traffic violation, so most people who get tickets either just ignore them, mail in the payment, or go to court and explain to the judge why they really didn't do what they did and beg for mercy. Judges will usually go for a reduction just to get a guilty plea and be done with the case. Volume matters to court administrators and guilty pleas matter to prosecutors. So on this night, the prosecutor first asked that all of the attorneys come into a back conference room to see if they could resolve their cases. Six or seven of us went to the conference room as the 250 defendants sat and waited.

It was the fall, and the *World Series* was underway. The conference room had a television, so the prosecutor and the lawyers watched the game for a bit while everyone cooled their heels out in the courtroom. After 20 minutes or so, we got around to business, and all of the lawyers negotiated agreements with the prosecutor. The lawyers, and their clients, were free to go home and enjoy the rest of the evening. The great unwashed masses would have to wait their turns.

To be a great lawyer, you have to absolutely love it. It has to define who and what you are. I never really loved it - it was a job, just like any other. When I managed to get out, a lot of my lawyer friends confided that they wished that they could, too.

CHAPTER 38

SATURDAY, DECEMBER 5, 1998

This was most likely the first time that I took Dylan to a Flyers game, since he had just turned seven years old in October. Dylan always loved hockey, so we decided to go to a game at what was then the First Union Center, originally called Spectrum II, then the CoreStates Center (1996-98), then the First Union Center (1998-2003). then the Wachovia Center (2003-2010) and finally the Wells Fargo Center (2010-present). Since the name is constantly changing, we just call it "the big house." Naming rights are important in the world of modern professional sports, with banks and insurance companies particularly vulnerable to the siren song of having a professional sports stadium or arena bearing their names. Philadelphia alone has three of them, all bearing the names of financial institutions.

Instead of classic names like Wrigley Field, Fenway Park, the Polo Grounds, Boston Garden or Sportsman's Park, we now have to deal with Quicken Loans Arena, Smoothie King Center, Minute Maid Park, the KFC Yum! Center and Crypt.com Arena. It is only a matter of time before the team names change, too. We could have the Sacramento Burger Kings, the Kansas City Crown Royals, the Los Angeles Dodge Rams, the Denver Golden Nuggets, or the Vegas Golden Corral Knights.

The owners of naming rights can be a little persnickety about their investments. When the Lincoln Financial Group first purchased the naming rights to Lincoln Financial Field, home of the Eagles, I seem to remember them issuing a slightly nasty press release admonishing fans not to call it "the Linc." No one calls it anything other than that.

For Dylan's first Flyers game, we had seats in Section 224, Row 7, and actually saw the Flyers win a game, which usually didn't happen, a 2-1 over the Washington Capitals, behind two goals from Rod Brind'Amour and 22 saves by Ron Hextall. It was the first of quite a few Flyers games that we have gone to at the Center, in addition to going to a couple of Philadelphia Wings indoor lacrosse games and one Philadelphia Soul Arena Football League game.

Dylan even got to play lacrosse at the big house once. With no Flyers, Sixers, Disney on Ice, Monster Truck Jam or concert scheduled, an indoor lacrosse tournament was held with teams from all over the place. Parents could come for free, so we spent the day watching kids play lacrosse in a nearly-empty arena. Maybe it's just me, but I think that me playing midget football in the Atlantic City Convention Hall trumps Dylan playing indoor lacrosse at the big house.

CHAPTER 39

B efore our lives began revolving around Dylan's lacrosse schedule, there was baseball. Dylan started playing with the Gibbsboro-Voorhees Athletic Association as soon as he was old enough, which was at five or six years old. There was a large baseball complex on Kresson Road, known as the Rabinowitz Baseball Complex, with six fields. Each spring, some weeknights and most Saturdays revolved around youth baseball.

While we all enjoy watching our kids play, youth baseball is simply excruciating. The youngest kids play what they call "T-ball," where a soft baseball is set onto a plastic/rubber tee about waist-high for the five or six-year-old kids to try to hit. Meanwhile, the other team stands in the field waiting for something - anything - to happen. The dutiful fathers who have volunteered to coach put the ball on the tee and pray that someone on their team will actually be able to hit it. More often than not, one of two things happens when the batter swings. The most likely outcome, no doubt, is that the batter will simply swing and miss. And will then swing and miss again. And will then swing and miss again.

The second most likely outcome for any given batter is that they will hit the tee, rather than the baseball, which results in the ball dropping straight down to the ground and the batter running to first base, or in whichever direction the batter chooses to run. When someone finally picks up the ball and throws it somewhere, an astute T-ball baserunner will simply keep running, while various fielders pick up the ball and throw it in random directions, as the runner ultimately circles the bases and is congratulated for the "home run," in front of his (or in rare cases, her) beaming parents.

For those kids who somehow still like baseball after surviving T-ball, the next challenge is "coach pitch," where one of the coaches tosses the ball, probably underhand, in a mostly-futile attempt to hit the bat of the kid at the plate. Because we would never allow a kid this young to actually strike out, it doesn't matter how many times he swings and misses, or simply stands there, he continues to bat until he hits the ball or the ball hits his bat. I have seen some at-bats which have taken 150-160 pitches before the ball somehow makes contact with the bat.

The real fun begins when someone actually hits a fair ball. When that happens, five of the nine fielders will have actually been paying attention, while the other four will be doing something more interesting, like picking their noses, tossing their gloves up into the air, sitting down, or watching a game going on on a nearby field. When a ball is actually put into play in coach pitch, it will always be hit to one of the kids who is paying absolutely no attention. In that case, the other five kids who are paying attention will all run to retrieve the ball, which will be resting four or five feet from the oblivious player. One of those players will pick up the ball and look for something to do with it.

The kids who hadn't been paying attention to the game are generally startled when a batter actually hits the ball. Aroused by all of the commotion caused by the batter, and by some of their teammates suddenly running around, they try to figure out what is happening. Meanwhile, whoever manages to pick up the ball after it is hit will often throw it in the general direction of anyone wearing a uniform. Others will pick up the ball and freeze, not knowing what to do with it now that they have it, but getting lots of conflicting advice from coaches and fans. Almost invariably, the batter will simply stop at first base and stand on top of the base, like a statue atop a pedestal, refusing to move.

Dylan, of course, played both T ball and coach pitch. Dylan was, to phrase it politely, a selective batter. He would, for nearly his entire baseball career (which only really lasted until lacrosse came along) take at least two strikes before swinging the bat. This is not the preferred way to hit, since even major league players have a collective batting average below .200 when batting with two strikes. Despite his batting flaws, he was a pretty good player, since he could pitch, catch and throw pretty well.

In his moment of greatest baseball glory, Dylan hit two grand slams over the fence in one coach pitch game at the baby field, which had a fence about 100 feet from home plate. Marc Friedant was coach-pitching and gave up both homers, but it probably took a couple of dozen pitches before Dylan actually swung the bat and hit them. Marc presented Dylan with a game ball, which I think we still have.

Nancy, Dylan and I all liked baseball at this point, so we decided to make the pilgrimage to the Hall of Fame - more precisely, the National Baseball Hall of Fame and Museum - in Cooperstown, New York. We visited the Hall on FRIDAY, NOVEMBER 10, 2000. Dylan was only 9 at the time, so we didn't stop to see and read everything in the museum nor all of the plaques for the players enshrined in the Hall of Fame. I could have spent a few days there looking at all of the memorabilia and photographs and reading all of the displays. But it was fun, anyway, something that any parent and child should do at some point before it's too late. I have an inkling that I may have gone with my parents when I was really young, but I don't specifically remember it. I should have taken Charlie as he was getting older, though. There are so many opportunities in life that we simply miss. He would have loved it.

Youth baseball parents, and fathers in particular, can be trying. Probably not as bad as soccer moms or hockey dads, but challenging in their own ways. In any given town, in any given state, in any given year, there are dozens, if not hundreds, of young boys destined for major league stardom. The only thing standing in their way is all of the lesser talents who insist on playing baseball, too, and slowing down the stars. Voorhees youth baseball was blessed with its share of future professional baseball players. The future major leaguers and their parents tolerated the regular baseball season, when they had to play with the lesser players, but the real action was with the tournament teams.

It is the highest honor that a young player can receive - to be selected to play on the top tournament team for your age. The collective psyche of the town seemed to ride on the performance of the "A" team. There was also sometimes a "B" team, for kids who were pretty good players but not headed for the major leagues, depending on whether there were enough kids interested and enough parents willing to coach and to spend summer weekends at tournaments. While people tried to be polite and refer to the top team as the "Blue" team and the other team as the "Red" team, in times of great excitement or anxiety, they let slip the "A" and "B" descriptors.

Since Dylan certainly was not headed for baseball superstardom, or even just stardom, he spent a couple of years on the Red ("B") Team, in 2003 and 2004. Marc Friedant was the manager of the team and his son, Adam, played on it. Marc and I knew each other a little bit, so when he asked if I would help coach, I agreed. There was a lot less pressure playing for the Red team. It was, by and large, fun, although we lost more games than we won. The first year was the most fun, since we were just out playing baseball and spending the summer traveling to various tournaments. The next year was not quite as much fun, since some different players, exiled from the Blue team, joined, and they (meaning their fathers) were a little bit more into the "gotta win" spirit.

Forty or so years earlier, I had made the tournament team in Westmont, although I wasn't really one of the elite players. I was OK, but not nearly one of the best. I think that there were 15 kids on the team, and I was probably somewhere between the 13th and 15th best. I didn't pitch, didn't hit for power, and had an average, at best, throwing arm. Nonetheless, I somehow made the team. I only remember us playing two games. We had a game at Knight's Park in Collingswood, where I played right field, and we had another game in Haddonfield, which I did not play in. My big contribution was helping one of our pitchers warm up in the bullpen. We lost the game in Haddonfield by 12-4, or some such score, but my friend Rich Gant did hit a home run for us.

According to one of the Blue team players in Voorhees, getting to the major leagues was hard, but getting to the minors was pretty easy. I didn't really follow his career through Babe Ruth, or American Legion, or high school, but I'm pretty confident that he never got drafted or made it to the minor, much less the major, leagues. Neither did anyone else from those teams. There was one kid that we saw play, though, who did manage to make it. There was a tournament being played at the Rabinowitz complex in Voorhees. Dylan and I happened to be there after one of our Red team games. Two kids in particular stood out in the games that we watched. One of the kids had a last name of Favatella, or something like that. The other kid, playing for Millville, New Jersey, was Mike Trout.

CHAPTER 40

SUNDAY, DECEMBER 31, 2000

The last day of the year. The last day of the 20th Century. Yes, the 20th Century ended on December 31, 2000, not December 31, 1999. The last day of the Second Millennium, in fact. The Eagles and Tampa Bay Buccaneers, kicked off the final NFL game of the century and millennium at 4:16 p.m. I was sitting in Section 628, Row 4, Seat 15 at Veterans Stadium, with Michael Dolich, a fellow lawyer, alongside. Mike had gotten the tickets. It was a cold day, 34 degrees, but with a wind chill of 11 degrees because of a steady wind, which would whip through the upper deck of the Vet. I had never been to an NFL playoff game. I remember driving into one of the stadium parking lots and being told that it was $40 to park. I told the attendant that I wanted to park my car, not have it detailed, and drove off to a more distant, cheaper lot.

The Eagles, at 11-5, had come in second in the NFC East and earned a wild-card berth in the playoffs. Tampa Bay, at 10-6, had come in second in the NFC Central and also earned a wild-card spot. Having the better record, the Eagles were the home team, although Tampa Bay was the slight favorite.

Despite giving up the first three points of the game, the Eagles won easily, 21-3. It was Donovan McNabb's first full year as a starting quarterback and he came in second to Marshall Faulk of the Rams in the MVP voting. It was also Andy Reid's second year as head coach. Eagles fans, by and large, hate Andy Reid, fueled by moronic sports talk show hosts who constantly complain about his inability to make "adjustments" and his clock management. Despite those criticisms, Reid is still, by far, the best and most successful coach in Eagles history, compiling a 130-93-1 (.583) record; winning six NFC East titles; making the playoffs nine out of 14 seasons; and having a winning record of 10-9 in the playoffs. Most Eagles fans much prefer Buddy Ryan, who compiled a 43-35-1 (.551) record as head coach, including losing all three playoff games he coached. But Ryan was full of bluster and braggadocio, so Philadelphia fans loved him.

In the playoff game against the Bucs, McNabb threw for two touchdowns and ran for another to help the Eagles advance to the divisional round of the playoffs. The loss plummeted the Bucs to 0-20 in games where the temperature was below 40 degrees. The excitement didn't last long, as the Eagles were bounced in the divisional round of the playoffs the next week, on SUNDAY, JANUARY 7, 2001, by the New York Giants at the Meadowlands by the score of 20-10. Three years later, Dylan and I would go to another Eagles-Bucs playoff game, this time with much more at stake and in even colder weather.

* * *

Y2K, the supposedly cataclysmic computer bug which was going to end civilization as we knew it, had passed without a whimper on SATURDAY, JANUARY 1, 2000, a full year earlier, ushering in the last year of the 20th Century. I watched the new year roll in, waited for the television to go blank, for the power to go off and for the world to come screeching to a stop, all because computers supposedly didn't know the difference between the year 1900 and the year 2000. Nothing. Computers are pretty smart.

CHAPTER 41

TUESDAY, SEPTEMBER 11, 2001

The world changed. In one morning, the entire world changed forever. I had just arrived at work on Kings Highway in Cherry Hill when I heard the news. I watched on a small television for a few minutes with Michael Dolich at the office, and when it became pretty clear that this was no random, horrific accident, which the first reports seemed to suggest, I headed home. No one knew what was going to happen next. I watched as the South Tower, and then the North Tower, collapsed. Nancy, who was teaching at Strawbridge School, called me at 11:30, just having heard the news. We discussed bringing Dylan home from Haddonfield Friends School, but decided that the best thing to do was to let him stay in school. All he would have done was watch the TV coverage, anyway.

I had only been to the World Trade Center once, in the 1980's, when I was in one of the towers, but I don't know which one. I was reviewing some documents in a lawsuit involving eight liquefied natural gas (LNG) tankers which had been built at the Quincy Shipyard in Massachusetts by General Dynamics. The tankers were massive, nearly 1,000 feet long and capable of carrying 125,000 cubic feet of LNG. There were eight of them - *LNG Aquarius, LNG Aries, LNG Capricorn, LNG Gemini, LNG Leo, LNG Libra, LNG Taurus* and *LNG Virgo*. Only the *LNG Taurus* was rumored to be haunted.

Now, I'm not a kleptomaniac, although I must admit that I may have pilfered some candy from a little store on New Jersey Avenue when I was a kid. While at the World Trade Center, though, I did help myself to an *LNG Taurus* coffee mug, which I stashed in my briefcase before departing. I'm a Taurus, so I just had to have it.

* * *

For days, then weeks, and even for a few months after 9/11, we were all a little bit nicer and a little bit kinder to each other. That didn't last long.

At the time, Carole Bennett (*nee* Couture, and later Carole DeAngelis) was married to Peter Bennett and lived in Plymouth, Massachusetts. Peter had a son the same age as Dylan - in fact, they shared the same birthday. Dylan and I both really like rollercoasters and so do Carole and our mutual friend, Martine Taylor. I invited them all to spend the Columbus Day (that's what it was called back then) weekend with us and to make a trip to Six Flags Great Adventure in Jackson, New Jersey. Great Adventure, as I always call it, is one of the great rollercoaster parks in America. By many accounts, it was the best twenty years ago, usually narrowly ahead of, or just behind, Cedar Point in Sandusky, Ohio. Whether it is first, second or third best doesn't really matter - the coasters are awesome. Our guests all headed down together on FRIDAY, OCTOBER 12, 2001, while Nancy and I readied Abbey Road for company.

By pure happenstance, Great Adventure was having a special on Saturday - donate some canned goods and admission was some ridiculously cheap price, like $8.00 per ticket. So we packed up some canned goods from our pantry and headed off for a day of coaster riding. Great Adventure was in an arms race, of sorts, with the other coaster parks, constantly tearing down old rides and putting up newer, taller, faster ones. We rode on Batman, the Runaway Mine Train, Skull Mountain, Superman, Rolling Thunder, Batman and Robin, Viper, the Great American Scream Machine, Medusa and Nitro. All of those are great rides. Dylan, Carole, Martine and I, being the most daring, wanted to ride everything as often as possible. Many of those rides no longer exist, including Rolling Thunder, Batman and Robin, Viper and the Great American Scream Machine.

Medusa was the first floorless coaster in the world, having opened two years prior to our visit. Viper was a nasty ride which eventually was removed since not too many people wanted to ride it and because it was constantly down for maintenance. The ride was incredibly rough, with riders banging their shoulders, torsos, heads and necks on the restraints and sides of the car. It was a little like being thrown into a large commercial dryer at a laundromat for three minutes. The Great American Scream Machine had opened twelve years prior as the world's tallest and fastest looping roller coaster, featuring a maximum speed of 68 mph and seven inversions and corkscrews. We rode all of them, usually multiple times (although not Medusa), but our favorite was Nitro.

Nitro is a "hypercoaster," meaning that it is over 200 feet high. In fact, Nitro tops out at 230 feet on the initial climb and then drops 215 feet, reaching a top speed of 80 mph. The ride itself is more than one mile long. Nitro is consistently rated as one of the top ten steel coasters in the world, and has been ranked as high as number three. I hope to ride on numbers one and two someday. The four of us waited in long lines to ride Nitro a few times. We even braved the longest line to wait for seats in the front car. By the time we got into the front car, it was late and dark, which made the ride even more harrowing, but more than worth the extra wait. By the time we finally headed home, we were exhausted, both from being on our feet all day and from the incessant adrenaline rushes from riding coasters all day.

On SUNDAY, OCTOBER 14, 2001, we were going to get some exercise and then settle down to watch football. First, we needed to have some breakfast. I asked the kids if they wanted green eggs and ham for breakfast. They said that they did, but I know that they weren't really expecting it. So while everyone was sitting around the table and chatting, I got out the eggs, added some green food coloring, and whipped up some green scrambled eggs. Making green eggs was fun, for me as much as for our guests.

Before settling in to watch football, we grabbed a frisbee and headed over to a park for a game of frisbee football. Since the Eagles had a bye that week, I had to settle for watching other teams. We may have watched the Patriots defeat the Chargers if it was being shown in Philadelphia, but I don't recall. I probably took a little nap during whatever games we were watching. Everyone got up early on Monday, packed, and headed back home to Massachusetts.

Dylan and I went to Great Adventure ourselves a couple of times after that weekend. We wanted to try all of the new coasters which had been added, including Kingda Ka and El Toro. This time we were smart and spent the extra money for a Fast Pass, meaning that we wouldn't have to wait in hours-long lines for rides that only lasted a couple of minutes. Kingda Ka had opened in 2005 and El Toro in 2006, which means that we went while Dylan was in high school. Kingda Ka is more than a hypercoaster. It is a "strata coaster," being more than 400 feet tall - 456 to be exact - or around 40 stories. At the time, it was both the tallest and the fastest coaster in the world. The entire ride lasts only 28 seconds, but it is more than worth it.

Kingda Ka launches riders down a quarter-mile track, going from zero to 128 miles per hour in 3.5 seconds. The acceleration actually hurts your face. The cars climb almost straight up the 456 foot tower and drop back down 418 feet before returning to the station. Naturally, we rode in the front car. A few times. El Toro, on the other hand, has the look and feel of a classic wooden coaster. El Toro is ranked in the top five wooden coasters for height, drop and speed (70 mph max). It also has the harrowing feel during one of the drops that riders will be decapitated by the wooden beams overhead. An excellent ride, but not quite the thrill of Kingda Ka's speed and height.

For a number of years, we tried to arrange a trip to Cedar Point in Sandusky, Ohio. Cedar Point has around 17 coasters and was voted the Best Amusement Park in the world for 16 straight years. Five of its steel coasters rank in the top 25 in the world. We never made that trip, with school, work, baseball, lacrosse, college and jobs filling our schedules. There is still time, though, and I really should make it happen.

CHAPTER 43

SUNDAY, NOVEMBER 17, 2002

The first Eagles game that Dylan and I went to together was in 2002, during the Eagles final season at the Vet. It was cold, in the low forties, and misting or raining for most of the game. No wonder Marc Friedant let us have his season tickets. Although the attendance was officially listed as 64,990, I don't think that there were half that many people there. Maybe a third by the time the fourth quarter rolled around.

The Eagles were good that year, and by the time they were finished with the Arizona Cardinals that day, they stood at 7-3. They decisively beat the Cardinals by the score of 38-14, with Donovan McNabb throwing four touchdown passes and completing 20 of 25 passes for 255 yards. Even though he broke his right ankle on the third play of the game, McNabb played the entire game, but would miss the rest of the regular season. The Eagles finished the year with either Koy Detmer or A.J. Feeley at quarterback, but managed to win five of their last six games and finish with the best record in the NFL at 12-4.

This is one of those "why do I remember this" things, but I know that Dylan was spending an overnight field trip with his classmates from Haddonfield Friends School somewhere in the Pinelands of South Jersey on MONDAY, NOVEMBER 25, 2002. We were both watching the Eagles game - me at home and Dylan in the Pinelands with his friends. I remember talking to Dylan on the phone about the game, maybe as it was happening. During the game, the Eagles' second-string quarterback, Koy Detmer, dislocated his elbow, which had to hurt, and he was replaced by third-stringer A.J. Feeley. Miraculously, the Eagles won that game, and the next four after it, to finish atop the NFC and secure home field advantage throughout the playoffs, which would end in calamitous defeat in January.

I had been to see professional football a few times before going to that first game with Dylan. Way back in the sixties, my father had taken me to an Eagles game at Franklin Field. If I had to guess, I would say 1964 or 1965. I'm basing that on conjecture, but my reasoning is that I think that Norm Snead was the Eagles' quarterback that day, and he played for the Eagles from 1964 to 1970. I also know that I was pretty young, not even in high school, so I'm going with 1964 or 1965. I'm leaning toward 1964, since I think that the Eagles lost, and I know that they won the 1965 game. If I'm correct about all of those things, it would be SUNDAY, NOVEMBER 1, 1964, against the Washington Redskins (now the "Washington Football Team;" oops, I mean the "Washington Commanders.") The Eagles lost, 21-10, as Snead threw two interceptions, and his replacement, King Hill, tossed another one, dropping the Eagles to 4-4 for the season.

I also went to a non-NFL professional football game once, and for the only time in my life became personally embroiled in a "gate" scandal. Nothing as big as the granddaddy of all of them, "Watergate." Not even as big as "Nipplegate," where Janet Jackson had her wardrobe malfunction during halftime of *Super Bowl XXXVII*. Or "Beachgate," which saw New Jersey governor Chris Christie lounging at a state-owned beach which was closed because of a statewide government shutdown. "Beachgate" spawned a boatload of hilarious Christie-in-his-beach-chair memes, which placed him in settings ranging from the beach at Normandy to the cover of a Wheaties box to Abe Lincoln's lap at the Lincoln Memorial. Nor was my "gate" as big as "Bridgegate," which also had Christie at its center, after members of his administration intentionally caused hours-long delays on the George Washington Bridge to punish the mayor of Fort Lee for not endorsing Christie. Or "Pizzagate," the widely-held Republican belief that Hillary Clinton and other Democrats run a child-sex-trafficking, blood-of-children-drinking, satanic cult out of a pizza shop. Sounds serious. Someone should investigate.

The scandal that I was associated with was "Papergate," and it involved the World Football League's Philadelphia Bell. I went to the Bell's very first game, a WEDNESDAY, JULY 10, 1974, game against the Portland Storm at JFK Stadium in South Philadelphia. I think that it was my high school friend and golf teammate Bob Siman who got the tickets, apparently for free. He wasn't alone. A crowd of 55,534 was announced. City tax records, however, showed that only 13,855 had actually paid. The rest of the tickets had been given away in an attempt to make the Bell seem more interesting than they actually were. The Bell had "papered" the crowd, an embarrassment for the WFL and the team. By their final game of 1974, only 750 people attended in a stadium that could seat 102,000 people. I did get to see future Eagle Vince Papale, the inspiration for the movie *Invincible*, and former Eagle and crazy person Tim Rossovich, who would do things like bite the tops off of beer bottles and eat them, set himself on fire, and eat spiders. Papergate caused the WFL, and the Bell in particular, to lose a lot of its credibility. The league folded midway through the next season.

Dylan and I went to the final NFL game ever played at the Vet - the NFC Championship Game on SUNDAY, JANUARY 19, 2003. The weather was cold, but not bitter, at 26 degrees for the 3:00 p.m. kickoff. The Eagles were favored, having beaten Tampa Bay four straight times, including the past two seasons in the wild card round of the playoffs. It never occurred to us that they might lose. The Bucs had never won a game when the temperature was below freezing and hadn't even managed a touchdown in the prior two playoff games against the Eagles. When Eagle Brian Mitchell returned the opening kickoff 70 yards, and Duce Staley scored a touchdown two plays later, I turned to Dylan and said, "We're going to the *Super Bowl!*" No, we weren't.

The Eagles only scored three more points the entire game, and the Bucs won, 27-10 to advance to the *Super Bowl*. I still remember the sight of Joe Jurevicius catching a pass over the middle and gaining 71 yards on a third-and-two as the aging Levon Kirkland and Blaine Bishop tried to catch him. With a little over three minutes left in the game, the Eagles were down 20-10, but had the ball at the Bucs' 10-yard line. With a touchdown, the Eagles still had a chance. But then Donovan McNabb threw an interception to Ronde Barber, who returned it 92 yards for a touchdown. I have never heard any stadium in any game go as suddenly and completely silent.

After losing the NFC championship to the Bucs in January, the Eagles moved to Lincoln Financial Field for the 2003 season. We had seen the Linc being built when we went to Phillies or Flyers games and were curious to see what the new place looked like inside. Somebody gave me tickets to the Eagles second preseason game on THURSDAY, AUGUST 28, 2003, against the New York Jets. It was a preseason game, and by definition horrible, but we had a fun time checking out the Linc.

For some reason, I think that Dylan and I went to the SUNDAY, JANUARY 18, 2004, NFC Championship game against the Carolina Panthers, but I'm really not 100% sure. I know that I have seen the Panthers play at the Linc, and I think that this was that time. Maybe we watched it on TV, but wherever we watched it from, it was a disaster. One week after the Eagles had beaten the Packers in the famous "4th and 26" game, on SUNDAY, JANUARY 11, 2004, they lost the NFC championship game for the third straight year, 14-3. Donovan McNabb threw three interceptions, all to Ricky Manning, Jr., and Koy Detmer chipped in one more in the Panthers upset victory.

The worst Eagles game that Dylan and I ever went to was certainly against the Jacksonville Jaguars on SUNDAY, OCTOBER 29, 2006. We had standing room tickets in the south end zone and rushed in as soon as the gates opened. With both of us standing at 5'5" or so, being in front was imperative. The only good thing that can be said about this game is that the weather was very nice. The Eagles lost 13-6 to a quarterback named David Garrard. They did not get a first down until halfway through the second quarter and, by halftime, there were plenty of good seats available, so we grabbed a couple.

As dreadful as the Jaguars game was, the game against the St. Louis Rams on SUNDAY, SEPTEMBER 7, 2008, was equally the opposite. It was nearly 80 degrees for the season opener and the Eagles absolutely demolished the Rams by a score of 38-3. The highlight of the game was Sheldon Brown blowing up Rams running back Stephen Jackson. You can still see that one on YouTube. Jackson caught a pass and was hit by Brown, which caused Jackson's helmet to fly off and various other pieces of equipment to come flying off of him as well. In the game itself, the Eagles led 38-0 before the Rams decided to avoid being shut out by kicking a field goal. This was Desean Jackson's first pro game, and he caught six passes for 106 yards, including a 47-yard reception on the second play of the game, and also returned a punt 60 yards.

We had tickets to the home opener for the 2009 season on SUNDAY, SEPTEMBER 20, 2009. The seats were in the very top row, possibly Section 213, on the south side of the stadium behind the end zone. Although they weren't the best seats for watching the game, they were great for the pre-game show. After the national anthem, there was a Navy jet flyover - F-15s maybe. They approached from the south, so from our top row seats we could look down toward the airport and see them coming until they passed by directly overhead. The speed and the roar were incredible. We could feel it as much as see it.

The game was not nearly as good as the flyover. Despite the game being tied at 7-7 in the first quarter and the Eagles only trailing 17-13 at halftime, the Saints scored 31 points in the second half on their way to a 48-22 beatdown of the Eagles. And we had to endure seeing Kevin Kolb quarterback the birds, while Drew Brees quarterbacked the Saints.

The strangest game that Dylan and I went to, along with Patrick and Sean Carlin, was against the Minnesota Vikings on TUESDAY, DECEMBER 28, 2010. Yes, Tuesday. It was the first NFL game played on a Tuesday since 1946 and the Eagles' first Tuesday game since 1944, when they played the Boston Yanks in their season opener. The game had originally been scheduled for 1:00 p.m. on Sunday, but was moved to *Sunday Night Football* because of its playoff implications. However, a blizzard was due to arrive in Philadelphia on Sunday evening, with a foot of snow projected, and around noon on Sunday it was announced that the game was being postponed until Tuesday night. Ed Rendell, the former mayor of Philadelphia and the sitting governor of Pennsylvania at the time, was critical of the decision to postpone the game, saying that it proved that we were "a nation of wusses."

The Eagles were 10-4 and had already clinched the playoffs, while the Vikings were 5-9 and going nowhere. Taking the place of Brett Favre, who was injured, was an unknown rookie quarterback named Joe Webb.

Making his first start ever in the NFL, Webb embarrassed the Eagles by going 17 for 26 with no interceptions, for 195 yards, in the Vikings' 24-14 upset. The loss locked the Eagles into the number three seed in the NFC playoffs, rendering the final game against the Dallas Cowboys the next week meaningless.

The next year, I got Dylan and I tickets for the SUNDAY, DECEMBER 18, 2011, Eagles-Jets game, a time when Dylan was home from college on break. We once again got standing room tickets and stood in the south section behind the end zone. The Eagles weren't very good that year, finishing 8-8 and missing the playoffs. They had been 4-8, but managed to win their final four games to end the season at .500. The Eagles crushed the Jets 45-19, but the game was mostly memorable because of Jets wide receiver Santonio Holmes. Holmes was a world-class knucklehead, having been repeatedly suspended by the league and his various teams, getting into arguments with teammates and coaches, and having various other off-the-field issues. In this game, he dropped an easy pass early in the game that probably would have resulted in a Jets touchdown. With the Jets trailing 28-3 late in the second quarter, Holmes managed to hold onto a touchdown pass and proceeded to incur a 15-yard unsportsmanlike penalty for flapping his arms like a bird, mocking the Eagles, a very smart move when your team is getting crushed. He was serenaded by the fans with chants of "asshole . . . asshole . . . asshole."

With Dylan living and working in Charlotte, North Carolina, Nancy and I went down to visit him one weekend. Dylan and I had timed the visit to coincide with the Eagles-Panthers game on SUNDAY, OCTOBER 25, 2015, as well as with our 28th wedding anniversary. The game was the *Sunday Night Football* national broadcast. The Eagles entered the game at 3-3, while the Panthers were undefeated at 5-0. It was a very entertaining game, even though the Panthers won 27-16. We got to see Sam Bradford, undoubtedly the luckiest man in the history of the NFL, quarterback the Eagles. Due to a confluence of circumstance and luck, Bradford made more than $135 million in nine years for the most mediocre of careers, never taking a team to the playoffs or making a Pro Bowl. He won 34 and lost 48 of the games he played in. He was quintessential Sam Bradford in this game, completing 26 of 46 passes, getting sacked five times, and throwing an interception.

Carolina finished that season 15-1 and won the NFC championship. Cam Newton won the league's MVP award, but the Panthers lost *Super Bowl 50* by the score of 24-10 to Denver in Peyton Manning's final game.

Dylan and I planned on going to see the Eagles-Bears game on SUNDAY, NOVEMBER 3, 2019. Once we had secured the tickets from Ray Carlin, who had season tickets, I checked to see whether the Flyers happened to be in town that weekend. As fate would have it, they were. Nancy, once she learned that Dylan and I were heading to Philadelphia for the weekend, arranged a little getaway of her own. She and her friends planned a trip to New York. I took Erin and Molly to the kennel, which they don't much care for, and we drove down to New Jersey from Maine on FRIDAY, NOVEMBER 1, 2019. We met Dylan up at the airport in Philadelphia.

We spent Friday night at the Carlins' house, drank some beer and chatted into the wee hours. On SATURDAY, NOVEMBER 2, 2019, I dropped Nancy off at Lori Sotland's house in Moorestown, spent some time on Abbey Road, and went with Dylan to the Flyers game at the big house against the Toronto Maple Leafs. The reason that they aren't the "Maple Leaves" is that the team is not named after the maple leaf, per se, but rather after the Maple Leaf regiment of the Canadian Army. Maple Leaf, being a proper noun in that case, means that the plural is, in fact, Leafs.

We saw a Flyers loss, as we usually do, but it was a pretty exciting game nonetheless. Tied at 3-3 after regulation, we watched a scoreless overtime period followed by 11 rounds of a shootout, the second longest shootout in the team's history. After seven rounds of the shootout, with the Flyers shooting first, neither team had scored. Sean Couturier, Claude Giroux, Oskar Lindblom, Jakub Voracek, Joel Farabee, Kevin Hayes and Shane Gostisbehere all failed before Travis Konecny finally scored in Round 8. It looked like the Flyers were going to win, but Toronto also scored in Round 8. Michael Raffl, James van Riemsdyk and Ivan Provorov then failed to score in the next three rounds, and Toronto scored to win the game. We should have known. Philadelphia is, by a wide margin, the worst shootout team in NHL history, losing an incredible 65% of the time.

We came back to the Carlins' house, talked for a bit, and went to bed. We had a big day ahead on Sunday.

Dylan and I got up early to head out to the Eagles game. We were meeting Joe and Kevin in one of the "No Tailgating" parking lots for a little pre-game tailgating. I had carefully curated a cooler full of New England beers and pumpkin beers. Dylan and Kevin preferred IPAs, Joe and I were going with the pumpkins. I had brought a whole bunch of IPAs and double IPAs, which Nancy and I judged the best of the best, including a lot of samplings from Tree House Brewing in Charlton, Massachusetts, one of the great (and freaking most expensive) breweries in the world. I once paid Tree House $134.00 for one case of beer.

The problem with most of the IPAs was that their ABV hovered around 8-9% or so, while the pumpkins checked in at around 6.5% on average. That may not seem like much of a difference, but, believe me, it is when you are having "a few" of them in three hours. While Dylan, being much younger, handled the IPA onslaught pretty well, and Joe and I handled the less-potent pumpkin beers without too much difficulty, Kevin struggled a little bit with the tailgating aftermath. We managed to lose him, or he managed to lose us, in the concourse on the way to our seats. After sitting and watching the beginning of the game with Dylan and Joe, I was dispatched to retrieve the missing Kevin, finally managing to corral him as he roamed the concourse in a state of confusion. We finally settled in and watched the final three quarters of the game, which the Eagles won 22-14.

Dylan had a 6:00 a.m. flight back to Charlotte on MONDAY, NOVEMBER 4, 2019, so we got a hotel near the airport. We had fun watching the Patriots lose to the Ravens on *Sunday Night Football,* ending their undefeated season. Four a.m. came early, I dropped Dylan off at the airport, and started the long drive back to Maine. There is nothing in the world like father-son time.

At least the dogs and I would have a few days to ourselves to recover from our respective weekends while Nancy and her friends were having a blast in the Big Apple.

CHAPTER 44

SUNDAY, MARCH 21, 2004

The implosion lasted 62 seconds, and Veterans Stadium was gone. The stadium Biz had let me sneak into through the courtesy gate; where I had tried out, quite unsuccessfully, for the professional softball team; where I had watched the Phillies win their first *World Series*; and where Dylan and I had watched the Bucs stymie the Eagles in their attempt to reach the *Super Bowl*. It reportedly took 3,000 pounds of dynamite to bring her down.

Nancy, Dylan and I arrived at Sue and Dave Glennon's apartment on South Columbus Boulevard in Philly well before the scheduled 7:00 a.m. demolition that morning. We could have stayed home and watched on television, but the Glennons' apartment was on the south side of the building, around the 10th floor, and was only a couple of miles from the stadium. We had all been to the Vet many times, and it was sad to see her go. It was rumored that one person had even lived in one of the concession stands for a time, but he was gone well before the demolition. The rats inhabiting the Vet were reported to be the size of leopards.

Sue was Nancy's best New Jersey friend, although Sue was more than 15 years younger than us. Nancy and Sue taught together in Haddon Township, worked together on curriculum for the Independence National Historical Park in Philadelphia, had a mutual intolerance for school administrators, spent hours after work laughing and socializing and liked beer. Sue was adventurous, even taking flying lessons and earning her pilot's license. She and Dave were big Eagles fans, like Dylan and I (Nancy, unfortunately, is a Patriots fan), and the implosion of the Vet was a big event. It had been at the heart of Philadelphia sports for more than 30 years, and though it was, indeed, a relic of the past, it would be remembered wistfully by most fans, although not by those who actually had to play there.

Sue loved Disneyworld and especially loved going to the beach and swimming in the ocean, so it wasn't a big surprise when she and Dave moved to Naples, Florida the next year. Nancy and Sue kept in regular and frequent contact over the years, although we never did go south to visit them in Florida.

On the day after Thanksgiving in 2009 - FRIDAY, NOVEMBER 27, 2009 - Nancy got a phone call from Dave. At age 39, Sue was suddenly, and very unexpectedly, gone. A fairly routine dental procedure, an infection, and an unfathomable loss. Nancy was devastated. Nancy, Dylan and I attended a funeral mass for Sue on SATURDAY, DECEMBER 12, 2009, at Saint Bernadette Church in Drexel Hill, Pennsylvania. The best funerals and memorials, not that any are good, are full of warmth and grace, and Sue's certainly was. There are so many things in life that make absolutely no sense. Sometimes, there is simply no answer for "Why?"

CHAPTER 45

SUNDAY, FEBRUARY 6, 2005

The New England Patriots cheated to beat the Eagles in *Super Bowl XXXIX*. Not that anyone should be the least bit surprised. The Patriots are notorious cheaters, as anyone not born north of Hartford knows. If you want some fun in New England, just mention the Patriots and their cheatin' ways to one of their fans and watch the flailing arms, protruding veins, beads of sweat on their foreheads and flying spittle. It makes for great sport at a party or in any group setting. And when they finally come around to admitting that the Patriots do, in fact, cheat, it is always with the caveat that "everybody does it" or that it's really just no big deal.

The Patriots' offenses, in no particular order, include:

Illegally videotaping a game against the New York Jets on SUNDAY, SEPTEMBER 9, 2007. That's merely the game where they finally got caught doing it. This offense became known as "Spygate." By taping the opponents' sideline, the Patriots were able to decipher offensive and defensive signals, relay that information, and gain a competitive advantage. For this offense, Head Coach Bill Belichick was fined $500,000, the team was fined $250,000, and the team's first-round draft choice was taken away by the NFL on SATURDAY, SEPTEMBER 15, 2007. It was the largest fine ever imposed on a coach by the NFL. It was not determined for how long the Patriots had been illegally videotaping opponents, but the NFL's report called it a "common practice" for the Patriots from 2002-07. *Super Bowl XXXIX*, against the Eagles, fell right in the middle of that time period.

Deflating footballs. This one is known as "Deflategate." Before the 2014 AFC Championship Game on SUNDAY, JANUARY 18, 2015, the Patriots deflated some footballs below the legal PSI limit because that was the way Tom Brady liked them. The Patriots, naturally, won that game against the Indianapolis Colts. The investigation revealed text messages implicating the team in the cheating and found Tom Brady destroying his cell phone before turning the remnants over to investigators. That's what innocent people do. For this cheating episode, the team was fined $1 million and its first and fourth-round draft picks were docked. Tom Brady was suspended for the first four games of the next season. Patriots fans will tell you that it was all a vendetta against the Patriots and Brady by the NFL. That makes sense. What league wouldn't want to take down its biggest star from its most successful team?

During the "Spygate" investigation, several Patriot employees admitted to stealing play sheets from opponents' locker rooms. The investigation also revealed that as early as 2001, there were handwritten diagrams and notes from prior to the AFC Championship Game showing Pittsburgh's defensive signals. Just coincidentally, I'm sure, Belichick had become the Patriots' head coach in 2000. The Patriots defeated Pittsburgh 24-17 in that game.

In 2019, a film crew from the Patriots videotaped the Cincinnati Bengals' sideline during a game in Cincinnati against the Browns. The Patriots just happened to be playing the Bengals the following week. The NFL fined the team $1.1 million and stripped them of their third-round draft pick in 2021. Belichick, naturally, knew nothing about it.

The Patriots have also been accused of falsifying injury reports, bugging locker rooms and interfering with headphone communications of their opponents. How dare people accuse them of such things.

So it really should not come as any surprise that the Patriots cheated to win *Super Bowl XXXIX* against the Eagles. The Eagles pretty much beat the Patriots up and down the field during the first half. By the second half, New England seemed to know every offensive play and defensive scheme the Eagles were running, scoring touchdowns on two of their first three possessions of the second half. I'm not bitter, I'm just sayin'.

The first time that I saw the Eagles and Patriots play in person was on SUNDAY, SEPTEMBER 14, 2003, at Lincoln Financial Field. It was just the second regular season game at the Linc, the stadium only having been completed earlier that year.

Dylan and I went to the Eagles-Patriots game in 2003 with Carole Bennett, one of our fellow rollercoaster riders at Six Flags Great Adventure, and Carole's friend, Beth. Both were huge Patriots fans and drove down from Massachusetts for the game. I had bought a little charcoal grill, picked up some crab cakes from Bobby Chez, and we got there early so that we could tailgate before the 4:15 game. Carole and Beth were in full Patriots regalia, including face paint. Marc Friedant sold me his season tickets for the game. In addition to the crab cakes, we had a little plastic Keyshawn Johnson figurine which we threw into the charcoal after the crab cakes were cooked, just because it was Keyshawn Johnson.

The Eagles were horrible, losing 31-10, on the heels of being shut out 17-0 by Tampa Bay in the season opener the week before. We were sitting on the Patriots' side of the field, and toward the end of the game, Carole and Beth made their way down to the railing right behind the bench. They were featured on the cover of the *Philadelphia Daily News* the next day. The Eagles recovered from their 0-2 start by winning 12 of their final 14 games to claim their third consecutive NFC East title and the top seed in the NFC playoffs. Following a bye week, the Eagles played the Green Bay Packers at the Linc on SUNDAY, JANUARY 11, 2004. After falling behind 14-0 early, the Eagles rallied, but trailed 17-14 with two minutes left. On their final possession of regulation, they faced 4th and 26 following Donovan McNabb getting sacked and throwing two incompletions. With just 1:12 left in the game, McNabb miraculously completed a 28-yard pass to Freddie ("FredEx," "First-Down Freddie," "Hollywood," "The Peoples' Champ") Mitchell, a completely pedestrian player with a bevy of nicknames, most of which he gave to himself, for the first down. The Eagles' David Akers kicked a field goal to tie the game and another in overtime for the win. The glory was short-lived, though, as the Eagles lost the NFC Championship game at home the following week to the Carolina Panthers, 14-3 - their third consecutive loss in the championship game, and a game that Dylan and I, unfortunately, went to.

I next saw the Eagles and Patriots on SUNDAY, NOVEMBER 25, 2007, at Gillette Stadium in Foxboro, Massachusetts. It was a night game, kicking off at 8:23 p.m. on NBC's *Sunday Night Football*. We had spent Thanksgiving in Massachusetts and were going to go to the game on Sunday night on the way back to New Jersey. Carole, who had gone to the game in Philly four years earlier, would meet us in the parking lot, along with Martine Taylor, the other Great Adventure coaster rider. We would tailgate (just a little for me, since I would have to drive 300 miles after the game) for a bit and head into the game.

By this point in the season, the Patriots were 10-0, while the Eagles were only 5-5. The Patriots were 22-point favorites in the game, partly, at least, because Donovan McNabb would not be playing due to injury, and journeyman quarterback A.J. Feeley would be starting in his place. It was also because the Patriots had won their previous 10 games by an average of more than 25 points. Dylan and I sat together in the stands, while the others stood in the standing room section.

On just the third play of the game, Asante Samuel intercepted a Feeley pass and returned it for a touchdown, giving the Patriots a 7-0 lead. It seemed like the inevitable rout was underway, but the Eagles surprisingly rallied behind Feeley, taking a 28-24 lead into the fourth quarter. Ultimately, though, the Patriots scored a touchdown with 7:24 left in the game, taking a 31-28 lead which they never relinquished. The Patriots went 16-0 during the regular season, becoming only the fourth NFL team to win every game in the regular season. They then defeated the Jacksonville Jaguars by 11 points and the San Diego Chargers by nine to reach *Super Bowl 50*, where I found myself in the extremely unfortunate position of actually rooting for the New York Giants to win. On the strength of David Tyree's miracle catch, the Giants did win, saving us all from an eternity of hearing about the Patriots' undefeated season.

The last time that I saw an Eagles-Patriots game in person was on SUNDAY, NOVEMBER 27, 2011, at the Linc with Nancy and Dylan, and we witnessed the Patriots destroy the Eagles, 38-20, on a beautiful 63-degree day in South Philly. Naturally, the Eagles played the game not only without their starting quarterback, but with their third quarterback. Kevin Kolb had been the starter that year, but got hurt. Michael Vick replaced Kolb and also got hurt. Vince Young replaced Vick. Although Young passed for 400 yards and ran for another 40, the birds were no match for New England.

So, I've been to three Eagles-Patriots games, and the Eagles have lost by a combined score of 100-58. If they ever play in another game that matters, I'll probably just watch on TV.

CHAPTER 46

MONDAY, AUGUST 29, 2005

Hurricane Katrina made landfall on August 29th, and Hurricane Rita followed less than a month later, on SATURDAY, SEPTEMBER 24, 2005. Katrina's major impact was on Louisiana, and particularly New Orleans, leaving more than 1,800 people dead. While Hurricane Rita caused far fewer deaths, it still destroyed more than 4,500 houses in southeast Texas and caused major damage to 14,000 more. Rita basically took a path straight up the Texas/Louisiana border.

Nancy heard on the car radio that the Red Cross was looking for volunteers to go down to Texas and thought that I might want to help. I called and registered to go to their training session in Pennsauken. The training wasn't much, maybe three hours, but I did get my official Red Cross disaster relief card. Camy Trinidad, a Red Cross employee, led the training. I cleared my calendar, and a couple of days later, I picked up my Red Cross vest, flip phone and plane ticket for Houston, where I would spend a week as a Community Relations Liaison.

After I returned, a few of us, including me, were interviewed by *South Jersey Magazine* for an article entitled, "Tales from the Gulf Coast" by Lori Garber. She wrote:

> *David Florig is an attorney who left the private practice of law to become 'more productive.' He now represents the best interests of children who are victims of abuse, neglect and other crimes. David read an ad in the Inquirer for Red Cross volunteers and was shipped out in October for East and Southeast Texas, which was primarily hit by Hurricane Rita.*

As a Community Relations Liaison, David's responsibility was to find populations left out of the relief efforts and financial aid assistance for various reasons. He traveled 250 to 300 miles a day, knocking on doors of churches, government offices, hospitals and senior citizen centers to spread the word about where and how to get aid for food and other services. 'The images of thousands of uprooted trees and blue tarps acting as roofs will never leave my mind,' he remembers.

David described lines with thousands of people in need of assistance. 'They stood in very hot conditions for food, diapers, water, juices and other essentials. Some were hit by Katrina, then migrated to Texas and were hit again by Rita. They were double victims and it was crowded and confusing. These were underserved areas with no power, electricity or phone lines.'

He continued, 'I found a woman who was living with her eight-year-old son in their house that was over 90 degrees. The boy was recovering from transplant surgery and was not doing well. I set them up in a hotel with air conditioning until more permanent accommodations could be found.'

David reiterates the common message. 'It was truly a rewarding experience. The Red Cross provided invaluable services under trying circumstances. Volunteers came from all over the country providing a wide variety of services. I was very happy to be one of them,' he said.

Neither the rudimentary training nor the news coverage did anything to prepare me for what I would see. Everywhere I went, there were uprooted trees - not splintered, but entire trees with 10 or 12 foot high root balls lying on the ground, a testament to the ferocity of the wind which had passed through. I did what I could, although I know that it barely made a dent in the suffering that was going on.

More than anything, people needed three main things - bleach, water and diapers. Some were going to be without power for weeks or months, and homes were already getting moldy. So I drove from Houston, where I was staying, to Galveston, took my car on the ferry to Port Arthur, and filled it up with those supplies at a relief depot run by FEMA. Each time, wherever I stopped, the supplies were gone in a couple of minutes. I remember making a stop in the town of Nocogdoches, Texas, and being swarmed by people looking for something, anything, to help them cope. It felt almost hopeless. We lost power in Maine for four days once, and we were miserable.

One of the towns that I drove through was Jasper, Texas, a rural town with a shrinking population of 7,500 people. I passed through, recognizing the name, but not being able to place exactly why I had heard of it. Jasper is known as the "Butterfly Capital of Texas," holding a butterfly festival each year on the first Saturday in October. The festival was probably cancelled due to Rita, but that isn't why I recognized the name.

On SUNDAY, JUNE 7, 1998, John William King, Lawrence Russell Brewer and Shawn Allen Berry, three white men, had offered James Byrd, Jr., a 49-year-old Black man, a ride home late at night while seeing him walking in Jasper. Byrd sat in the bed of their pickup truck while they drove to the outskirts of Jasper. The three men proceeded to beat Byrd, spray paint his face, and chain him by the ankles to the back of the truck. They then drove three miles along the paved Huff Creek Road, dragging Byrd behind them. While being dragged, Byrd struck a culvert and his right arm, shoulder, neck and head were severed. The men continued to drag the rest of Byrd's body, stopping only to dispose of it in Jasper's segregated Black cemetery. The story made national news.

The three white men were convicted of murder. By the way, why do notorious white murderers seem to go by three names - Lee Harvery Oswald, John Wilkes Booth, James Earl Jones, Mark David Chapman? Berry received a sentence of life in prison after cooperating with the investigation. King was executed by lethal injection by the State of Texas in 2019. Brewer was executed in 2001. They were the first white men in Texas sentenced to death for killing a Black man. On the day before his execution, Brewer told KHOU 11 News in Houston, "As far as any regrets, no, I have no regrets. No, I'd do it all over again, to tell you the truth."

I have always been opposed to the death penalty, but I might be willing to compromise on that sometimes.

CHAPTER 47

SATURDAY, MARCH 17, 2007

E rin is from Virginia, or so we were told. But her name wasn't Erin - not yet. She had four sisters - Abigail, Allison, Agatha and Annie. They were all adorable black lab puppies, although Dylan was most smitten by Erin. They were all also very excited to see us, but they were probably excited when anyone came by their cage at the Voorhees Animal Shelter. Amy, as she was then named, was the shyest of the five girls, nosed out by the other four for the best spots to greet and woo potential adopters.

Naming a dog is a big decision which is rightfully made by the entire family. Amy wasn't a bad name, it just wasn't what we wanted her name to be. Finally, because she was born on St. Patrick's Day in 2007, the three of us decided that it would be Erin. And so it was.

Erin grew up to be a big girl, weighing in at around 75 pounds in her prime. We already had Fenway, but two dogs are way better than one, and Fenway was really my dog. We wanted to get another that would be Dylan's. So Erin left her sisters at the shelter for life with us on Abbey Road. While Fenway went by several names - Mr. Fenner, Fennerman, Super Fen - Erin was just Erin, although, occasionally, she was simply called "E." Fenway and Erin would have epic battles with their knotted rope toy, utilizing different strategies. While Fenway would clamp down on the rope and shake his head furiously to get it from Erin, Erin would simply brace herself and hold on, waiting for Fenway to give up and let the rope go.

Erin is probably the only Black Lab who doesn't like to swim. Try as we might to convince her otherwise, she hated going in the water. Dylan and I would sometimes carry her into the pool to try to get her to adapt, but it just didn't work. She always swam a straight line for the stairs to get out, and generally spent the rest of the day sulking as far away from us as she could get, refusing to get anywhere near the dreaded pool.

Fenway didn't care for the water, either, but he had an excuse - he wasn't a water dog. He was probably mostly Rottweiler, given the markings. Although Rotties are supposed to be tough guys, Fenway, at least, was a bit of a baby. He was terrified of thunder and would find anyplace that he could to escape. Often, he ended up behind the couch against the wall, where he would stay for hours even after the thunder had ended. Nancy is no fan of thunder and lightning, either, and she would often end up cowering on the floor in the kitchen with Fenway, as far away from any windows as they could get.

Fenway was cremated at Pet Memorial Services in West Chester, Pennsylvania on TUESDAY, SEPTEMBER 10, 2013. He had been sick for a while, had extreme difficulty going up and down the two steps into our backyard, and for three or four days he hadn't eaten. By Friday night, he couldn't stand up on his own. We were giving him some meds, but they weren't helping. On Friday night, I made the decision that we would give it the weekend to see if there was any improvement, and, if not, that we would do what no dog owner ever wants to do come Monday.

When we came downstairs on SATURDAY, SEPTEMBER 7, 2013, it was clear that it was time. There was no good that could come from waiting until Monday. And so I carried Fenway into the veterinarian's office, placed him on the table, petted and talked to him while they shaved a small patch of fur from his front leg, sterilized it, and inserted the first, and then the second, needle. Silently, he stopped breathing and his heart stopped beating. I stayed for another minute or two, told him what a good boy he was, petted him for the last time, and said my final goodbye.

That time is coming soon for Erin. Although she has always been a pretty nervous dog, the past year has seen her mental, and physical, health decline. She sometimes gets manic at night, pacing, panting, barking and moaning. She randomly barks at "ghosts." The vet prescribed some pills to help calm her down, which we give her sporadically. We also give her melatonin many nights. Her back legs have weakened to the extent that we don't let her go down the five steps from the deck to the back yard, because she can no longer climb back up. And she has started to leak at night. None of those are good signs, and I know that it will soon be decision time once again.

Mainly, I wanted her to make it at least until Dylan came to visit over the Fourth of July holiday in 2021. She did, but we all believed that it would probably be the last time that he saw her.

CHAPTER 48

SUNDAY, MAY 4, 2008

My birthday is on 5/4/54. Nice and symmetrical. May the 4th is a fairly uncommon birthday, ranking 327th among the 366 possibilities. For my 54th birthday in 2008, we decided to go to the Lone Star Steakhouse that was maybe a half mile from our home.

We liked going to Lone Star, since it was nearby, had pretty decent food (including an outstanding Bloomin' Onion), and served peanuts. Once you got there, you could grab a basket of peanuts, still in their shells, to eat while you waited to be seated, or you could take them to your table if you were seated right away. The floor was always covered with peanut shells, which patrons were encouraged to just drop on the ground. It gave the place a little character, with the crunching sound made as people walked over the shells.

The peanuts were discontinued at some point. Although Lone Star claimed that the shells presented a slip and fall hazard, I suspect that the peanut police had something to do with it. It seems that half of the kids in the country suddenly developed deadly peanut allergies in the 2000's. The only joy in flying on an airplane - getting a half-ounce bag of peanuts - fell victim to the nut allergies. Now, we're lucky to get a stinkin' bag of pretzels. There were petitions to get airlines to stop serving peanuts, which they finally caved to. We ate peanuts all the time as kids - shelled peanuts, Planter's peanuts, peanut butter sandwiches, peanut butter crackers, peanut butter candy - and I never saw a single person in distress over it. In fact, they all looked happy while eating peanuts. What happens when someone develops an allergy to Cheese Curls? Do we pull the plug on them, too?

On my 54th birthday on 5/4/54, Dylan had a San Antonio Sirloin, Nancy had a Sweet Bourbon Salmon, and I had a Texas Ribeye at Lone Star. And we ate peanuts. The bill came to $54.54. I kept our receipt as proof.

C harlie died six days short of his 87th birthday at Our Lady of Lourdes Hospital in Camden. Unlike with my mother, I was there when it happened. On WEDNESDAY, MAY 28, 2008, like Marge, he was cremated at the Harleigh Cemetery & Crematory (Certificate No. 26913), and, like Marge, his memorial service was held at the First Baptist Church of Collingswood. Dylan and I both spoke at the 11:00 a.m. service on THURSDAY, MAY 29, 2008. I hadn't been in the church since 1995, when I was there for my mother's memorial service. We stopped and looked at the plaque which Charlie had purchased honoring my mother on the church's sign on Frazier Avenue. The Reverend Robert Santilli, who I did not know, officiated Charlie's service. Lorraine Carlson, who I also did not know, was the organist.

Eighty-five people signed the guestbook. A much smaller crowd than for my mother's service, only half the size, but understandable, since 13 years had passed, as had many of the folks who had attended Marge's service.

While Marge's death was slow and not at all unexpected, Charlie's was quite the opposite. Charlie was pretty robust for an 86-year-old man, still golfing occasionally and living independently in his assisted living apartment. Of course, he had problems with things like remote control buttons and cordless phones, but he was pretty spry nonetheless. He did use his walker quite a bit, and keeping a checkbook was an issue, but not too bad in the scheme of things.

One of the wonders to behold at the assisted living facility was mealtime. Old-timers like to eat when they like to eat, which is usually early. As mealtime approached, the seniors made their way toward the dining room, which only had one door that didn't open until the appointed hour. Almost all of them used walkers and weren't shy about using them. The crowd would get as close to the door as they could, jockeying for position. It was reminiscent of some combination of cattle shoot, roller derby and demolition derby, the metal walkers bumping, jostling and clanging as they tried to gain early advantage for entry to the dining room.

Over the weekend, Charlie had fallen in his apartment a couple of times and had been taken by ambulance to Our Lady of Lourdes Hospital. They didn't find anything wrong and sent him home after a couple hours of observation. On Sunday, though, he fell again and was once more taken by ambulance to the emergency room. I spent the weekend shuttling back and forth between home, Charlie's apartment at the Collingswood Manor, and the hospital. On Sunday afternoon, he was admitted to the hospital. Nancy and Dylan went to visit Charlie. When they arrived, he was unresponsive. Nancy summoned a nurse, because something was obviously very wrong. She called me at home, and I immediately jumped into the car for the 25-minute drive.

About halfway into the drive, my phone rang. It was the doctor. I pulled over to talk. He advised me that things were serious and asked if I wanted Charlie put on life support. He explained, though, that since Lourdes was a Catholic hospital, once a patient was placed on life support, that it couldn't be removed. As Charlie wished, I told the doctor no, but that I would be there in 15 minutes. Oddly, this conversation took place just a half-mile from where I had seen the lightning and heard the thunder when my mother died.

I got to the hospital, and Nancy and I consulted with the doctors. Charlie had suffered a significant stroke and that there really wasn't much that could be done. They did say that we could have him airlifted to the University of Pennsylvania Hospital, but they didn't really think that that would accomplish much. When I asked how long it might be until he passed, they were very non-committal, as doctors usually are in those circumstances. And so, there was nothing to do but wait.

We didn't have to wait very long, though. I'm not sure how all of the logistics went, but by the early nighttime, Nancy, Dylan, Joan Rogers (Charlie's companion of the last few years) and I were all on one of the upper floors where they had brought Charlie. One by one, each of the other three went into the room, which I remember was dark, and said their goodbyes. They all finally went home. It would be just me and Charlie at the end. I had prepared to stay there for however long it was going to take. I brought a John Grisham book with me and went into the room to sit with Charlie and to wait. His breathing was low and sometimes erratic. I talked to him a little bit, but mostly just sat in a chair next to the bed. At one point, I thought that he had stopped breathing and called a nurse in. She checked, said that he was still breathing, and left.

Not long after, he did stop breathing. And just like that, it was over. The father who had taken me to see the Phillies at Connie Mack Stadium, who had let me sit in the captain's chair on the *Dendave*, who got my Opel up and running, who I golfed with most Saturdays as a teenager, who picked up box turtles when he passed them on the road and brought them home for me, who took me to Alloway Lake and taught me to fish, who bought an extra bag of fries at McDonald's for us to share, and who babysat Dylan on Friday nights, was gone. On MONDAY, MAY 26, 2008, we went to the funeral home to make arrangements.

Nancy saved the eulogy that Dylan gave at Charlie's service:

The one thing I'll never forget about my Pop Pop was his good heart - both literally and metaphorically. Literally, he had the heart of a young man - he was playing golf into his 80's. Metaphorically, he was one of the most caring men I've ever known. Even though I can't remember my earliest experiences with him because I was too young, there are many things I'll never forget . . .

Like spending the 4th of July at his apartment. From the balcony (or the bedroom window when I was too afraid of the noise) of the 15th floor overlooking Haddon Township High School, Pop Pop's apartment was the perfect place to see the fireworks. When I was younger I thought we weren't safe because they were too close! The 4th of July was my favorite family tradition. I loved the fireworks, the food and spending time with my family, and especially my grandfather.

I remember how Pop Pop came to every one of my baseball games. Whether hot or cold, I always knew I'd have my biggest fan at all of my games. I remember one time when I was 8 years old after I hit two home runs in one game, Pop Pop was there congratulating me and wanting to pay me for my performance. That may be why over the past few years he has told people that I was being scouted by the major leagues.

Telling Pop Pop that I no longer played baseball was tough; I knew he would be disappointed that there would be no more games to go to. But he even wanted to come to several of my lacrosse games, even though he didn't understand the game. This made it clear to me that what he really cared about was seeing me at my best and at my happiest, regardless of what I was doing.

I remember the times when I was home sick and he'd come to take care of me. Even though I was sick, I used to love when he came over. He'd always pick up lunch for us and we played a few games of checkers every time. I loved this.

My Pop Pop loved the game of golf. When I was just 3 years old, Pop Pop cut a putter down to fit my sub-3-feet tall size.

Another thing I remember is the little tin box of coins he saved for me at his apartment. Every time we spoke on the phone, he'd tell me, "You better come down here soon because that little box I have for you is starting to get heavy."

Pop Pop took me anywhere I wanted to go when I was younger. Sure, it made my mom nervous, but I loved going places with Pop Pop. He took me everywhere - errands, restaurants, and even to buy me gifts.

Pop Pop was a man who cried. He teared up at my accomplishments or when he heard about how much I enjoyed something. It always felt good to know that I had made Pop Pop proud.

For all of Pop Pop's latest years, I knew one thing would be constant - his heart would never, ever give in, and it didn't. Whether it was being passionate or compassionate, my Pop Pop always had the biggest heart of anyone I knew. In the last few years, Pop Pop had begun to forget a lot of things, but not once did he ever forget who I was - my place in his heart was always too big to be forgotten, and I will forever keep a place in my heart for him.

After the service, Nancy and I greeted the guests who had come to the service. It was good to see everyone and to thank them for coming. When it was over, Nancy and I, Dylan, Joe and Julia, Kevin and Martine went out for lunch at P.J. Whelihan's in Haddon Township. Martine had driven all the way down from Massachusetts for the service, and I had been surprised to see her. We ate, had a beer, reminisced about Charlie, laughed and finally went our separate ways. He was a good father, a good man and Nancy's best friend. As usual, Dr. Seuss was right when he wrote - "Don't cry because it's over. Smile because it happened."

On FRIDAY, JUNE 20, 2008, the Camden County Surrogate's Court named me Executor of Charlie's estate, and I set about the sad business of settling his affairs.

CHAPTER 50

I had never seen so many people peeing at the same time. I've seen upwards of 50 or so men urinating into a trough at Wrigley Field or Fenway Park or the Palestra or Franklin Field. But never a co-ed pee-fest.

Kelly Tierney, Nancy's niece and the daughter of Billy and Linda Tierney, got married to Patrick Longley in Vermont the last Saturday in August of 2008. Nancy, Dylan and I made the drive from New Jersey to Vermont the night before. Kelly and Patrick had reserved cabins for guests at the resort where they were getting married near Burlington. On Friday night, everyone basically sat around outside, drank, and partied like MacDonalds.

The wedding wouldn't be until later in the afternoon on Saturday, so people were just hanging out and chilling before the wedding. Some of us went horseback riding on some rather old and tired horses. Dylan took off with some uncles and cousins, apparently heading for a nearby park. When he returned, he told me that I had to put on a bathing suit and go back to the park with him. And so I did.

We drove just a couple of miles to the park, and then had to hike perhaps ¼ or ½ mile into the woods. Finally, we arrived at a small clearing. There were quite a few people around. There was a waterfall, 50 or 60 feet high, that emptied into a crystal-clear pool at its base. The pool was 20 feet or so deep. It was the clearest water I had ever seen, with round river rocks covering the bottom. I think that it may have been one of the Bolton Potholes.

On the far side of the pool was a rock ledge from which people were jumping into the water. The ledge was only about 15 feet above the water, although it seemed higher as I stood on it preparing to jump. It was obviously not dangerous to jump, since lots of people were doing it and surviving. Dylan went first and jumped in. I followed, hesitating for just a moment to figure out which direction and how far out I was going to jump. After a few seconds, I went in. Even though it was August, the water from the mountains was absolutely freezing - no more than 33 degrees at most, if I had to guess. When I came to the surface, I tried to say something to Dylan, but nothing would come out. It was a little bit unnerving, and it took nearly a minute before I was able to speak.

I didn't know anything about *cold water shock* at the time, but apparently it's a very real thing. There is even a National Center for Cold Water Safety in Spotsylvania, Virginia. It seems that anything below 77 degrees is technically considered "cold water," since at that temperature the human body doesn't generate enough heat to keep itself warm, but the real danger of cold water shock begins at around 59 degrees. In either case, the water that I had jumped into more than qualified.

Cold water shock causes the blood vessels in the skin to close, which increases the heart rate, which causes blood pressure to go up. The sudden and shocking cooling of the skin also causes an involuntary gasping reflex, which often leads to inhaled water and drowning. The National Center for Cold Water Safety takes cold water shock quite seriously. Its home page warns:

> Cold shock is a lot more complicated and dangerous than just gasping for air. The instant that cold water makes contact with your skin, you will experience a number of *potentially lethal shock responses.* These fall into 3 categories: Loss of Breathing Control, Heart and Blood Pressure Problems, Mental Problems. [emphasis in original]

> Breathing problems include gasping . . . If your head is underwater when you gasp, *you will immediately drown, and you will head straight to the bottom* [emphasis added]. Before cold water shock was identified as the cause, this phenomenon was known as Sudden Disappearance Syndrome . . . Gasping is immediately followed by hyperventilation . . . The result is swimming failure. If you're not wearing a PFD, you will drown.

> The moment you hit the water, cold shock causes a huge reduction in your ability to think and function. This can continue for a long time - even after you get out of the

water. Problems include:

Disorientation

Fear

Panic

Inability to think clearly

Inability to evaluate options

Inability to carry out a plan of action

Freezing in place

Failure to act

Helplessness

Lethargy

If the water temperature is below 40 F (5C) add Severe Pain to the list.

Cold water shock may help to explain much of my behavior over the past 14 years since I jumped into that water, because I have had every single one of those symptoms at some point during that time. And it does warn that symptoms "can continue for a long time." The next time that I am unable "to think clearly," I'm blaming it on the cold water shock that I experienced in Vermont.

As we were driving home from the wedding on Sunday, winding our way through the beautiful mountains and hills of Vermont, we got stuck behind a bicycle race. There were seemingly hundreds of riders in serious biking gear and wearing numbers. Although they were good riders, they still slowed us down, which was annoying since it was probably a nine or 10 hour car ride home even without delays. Suddenly, in a motion that I can best describe as a flock of flying birds who suddenly, and without warning, simultaneously turn together (it's called a "murmuration"), the bikers drove off the road, dismounted, and dropped their bikes in a culvert. Although starlings are known to murmurate in flocks of up to 10,000 birds, I had never seen people murmurate.

As it turns out, the bikers had to murmurate to urinate. All of them, men and women, squatting or standing, taking care of their business together in the culvert. We were able to pass them now, and watched in the rear-view mirror as they remounted, now refreshed, and continued the race.

Despite the cold water shock and its aftermath, Kelly and Patrick's wedding was one of my favorites ever. I tell them almost every time I see them. Beautiful weather, the whole family gathered, and a great, great band.

CHAPTER 51

WEDNESDAY, JUNE 3, 2009

It was easily the longest night of my life. I attended something called the "Eastern Camden County Regional School District 27th Annual Academic Awards" at the Eastern Center for the Performing Arts - the school auditorium - beginning at 6:45 p.m. The program kicked off with a salute to the flag; followed by "Congratulatory Remarks" from Superintendent of Schools Dr. Harold Mellby, Jr.; followed by "Welcome/Introductions" by Intermediate High School Principal Dr. James Talarico and by Senior High School Principal Mr. Robert M. Tull, Jr.

After the opening festivities came the "Presentation of Freshman and Sophomore Plaque Awards and Achievement Medallions, and Special Achievement Awards." I'm not completely familiar with the precise distinction between plaque awards, achievement medallions and special achievement awards, but apparently there is one. In order to accept their plaque awards, achievement medallions and special achievement awards, the students had to line up in the proper order and parade across the stage to secure their bounty as their names were announced. There were some seven or eight hundred different categories of awards, including:

Freshman Distinguished Honor Roll for 3 Marking Periods
Academic Achievement Freshman and Sophomore Medallion Award - Music - Basic Musicianship (2 Awardees)
Academic Achievement Freshman and Sophomore Medallion Award - Music - Handbells I (2 Awardees)
Academic Achievement Freshman and Sophomore Medallion Award - Family & Consumer Science - Fashion I
Academic Achievement Freshman and Sophomore Medallion Award - Family & Consumer Science - Fashion II (2 Awardees)
Academic Achievement Freshman and Sophonore Medallion Award - Industrial Arts - Wood Technology I

Academic Achievement Freshman and Sophomore Medallion Award -
Prettiest Backpack Decoration (2 Awardees)
Academic Achievement Freshman and Sophomore Medallion Award -
Cafeteria Workers' Award for Best Presentation of a Brown Bag Lunch

Whether it is really necessary to hand out two awards for first year handbell students is a fair subject for debate among school administrators, I suppose. I tend to come down on the side of sure, give the kids their awards, but do I really have to watch?

In many cases, such as for the "Student Council Certificates for Outstanding Service and Leadership to the School," there were seemingly scores of recipients. Since there were hundreds of award categories, across multiple grade levels, most with multiple recipients, it meant that basically all of the students were accepting their awards and then quickly finding the next group that they were supposed to line up with so that they could again take the stage and accept their next award. The scene was reminiscent of Dr. Seuss's *The Sneetches*, with students rushing around the auditorium to either have a star stamped upon thars or to have a star removed from thars.

After a few hours of watching hundreds of kids I didn't know, and two or three that I did, parading back and forth across the stage, I decided I needed a break and went home, watched a Phillies game, took a quick nap and then headed back to the awards ceremony. Thankfully, by this time they were now more than halfway through the freshman and sophomore presentations. The line for the mens' room stretched out into the parking lot. Finally, they got to the junior and senior awards. As the sun was coming up, the ceremony ended and we headed off to work. Some of the parents, who had obviously been through this ordeal before, had the foresight to bring tote bags in which to lug home the awards, medallions, plaques and certificates bestowed upon their exceptional children. Much like at Lake Wobegon, all of the children in Voorhees are above average.

We had to wait a whole year until the "Eastern Camden County Regional School District 28th Annual Academic Awards," presented on WEDNESDAY, JUNE 9, 2010. For some reason, I was unable to attend. I might have had softball that night. Or I really, really, really had to stay late at work. Or I was coming down with an extremely bad case of poison ivy. Or my car got a flat. Or a dead battery.

CHAPTER 52

WEDNESDAY, JUNE 23, 2010

Graduation for the 512 students in the senior class at Eastern Senior High School in Voorhees was held at 3:00 p.m. at the Frank J. McAleer Memorial Stadium behind the school. It was a warm 93 degrees in the visiting team bleachers. I'm not really sure what the rationale for a mid-afternoon graduation outdoors at the end of June was, but we wouldn't have missed it if it were 110 degrees in the shade. The graduation program listed the following scholarships and awards for Dylan:

- *National Merit Scholarship Program Commended Student*
- *Congressman Robert Andrews First Congressional District Scholarship*
- *VFW-ANMAC Post & Ladies Auxiliary No. 6253 - "Voice of Democracy Scholarship"*
- *82nd Airborne Division Association, Inc. Scholarship*
- *Edward J. Bloustein Distinguished Scholar Award*
- *President's Excellence in Education Award*

I know, I know . . . I spent most of the last chapter bloviating about all of the awards handed out to all of the exceptional students at the Annual Academic Awards. I recognize, with some embarrassment and a slight sense of hypocrisy, that listing all of Dylan's awards is perhaps a tad inconsistent. But awards are only boring when other people's kids get them.

Thirteen-thousand eight-hundred and eighty-seven days (very nearly 20,000,000 minutes) after I graduated from my high school, Dylan graduated from his. Twenty million is a lot of minutes, but they flew by awfully fast.

CHAPTER 53

I had a date at World Cafe Live at 3025 Walnut Street in Philadelphia with approximately 160 women. It was the annual meeting of *Impact100 Philadelphia*, a group of mostly well-off, mostly suburban women who each contributed $1,000 to pool and donate to charity. Since they had 164 members in 2011, tonight they were going to award $100,000 to one lucky nonprofit, $20,000 each to two others, and $12,000 each to two more, for a total of $164,000.

I had only been the Executive Director of the *West Philadelphia Alliance for Children* ("*WePAC*") for a year at the time. *WePAC* is a nonprofit organization in the business of recruiting and training volunteers to open and staff elementary school libraries in West Philadelphia public schools, although we did have some other literacy-based programs as well. By 2010, hardly any elementary schools in Philly had functioning libraries, let alone librarians on staff, mainly due to the ever-present financial crises faced by the Philadelphia School District.. Most schools still had library rooms, and most had some books, but no budget for a librarian. I volunteered to take on the Executive Director job, which no one else did, after the previous Executive Director had been fired by the Board. I had only been working at *WePAC* for maybe a year when I got the promotion. At that time, we may have been running three or four elementary school libraries.

Most Executive Directors spend the majority of their time worrying about money and raising money. It is helpful if the nonprofit's Board of Directors also does those things, but that isn't always the case. So I spent a lot of time researching and writing grants and soliciting donations from anyone even remotely connected to, or interested in, *WePAC*. We managed to keep afloat during my first year. Our entire budget, for rent, insurance, office supplies and salaries was only $170,000, so winning $100,000, $20,000, or even $12,000 would be a big help.

Impact100 announced that it was seeking applicants for its annual grants early in 2011. Grants would be awarded in each of five focus areas -

Education, Arts & Culture, Environment, Family, and Health & Wellness. We fit into the Education category. The first part of the granting process was the easiest - a two-page letter to *Impact100* describing what we would do with the grant money and why our organization deserved to be a recipient. I spent a few days crafting the letter and eventually submitted it - as did more than 150 other nonprofits in the region. From all of the initial applicants, *Impact100* would narrow the list down to 25 semi-finalists, five from each focus area. I figured that we had at least a chance of making the first cut, since our library-opening program was certainly unique and valuable.

As I pointed out every chance I got, before whatever group I was speaking to, while schools in Philadelphia are not required to have a library or a librarian, every prison in Pennsylvania is required to have a library, a librarian with a degree, books and computers. I was in favor of the prison requirement, but appalled that schools didn't have one as well. It always got some kind of reaction from the audience. It was my go-to fact. The failure of our schools, particularly schools in low-income communities, feeds the school-to-prison pipeline. As it turned out, *Impact100* chose *WePAC* as one of its five semi-finalists in the Education area. It was about to get much more competitive, as *WePAC* and four other education-focused nonprofits would compete for the Education spot among the five finalists.

Impact100 required that we now submit a full-blown grant proposal, complete with financials, a project budget, project goals, IRS Form 990s, timeline, and everything else necessary to make an informed judgment about awarding the grants. Full grant proposals are neither easy to present in a compelling way nor that much fun to write. There is a whole cottage industry of grant writers and grant consultants, although we certainly didn't have room in our budget to hire any of them. Grant applications often have specific length or word count limitations and each seems to have a particular format in which it must be submitted. After a couple of weeks and many, many rewrites, I submitted ours. The next step was an in-person meeting with the Education committee from *Impact100*, which would evaluate the five proposals, interview the organizations, and select one as the Education category finalist. *WePAC* was invited to bring whomever they wanted to the meeting and to schedule it wherever we would like.

I decided that I would schedule the meeting for the Lewis C. Cassidy School on Lansdowne Avenue. One of the first libraries which *WePAC* had opened, and which we were still running, was in the Cassidy School, and I wanted the *Impact100* women to see it, rather than just sit around in an office. So we took a look at the small library in the basement at Cassidy, then assembled around a couple of folding tables on the stage in the school auditorium, right across from the school office. There were probably three or four women from *Impact100* there, along with me; Anita Allen, the president of our Board of Directors and a law professor at Penn; and Laurie Robinson, one of our original volunteers who volunteered in the Cassidy library. It's likely that Siobhan Reardon, the president of the Free Library of Philadelphia, who was recruited to the *WePAC* board by Anita and I, was also there, but I can't be sure. Steve Mygatt, another board member, was probably there as well, since he came to almost everything.

As the meeting was ending, I remember that I wasn't feeling all that great about how it had gone. It seemed a little uneven and didn't flow very well, but we had, at least, described what we did and how we intended to grow. I just didn't feel like we had wowed them. What happened next, had I planned it, would have been an absolute stroke of genius. I don't know why I hadn't thought of it beforehand, because I should have. But I didn't. Beverly Crawl, who was the school principal and very supportive of what *WePAC* was doing in her school, happened to be walking by, having just returned to the school from a meeting. I asked the *Impact100* women if they wanted to hear from the principal, and they said yes. I had no idea what Beverly would say, but I explained to her what we were doing and I asked if she would mind stepping in and saying a few words. I was later told that what she said had elevated us into the finals for the grant. At least I knew that we were guaranteed a minimum of $12,000.

Principal Crawl told the women that her school's reading scores had risen dramatically in the past year and that the School District of Philadelphia had removed Cassidy School from its list of "failing schools." She told the women, and I have no idea how she came up with this number, that she gave "65 percent of the credit" for that to *WePAC*. Shortly thereafter, we were notified that we were finalists. It was a great feeling to hear that our work had paid off, but we would now be competing with the best of the best - four other organizations which had been chosen to represent their focus areas.

The rules for presentations at the *Impact100* Annual Meeting in June were very specific. Each organization had nine minutes, which would be timed and strictly enforced, to make its presentation to the assembled members at World Cafe Live. Absolutely no handouts or visuals were permitted. At least we were spared the indignity of having to prepare a Powerpoint presentation. There was to be no lobbying during the cocktail hour or dinner before the presentations. The five finalists were:

Environment - *Urban Tree Connection*

Education - *West Philadelphia Alliance for Children (WePAC)*

Family - *Northwest Philadelphia Interfaith Hospitality Network*

Health & Wellness - *CHOICE*

Arts & Culture - *Community Arts Center in Wallingford*

By the luck of the draw, we presented last. Given the "Primacy and Recency Effect," going either first or last was an advantage. The other four finalists all gave great presentations from either their Executive Director and/or one of their board members. Going last, I had plenty of time to get nervous, as did my co-presenter. I had convinced myself that if I could get an emotional reaction from the women, that *WePAC* could win. So I worked with a couple of our volunteers to find a student who was willing to speak at the event. We selected Lady Eugenia, a sixth-grade student at the Cassidy School, and convinced both her and her mother that she should speak, even though it was a weeknight.

We went up onto the stage together after the other four presentations. I spoke for three or four minutes about how many school libraries we were running, how many more we might run if we got the grant, and, of course, the prison library mandate. I then turned it over to Lady Eugenia, who was great. She talked about her love of reading and what being able to use the school library meant to her. She went past the nine-minute time limit, so I had to cut her off, and I didn't even give the closing which I had prepared. It didn't matter, though, because I saw a few of the women wiping their eyes.

All of the finalists had to wait around for the 20 or 25 minutes that it took the *Impact100* women to vote and for the votes to be tallied. We were all then called back onto the stage and we stood there, like Miss America contestants, while they announced their decision, in reverse order of grant size. *CHOICE* and *Community Arts Center* were each awarded $12,000 grants. That left three of us. *Urban Tree Connection* received one of the two $20,000 grants. That left two of us. When the second $20,000 grant was awarded to the *Northwest Philadelphia Interfaith Hospitality Network*, I turned to Lady Eugenia and said, "We won."

Winning the grant was the easiest part. We now had an obligation to use the grant money to achieve the goals that we had outlined in our application and at the annual meeting. On TUESDAY, OCTOBER 4, 2011, four months into the 15-month grant cycle, I was invited to join *Impact100* at the Bala Golf Club for their opening reception for the new membership year. Past members and prospective members were invited to learn about *Impact100* and were encouraged to join for 2012. Part of their presentation was an update on what *WePAC* had accomplished with its grant.

Honestly, I don't remember a whole lot about the reception, but the *Impact100* newsletter reported it as follows under the headline, "WePAC Meets Grant Objectives in Just Four Months":

At the reception on October 4, West Philadelphia Alliance for Children, or WePAC, gave an update on the $100,000 project grant awarded in June 2011. Executive Director David Florig spoke about the **Open Books Open Minds** *library initiative and the effect of the grant.*

'WePAC opens closed public school libraries,' Florig began. 'You may be surprised to know that almost no public elementary school in Philadelphia, particularly in West Philadelphia, has an open library. Many have the space, many have the books, but they don't have anybody to run them. That has been the trend for 25 years - **the elimination of libraries** *- that was exacerbated this past year, with the budget situation in Philadelphia.'*

Florig described what happened after receiving the Impact grant: Summer meetings with 16 principals at 16 new schools, and **WePac's selection of five new libraries to open** *in September and October. The last of these, William Longstreth School, was to be opened October 5, the day after the Impact reception. Florig said Longstreth School's library space had been renovated ten years ago and was beautiful, but had never been used. 'There were maybe 100 books there,' he said. 'We have donated several thousand, shelved them and catalogued them and gotten them ready, and tomorrow morning students will be coming through and enjoying the benefits of a library in their school.'*

*During the 15-month Impact grant period, WePAC's stated goals were to serve 5,000 students in 10 to 12 schools. Florig said that with the opening of Longstreth's library the next day, those goals would be met. 'I know you have high expectations of WePAC,' he said, 'but you cannot possibly have higher expectations than we have for ourselves. **We will exceed what we told you we would do.**'*

'Nothing has changed WePAC more than this grant,' Florig said. 'It put the issue of school libraries being closed on the map . . . That has enabled us to gain visibility, gain credibility, attract more volunteers, attract additional funding. It has probably been the most significant event that ever happened to us.'

*Florig spoke to the individual women in the room, saying, '$1,000 at a time, when pooled, and when joined together with a small, innovative nonprofit that is able to make things happen very quickly, it is a game-changer.' Florig said that the Impact100 grant process '**makes small organizations really think about the great things they can accomplish.**'*

Things got a lot busier after we were awarded the *Impact100* grant. We hired staff and were opening more school libraries quickly, eventually opening 17 while I was there. On FRIDAY, OCTOBER 12, 2012, we opened the library at the Morton McMichael school on Fairmount Avenue, the final library opening during the *Impact100* grant period. I always sent out press releases and invited our Board and others to come and join the celebrations.

In early 2012, I was invited to enroll in the Bryn Mawr College Graduate School of Social Work and Social Research's "Nonprofit Executive Leadership Institute." NELI was a pretty intense course that was conducted on five weekends over the course of five or six months. There was a lot of reading, surveys to fill out about things like management style and personality traits, presentations to plan and group activities. Honestly, it isn't really the kind of setting that I thrive in, but I soldiered through, and did meet some great nonprofit leaders from the area. One of the foundations which supported *WePAC*, the Patricia Kind Family Foundation, gave me a scholarship of around $3,000 so that I could attend. On SATURDAY, NOVEMBER 3, 2012, I was awarded my "Certificate in Executive Leadership."

Cherri Gregg was a reporter for KYW Newsradio 1060, Philadelphia's most listened-to news radio station. I had been interviewed by Cherri a number of times and she had covered a few of our events and library openings for the station. I was a bit of a media whore, frequently sending out press releases, and garnered a fair amount of radio, television and newspaper coverage for *WePAC*. For *Black History Month* in 2013, Cherri was putting together a series called "GameChangers," which spotlighted "individuals or organizations that have used their volunteer efforts and community influence to make a significant, positive change for people of color." When I was the Executive Director of *WePAC*, we were named to the first group of ten "GameChangers" by KYW. The story ran on MONDAY, FEBRUARY 4, 2013. It was my proudest moment at *WePAC*. The online version of the story read:

> *The West Philadelphia Alliance for Children is all about literacy.*

> *'Studies show that if a child is not reading well by third grade, their chance of graduating high school is greatly diminished,' says David Florig, WePAC's executive director. 'Early reading and a love of reading is important.'*

> *It's no secret that Philadelphia's public schools have had a rough time over the past few years. School district budget cuts have forced many principals to eliminate the position of librarian to save money, which resulted in school library closures.*

'In Pennsylvania by law, each of the state prisons is required to have a librarian with a master's degree and a large collection of up to 5,000 books,' says Florig. 'No such requirement exists for schools.'

Over the past 3 ½ years, WePAC has reopened 16 libraries in elementary schools in West Philadelphia, which have a population that is mainly African-American. Four of those schools have since been shut down, but the remaining twelve have libraries that remain open, manned by WePAC volunteers.

'The schools we're in have a population of about 5,000 students,' says Florig. 'We see about 3,000 of them on a daily basis. We've donated about 48,000 books.' And WePAC volunteers have donated 10,000 service hours, acting as stand-in librarians for kids in grades K through 4.

'The exposure is really good for them because some of the children don't read much at home,' says Jennifer Darby, who teaches kindergarten at the Add B. Anderson Elementary School, on South 60th Street in West Philadelphia, where WePAC operates a library. 'It's critical at this age that they have exposure to letters, sounds,' says Darby. 'We give them books to read for homework and then this library exposes them to more literature.'

Florig says he hopes WePAC will not just change the lives of young people one book at a time, but also the fabric of West Philadelphia, 'West Philadelphia was historically the educational and cultural and social hub of Philadelphia,' says Florig. 'Over the years that has declined a little bit. We want these children to graduate high school, to go on to college, have great careers, and reinvest and open businesses in West Philadelphia, raise families there, and really rebuild the community.'

Without a doubt, the worst part of running a nonprofit organization is the constant need to raise money. I had been fairly successful after the *Impact100* grant in keeping *WePAC* in a pretty sound place financially. We were living off of $1,000 - $5,000 grants from foundations like the Claneil Foundation, Christopher Ludwick Foundation and Union Benevolent Association, with an occasional $10,000 from someone like the Patricia Kind Family Foundation. We decided to hold our first big fundraising event on THURSDAY, APRIL 18, 2013.

I scoped out a few possible venues and finally settled on the Simeone Foundation Automotive Museum in Philadelphia. The museum houses an historic collection of vintage racing sports cars, including Ferraris, Alfa Romeos, Bugattis, Mercedes, Jaguars, Bentleys, Porsches and Aston Martins from 1908 through 1970. The concept for the fundraiser was to have sponsors for individual tables, at $2,500 apiece, and the sponsors could invite people who might become donors to fill the table. I worked with my friend Lauren Dodington, who had worked on a similar fundraiser for *Summer Search* in Philly.

Lauren had been my mentor of sorts when I first joined *WePAC* to run its library program. She was one of the people who interviewed me for the job, along with Hannah Godfrey and Dylan Snow. Lauren was the one that I usually went to for help and advice, even though she is much younger than I am. She is whip-smart and very well-versed in both the educational and nonprofit worlds. I trusted her advice and counsel. She also served as my sounding board and outlet for various ideas and frustrations. Sadly for me, Lauren left *WePAC* right around the time that I took over as Executive Director in 2010, but she later served as president of the Board, at my urging, or, more precisely, begging.

That didn't turn out all that well for Lauren. One of the Board members directed some very underserved vitriol at Lauren over some perceived slight. I think that Lauren ultimately decided that she didn't need the grief, stepped down, and moved on to better things in life, including starting a family. I can't really blame her.

As they say, getting everyone pulling in the same direction is like herding cats. Despite Lauren and I coming up with a very detailed plan for how the event at Simeone would work, and presenting it to the Board, it rather quickly devolved into something else. It was incredibly frustrating to me trying to get the Board to engage by finding sponsors and raising money. In the end, we raised around $70,000, with more than $50,000 of that coming from my efforts. Although the Board members themselves were generous with their personal money, they were always quite resistant to reaching out to others about funding. I get it - asking for money isn't easy. Although it was not part of the plan, we ended up selling tickets to the event, which I guess helped.

Something that Nancy once told me has stuck with me ever since. She told me that one of my best - and worst - traits are one and the same. She told me that it seemed that I don't really care whether people like me or not. In my estimation, that observation is dead on. It's a good thing, in that I don't spend my time constantly trying to please people and get them to like me. It allows me to be free and to be mostly frank and honest with people. On the other hand, it can certainly make me seem distant and a little uncooperative. It's probably why I might be perceived as a challenge to work with. Regardless, I simply don't spend my time trying to make other people like me. I prefer that they do, but don't worry too much if they don't.

I had been working on getting Heidi Hamels and the Hamels Foundation involved with *WePAC* for a couple of years, but had never been able to pull it off. Heidi and her husband, Cole Hamels, who pitched for the Phillies, had started the Hamels Foundation to help with educational issues in Philadelphia and Malawi, where they had honeymooned. I was finally able to book her to speak at our event. [*Pictured from left to right at the event are Nancy Florig; me; Heidi's assistant, whose name I have forgotten; Heidi Hamels; Lori Wilson; and Kelly Parker*]. My favorite thing about the picture is that it makes me look tall. Having Heidi Hamels as the featured guest was certainly a draw for the event. Having Lori Wilson, an anchor at NBC10 in Philadelphia as the emcee helped as well. I had recruited Lori to serve on our Board of Directors and Kelly was the principal at one of our library schools.

Cole Hamels was a modern Phillies legend. When they won their first-ever *World Series* title in 2008, Hamels was named the Most Valuable Player of both the National League Championship Series and the *World Series* at just 24 years of age. By 2015, everyone knew that he was going to be traded before the trade deadline. On SATURDAY, JULY 25, 2015, we watched on television as Hamels pitched a no-hitter against the Chicago Cubs, striking out 13 batters. It was his final game as a Phillie, and the best era of Phillies baseball unofficially ended six days later, on FRIDAY, JULY 31, 2015, when he was traded to the Texas Rangers for a bunch of players who never amounted to much.

I don't remember much of what Heidi spoke about, other than her experience working in Malawi. She was, however, a wonderful person, very down-to-earth. Not what I had expected, given how difficult it had been to book her, the fact that she was a celebrity, being married to a *World Series* MVP, having starred in Season 6 of *Survivor: The Amazon,* and having been on the cover of *Playboy.* We sat at a front table and she talked about growing up on a farm in Missouri and about education in Philadelphia. When she was finished speaking, she excused herself to go home, since she had just flown into Philadelphia that night.

I had applied to the Hamels Foundation for a *Partners in Education* grant, and shortly after the fundraiser, we were notified that we were being awarded $10,000. Heidi made it pretty clear that the foundation was extremely selective in who they chose to support. I thought that receiving the grant was a great achievement, since every educational nonprofit was trying to win the foundation's support, but I remember one Board member in particular saying that it should have been more. *WePAC* nerves, especially mine, were getting frayed.

One of the ideas which I came up with at *WePAC* centered around National Library Week, which is held each year in April. I decided to see whether I could find any local childrens' book writers or illustrators who would be willing to take an hour or two to come to one of our school libraries to read one of their books or do some demonstration of illustrating a book. Kids are fascinated with drawing or painting. So I started looking around to see if there were any such people in the Philadelphia area. I stumbled upon the *Society of Children's Book Writers and Illustrators* website and found the Pennsylvania East chapter.

The Pennsylvania East chapter made the mistake of listing its members and providing email addresses for many of them. To my surprise, there were hundreds of members. So I did what any enterprising Executive Director would do and I started sending emails to the authors and illustrators who seemed the most promising, judging by the kinds of books that they had written illustrated. I invited them to come to Philadelphia one day during National Library Week to see kids in a school library. Frankly, I was hoping that maybe I could cajole four or five of them into doing it.

By the time I finished compiling all of the invitations and acceptances, I had around 40 authors, illustrators, local newspeople and politicians volunteering to come to West Philadelphia and read to the children in the school libraries that *WePAC* was running. Beginning on MONDAY, APRIL 9, 2012, and ending on FRIDAY, APRIL 13, 2012, stretched across 12 elementary schools, we scheduled the authors and readers to see a class or two in the school libraries. It was extremely complicated to organize. Each school was on a different schedule and had different classes coming to the libraries at different times and for different lengths of time. It took weeks to put together a workable schedule, but I did it, and the kids and the authors loved it. We repeated the process the next year, from MONDAY, APRIL 22, 2013, through FRIDAY, APRIL 26, 2013, even though National Library Week was technically the week before.

Among the authors and illustrators who joined us were some of the most accomplished in their fields. Although I have forgotten some, all of the people listed below participated:

David Wiesner (three-time Caldecott Medal winner for *Tuesday, The Three Pigs,* and *Flotsam*)

Alexander Stadler (author of the *Beverly Billingsly* and *Julian Rodriguez* series)

Judy Schachner (first winner of the E.B. White Read Aloud and author/illustrator of *Bits & Pieces* and the *Skippyjon Jones* books)

Dan Gutman (author of the *Baseball Card Adventures* and the *My Weird School* series)

Debbie Dadey (co-author of the *Bailey School Kids* series)

Matt Phelan (author/illustrator of *The Higher Power of Lucky, If Wendell had a Walrus,* and *Turtle Walk*)

Brian Biggs (author/illustrator of the *Tinyville Town* books, *Everything Goes,* and *Bike & Trike*)

Alice Ozma (author of *The Reading Promise*)

Eileen Spinelli (author of *When You are Happy, In Our Backyard Garden, Three Pebbles and a Song,* and dozens of others)

Mara Rockliff (author of *Mesmerized: How Ben Franklin Solved a Mystery That Baffled All of France, Jefferson Measures a Moose,* and *Gingerbread for Liberty!*)

Adrienne Wright (author/illustrator of *Hector: A Boy, a Protest, and the Photograph that Changed Apartheid*)

Gene Barretta (author/illustrator of *The Secret Garden of George Washington Carver* and *Now & Ben*)

Donna Jo Napoli (author of *The King of Mulberry Street,*

Stones in the Water and *Mama Miti*)

Andy Myer (author/illustrator of *Pickles, Please*; *Delia's Dull Day*; and *Henry Hubble's Book of Troubles*)

Becky Birtha (*WePAC* volunteer and author of *Far Apart, Close in Heart*; *Grandmama's Pride;* and *Lucky Beans*)

Bob McLeod (legendary illustrator for Marvel Comics)

Zach O'Hora (author/illustrator of *Wolfie the Bunny*; *Stop Snoring, Bernard!*; and *No Fits, Nilson*)

J.D. Holiday (author/illustrator of *Janoose the Goose* and *The Great Snowball Escapade*)

Pamela Tuck (author of *Mother of Many*, *As Fast as Words Could Fly* and *Color Struck*)

Kate Garchinsky (illustrator of many books about animals, including *Belle's Journey - An Osprey Takes Flight* and *The Secret Life of the Little Brown Bat*)

Amy Ignatow (author of *The Popularity Papers* book series)

Catherine Nichols (author of more than 80 books, including *Dolphin Rescue* and *Alice's Wonderland: A Visual Journey Through Lewis Carroll's Mad, Mad World*)

Marisa de Jesus Paolicelli (author of *There's a Coqui in My Shoe!* and *Lightkeepers to the Rescue!*)

Greg Pizzoli (author/illustrator of the *Baloney and Friends* graphic novels as well as *The Watermelon Seed* and *The Book Hog*)

They came in costumes, brought copies of their books, showed movies and pictures, drew characters, answered questions, talked about reading and writing, and were absolutely fabulous with the kids. I will never really know what kind of impact they made, but I'm sure that they did. Although these people usually charge hundreds, if not thousands, of dollars for school visits, not a single one of them asked for so much as a dime. They did it because they could and because they wanted to.

I even managed to get a few local "celebrities" to come and read in the libraries, like Tamala Edwards, morning anchor for 6ABC Action News; Lori Wilson, anchor for NBC10 (and who later joined WePAC's Board of

Directors); Lynne Adkins, Kim Glovas and Carol MacKenzie from KYW Newsradio; and political commentator Michael Smerconish (who brought an autographed copy of Barack Obama's book for the kids to see).

I mentioned that I became a bit of a media whore while working at *WePAC*. I always thought that getting our name out there and creating more visibility was good both from a volunteer recruitment and a fundraising perspective. I got *WePAC's* name in the crown lights atop the PECO building one day. I got up very early, while it was still dark out, took my video camera to the steps of the art museum, where *Rocky* had been filmed, and filmed the PECO lights in the early, early morning darkness.

On THURSDAY, JUNE 20, 2013, the *Philadelphia Inquirer* ran an open letter which I had written directed to residents, businesses and foundations in greater Philadelphia. I secured more than 60 co-signers, including authors, school principals, elected officials, business leaders, religious leaders, other nonprofits, and the Philadelphia Superintendent of Schools. The letter was entitled, "The Best Library in the World," and read:

You Are Part of the Solution

Every state prison in Pennsylvania is required to have a library and a librarian with a Master's degree, but there is no such requirement for our schools. Next year, nearly all Philadelphia elementary school children will return to a school without a library.

WePAC addresses the problem of closed school libraries by opening and running elementary school libraries with volunteers. During the 2012-13 school year, WePAC staffed and ran 12 elementary libraries in schools serving 5,100 students. We are the only nonprofit in the city providing this kind of service. With your help, we will do much more.

'This is the best library in the world.' That's what one second grade student said as she checked out a book from a small basement library run by WePAC. And to her it is, because it is the only library she uses.

Ten-Thousand Hours

WePAC asks you to join us in promoting childhood literacy. Please volunteer with WePAC to support students, teachers, and public schools in Philadelphia. By giving just a few hours a week, you can support early reading and make a lifelong difference in the lives of our children. WePAC library volunteers read aloud with children and work in teams to help students check out books.

This past year, WePAC's amazing volunteers provided more than 10,100 hours of service to school children. Please help us double or triple our volunteer impact next year. WePAC provides these services at no cost to the School District of Philadelphia.

The Fierce Urgency of Now

Nothing is more important to children's futures than reading. In fact, the chances of a child graduating from high school can be predicted by knowing the child's reading score at the end of third grade. A child who is not at least a moderately skilled reader by then is unlikely to graduate. With a dropout rate near 40% in Philadelphia, we must act now. The alternative is unacceptable. School libraries enrich learning and encourage young students to read by making reading fun and books easily accessible. When reading becomes part of a child's life, a world of possibility and opportunity opens to them.

Dr. King spoke of 'the fierce urgency of now.' We ask each of you to support WePAC and our city's children . . . now.

As a nonprofit, WePAC relies on the extraordinary generosity of the greater Philadelphia community. To grow and to serve thousands more students, we ask you as an individual, business, or foundation to support WePAC's volunteers and our commitment to literacy. Your donation is an investment in the future of our young people and our great community. Our children need you.

Sincerely,

David Florig, Executive Director

Three days later, on SUNDAY, JUNE 23, 2013, the *Main Line Times* published the same open letter.

Each year, *WePAC* would host its "Volunteer Kick-Off" to start the new school year, a tradition since before I arrived. The last one that I was involved in was held on MONDAY, SEPTEMBER 16, 2013, at Main Line Reform Temple in Wynnewood, Pennsylvania. We had a few volunteers from Main Line Reform Temple, the temple had been a generous financial supporter, and they were kind enough to host our event. *WePAC's* program coordinators did most of the heavy lifting for the kick-off, although I did say a few words. The volunteers seemed to enjoy these events, where they got to see their fellow volunteers, many of whom they hadn't seen all summer. They always had new and creative ideas for how to make the library experience better for the kids. And with that, I began my final six months at *WePAC*.

I always put together something for our staff, volunteers and outside groups to do on the annual Martin Luther King, Jr. National Day of Service. Usually, we did things like collect books from book drives or catalogue books which had been donated so that they could be distributed to our school libraries. For MLK Day on MONDAY, JANUARY 20, 2014, I put together something different. We had been talking around the office about joining the Little Free Library movement. Little Free Libraries are public book exchanges, where a person can leave a book and take a book. There are nearly 100,000 Little Free Libraries around the world.

We didn't have the money to buy the ready-to-assemble kits from the Little Free Library organization, so I enlisted the help of Marty Butler, the husband of Nancy's friend and fellow teacher, Marie Butler. Marty is a craftsman and artist, building model ships from scratch, with beautiful and painstaking attention to detail. I explained to him that we would like to build around ten Little Free Libraries for MLK Day, and he basically took it from there. Marty bought the wood, glue, fasteners, hinges, windows and all of the other parts needed to build them, cut all of the pieces exactly as needed so that they could be assembled, and wrote explicit instructions on how to do the assembly. He divided the parts up into kits that could be assembled on MLK Day.

Not only did I want our volunteers and supporters to assemble the Little Free Libraries, but I also wanted them painted and decorated. Not knowing the artistic skills of those who would be working with us, I emailed a few of the illustrators that I knew from our National Library Week events and asked if they would like to join us and paint a Little Free Library on the holiday. Several of them did, not surprisingly.

Early on the morning of January 20th, Marty and I loaded up the materials and headed over to one of the schools in Philly, where I had arranged for the event to take place. *WePAC* had purchased paint and brushes, and we brought tools so that the little libraries could be assembled and decorated. With Marty's detailed instructions and help, we were able to quickly build them, and moved on to the painting. The professional illustrators did some amazing work and the rest were painted by our board, staff and volunteers.

When we were done, we took all of the Little Free Libraries back to our office. They were pretty big, probably about 2-3 feet long, wide, and tall. We found places to store them until we could find good locations near some of the schools we worked in. I don't know what became of those ten or so that we made and decorated. They were still sitting in our office when I left. I can only hope that they were eventually put to their intended use.

On SATURDAY, MARCH 8, 2014, the *Philadelphia Inquirer* published an op-ed piece which I had written, entitled, "Literacy Should Not be an Elective." It was similar to the open letter, but also mentioned the fact that 30 years ago, every school had an open library and talked about the school-to-prison pipeline. By this time, everyone's nerves were seriously frayed and there was a good deal of tension, particularly between me and the Board of Directors. We had scheduled a strategic planning retreat for Saturday, the same day that the *Philadelphia Inquirer* op-ed was published.

In advance of the retreat, someone had developed an anonymous questionnaire for the Board to complete. The responses were compiled, and a copy was given to me a few days before the retreat. In addition to some helpful comments and suggestions, under "Identify 3-5 greatest strengths, weaknesses, and opportunities to be addressed," one Board member wrote:

Replace the executive director

Later, under "objectives," someone (maybe the same person, maybe not), wrote:

Find a more inspirational and collaborative executive director

As you might imagine, that didn't land well with me. I wasn't thrilled to read those anonymous comments, and to this day I don't know who wrote them, although I have a couple of educated guesses. In a business setting, I am not necessarily one who minces his words. I spoke to the president of the board and told him that the board should begin the strategic planning meeting without me and decide whether they wanted me to continue as the Executive Director or not. I also told him that I did not want to be participating in a process in which I didn't know who wanted me there and who didn't. I told him that I would be in the *WePAC* office on Saturday morning and would wait for him to call with their decision. If they wanted me to continue, I could then get to the meeting in a couple of minutes. If not, no need for me to go. The president told me that it would only take a half hour or so, and that he would call.

I went into the office on Saturday morning and waited. One hour . . . two hours . . . three hours. After nearly four hours, the president called, told me nothing, and said that he would come by on Monday to talk. In rather certain terms, I told him that I had been waiting all day for an answer and that I found it very unfair to have to wait two more days. I strongly suggested that he come to the office immediately, which he did. Although he was very hesitant to talk about what had transpired, I finally just asked whether they wanted to replace me or not - and it turns out that they did. Although I was never told why I was being replaced (a nice euphemism for fired), I suspect that my enduring unhappiness with the board was both quite apparent and unappreciated. I informed him that I was willing to stay on for a limited period to help with the transition and to negotiate a separation agreement.

Although the board president was anxious to leave, I told him that there were some things which had to be taken care of immediately, such as changing the usernames and passwords for all of our financial and accounting programs. When there is an acrimonious parting of employment ways, the last thing any organization needs is a disgruntled employee with access to the money. The president said that we could do all of that the next week, but I said that we would do it right then and there. So we went into my office, changed all of the passwords to all of the financial accounts and started to plan my departure.

You might think that I wouldn't be working on weekends any longer, but on SUNDAY, MARCH 9, 2014, I went to the office and started writing exit memos to make sure that I wasn't going to be on the hook for anything that might be missing or that might go wrong. By the time that I left *WePAC* for good, I had written 26 of them.

During this first week after the board decided to get rid of me, I was working on a Separation and Release of Claims Agreement with the board, specifically with the president. My belief is that they were very much afraid that I would sue *WePAC*, in either the form of an age or racial discrimination claim, or both. We reached an agreement on FRIDAY, MARCH 14, 2014, which both parties signed. *WePAC* gave me pretty much everything that I asked for in terms of payment for accrued vacation days, IRA contribution and salary payment beyond my last day of work. Maybe my allusion to a lawsuit worked, or maybe they were just so anxious to get rid of me that they would have given me anything I asked for. We agreed that my last day at work would be TUESDAY, APRIL 15, 2014, and so it was.

During that final month, I was making sure to document every single thing I did and every conversation I had. If there was a board meeting, for example, I made sure to ask if I was expected to attend (which, fortunately, I wasn't) and confirmed the response in an email. The rest of my tenure was basically spent deferring on making any decisions, except for the most minor ones, sitting in my office counting the days, answering any questions people had and churning out CYA memos. On MONDAY, APRIL 15, 2014, I left my keys and closed the door behind me.

Amidst all of this chaos and mistrust, *WePAC* was in the middle of planning its second major fundraising gala, this time at the Merion Tribute House. By the grace of God, I wasn't very heavily involved in planning it even before all of this hit the fan, and wasn't involved at all afterwards. My one contribution was securing Lauren Hart to attend and sing a couple of songs. Lauren Hart is an incredibly talented singer and musician who, for years, has sung the National Anthem or "God Bless America" before Flyers' games. She also has written music for TV shows like *Joan of Arcadia* (one of my personal favorite shows) and *Party of Five*. Somehow, I managed to convince her to play some music at the gala. The sad thing is, I never got to see her perform. The board and I decided that it would be best if I didn't attend.

As my last day wound down, I chatted with the employees, all of which I had hired, and said goodbye. The board president was in the office, too, as he had been nearly every day for the past month. We said icy goodbyes, and I left. I never heard from anyone on the board (other than the president) from the Saturday I was told I was being "replaced" until this day. Not a "thanks," not a "sorry it didn't work out," not a "good luck."

Nothing, even though I was the one who had recruited almost all of them to the board, including two school principals where *WePAC* was running their libraries. On the other hand, I never thanked them for their service or wished them good luck, either.

I had been the longest-tenured Executive Director in the organization's history, and I think that they have burned through about five more in the seven years since I left. Looking back, I'm proud of the work I did and what we accomplished. The only person from my *WePAC* days that I have stayed in any contact with is Lauren, without whom I probably wouldn't have gotten the job or survived in it for as long as I did. In fairness, though, that's just my side of the story, and every story has two sides. I'm sure that the board's side would be quite different (but far less accurate). Am I bitter? Yeah, maybe a little bit.

CHAPTER 54

The Lee-Jackson Lacrosse Classic is the annual fall lacrosse game between Virginia Military Institute and Washington and Lee University in Lexington, Virginia, and the 26th annual game was held in 2012. College lacrosse is a spring sport, but the NCAA allows teams some limited practice time in the fall. Teams are also allowed to play one game against another school, and it is traditional for VMI and WLU to play each fall. Unfortunately, the game is named after two Confederate generals, but that's another story for another time. Robert E. Lee had been the president of Washington College (later Washington and Lee University) after the Civil War and Thomas "Stonewall" Jackson had taught at VMI. Lee is buried beneath Lee Chapel at Washington and Lee University and Jackson is buried about a mile away in Lexington. Regardless, they *were*, nonetheless, Confederate generals.

From the time that Dylan was in sixth grade, our lives (and finances) revolved around lacrosse. He was always involved with some kind of team or going to some kind of lacrosse camp or tournament. For the first couple of years, he played on the Voorhees town team, known as the Vortex. Back then, he was splitting time between playing attack and playing goalie. Later on with the Vortex, he transitioned to full-time goalie, partly because he was very good at it and partly because nobody else really wanted to play goalie. Brendan Canavan and Jeff Grabowski, who each had boys Dylan's age, had started the town program, and Dylan was introduced to the game when he and Patrick Carlin went to a "Learn to Play" clinic.

The summer before his freshman year of high school, in 2006, Dylan joined All State Lacrosse, a travel team which went to four or five tournaments in the mid-Atlantic during the summer. A few of his future teammates at Eastern High School also played for All State, alongside kids from other towns. By the time the school year rolled around, Dylan had decided that he wanted to be a goalie and play in high school. In 2007, he attended the Chris Sanderson Goalie Camp in Pennsylvania. Chris Sanderson was a lacrosse legend and Canadian lacrosse hero. He played for

Canada in the world lacrosse championships in 1998, 2002, 2006 and 2010, helping them win gold in 2006. Three times he was named Outstanding Goalie in the tournament, including in 2010, while suffering from brain cancer. Dylan loved going to Sanderson's camp. Just two years after being named Outstanding Goalie in the world championships, Sanderson passed away on THURSDAY, JUNE 28, 2012 at the age of 38. Dylan continued his summer travel schedule with All State in the summer of 2007.

By the summer of 2008, Dylan had a year of JV lacrosse and a year as the full-time varsity goalie for Eastern under his lacrosse belt. He continued to play for All State Lacrosse that summer, playing in LaxMax in Maryland, Jersey Shootout in New Jersey, STX Invitational, Syracuse Shootout in New York, East Coast Lacrosse Wars, Summer Sizzle in Maryland and Rutgers MVP in New Jersey. We also found the time to send him to the Players Choice Chris Surran Goalie Camp in Massachusetts from MONDAY, JULY 28, 2008, to THURSDAY, JULY 31, 2008. Dylan was most impressed by the college kids he had watched on TV serving as coaches, like Kip Turner, the goalie from the University of Virginia.

If anything, the summer of 2009, before Dylan's senior year, was even busier. This was the summer when we would be narrowing the list of possible colleges and trying for one final time to get noticed by the coaches. We had already made a DVD and sent it around with Dylan's transcript to a long list of possible schools. The next step was getting in front of the coaches so that they could see him play. Dylan was scheduled to play in two showcase camps - Top 205 in Maryland and Elite 180 in Keene, New Hampshire. Top 205 was attended by coaches from virtually every college lacrosse program in the country and was designed for serious high school players who wanted to play college lacrosse. To get into Top 205, Dylan needed a letter from Coach Picot and an invitation, both of which he got. I dropped him off for the start of camp on WEDNESDAY, JUNE 24, 2009.

Top 205 ended on the same day that Elite 180 in New Hampshire started, SATURDAY, JUNE 27, 2009. So I picked Dylan up in Maryland and drove to New Hampshire, where we checked in late. Elite 180 was a little different from Top 205 in that Elite 180 was geared more toward smaller, Division III, liberal arts schools. The NESCAC ("New England Small College Athletic Conference") was heavily represented, as was the North Coast Athletic Conference and the Centennial Conference. Although I hadn't stayed to watch all of Dylan's games at Top 205, I did stay for the entire Elite 180 camp. The Kenyon College coach, Doug Misarti, seemed particularly interested in Dylan. We had visited Kenyon, along with four other Ohio schools - Oberlin, Ohio Wesleyan, Wooster and Denison - on a whirlwind trip over the winter. After seven days of lacrosse camps, Dylan and I headed home on TUESDAY, JUNE 30, 2009.

Dylan no longer played summer lacrosse with All State Lacrosse, having joined Braveheart Lacrosse for the 2009 summer season. Once again, we spent most summer weekends at one lacrosse tournament or another.

As a recruit, Dylan was invited to the Lee-Jackson Classic to stand on the sideline with Washington and Lee for the 23rd Lee-Jackson Classic on FRIDAY, OCTOBER 2, 2009, at Wilson Field, which Nancy and I attended. Nancy, Dylan and I also traveled to Lancaster, Pennsylvania, on SATURDAY, MARCH 13, 2010, for a game that Washington and Lee was playing against Franklin and Marshall. By this time, Dylan had been accepted at W&L and was getting ready to start his senior season in high school. W&L was ranked #8 in the country heading into the game, but lost 7-5 at Tylus Field on the Franklin and Marshall campus.

Nancy and I traveled down to Lexington for the 24th Annual Lee-Jackson Classic on SATURDAY, OCTOBER 23, 2010, during Dylan's freshman year. Joe and Julia also went to the game with us, which was held at Foster Stadium on the VMI campus at 1:30 p.m. I also attended the 25th Lee-Jackson Classic on FRIDAY, OCTOBER 21, 2011, at Wilson Field during Dylan's sophomore year.

Before settling on Washington and Lee, Dylan had visited Amherst College, Catholic University, The College of Wooster, Connecticut College, Denison University (after visiting Denison, Dylan received a handwritten note from Head Coach Mike Caravana, which read, "Dylan, Here's a note to wish you all the best with your upcoming games. Think Denison as you move forward with your college choices . . . We have you at the top of our recruiting list! All the best, Coach Caravana"), Drexel University, Dickinson College, Franklin and Marshall College, Hamilton College, Haverford College, Kenyon College, Muhlenberg College, Oberlin College, St. Mary's College of Maryland, Swarthmore College, Trinity College, Wesleyan University and Williams College. Washington and Lee was the next to last recruiting visit we made in the summer of 2009. Mike Kruger was the Defensive Coordinator and Recruiting Coordinator and had been an All-American goalie at Fairfield University. He took Dylan and I on a tour of the athletic facilities and seemed to really want Dylan.

By the time we were done with the admissions tour and the recruiting visit with Kruger, Dylan had made up his mind. Washington and Lee it would be. Since only Dylan and I went on the first trip to W&L, we went back three weeks later with Nancy. While Dylan was doing an interview with Admissions, Nancy and I met with Financial Aid. We all took the Admissions tour again and had lunch with Gene McCabe, the Head Coach. Nancy didn't care much for him, and he seemed much more interested in eating than in recruiting.

Dylan applied early decision to Washington and Lee, which meant that. if accepted, he was obligated to attend. High school kids who really know where they want to go to college often apply for early decision, since it somewhat increases the odds of being accepted. College coaches like athletes that they recruit to apply for early decision, since they find out earlier who will be granted admission and be on their teams.

The road to Washington and Lee was paved with four years of high school lacrosse. As a freshman in high school, Dylan played goalie for the junior varsity team, splitting time with the other goalie, sophomore Derek Metallo. The JV team played the following games:

THURSDAY, APRIL 5, 2007 versus Cherokee

TUESDAY, APRIL 10, 2007 at Cherry Hill East

THURSDAY, APRIL 12, 2007 at Clearview

SATURDAY, APRIL 14, 2007 versus Washington Township

MONDAY, APRIL 16, 2007 versus Rancocas Valley

WEDNESDAY, APRIL 18, 2007 at St. Augustine Prep

TUESDAY, APRIL 24, 2007 at Washington Township

THURSDAY, APRIL 26, 2007 at Cherokee

SATURDAY, APRIL 28, 2007 at Lenape

WEDNESDAY, MAY 2, 2007 versus Cherry Hill East

FRIDAY, MAY 4, 2007 at Rancocas Valley

SATURDAY, MAY 5, 2007 versus Holy Cross

MONDAY, MAY 7, 2007 at Seneca

WEDNESDAY, MAY 9, 2007 versus Lenape

THURSDAY, MAY 10, 2007 at Cherry Hill West

WEDNESDAY, MAY 16, 2007 versus Camden Catholic

FRIDAY, MAY 18, 2007 at Shawnee

Dylan's high school lacrosse career went far better than we could have imagined. He became the starting goalie before his sophomore season and played virtually every minute of every game for three years. Eastern High School was good at lacrosse, always in the Top 10 in South Jersey, but rarely quite good enough to beat the likes of Shawnee, Moorestown or St. Augustine Prep, except for Dylan's freshman year, when Eastern had ended the season ranked No. 1 in South Jersey, finishing at 18-3 and winning two state tournament games.

The *Courier-Post* ranked Eastern No. 3 heading into the 2008 season, with this preview:

*No team lost more talent than the Vikings, last year's No. 1
team. But this is an established program that should reload
as much as rebuild. Senior attacks Mike Lane (20 goals in
2007) and Steve Adelman (47) lead the way, while senior
Josh Reese anchors a sturdy defense. Look for a big impact
from junior attack Tyler Costantino.*

Nancy and I went to virtually every one of Dylan's high school lacrosse
games. Steve Picot, the lacrosse coach at Eastern, had told me after the
preseason parents' meeting that Dylan had beaten out the other kid trying
out for goalie, and would be the starter to begin his sophomore year.
Eastern's first game of the 2008 season was at Kingsway High School, on
WEDNESDAY, APRIL 2, 2008. Eastern won 12-0, with Dylan making three
saves, picking up three ground balls, and recording a shutout in his first
high school varsity game. When the game was over, I walked onto the field
and picked up the game ball. Dylan still has that ball. Our lives for the
next two months would revolve around going to work, picking Dylan up
after practices, going to games, and bringing him home afterwards.

As nearly as I can figure it out, the rest of the 2008 Eastern season went
like this:

THURSDAY, APRIL 3, 2008: **Eastern 12**, Cherry Hill West 10

SATURDAY, APRIL 5, 2008: **Eastern 8**, Cherokee 5. Eastern
got three goals from Tyler Costantino, two from Steve
Adelman, and one each from Chris DiNote, Dylan Fox, and
Mike Lane. Dylan made 12 saves and picked up three
ground balls.

TUESDAY, APRIL 8, 2008: **Eastern 14**, Cherry Hill East 5

THURSDAY, APRIL 10, 2008: **Eastern 11**, Clearview 8. Dylan
made 13 saves and picked up three ground balls.

MONDAY, APRIL 14, 2008: **Eastern 15**, Rancocas Valley 1.
Dylan recorded four saves.

WEDNESDAY, APRIL 16, 2008: **Eastern 9**, Holy Cross 2

MONDAY, APRIL 21, 2008: **Eastern 12**, Washington
Township 7

THURSDAY, APRIL 24, 2008: Cherokee 13, **Eastern 6**

SATURDAY, APRIL 26, 2008: Lenape 7, **Eastern 6**

TUESDAY, APRIL 29, 2008: **Eastern 9**, West Deptford 5. The game was reported in the *Philadelphia Inquirer* as, "Eastern improved to 9-2 with a 9-5 victory over visiting West Deptford. Steve Adelman's four goals and Mike Lane's three accounted for most of the Vikings' offense, and goalie Dylan Florig made 15 saves."

WEDNESDAY, APRIL 30, 2008: **Eastern 16**, Cherry Hill East 0

FRIDAY, MAY 2, 2008: **Eastern 17**, Rancocas Valley 2

MONDAY, MAY 5, 2008: **Eastern 12**, Seneca 5. Tyler Costantino scored four goals and Dylan made six saves.

WEDNESDAY, MAY 7, 2008: **Eastern 12**, Lenape 5

THURSDAY, MAY 8, 2008: **Eastern 17**, Washington Township 5

MONDAY, MAY 12, 2008: St. Augustine Prep 8, **Eastern 5**. The *Philadelphia Inquirer* reported:

There is no official title as the best boys' lacrosse team in South Jersey. Unofficially, the heavyweight belt belongs to St. Augustine Prep. The Hermits claimed the crown yesterday with an imposing 8-5 victory over Eastern on a cold, rainy afternoon on the Vikings' home field.

With victories over Eastern (14-3) as well as Burlington County powers Shawnee and Moorestown, St. Augustine has bragging rights as the best team in the area, at least in the regular season . . . The NJSIAA boys' lacrosse state tournament will begin next week, with St. Augustine likely to be the No. 2 seed in Non-Public A.

Chris DiNote and Dylan Fox each had a goal and an assist and sophomore goalie Dylan Florig made 13 saves for Eastern, which rallied in the second quarter to forge a 3-3 tie at halftime.

<u>WEDNESDAY, MAY 14, 2008</u>: **Eastern 14,** Camden Catholic 4

<u>FRIDAY, MAY 16, 2008</u>: Shawnee 8, **Eastern 6**

Eastern finished the regular season with a record of 15-5 and qualified for the New Jersey state playoffs. The playoffs back then were statewide, not regional, so it was possible to play a team from two hours away. Eastern was in Group IV, the group for the largest public schools in the state. The first round of the playoffs was against Toms River North. In his first playoff game, on WEDNESDAY, MAY 21, 2008, Dylan made 11 saves in a 7-4 Eastern win. The *Courier-Post* reported on the game under the caption, "Easier said than done":

Everyone who watches lacrosse knows that goalies are a little crazy. With a small rubber ball coming at them multiple times at speeds capable of reaching 100 miles per hour, they have to be.

*No. 5 Eastern's goalie **Dylan Florig** is one of those people. At about 5-8, Florig barely fills up the net. But that didn't stop him from making 11 saves in his postseason debut. 'His size doesn't really fill up the net,' said Eastern coach **Steve Picot**. 'But his quick hands and good reaction skills make up for what he lacks in size.'*

Florig held Toms River North to just four goals in Eastern's 7-4 victory in the first round of the South Jersey Group 4 playoffs. 'He has been doing great every game,' said Picot.

'And with over 156 saves and an average of only five goals against, he has kept us in a lot of big games.'

Florig has a knack for handling opposing players one-on-one. He did it twice against Toms River North, and both times came up with a save. 'He is really good when it is just him and the shooter,' said Picot. 'He will sacrifice his body and do whatever it takes to make the save.'

Florig didn't only earn his coach's respect, but the respect of his senior defensemen. 'He has seniors in front of him and they listen to every word he says,' said Picot. 'He controls our defense and they have the utmost respect for him. It's a great atmosphere.'

For the record, Dylan is not even close to 5'8". The next game wouldn't be quite as easy. Eastern had to travel nearly 100 miles north to play perpetual lacrosse powerhouse Montclair. Schools in North Jersey, like Montclair, had been playing high school lacrosse for decades. High school boys' lacrosse didn't exist in South Jersey until recently, and didn't have the youth programs as feeders that the northern schools did. As a result, North Jersey schools dominated South Jersey when they met in the playoffs. That was certainly the case when Eastern had to play Montclair. Given the difference in experience and pedigree, the result was not surprising. On FRIDAY, MAY 23, 2008, Montclair eliminated Eastern 9-3, ending their season.

Eastern finished the 2008 season ranked No. 5 in South Jersey, behind No. 1 Moorestown, No. 2 St. Augustine, No. 3 Shawnee and No. 4 Cherokee. That would become a familiar theme.

Following his 2008 sophomore season, Dylan was named Second Team All-Conference and Honorable Mention All South-Jersey. The Spring 2008 Athletic Awards ceremony was held on TUESDAY, JUNE 3, 2008, at 7:00 p.m. in Gym #1. Dylan received his varsity letter, as did his teammates Steve Adelman, Matt Bittner, Joe Casole, Tyler Costantino, Mike D'Olio, Nick Dadarrio, Tom Daley, Chris DiNote, Shane Flannery (Capt.), Dylan Fox, Jake Goodman, Christian Kramer, Mike Lane, Michael Leung, Derek Metallo, Josh Reese (Capt.), Frank Sirch, Michael Stoner (Capt.), Lance Vernon and Mike Wahl. Tyler Costantino, Jake Goodman,

Josh Reese and Michael Stoner all made All-Conference, while Steve Adelman, Chris DiNote and Mike Wahl, in addition to Dylan, made Second Team All-Conference.

The *Courier-Post*'s "team outlooks" for 2009 had this to say about Eastern:

> *Coach: Steve Picot (7 years, 81-32). 2008 record: 16-5. Players to watch: Dylan Florig (Jr., goalie); Shane Flannery (Sr., defense); Christian Kramer (Sr., defense); Frank Sirch (Jr., defense); Mike Stoner {Sr., LPM}; Tyler Costantino (Sr., attack); Nick DiNote (So., mid); Dylan Fox (Jr., mid); Mike D'Olio (Jr., attack); Mike Jevic (So., attack). Coach's quote: "Our strong point is goalie Dylan Florig and leading attackman Tyler Costantino. We are young on offense.'*

The *Courier-Post* preseason rankings for 2009 had Eastern ranked No. 5 again. The newspaper wrote, "The Vikings always have lots of depth and talent, and this should be no exception." The *Philadelphia Inquirer* also ranked Eastern No. 5 in South Jersey in its preseason rankings:

> *The Vikings lost a ton of talent, but this is a burgeoning program, with the Olympic Conference's first freshman team. Senior middies Tyler Costantino and Dylan Fox along with senior defender Shane Flannery will keep Eastern in the mix. Junior goalie Dylan Florig gained valuable experience last season.*

Dylan's junior season began on WEDNESDAY, APRIL 1, 2009, against Bishop Eustace. Bishop Eustace was coached by Ray Carlin, our friend and neighbor from two doors down on Abbey Road. Patrick Carlin, Dylan's best friend, played for Bishop Eustace. Eastern won the season opener 14-4. The second game was on SATURDAY, APRIL 4, 2009, against St. Augustine Prep, the best team in South Jersey. It was a cold and very windy day. Eastern was awful, losing 10-2. It could have been worse, but I think that St. Augustine's coach, J.C. Valore, took it easy. The game was so one-sided that Eastern didn't even get a shot on goal until the fourth quarter, and

Dylan had to make 16 saves on 26 shots on goal. The rest of the regular season went like this:

<u>WEDNESDAY, APRIL 8, 2009</u>: **Eastern 9**, Lenape 1. The *Courier-Post* reported on the game under the headline, "Led by Florig, Eastern defense shines":

One of the factors that is sometimes overlooked when evaluating the abilities of a team in the high-scoring world of boys' lacrosse is the overall ability to play defense. But Eastern High School showed the value of scoring timely goals while playing shutdown defense Wednesday as the Vikings turned back Lenape 9-1 in an Olympic Conference American Division game.

Goalie Dylan Florig was credited with five saves, and he allowed only one score - on a shot by Kevin Rapp. But, thanks to two goals by Mike Jevic, the Vikings were up 4-0 at that point in the third quarter. A junior who has taken a leadership role on a young team, Florig credited his defense with helping set the stage for a victory. 'It's kind of easy for me when the defense plays as well as it did today,' he said. 'We're kind of new back there after losing two seniors who were all-conference players. But I think we're starting to come together really well.'

The replacements - senior Chris Kramer and junior Frank Sirch - are both starting for the first time as varsity players, but Florig suspects they will improve with each game. 'They know their stuff for the most part,' he said. 'As the goalie, I'm the leader of the defense, and the more I'm talking to them the more I can help them out. But they're both pretty good.'

Coach Steve Picot was happy to see his team respond so well because the Vikings were defeated by highly-regarded St. Augustine 10-2 in the last outing. He didn't want his team to have its confidence shaken any further. 'This was our first divisional game, and I know in this game we had to come out hard,' he said. 'I think this was a good bounce-back game for us. We came out much better than we did the last time (against St. Augustine). I thought this was a good solid win and (they) played hard and they played together. That's what we've been talking about.'

As the game developed, Florig probably didn't have to be quite as sharp as he was because his team gave him plenty of late breathing room. Sparked by three goals by Mike D'Olio, all coming within a span of six minutes over the last part of the third quarter and the first part of the fourth, the Vikings put the game out of reach.

SATURDAY, APRIL 11, 2009: Cherokee 8, **Eastern 6**

TUESDAY, APRIL 14, 2009: **Eastern 3**, Clearview 2 (OT). On a rainy, windy, miserable day, Eastern won in overtime on a goal by Mike Jevic, against one of the best goalies in South Jersey, Eddie Stubits. Dylan made a save in overtime on a shot by All South-Jersey player Nick Philippi. *NJ.com* reported that, "In a defensive battle that resulted in just five total goals, Eastern edged Clearview, 3-2 in overtime. Dylan Florig had a great game in net for the Vikings, stopping 14 Clearview shots."

FRIDAY, APRIL 17, 2009: Shawnee 15, **Eastern 4**

FRIDAY, APRIL 24, 2009: **Eastern 15**, Cherry Hill East 0

MONDAY, APRIL 27, 2009: Cherokee 5, **Eastern 1**

WEDNESDAY, APRIL 29, 2009: **Eastern 16**, West Deptford 3

MONDAY, MAY 4, 2009: Moorestown 8, **Eastern 7**

WEDNESDAY, MAY 6, 2009: **Eastern 9**, Seneca 2. In a game played at Seneca High School, Eastern won behind four goals from Mike D'Olio, three from Mike Jevic, and two from Tyler Costantino. Dylan stopped 10 of 12 shots on goal.

THURSDAY, MAY 7, 2009: **Eastern 9**, Washington Township 2. The *Philadelphia Inquirer* reported, "Mike Jevic's five goals sparked the Eastern attack, while goalie Dylan Florig made nine saves to back the Vikings' defense in a 9-2 home win over Olympic Conference rival Washington Township."

MONDAY, MAY 11, 2009: West Windsor-Plainsboro North 6, **Eastern 4**. Dylan had 13 saves in the loss.

WEDNESDAY, MAY 13, 2009: Peddie 8, **Eastern 7**

FRIDAY, MAY 15, 2009: **Eastern 7**, Washington Township 3

MONDAY, MAY 18, 2009: **Eastern 9**, Lenape 5

Eastern again qualified for the state playoffs and drew Jackson Memorial in the first round. On WEDNESDAY, MAY 20, 2009, in a home game, Eastern won 10-3. The *Philadelphia Inquirer* reported on the game under the headline "Costantino sets Eastern goals record":

> *Tyler Costantino broke the Eastern school record for career goals by scoring six in a 10-3 first-round win over visiting Jackson Memorial in the NJSIAA state Group 4 boys' tournament. Costantino's final goal boosted his total to 112 goals, topping the 2007 record of 111, set by Mike Feldberg. Eastern goalie Dylan Florig made 11 saves.*

The season would come to an abrupt and inglorious end on SATURDAY, MAY 23, 2009, at Bridgewater-Raritan High School. Bridgewater-Raritan, a perennial lacrosse power in New Jersey, won in dominating fashion, 11-3, and went on to win the New Jersey Group IV state championship.

Following the 2009 season, Dylan was named first team All-Conference and second team All-South Jersey.

In the *Newark Star-Ledger*'s 2010 season preview, Dylan was named one of the Players to Watch - "Dylan Florig, Eastern, Sr.: Talented goalie expects to anchor the defense for one of South Jersey's top teams. Will go to Washington & Lee."

The *Courier-Post*'s 2010 season preview had Eastern ranked No. 3 in South Jersey, after finishing 2009 at No. 6 with an 11-8 record. The preview said, "It was supposed to be an off season for the Vikings last year, but coach Steve Picot still kept them near the top of the rankings. This should be another good season." Among the "Players to Watch" was Dylan, "Was second team All-South Jersey last year. Aims for the top spot this year."

The *Philadelphia Inquirer*'s season preview had Eastern ranked No. 5 in South Jersey, behind St. Augustine, Moorestown, Lenape and Shawnee. Its preview stated:

> *The Vikings are expected to have one of the top defensive teams around, led by senior defender Frank Sirch, an Inquirer first-team all-South Jersey selection. Sirch, along with goalie Dylan Florig and senior attack Mike D'Olio, were first-team all-Olympic American Conference selections. Florig made 165 saves, and D'Olio contributed 34 goals and 12 assists. Junior midfielder Nick DiNote was a second-team all-conference selection. Classmate Mike Jevic scored 25 goals. Two other key returning seniors are midfielders Matt Bittner and Nick Daddario, a face-off specialist.*

Dylan was also named one of the *Inquirer*'s "Players to Watch."

The *Voyager*, Eastern's school newspaper, did a feature on Dylan shortly after the 2010 season began - "Athlete Spotlight: Dylan Florig, Senior - Lacrosse":

> *Senior Dylan Florig has been a starter on the varsity lacrosse team since his sophomore year. He is the all time leader in saves for Eastern lacrosse goalies. In 2008 he was Honorable Mention All-South Jersey and Second Team All-Conference. In 2009 he was a team captain, named Second Team All-*

South Jersey, and First Team All-Conference. This year he is a captain again and a Star Ledger "Player to Watch." Next year, he will continue his career at Washington and Lee University.

Favorite Food? Buffalo Chicken Nachos from The Fours in Boston.

Favorite TV show? The Office and 30 Rock.

What is your most memorable moment from lacrosse? It's hard to pick just one. My most memorable game was the one against Clearview last year. We won 3-2 in overtime, and the defense held a shutout for the last three quarters. I also had a shutout in my first varsity game. That was pretty awesome.

When did you first realize lacrosse was a sport you could have success in? In sixth grade, when I started playing, I wasn't even sure if I would stick with it in high school. My first sport up until eighth grade was baseball. In eighth grade, when I made the top Vortex team, I knew that I'd be committed in lax. I knew I'd be successful when I won the starting varsity job sophomore year.

Who is your biggest rival? Our biggest rival is Cherokee. Last year, we dropped two tough games to them and that cost us the division title. They always come ready to play us. This year we beat them 11-2 in our first matchup.

Why did you choose Washington & Lee? I knew I wanted to go to a competitive liberal arts school whether I'd be playing lacrosse or not. W&L has a great campus and one of the best

Division III teams. It's also great for political science and history.

How did you decide to play goalie? In baseball I played catcher, so I guess there are some similarities. In my first game ever I volunteered to play the first half. I played half goalie and half attack in sixth and seventh grade.

Do you have any advice for new or incoming players? Make sure you understand that at Eastern, lacrosse is a year-round commitment. You need to be working out and playing in the offseason in order to have a chance to play. Join a summer team and just work hard in general.

Dylan was named one of the Eastern team captains for his senior season. For the second straight year, Eastern opened its schedule against Bishop Eustace. On THURSDAY, APRIL 1, 2010, Eastern won 13-2. The rest of the regular season went like this:

TUESDAY, APRIL 6, 2010: Shawnee 11, **Eastern 10**

WEDNESDAY, APRIL 7, 2010: **Eastern 10**, Cherry Hill West 3

FRIDAY, APRIL 9, 2010: **Eastern 10**, Cherokee 2

MONDAY, APRIL 12, 2010: **Eastern 11**, Cherry Hill East 0

WEDNESDAY, APRIL 14, 2010: **Eastern 11**, Clearview 1

MONDAY, APRIL 19, 2010: **Eastern 14**, Holy Cross 0. The *Courier-Post* recap noted: "Mike D'Olio and Mike Jevic both scored three goals, but goalie Dylan Florig stole the show with a rare shutout." Leading up to the next game, Eastern was ranked No. 3 in South Jersey by the *Philadelphia Inquirer*, with a 6-1 record. The paper previewed the game against No. 7 Lenape: "Lenape has won four of its last five, with the lone loss by a 5-4 score to No. 2 Shawnee. The Indians have a balanced offense . . .

Eastern's only loss was by 11-10 to Shawnee. The Vikings have talented scorers in Mike D'Olio (20) and Mike Jevic (18), but the team's strength is a sturdy defense led by Frank Sirch and goalie Dylan Florig."

WEDNESDAY, APRIL 21, 2010: **Eastern 7**, Lenape 4. The *Philadelphia Inquirer* wrote, "Mike Jevic scored three goals and goalie Dylan Florig made 11 saves as Eastern beat visiting Lenape 7-4."

THURSDAY, APRIL 22, 2010: Washington Township 6, **Eastern 5**. In a game at Washington Township, the Minutemen scored the game-winning goal with eight seconds remaining for the win.

TUESDAY, APRIL 27, 2010: **Eastern 13**, Cherokee 6

THURSDAY, APRIL 29, 2010: **Eastern 13**, West Deptford 5

FRIDAY, APRIL 30, 2010: Peddie 7, **Eastern 6**. Mike Jevic led Eastern with three goals and Dylan made eight saves on 15 shots on goal.

TUESDAY, MAY 4, 2010: **Eastern 13**, Cherry Hill East 1

WEDNESDAY, MAY 5, 2010: Moorestown 9, **Eastern 2**. Dylan made 9 saves in the loss against the No. 3 ranked team in South Jersey. Eastern was ranked No. 4.

FRIDAY, MAY 7, 2010: **Eastern 8**, Seneca 7

TUESDAY, MAY 11, 2010: Lenape 5, **Eastern 2**

The playoffs began on TUESDAY, MAY 18, 2010, against Clifton, with Eastern as the sixth seed and Clifton as the fourteenth seed. Eastern won 7-1, behind four goals by Mike D'Olio and 14 saves by Dylan. Following that win, Eastern was ranked No. 5 in South Jersey by the *Philadelphia Inquirer*, which previewed the "Boys' Game of the Week": **North Hunterdon at Eastern, Thursday, 4 p.m.**:

Sixth-seeded Eastern has a clear path to the semifinals of the Group 4 state lacrosse tournament. The Vikings' offense is led by senior attack Mike D'Olio and junior midfielder Mike Jevic; each has 39 goals. Senior goalie Dylan Florig anchors a sturdy defense. North Hunterdon, the No. 14 seed, advanced with an upset of third-seeded Hunterdon Central. The winner of this game likely will face second-seeded Montclair in Saturday's state semifinals.

Eastern did indeed advance with a 12-7 win, with Dylan again making 14 saves against North Hunterdon on Thursday, May 20, 2010.

For the second time in three years, we drove 100 miles north to watch Montclair end Eastern's season, winning 12-4 on Saturday, May 22, 2010. And just like that, Dylan's high school lacrosse career was over.

At the conclusion of the 2010 season, Dylan was named first team All-Conference and first team All-South Jersey. He was also named Eastern's Defensive Player of the Year. He set Eastern records for most saves in one season (217) and most saves in a career (563). His 3-year stats were 563 saves, 4.9 goals against average, and 105 ground balls.

Laxrecords.com lists Dylan as having the 40th most career saves among high school goalies in New Jersey with 563.

Dylan's college lacrosse career at Washington and Lee was nothing like his high school career. As a freshman, he played in only two games, both in mop-up duty. On Wednesday, March 23, 2011, he played 4 minutes and 17 seconds in an 11-1 win over Guilford College, making no saves and giving up no goals. On Saturday, April 2, 2011, he played 8 minutes and 17 seconds in a 13-4 win over Randolph College, making no saves and giving up one goal.

Although I went to quite a few games when Dylan was a freshman, the most memorable was on Tuesday, March 29, 2011, when W&L played a night game against Middlebury College in Washington, D.C., at Georgetown's stadium. Nancy and I made the long drive down to Georgetown to watch. Middlebury was ranked No. 7 in the country, and always had a good lacrosse program. Although W&L jumped out to a 4-2 lead after the first period, they only managed one more goal the rest of the way, and lost 6-5.

We had much higher hopes heading into his sophomore season. The two senior goalies had graduated and Dylan was competing with Patrick Jennings, another sophomore, for the starting job. W&L had also recruited another goalie, Warren Berenis, who joined the team as a freshman. Berenis was bigger than either Dylan or Jennings, and it was clear from early on that head coach Gene McCabe loved him. Defensive coordinator Mike Kruger had left W&L to coach at Shenandoah, so Dylan's biggest advocate was gone. One or two days before the season started, Dylan suffered a high ankle sprain, which knocked him out of practice and games for the first six weeks of the season. By the time Dylan had recovered, Jennings had played poorly enough to be replaced and Berenis took over.

Dylan only played in two games that year, the first being 15 minutes against Randolph College on SATURDAY, MARCH 31, 2012, during which he did not face a single shot in a 21-2 Washington and Lee victory. The second was on WEDNESDAY, APRIL 18, 2012, against Greensboro, when Dylan played 8 minutes and 8 seconds during a 14-4 win, making two saves and giving up one goal. Months of training and practice, hours and hours of bus rides, to play 23 minutes and 8 seconds of college lacrosse. It took a good deal of convincing to talk Dylan into playing again during his junior year.

The Generals Lacrosse website at WLU said this about Dylan in its 2013 Season Preview:

> *2013: "Two-year letter winner . . . expected to compete for playing time in the goal again this spring . . . had a tremendous fall, which was capped by being named W&L winner of the Worrell-Fallon Award as the game MVP of the Lee-Jackson Lacrosse Classic . . . recorded 13 saves in a 19-8 win over the Keydets" 2012: "Saw action in two games, playing a total of 23:08 . . . posted two saves with one goal allowed for a .667 save percentage . . . logged a 2.59 goals- against average . . . played the third quarter of a 21-2 win over Randolph (3/31) holding the WildCats scoreless across the 15 minutes." 2011: "Played in two contests, seeing 12:34 of game action . . . did not record a save and allowed just one goal for a 4.77 goals-against average . . . helped the Generals rank 19th in Division III with a 7.06 goals-against average."*

His junior season turned out to be only marginally better than the first two, and also proved to be his last. Having played only 12 minutes and 34 seconds as a freshman and 23 minutes and 8 seconds as a sophomore, Dylan managed to play 89 minutes and 16 seconds as a junior, although it all came at meaningless times, as W&L easily won each of the games Dylan played in.

TUESDAY, FEBRUARY 12, 2013: During W&L's season-opening 23-4 victory over Ferrum College, Dylan logged 12:17, allowing one goal and making no saves. Regardless of whether he played or not, it was always good to see Dylan. We would usually go to the luncheon or barbeque after a game with the team and the parents, and if there was time, would head to an ice cream shop near the campus.

SATURDAY, FEBRUARY 16, 2013: Naively, I suppose, I was always hopeful that Dylan would get a chance, so I went to a lot of games where I watched other people's kids play. One of those was W&L's game against Christopher Newport University in Lexington, a 12-9 afternoon win.

WEDNESDAY, FEBRUARY 20, 2013: It was certainly the best W&L lacrosse game that I attended. Salisbury University was the most dominant team in Division III men's lacrosse and had been for some time. Salisbury won national championships in 1994, 1995, 1999, 2003, 2004, 2005, 2007, 2008, 2011 and 2012, and was ranked No. 1 in the country heading into the game. Nancy and I drove down and saw W&L knock off Salisbury in double-overtime, when senior midfielder Luke Heinsohn scored a goal with nine seconds left for the win. We got to see Dylan, who of course did not play, for about three minutes after the game, since the team was heading straight home to Lexington. I'm all but certain that it was on this trip that we stopped for foot-long hot dogs in Wilmington.

SATURDAY, MARCH 2, 2013: Nancy and I drove to Chestertown, Maryland, only to see W&L lose to Washington College, 8-4, at Roy Kirby, Jr. Stadium. We had gone to the game at Washington College when Dylan was a freshman, too, on SATURDAY, MARCH 5, 2011, meeting Joe and Julia there. W&L went into the game ranked No. 9, while Washington College was ranked No. 13. W&L won, but barely, by a score of 5-4. We went to the post-game luncheon outside of the athletic building, chatted with Dylan, and then he boarded the bus back to Lexington. We decided to walk around Chestertown for a bit with Joe and Julia and stopped into a little place for some fried oysters and beer.

WEDNESDAY, MARCH 20, 2013. W&L defeated the University of Mary Washington, 9-4, as Dylan played 3:16, allowing one goal and making no saves.

SATURDAY, MARCH 23, 2013: W&L entered the game ranked No. 8 in Division III. I went down for the game, which was played on the turf field mostly used for field hockey, knowing that Guilford College wasn't a very good team, and hopeful that Dylan might at least get in toward the end for some mop-up duty. He didn't, even though Berenis didn't play very well, only making five saves on ten Guilford shots. I was certain that Dylan was going to go in at, or before, halftime, but Coach McCabe stuck with Berenis, as he always did.

WEDNESDAY, APRIL 3, 2013: Dylan played 23:55 in W&L's 27-1 win over Bridgewater College, making three saves and giving up Bridgewater's lone goal.

SATURDAY, APRIL 13, 2013: W&L defeated Randolph College 27-6, with Dylan playing 22:01, while allowing one goal and making no saves. I know that I went to this one, since I have a copy of the program. Heading into the game, W&L was ranked No. 8 in the country in Division III.

WEDNESDAY, APRIL 24, 2013: Dylan played 21:00 as W&L defeated Shenandoah University 14-3, allowing one goal and making one save.

SATURDAY, APRIL 27, 2013: I drove down to Hampden-Sydney College for the game. I remember listening to Day 3 of the NFL draft on the drive down, when the Eagles traded up to select quarterback Matt Barkley. That didn't work out too well. This was the final game of the regular season and W&L went into the game ranked #12 in the country. In an odd coincidence, one of the women I had hired at *WePAC* had a son who played goalie for Hampden-Sydney, although he, too, didn't get to play much. I saw her at halftime of the game, tailgating with the other Hampden-Sydney parents. Berenis didn't play particularly well for W&L, making only eight saves while surrendering ten goals in an 11-10 W&L win. By this time, I had finally given up on the fanciful notion that Dylan might ever get to play in a game when it mattered.

SATURDAY, MAY 4, 2013: A week later, I drove down to Salem, Virginia, to the Roanoke College campus, for the Old Dominion Athletic Conference ("ODAC") lacrosse playoffs. W&L ended the regular season with a 15-3 record, finishing in second place in the ODAC. W&L was ranked #12 nationally, while the University of Lynchburg was ranked #13, with a 12-4 record. In a game that was tied after regulation, Luke Heinsohn scored the overtime goal for W&L, sending them into the conference championship game the next day against the top seed, Roanoke College. Heinsohn had quite a season - he had also scored the overtime goal against top-ranked Salisbury earlier in the year. As W&L celebrated on the field, Dylan ran down to the other end, where Heinsohn had scored, picked up the ball, and brought it back to give to Luke.

SUNDAY, MAY 5, 2013: I stayed overnight in Salem and went to the championship game on Sunday at 3:00 p.m. Roanoke entered the game at 14-3 and ranked number 7 in the country. Despite trailing 9-5 midway through the third quarter, W&L rallied, only to lose by a 10-9 score. Dylan stood on the sidelines the entire weekend.

W&L made it to the NCAA lacrosse tournament in 2013. Dylan played 6 minutes and 47 seconds during W&L's 19-6 first-round NCAA Division III playoff win against Sewanee - The University of the South, on WEDNESDAY, MAY 8, 2013. He made three saves on three shots. I joke that he holds an NCAA lacrosse playoff record with a 0.0 goals against average and a 1.000 save percentage. It was the last lacrosse game he ever played in.

SATURDAY, MAY 11, 2013: Three days later, W&L headed into the second round of the NCAA tournament favored over perennial-power Salisbury. I once again made the 300 mile drive down to Lexington for the game. W&L had beaten Salisbury earlier in the season and was ranked No. 8, with Salisbury ranked No. 12. Nonetheless, Salisbury scored the first four goals of the game, led 5-2 at halftime and 6-2 after three quarters en route to a 7-4 win, knocking W&L out of the NCAA tournament. It was the last game Dylan suited-up for, having decided that it was better to enjoy his senior year than to just stand on the sidelines watching during his final semester of college.

For their respective Washington and Lee lacrosse careers, Berenis, Jennings and Dylan ended up with the following statistics:

Patrick Jennings: Goals Against Average - 9.63, Save % - .458

Warren Berenis: Goals Against Average - 7.55, Save % - .572

Dylan Florig: Goals Against Average - 3.39, Save % - .563

Why Dylan never got a chance to play in a meaningful game will forever remain a mystery. Dylan told me that after the 2013 season, Coach McCabe had individual meetings with each of the players to go over the season and make plans for the next year. Dylan told me that McCabe had asked him what kind of season he thought that Warren Berenis had. Dylan said it was OK, but that he would have had a better one. No one will ever know. And with that, Dylan said goodbye to college lacrosse as a player, although he did become a color commentator for the livestream of the games in 2014 on WLUR radio, the campus station.

* * *

Washington & Lee won the 26th Annual Lee-Jackson Lacrosse Classic against the Virginia Military Institute that October Friday night in 2012 by a score of 19-8. Dylan had called me the day before and said that Berenis, the starting goalie, was sick and that he thought that he would get to start. I hadn't planned on making the trip, but changed my mind when I heard the news. I drove down and watched the game at Wilson Field, along with a couple thousand other fans. Dylan made 13 saves while allowing only seven goals and won the Worrell-Fallon Award as the game's Most Valuable Player. His name is on the plaque in the Washington and Lee gym. It didn't make any difference come the spring, as Berenis started every game.

CHAPTER 55

FRIDAY, DECEMBER 14, 2012

It is impossible for me to even conceive of what happened at Sandy Hook Elementary School in Newtown, Connecticut. It is equally inconceivable to me that anyone involved - parents, first responders, doctors, teachers, other students - could come out the other side whole. Ask *them* whether it was all made up and staged by "crisis actors." I have driven through Newtown dozens, if not hundreds, of times since the shootings, and every single time I think about what happened that day.

It wasn't much, but Nancy and I felt like it was the least that we could do. On SATURDAY, MARCH 24, 2018, we drove to Portland for one of the *March for Our Lives* protests. About 5,000 people marched on Portland City Hall. The Portland march was one of more than 800 such events around the country that day, with the largest in Washington, D.C., which was attended by 500,000 people. *March for Our Lives* was a response to the shootings at Marjorie Stoneman Douglas High School on Valentine's Day in 2018, which left 17 people, 14 of them students, dead. During the march, the NRA posted a fundraising video claiming that, "Gun-hating billionaires and Hollywood elites are manipulating and exploiting children as part of their plan to DESTROY the Second Amendment." I can personally assure you that Nancy and I are not billionaires, nor are we Hollywood elites. I know that we don't manipulate and exploit children. I've never even been to Hollywood, although I was in *Rocky*.

Rick Santorum, former Republican senator and perennial presidential wannabe, offered the helpful suggestion that, rather than marching, students should be learning CPR. Santorum, of course, holds any number of enlightened positions on social issues:

- He has called climate change "junk science" and a "beautifully concocted scheme" by liberals

- He has compared homosexuality to beastiality

- He would ban gays from military service

- He opposes same-sex marriage and has said that he would not attend a same-sex wedding

- He has compared pro-choice people to German Nazis

- He opposes cultural diversity because, "Diversity creates conflict. If we celebrate diversity, we create conflict"

Of course, nothing changed after *March for Our Lives*. We should have known as much. If politicians weren't willing to do something - ANYTHING - after Sandy Hook, then they were never going to. If 20 six and seven-year-olds shot and killed in their classrooms wasn't enough to motivate some reasonable action, nothing ever will be. Certainly not 14 dead high school kids at Marjorie Stoneman Douglas High School.

For Christmas that year, I asked Nancy and Dylan to forego giving me presents and to send a donation to a gun violence advocacy group. They made the donation to the *Coalition to Stop Gun Violence* in Washington, D.C. I'm sure that they still gave me some other gifts, but that one was my favorite, pointless though it seems to have been.

CHAPTER 56

SATURDAY, JANUARY 25, 2014

It cost Nancy and I $0.35 more to adopt Molly than it cost my parents to adopt me. And there weren't even any lawyers' fees involved. The major difference between Molly and me is that Molly is a dog. We adopted her on SATURDAY, JANUARY 25, 2014 for $125.35, while my adoption had cost exactly $125.00. Even with our 20% discount, she was more expensive. Her name wasn't Molly when we adopted her, it was Julie, which is a perfectly fine name for a woman, but not that great for a dog. Fenway had been gone for four months, I was ready to have two dogs again, and we already had seven-year-old Erin. I had been secretly visiting the Voorhees Animal Orphanage periodically to scope out who was there, and through a little bit of obfuscation, convinced Nancy to take a car ride with me. We wound up in the parking lot of the animal shelter. Over some objections, she went in with me and wound up being the one who actually picked Molly.

Julie was a southern girl. She was picked up as a stray at 3979 Soapstone Road in Decatur, Georgia, on THURSDAY, JANUARY 16, 2014, and was taken to the DeKalb County Animal Shelter. Being a stray, and obviously not carrying her paperwork with her, no one really knows her birthday. It is listed in various places as WEDNESDAY, JANUARY 16, 2013; THURSDAY, JANUARY 24, 2013; or FRIDAY, MARCH 1, 2013. Those dates seem to have been chosen based on the shelter's guess that she was about one year old, and reflect the day she was picked up, the day she arrived in Voorhees, and the day of her first visit to our vet. We have never really settled on an official birthday. Dogs don't really understand birthdays, anyway, although they very much appreciate getting treats.

She arrived from Georgia at the Voorhees Animal Orphanage at 10:18 a.m. on FRIDAY, JANUARY 24, 2014. Not only do we not know her birthday, we also don't really know what kind of dog she is, other than a mutt. Based on her size, floppy ears and color, she is listed in different places as "beagle mix" or "shepherd/beagle mix." She will sit for hours watching for chipmunks, squirrels and birds, oblivious to other sounds and calls, like a good, focused hound. They call this trait "selective deafness," a trait which I share with her. If there is enough excitement, she can also howl. Strangers who meet her think that she is a shepherd puppy. After a meet-and-greet, we adopted her, but we very nearly didn't keep her.

Nancy let the kids in her fifth-grade class help with picking a name, and we settled on "Molly." Molly was very different from the other dogs we had adopted - Jesse Jackson, Fenway or Erin. For one thing, she was much smaller, only weighing around 30 pounds, compared to the others' 60 or 70. For another, she was fast - like greyhound fast. She was also far more hyper than the others. And she licked. And she licked. And she licked. To this day, she is a compulsive and annoying licker, flicking her tongue at anything nearby, like a lizard catching bugs. She can also jump straight up and look you right in the eye.

We had a fenced-in backyard because of our pool, but that really didn't deter Molly much. Twice within the first week, she jumped over the four-foot section like it wasn't there, and took off. I had to chase her for a couple of blocks before I managed to corral her, and then had to add an extra two feet to the fence. When I took her to a new veterinarian, the vet looked at her, looked at me, and said, "Well, we know who the athlete in the family is." She didn't mean me.

Between the licking, fence-jumping and hyperactivity, "we" decided that Molly wasn't really a great fit and that "we" would have to return her to the shelter. I didn't really want to, but, reluctantly, I put her in the car and drove back to the shelter. I told the worker that we had adopted her, but that we didn't feel like it was a good fit. I actually had to sit down and fill out some paperwork and answer some questions about traits and behaviors. When we were done, I was told that there was no room in the shelter and that I would have to take Molly home and wait for them to call so that I could bring her back. Silly me, I thought that I could just bring her back and that would be that.

Eight years later, we still have her. The shelter had called and told me I could bring her back for surrender, but by then, we just couldn't do it. She was part of the family.

CHAPTER 57

THURSDAY, MAY 22, 2014

Graduation from Washington and Lee University was at 10:00 a.m. There were only 450 students in Dylan's graduating class, so it wasn't an enormous event. In fact, there were more students in his high school class than in his class at W&L. It was hot and sticky in Lexington, Virginia - 83 degrees and 53% humidity by 11:00 a.m., so we arrived early to find some seats in the shade. The ceremony was held on the campus "front lawn" in front of Lee Chapel and Museum. Robert E. Lee, his wife, father, mother, children and other relatives are buried in the family crypt under the chapel. Lee's favorite horse, Traveler, is buried outside the chapel.

Eventually, I think, the name of the school is going to change. It takes its name from George Washington, who made a sizable donation to the school, and from Lee, who served as the school's president after the Civil War. A few years ago, students were successful in having replica Confederate battle flags removed from the Museum, although I think that some real ones remain. I am constantly amazed, when driving through the South, at how many memorials to leaders of the Confederacy there are, from street names to town names to statues to buildings. That's a discussion for somewhere else, but time and history are on the side of change. So far, the university hasn't been willing to make that change. It will.

After the commencement, we went out to lunch with Dylan, Alexandria Hensleigh (Dylan's girlfriend) and Alex's parents. Dylan and Alex had been dating since the first semester of their freshman year. We first met her during Parents' Weekend during the fall of that year. The post-graduation lunch was the last time that we saw them all, including Alex, since she and Dylan broke up shortly after graduating. A misapplication of judgment, perhaps, spending your entire college career with just one girlfriend.

Parents' Weekend was my first real exposure to life at Washington and Lee. During the admissions tours, Greek life was downplayed quite a bit, in my opinion. As it turned out, almost everyone at the school joined a fraternity or sorority of some kind. There is a whole street that seems to be filled with nothing but frat houses, which are not included on the Admissions tour. The only Parents' Weekend that we went to was during Dylan's freshman year in 2010. On SATURDAY, NOVEMBER 6, 2010, all of the frat houses were opened up for students and parents. Most of them had music and food - all of them had plenty of beer and drink. We went from frat to frat, sampling what was going on, kind of like college kids on a Saturday night. It just felt a little odd to me, all of these college kids and their parents drinking and partying together. It felt especially odd to see some of the fathers playing beer pong with the co-eds. Are women students even called co-eds anymore, or am I showing some age?

Washington and Lee is one of the top liberal arts colleges in the country, and Dylan got a magnificent education there. It's just a bit too southern for my taste. They have things like cotillions, which mold young college kids into fine, well-mannered young men and women, and cost lots of money for gowns and flowers and such. Not that a lot of W&L parents are cash-strapped. "W&L" is rumored to mean "white and loaded." The women students often wear dresses and boots to the home football games. Anywhere you travel in Virginia, there are Confederate memorials and reminders. It almost seems like they're still fighting the war in some ways. I'm a northeast liberal, so it's all just a little outside of my comfort zone.

Dylan got to do some pretty cool things at W&L. He was a DJ at WLUR, the campus radio station. Not much talking, just basically playing whatever music he felt like playing. Nancy and I would listen on the computer at work when we could. He also participated in the W&L Mock Convention, which is held on campus every four years, during the early stages of presidential primaries. The Mock Convention runs like a real political convention, with delegations and speakers and, occasionally, a real candidate like Harry Truman, Jimmy Carter or Bill Clinton making an appearance. It is usually televised on C-SPAN. The convention is always held for the party which is not in control of the White House, so during the 2012 Mock Convention, Dylan chaired a Republican delegation, I believe from Arizona. As it nearly always does, the convention got it right, nominating Mitt Romney as its candidate against incumbent Barack Obama. Since 1952, the Mock Convention has never been wrong about the Republican nominee. Nancy and I watched as much as we could online, including the parade of state floats down the main street in Lexington.

During one of our visits to Washington and Lee, the three of us came across a place called "Foamhenge," in Natural Bridge, Virginia. Foamhenge is (or was) a full-sized replica of Stonehenge, but made entirely out of styrofoam, which some guy had erected on his land. You can't make this kind of thing up. Unfortunately, Foamhenge was dismantled a few years ago, but I've heard that it has popped up again in Centreville, Virginia, and is part of the Fall Festival of Fear.

On WEDNESDAY, MAY 21, 2014, the day before graduation, Nancy and I, along with Dylan, went to the W&L Alumni Association luncheon and the President's Reception in the afternoon. We also attended the Williams School of Commerce, Economics, and Politics Reception and Ceremony on Wednesday, where Dylan was a member of *Pi Sigma Alpha*, a national honor society seeking "to stimulate scholarship and intelligent interest in political science.' At some point, either on Wednesday or Thursday, we stopped at the Blue Lab Brewery in town for a beer. Dylan and I each had a smoky red ale. Nancy and I still have a Blue Lab growler on our kitchen counter. After graduation, we packed up Dylan's stuff and headed home for a couple of weeks for Dylan's last real extended stay on Abbey Road. He was going to start his job with Wells Fargo in Charlotte, North Carolina, in early June. He's been in North Carolina ever since.

CHAPTER 58

THURSDAY, NOVEMBER 6, 2014

We bought our current home in Ocean Park, Maine, in November, 2014, although it would be more than a year-and-a-half before we moved in. We had talked about moving to Maine for a few years. Nancy and I would often come for a long weekend in November during the teachers' convention in New Jersey, when she would have a couple of days off. Jeff Chute, a realtor friend from Ocean Park, was looking for houses that we might be interested in buying. I had looked at quite a few when Jeff called and said that a house on West Tioga was going up for sale, and wanted to know if I was interested in taking a look. I drove up the next day and I really liked the place, although it needed lots of work. Nancy and I came up to see it together shortly thereafter and eventually made an offer. Haggling took a couple of months, but we finally made an offer that the owners accepted. Our life was going to require serious downsizing, since the house is 992 square feet with no basement, no garage and only a small attic.

Before we could move in, there was a lot of renovation to be done. I had never done a serious renovation before. Although it is small, it does have two full bathrooms, which is a big plus, and is a year-round house, as opposed to a seasonal cottage, like most of the houses in town. By the time of settlement in November, the water had been shut off so that the pipes wouldn't freeze. Betty Turner, who had lived there most recently, had passed away and the house was unoccupied. None of her children wanted the house.

We set about figuring out what we wanted the place to look like inside. I even built a scale model out of Dylan's Legos. The biggest dilemma, by far, was the kitchen. When we bought the house, the kitchen was right by the front door. You would walk in, and to the left was a tiny kitchen, no more than 90-100 square feet. We debated for weeks about what we would do about the kitchen, never really solving the problem. There was no way to make it larger where it was. Finally, one of my friends, Anne Polak, who had come through the house earlier, suggested that we simply relocate it to what was then a den with a slider leading onto the back deck. With that puzzle solved, renovations could begin.

Shortly after we bought the house, I began coming up for occasional long weekends to work. A lot of the house had carpeting which was old, so I ripped out all of the carpeting and padding, along with the carpet tack strips along the walls. Tearing out and removing old carpet and carpet padding is a dusty, dirty job, and the tack strips are a pain in the arse to remove, but I eventually managed to get rid of all of it and hauled it outside into the carport. A far more difficult and nasty job awaited.

There is a special place in hell for whoever invented particleboard. The entire house, except for the bathrooms and the one room where we were going to put the kitchen, had particleboard underlayment under the carpeting. Mrs. Turner had cats, and maybe a dog, and they probably had some "accidents" in the house over the years. The first problem with particleboard is that it absorbs any moisture whatsoever and holds odors in forever. So even though the old carpeting was gone, the house still had an obnoxious odor from old particleboard soaked with years and years of spillage and animal pee.

The other problem with particleboard is that it is almost impossible to remove in any reasonable manner. First of all, each individual piece, probably 4 x 8 feet, is nailed down with scores of nails, resulting in thousands of individual nails holding down 600 or 700 square feet of the stuff throughout the house. To remove it, I had to use a crowbar to try to pop the nails and raise the particleboard. If I was lucky, I could get maybe a ten-inch square piece of the stuff to break off. And since it was old, it would leave small pieces and lots of dust all over the place when I finally did manage to pry it loose. Usually, the nails stayed in place so that I had to go one-by-one and pull up the thousands and thousands of nails left sticking up behind. The stuff only smelled worse after it was broken apart. I think it took two or three weekends to finally, mercifully, get all of the disgusting stuff ripped up and out of the house. The entire house stank of dust, must, and decades of whatever had been absorbed by the particleboard.

I ordered some shiplap to use as flooring in the master bedroom; some 5" tongue and groove oak for the living room, guest bedroom and hallway; and cabinets for the kitchen so that actual renovation could start. I'm not even sure which order I did things in, but I finally started laying down flooring. In the master bedroom, we decided to try shiplap, which is a little bit unconventional for flooring. Shiplap is basically an 8" wide board with cutouts on each side so that pieces can fit together. It was painstaking work, cutting and screwing down each individual board. That was the easy part. We decided to pickle the boards after they were down, which is a meticulous process involving brushing on a white stain (no rolling, please), waiting a couple of minutes, and then wiping the excess stain with a rag. The fumes made me a little swimmy. Unlike painting, pickling allows the grain and the knots in the wood to show. It took days, one section of shiplap at a time, on hands and knees.

The problem is that pickling offers no protection for the wood, meaning that the entire floor had to be covered with polyurethane in order to be protected. Again, on hands and knees, with a brush, I applied three coats of polyurethane. It took a couple of weekends to finish the job, but it looks pretty good.

Installing kitchen cabinets is not a one-person job, and definitely not for someone who doesn't know what they're doing, so I hired Frank Polak to install them, with me serving as a helper. Nancy and I picked out some white beadboard cabinets and ordered them. I had measured the kitchen over and over again to get it right. There is a set of pulldown attic stairs in the kitchen, so it was crucial to get the measurements just right so that the stairs could be pulled down without hitting a cabinet or countertop. Of course, I was off by a couple of inches, which meant that I had to order one more 9" base cabinet and wait for it to be delivered before we could actually finish the installation. After it finally arrived, and we finished putting in the cabinets, sink, oven, dishwasher and microwave. Nancy picked out the hardware for the cabinets. We had granite countertops installed, and, with that, we had a brand new working kitchen.

In order to install the kitchen cabinets, I had to remove an entire wall of 5" knotty pine boards. In so doing, I discovered two things. First, I found the original back of the house underneath. It was barn red. The room which we had converted into the kitchen used to be a porch on the back of the house. I liked finding the old exterior and left some of it exposed next to the cabinets as an homage to the house's origin as a seasonal cottage. The second thing that I discovered was that underneath the knotty pine was a cutout for what used to be a window. That would be a little trickier to deal with. Nancy saved the day by suggesting that we put a piece of pegboard in what used to be the window, and we hung kitchen utensils on it, *a la* Julia Child.

Before I could lay down the living room floor, there was the small problem of the brick hearth in front of the fireplace. The living room had a wood-burning fireplace, which we didn't intend to use as such. We were going to have a gas fireplace installed inside of the firebox to use as the primary heat source in the front of the house. Therefore, we wouldn't be needing the brick hearth. I figured that it would take me an hour or two to break it apart and dispose of the bricks and mortar. It's no wonder that the big bad wolf couldn't blow down the third little pig's house.

Whoever built the chimney and hearth did a damn good job. I started pounding away at the hearth with a mortise chisel and hammer. The pounding went on for hour after hour after hour. At one point, the next-door neighbor rang the doorbell to see what was going on. I apologized for the racket, continued long into the evening, and finally got the last brick out. Exhausted, but quite pleased with myself, I went to bed.

Most of the time that I was working seemed to be in the fall, winter and spring, when the house had no running water. That wasn't usually much of a problem, since I could bring water with me. We had electricity, so that I had heat and could make coffee in the morning. And I could pee in the woods, so that wasn't a problem, either. However, one night, around 2:00 a.m., I had to do more than pee, which presented a challenge. Fortunately, two doors down, a new house was being built and there was a port-a-potty on site. So I got dressed (warmly, because it was about 5° Fahrenheit outside) and trudged through the snow, flashlight and toilet paper in hand, to answer nature's call. The seat was cold.

With the hearth out of the way, I installed the oak flooring in the living room, hallway and guest bedroom. It was hard, tedious work with a manual nailer and mallet, but good exercise. I rented the nailer from Home Depot to put a little time pressure on myself. Everyone loved our floor, especially Nancy's father, Jim, but he would only see it once.

There were other, smaller, projects that had to be done. Lots of painting, installing a subway tile backsplash in the kitchen, putting insulation in the attic, and such, but it was fun and I enjoyed fixing up the place, since I had never really done anything like it before. I got a surprise when I was taking out the drop ceiling tiles in the living room, when I removed one and was showered with several pounds of mouse droppings. The little critters had apparently been living there for quite some time.

Once we moved in and got somewhat settled, Nancy and I began exploring the many awesome places and sites in Maine. One of the first places we found was Cowshit Corner, in Newcastle. How we found it, I don't know, but it may have been after a day of visiting Damariscotta, and I think that it was on my 63rd birthday, on THURSDAY, MAY 4, 2017, my first birthday since arriving in Maine. Cowshit Corner is located on Route 194, the site of a dairy farm, and is named, obviously, for what the cows leave behind as they wander the farm.

On the fourth Saturday in March of each year, Maine's maple producers hold "Maine Maple Sunday." Nancy and I decided to go on SUNDAY, MARCH 26, 2017. We hopped in the car and drove west, not really having too much of a plan for what we were going to do. We stopped at a number of sugarhouses, sampled ice cream with maple syrup, and bought a few bottles of syrup. At one farm, Hilltop Boilers in Newfield, the barn was open so that people could walk through and see the animals. The cows were in the barn, and one of them was about to do what the cows at Cowshit Corner were known for. There were some kids in line in front of us, and an old-timer was sitting on a stool next to the cows. The old-timer tugged at the cow's tail and, to the kids' amazement, the cow dropped a cow pie. The kids were both amused and impressed.

In 2018 and 2019, we didn't make it to Maple Sunday for whatever reason, and in 2020 it was cancelled because of the pandemic. We did go on SUNDAY, MARCH 28, 2021, a chilly and rainy day, and bought four more bottles of maple syrup from different sugarhouses. The highlight, though, was stopping at a turkey farm and buying a homemade turkey pie, which I proceeded to cook as soon as we got home.

There are so many beautiful places in Maine, it would be next to impossible to visit them all, although we're trying. On FRIDAY, JUNE 16, 2017, we took a trip up the coast to Bailey Island and Orr's Island, located in Harpswell. The islands are joined by the Bailey Island Bridge, the only cribstone bridge in the world, made from 10,000 tons of granite cribstones, which allow the tides to flow through freely. We walked the beaches and ate lunch at a little restaurant. Three years later, the only fatal shark attack in Maine history happened just 20 yards from shore at Bailey Island, when a great white shark killed a 63-year-old woman.

Autumn is by far the best time of year in Maine, when most of the tourists have gone home and things are pretty quiet. It's not that we dislike the tourists, since they help to pay the bills, it's just that there are a lot of them. In the summer, every other license plate you see is from out of state. And almost all of the tourists seem to be very happy to be in Maine and not in whatever God-forsaken state that they came from. Nancy and I know that we will never be true Mainers, but will always be "from away," since neither we, our parents, nor our grandparents were born and raised here. That aside, we went to Fort Popham, a 19th-Century fort at the mouth of the Kennebec River in Phippsburg on THURSDAY, OCTOBER 19, 2017. We walked around the fort, walked onto Popham Beach, and enjoyed the long, beautiful sandy shore. On the way out, we saw a sign for Fort Baldwin, and made the climb up a steep hill to see the fort, which was manned during WWII to watch for enemy ships in Casco Bay.

One of the things that I'm not good enough at is just taking the time to sit back and enjoy the moment. In the words of Fred Rogers ("Mr. Rogers"), I'd like to be a "better appreciator." On the way home from one of our road trips, maybe to Norway (Maine, not Europe), we passed by a frozen, snow-covered lake in Waterford on SATURDAY, APRIL 7, 2018. In addition to Norway, Maine features places named Belfast, Belgrade, China, Denmark, Frankfort, Limerick, Lisbon, Mexico, Moscow, Naples, Paris, Peru, Poland, Rome, Stockholm, Sweden, Vienna and York. I pulled over to the side of the road, we got out, and just sat on a bench, enjoying a quintessential Maine view - it was "The Way Life Should Be."

CHAPTER 59

SATURDAY, JULY 4, 2015

On the Fourth of July, Nancy and I were driving south while Joe and Julia were driving north. Although we had not yet moved to Maine, we were taking a little vacation and doing some work on the house that we had purchased eight months prior. We were going to go to the Fourth of July parade, a typical little small town parade, complete with kazoo band, in the morning before Joe and Julia arrived from Pennsylvania in the early afternoon. All of that changed on Saturday morning.

Nancy's mother, Doris MacDonald, was born in Lowell, Massachusetts, on WEDNESDAY, AUGUST 26, 1931, to Ovide and Eva Couillard. She was raised speaking French and it showed. She would say things like, "Throw (pronounced "Trō") me down the stairs my hat," and once said of me, "He got nice hair, him." She was also very Catholic. Doris gave birth to five girls - Nancy, Annie, Linda, Donna and Cindy, before she finally gave Jim a son, Mark. I'm not sure Jim was going to give up until Doris spit out a boy.

Doris, who we called "Dot," liked to dance and she and Jim went out dancing in Dracut a lot. I think that dancing was her second favorite thing, behind talking on the phone, or just talking. She was always on the phone with someone, and it seemed like whenever we were there visiting, the only time the phone stopped ringing was when Dot was already on it. But there are worse vices, I suppose.

Whenever we visited for Thanksgiving or Christmas, we always took home a meat pie or two that Doris had baked. The holidays meant meat pies, especially to French-Canadians. Nothing says Quebecois like a pie filled with ground pork, beef and, occasionally, potatoes. I didn't have to have my arm twisted to accept as many as were offered, and I usually had some within 10 minutes of arriving back home after the holiday. Nancy makes me meat pies once or twice a year, but between us, they're not as good as her mother's.

Dot was not the most patient person in the world, but the pot shouldn't call the kettle black. When she was at home and largely confined to her bed, Jim had given her a bell to ring if she needed anything. The bell rang a lot. A bell was required because Jim always had the television on in the living room, usually at a decibel level approaching that of a motorcycle rally, and couldn't always hear her calling. Due to what Jim deemed overuse of the bell, he took it back. Once, while we were all sitting around Jim and Dot's kitchen table, Dot asked Jim to get her some ice cream. Jim got right up and was behind Dot in the kitchen, taking the ice cream carton out of the freezer. Not ten seconds later, Doris asked, "Jimmy, where's my ice cream?"

Dot had Parkinson's disease, and ended up in the Town & Country Nursing Home. The last time that I saw her, she was playing bingo as Nancy and I visited with her. Dot wasn't doing well, and Nancy would visit whenever she could, but we were still living in New Jersey. On the Fourth of July in 2015, Nancy woke up feeling strange. We had been planning on Joe and Julia's visit for a few weeks and they were supposed to arrive that afternoon, but Nancy had an odd feeling. Her mother hadn't improved since being moved to D'Youville Manor Life & Wellness Community. After checking with one or more of her sisters, Nancy told me that she wanted me to drive her down to Dracut right away, so I did, dropping her off at Cindy's house.

I didn't stay, but headed straight back to Maine, trying to get there before Joe and Julia arrived. Nancy, meanwhile, was getting a ride from Cindy's house to D'Youville when she got a call from her brother-in-law telling her that Dot had died. Just like me, she was in the car on the way to see her mother and wasn't there when it happened. In addition to her six children, Dot left 13 grandchildren and 20 great-grandchildren. Nancy called me while I was driving home to tell me the news. Joe and Julia arrived in Maine about 10 minutes after I did.

The family planned an open casket Celebration of Life for TUESDAY, JULY 7, 2015, at the McKenna-Ouellette Funeral Home in Lowell from 4:00 - 8:00 p.m. A lot of people came through, and Nancy and her siblings spent the entire night greeting people. Four hours is a long time. I, and the other in-laws, spent most of the night in the back, sitting and talking. I'm not personally a big fan of open caskets, and, thankfully, neither were my parents. On their way home from what turned into a brief visit to Maine, Joe and Julia stopped in at the funeral home.

The next morning, WEDNESDAY, JULY 8, 2015, was the funeral mass at the Ste. Therese Church in Dracut. Dylan served as a pallbearer. As the funeral procession was making its way to the cemetery, it made a detour onto Turgeon Avenue and stopped for a minute in front of Jim and Doris's house. While in the nursing home, Doris had always said that she wanted to go home.

The procession ended at Oakland Cemetery, where Doris and Jim had plots. Someone played a recording of "Spanish Eyes," Doris' favorite song, and she was laid to rest. We went for a "mercy meal," a tradition that I was not familiar with, at the Village Inn after the funeral. Mark, Nancy's brother, had everyone over to his backyard afterwards. Jim was largely just sitting around, looking, understandably, a little lost and out-of-it. After an hour or so, Dylan asked him if he wanted to go to his favorite ice cream place, Sullivan's. Jim accepted, because he loved ice cream, didn't get to see Dylan very often, and had been surrounded by people for the last four days. So we took off, drove to Sullivan's, and sat at a picnic table doing what we liked to do. I think Jim enjoyed getting away for an hour.

It was a nice send-off for Doris. She would have absolutely loved all of the fuss being made over her. It wouldn't be too long before we were back at the McKenna-Ouellette Funeral Home.

CHAPTER 60

MONDAY, MAY 30, 2016

Jim, Nancy's father, and Linda, one of Nancy's four sisters, came to our house in Maine on Memorial Day in 2016. Although we had purchased the house on THURSDAY, NOVEMBER 6, 2014, it definitely needed some work to get ready and we needed to sell our house on Abbey Road. We sold Abbey Road on THURSDAY, MAY 19, 2016, to James and Tara Bach, and took Nancy's blue Jeep Liberty, along with Erin and Molly, to Maine the next day, moving in for good on FRIDAY, MAY 20, 2016. There was a lot of work yet to come for our Maine house, but it was liveable. We hadn't had all that much time to prepare for the move.

We listed Abbey Road for sale on THURSDAY, MARCH 10, 2016, and the Bachs toured the property over the weekend. On MONDAY, MARCH 14, 2016, they made an offer, and, after some haggling, we signed an Agreement of Sale on WEDNESDAY, MARCH 16, 2016. Closing was scheduled for May 19th. We had two months to leave our home of 27 years. The Bachs' asked us a couple of times if we would like to move up the closing date, but we needed the time to get ready.

I had already done a lot of work inside of the Maine house over the past year and a half. I had already put down the 5" oak flooring in the living room, hall and guest bedroom. When Jim and Linda came up on Memorial Day, Jim spent most of the time sitting in our living room on one of the Queen Anne chairs that Nancy and I had inherited from my parents and that I had grown up with on Burrwood Avenue. Apparently, Jim liked the floor a lot, because he made a few comments about it. I later learned that he was still talking about the floor to Linda on their ride home.

Most of our belongings, at least those that were left after we donated much of it to Goodwill and Habitat for Humanity, or thrown out, were sitting in a POD in our driveway when Linda and Jim arrived. I was determined to empty the POD slowly and systematically, so that we could unpack our stuff and try to figure out where to put it in our much smaller house. I would bring in boxes and furniture, and try to at least get them into the correct room. Linda had other thoughts. She was determined that we were going to empty that POD while she was there, so she was constantly bringing things into the house. I finally had to gently tell her to stop. To Linda's chagrin, we didn't finish emptying the POD until a few days later, when Nancy's sister Donna visited and we completed the job.

I had known Jim, of course, for 30 years, ever since Nancy and I met. Jim was born in Lowell, Massachusetts, on TUESDAY, JUNE 3, 1930, and was adopted by Joseph and Mary MacDonald. Yes, Joseph and Mary. My first real memory of him is from the Jingle Bell Run in Boston on SUNDAY, DECEMBER 21, 1986. The Jingle Bell Run was a big deal in Boston back then, and maybe it still is. It was sponsored by the Bill Rodgers Running Center, a running apparel store at Faneuil Hall, and consisted of a 5K evening run through the streets of Boston, ending with a party and dance in the parking garage of the Sheraton Hotel in the Back Bay.

I hate distance running - always have and always will, but I knew that Nancy and Jim ran together, so I decided to show off and do it. The run wasn't just any old run - most of the hundreds of runners were in costumes of one kind or another. Some just wore Christmas hats or antlers, others wore Christmas sweaters, some carried sleigh bells, and some really got into it. Nancy, of course, wanted to run in costume. She dressed as the Grinch, while I was consigned to the role of Max, the Grinch's dog.

Anyone who has seen or read the story knows that Max had to pull the Grinch's sleigh on its trip to Whoville. They also know that in order to pass as a reindeer, Max had to wear a stick, fashioned as an antler, tied on top of his head. So Nancy bought a pair of tan long johns (since Max was tan), we found a leash and a collar, and I suffered the indignity of running through Boston in long underwear, with a collar, fastened to a leash, in snow flurries. When you're youngish and in love, you do stuff.

Jim liked to dance and he was a good dancer. He was usually a hit with the younger ladies, so it wasn't surprising to see him dancing with a group of younger people at the party in the parking garage after the run. Nancy and I, meanwhile, won either first or second place for "Best Costume" that night. I think we received a $100 gift certificate to the Bill Rodgers Running Center.

Jim could also be quirky, like all of us. He really liked doughnuts, so on one of our visits to Dracut, Nancy and I brought him a 10-inch cream-filled doughnut from McMillan's Bakery in Westmont, where my father had frequently gotten our family cinnamon buns and cream doughnuts when I was a kid. Their cream doughnuts are legendary, and we really thought that Jim would love the oversized one we had bought. He wanted nothing to do with it, leaving Nancy flummoxed, but not surprised.

That Memorial Day was the one and only time that Jim saw our house in Maine. It was also the last time that I saw him alive. He was very tired and didn't feel too well. Mostly, he sat in the Queen Anne chair while

Nancy, Linda and I busied ourselves unpacking and organizing. Finally, we took a ride around to show Jim the beach and the area where we were now living. We stopped and bought Jim an ice cream cone from Garside's in Saco, probably maple walnut, and we ate outside at a picnic table. We finally came home and Linda and Nancy helped Jim into Linda's Jeep for the ride back to Massachusetts.

By FRIDAY, JUNE 3, 2016, just four days later, Jim was in the hospital, and the prognosis wasn't good. He had congestive heart failure and all of his children, various grandchildren and I were there. We met with someone from the hospital in a room down the hall from Jim. There was little hope that he was going to recover. I asked how long we were looking at, since no one else did. The woman was fairly noncommittal, but you could tell that it wouldn't be long. I didn't go into his room to see Jim that day. I had just had ice cream with him on Monday, and that's what I preferred to remember.

I left, but Nancy stayed behind with her family. I was going to drive down to New Jersey to empty the last of our things out of storage and bring them back to Maine. While I was in New Jersey, Nancy was spending time at the hospital with most of the family. Jim had a Facetime chat with Dylan on SATURDAY, JUNE 4, 2016. Since I was in New Jersey, I had made plans to play softball on SUNDAY, JUNE 5, 2016 with my old team. I kept my cellphone on me all the time, and while sitting in the dugout during one of the games, it rang. It was Nancy with the news.

Jim left behind his six children and 13 grandchildren, the same as Doris. By this time, though, there were 21 great-grandchildren, one more than Doris's 20.

We went through the same ritual as we had gone through 11 months earlier with Doris. A four-hour Celebration of Life at the McKenna-Ouellette Funeral Home on TUESDAY, JUNE 7, 2016, and the mass at Ste. Therese Church on WEDNESDAY, JUNE 8, 2016, followed by the burial and a mercy meal. Joe made the drive up from Pennsylvania, even though I had assured him that it wasn't necessary. And with that, Nancy and I had said goodbye to our four parents.

CHAPTER 61

Nancy and I both like history and both like politics, but we just couldn't do it. The inauguration which we had dreaded for more than two months was happening and neither of us had the stomach to watch. Some people held out hope that maybe, somehow, someway, by some miracle, he would actually be able to rise to the office. That turned out to be just fantastical thinking. A long, dark journey was about to begin.

We didn't turn the TV on, had coffee, and headed somewhere, anywhere, where we wouldn't have to actually see it. Maybe if we didn't actually see it, it wouldn't truly be real. It was. Dear God, it was.

CHAPTER 62

We invited everyone who was at our wedding and still alive to our 30th anniversary celebration. I bugged Nancy over the years to have an anniversary party on a boat, just as we had had our wedding on the boat in Boston Harbor. Finally, after we moved to Maine, I convinced her to do it. We chartered the *M/V Islander*, a boat very similar to the one we had gotten married on, from Portland Discovery Land & Sea Tours in Portland. Although we had married in Boston, we would celebrate our anniversary in Portland. Using our memories and a list of the people we had invited to our wedding, we began sending save-the-dates to all of our living wedding guests. Gifts were strictly forbidden and we warned our guests that they (the gifts, not our guests) would be jettisoned.

In addition to the original wedding guests, we invited a bunch of other people as well. We added all of Nancy's nieces and nephews, who were little kids or not even born yet in 1987, but who were now in their 20's, 30's, or 40's, and some friends we had picked up during our married years. The boat was crawling with all of Nancy's siblings and their children, as well as some friends I hadn't seen for years, or even decades, like Tom and Mary Beth Bryant, Blane and Betty Ann Petterson, Bret Turner, and some Ocean Parkers like Earl Norman, Jeff and Pam Chute, Barry and Lynne Jackman, and Jan and Ed Hryniewicz. Joe, Julia and Kevin came up from Pennsylvania, and Dylan and Elizabeth came from North Carolina.

The weather was eerily similar to the weather of our wedding night thirty years earlier. It was 72 degrees at 5:00 when the *Islander* left Long Wharf and 64 degrees when it returned at 8:00 p.m. There was a small breeze with a waning crescent moon. It was perfect. We selected 5:00 p.m. because that had been the time of our wedding. Sunset sails on Casco Bay in Maine are pretty damn awesome.

Planning an anniversary party is more work than one might think. Finding a caterer who would, and could, work on a boat was the first challenge. Because we were in Maine, we knew that we wanted to serve lobster, but also knew that cooking and serving whole lobsters would be too difficult, since there really wasn't room for tables for a sit-down meal. Besides, the star of the show was Casco Bay, with its islands, like Peaks Island, Cushing Island, Little Diamond Island, Mackworth Island and Ram Island; its rocky coastline; its views of the Portland skyline; and, of course, its lighthouses - Spring Point Ledge Lighthouse ("Bug Light"), Ram Island Ledge Light Station and the transcendent Portland Head Light, first lit in 1791, allegedly the most-photographed lighthouse in the country, if not the world.

Since lobster dinner was not practical, we decided that we would serve the other signature Maine food - lobster rolls. Finding someone who would prepare fresh lobster rolls on a boat wasn't easy, but Nancy and I finally visited Linda Kate Lobster Company in Portland, met with the owner, and settled on hiring them. We ordered 50 lobster rolls to be prepared on the boat - half butter (Connecticut style), half mayo (Maine style), along with two pans of lobster mac 'n' cheese (serving 25-30 people each), 50 cheeseburger and veggie sliders, and potato salad. Apparently, we over-ordered on the lobster mac, since we ended up bringing several pounds of it home. Over the next two months, I ate lots and lots of lobster mac, but that's nothing to complain about. For dessert, we procured a few dozen whoopie pies from Wicked Whoopies in Freeport.

We also had to find housing for Nancy's family, as well as for Joe, Julia and Kevin, since there wasn't much room at our house, with Dylan and Elizabeth staying with us. We found four cottages, of varying size and quality that guests could rent, and put up most of Nancy's family in them.

I spent a couple of months carefully curating a playlist of songs for the cruise, put them in order and timed them to last for the night. Having worked on the playlist and meticulously chosen and placed the songs in the proper order on my phone, we had the music which Nancy and I liked, and didn't accommodate requests, although we got a few. Most people were dancing, enjoying a beer or two, and taking hundreds of pictures of Portland Head Light as we pulled near. We danced, reminisced, enjoyed drinks and laughed. We pulled back to the dock as everyone sang the obligatory "Sweet Caroline."

Everyone was invited back to our house, where we discovered that our new deck could, in fact, support 30 or 40 people at a time. We showed people around our house, showing off the work which we had done. Bret Turner, who had spent a lot of time at the house as a kid in the 1960's and 70's, explained what it used to look like and how our kitchen used to be an enclosed back porch. People slowly departed, either for home or for their rentals, leaving Nancy and I, Dylan and Elizabeth, Joe and Julia, and Kevin to sit around the fire pit and finally relax.

It was a glorious evening, and so much fun to celebrate 30 years. I want to do it again for our 35th, but there's this virus going around, so we'll see if that actually happens.

CHAPTER 63

SUNDAY, FEBRUARY 4, 2018

The Eagles finally got their rematch with the Cheatin' Patriots after losing *Super Bowl XXXIX* to them in 2005. The Patriots no-doubt somehow cheated in *Super Bowl LII*, just like they had in the previous match-up, since that's what the Patriots do. Whatever they did this time, it was to no avail.

It was the tenth *Super Bowl* appearance for the Patriots, but only the third for the Eagles. Both teams had gone 13-3 during the regular season, and had each won their two playoff games to advance to the *Super Bowl*. The Eagles, however, had a serious problem. After starting the season 10-2, second-year quarterback Carson Wentz, at that time the favorite to win the league MVP award, tore his ACL in game 13 against the Rams and was finished for the season. He was replaced by Nick Foles, a journeyman quarterback in his second stint as an Eagle. Nonetheless, the Eagles won three of their last four games. Although they were underdogs in each of their playoff games, the Eagles defeated the Atlanta Falcons 15-10 on SATURDAY, JANUARY 13, 2018, and crushed the Minnesota Vikings 38-7 on SUNDAY, JANUARY 21, 2018.

New England (the region, not the team) prepared for the game in all of its self-righteous, pompous, entitled glory. The *Maine Sunday Telegram*, on the morning of the game, ran the headline, "Prep the Duck Boats," referencing the Patriots' traditional parade after *Super Bowl* victories. Dan Shaughnessy, the *Boston Globe* sportswriter known best for not always being right, but for always being certain, wrote this, for example, on SUNDAY, AUGUST 29, 2021:

> *Cam and Mac. Mac and Cam. It's been a sports radio talk-a-thon, a gridiron soap opera, getting us through a hot/rainy August while waiting for games that finally count in September.*

Why did we waste our time wondering?

The Patriots final preseason game was Sunday night in the Meadowlands against the Giants (a 22-20 Patriot win) and it's clear there was never any real competition for the job of Patriots' starting quarterback.

[I]t's clear by now that there is nothing that's going to make Belichick turn to a rookie quarterback to start the season . . . He'd rather stick needles in his eyes than turn to a rookie quarterback . . . Cam Newton is the starting quarterback of the Patriots. As a wise man once said . . . it is what it is.

Less than 48 hours later, the Patriots released Cam Newton and named rookie Mac Jones their starting quarterback.

We should have known that the Eagles had a good chance in the *Super Bowl* when Shaughnessy wrote this before the game:

Not to go Full Tomato Can on you, but I think by now we all have concluded that there is no bloody way that the Eagles' Doug Pederson and Nick Foles are going to beat Bill Belichick and Tom Brady in a Super Bowl. Those of us here from the Globe will do our best to provide comprehensive coverage of the event, and we will feign interest in manufacturing some pregame drama, but I think we all already know how this is going to end.

Clever of the Red Sox to schedule Truck Day for next Monday — the day after the Patriots win the Super Bowl and the day before another duck boat parade.

Dylan traveled from Charlotte to Philadelphia to watch the game with the Carlins, while I was stuck in Maine. We texted and talked throughout the entire, wildly entertaining, game. The progression of scores looked like this:

3-0 (Eagles)

3-3 (Tie)

9-3 (Eagles)

15-3 (Eagles)

15-6 (Eagles)

15-12 (Eagles)

22-12 (Eagles)

22-19 (Eagles)

29-19 (Eagles)

29-26 (Eagles)

32-26 (Eagles)

33-32 (Patriots)

38-33 (Eagles)

41-33 (Eagles)

The relatively odd scores - 12, 15, 22, 29, 33 - were the result of both the Eagles and Patriots missing extra point kicks early in the game and the Eagles also failing on a two-point conversion, trying to make up for the missed extra point. Early in the second quarter, the Patriots attempted a trick play, which resulted in Tom Brady dropping an easy pass, leading to the Patriots turning the ball over on downs to the Eagles on the next play. At the end of the first half, the Eagles ran what would become the most famous single play in the team's history, "Philly Special," which resulted in a touchdown catch by quarterback Nick Foles (which Brady probably would have dropped) on a pass thrown by third-string tight end Trey Burton.

When New England finally took their first lead of the game, 33-32, with just over nine minutes left, I was not feeling particularly optimistic. Somehow, miraculously, the Eagles pulled off a seven-minute drive and scored a touchdown with 2:21 left in the game, to retake the lead at 38-33. Now it was time to sweat. The Patriots would have all the time they needed to march down the field, score a touchdown, and again deny Philly a *Super Bowl* win. This time, the Hoodie and the GOAT wouldn't have their way. Brady fumbled, the Eagles recovered and kicked another field goal, and time expired as Brady's Hail Mary pass fell incomplete.

Since Dylan was in Philadelphia, we talked about me driving down and going to the victory parade together, thinking that it would probably be held on Tuesday. When it was announced that the parade wouldn't be until THURSDAY, FEBRUARY 8, 2018, Dylan decided that he simply couldn't miss an entire week of work and headed back to North Carolina. We settled for watching the parade on TV. Somehow, I have never managed to make it to any of the championship parades in Philadelphia - not the two for the Flyers, nor the two for the Phillies, nor the one for the Sixers, nor the one for the Eagles. The way things look for all of those teams, I might have to wait quite a while for my next chance.

CHAPTER 64

FRIDAY, MAY 4, 2018

For my birthday in 2018, Nancy and I went to Charlotte for the weekend to visit Dylan and Elizabeth. Nancy, Dylan and I spent the early part of the day walking around Freedom Park, a large urban park with a lake and walking trails. In the afternoon, we headed to the United States National Whitewater Center, a 1,300 acre site with 50 miles of trails, ziplines, ropes courses, rafting, and dozens of other outdoor activities. None of us were really up for any great adventures, so we just walked around the site and found a spot to sit down and listen to some live music. It was a great way to spend a birthday.

I have been to Charlotte a number of times, since Dylan has been living there for the past eight years after graduating from college (except for a brief stay in Winston-Salem, which I never visited). In June of 2014, I had driven down with him to get him set up in his apartment as he started work at his first post-college job at Wells Fargo. As you might expect, it was a miserable, hot, humid day in North Carolina in June, not great for moving, but pretty good for sweating.

Later that month, Nancy and I went down to visit. On SATURDAY, JUNE 28, 2014, we went to Memorial Stadium in Charlotte to watch the Charlotte Hounds and Boston Cannons lacrosse game. It might have been on this trip that we went to Midwood Smokehouse, which Dylan assured us had excellent 'cue. It's tough to get good barbeque in New Jersey or Maine. As advertised, it was awesome, as confirmed by the fact that a couple of years later, President Obama himself made a point of going to Midwood when he was campaigning in North Carolina.

One year, Nancy and I spent Thanksgiving in Charlotte, where Dylan had smoked a turkey for Thanksgiving Dinner. The next night, we went to the Belk Theater to watch *Home Alone* as the Charlotte Symphony Orchestra played the score live. It was a fun night, except for the couple in front of us who used the occasion to make out for nearly the entire performance.

A couple of times, while visiting in North Carolina, we've made the two-hour drive west to Asheville, a charming little city full of artists, hippies, street performers and quirky shops. We toured the Biltmore House, a mansion built by George Washington Vanderbilt II in the 1890's. Biltmore House is the largest privately-owned "house" in the United States, with 189,926 square feet, 250 rooms, 43 bathrooms, 65 fireplaces and 3 kitchens. The Vanderbilts had some money. Naturally, we've visited most of the breweries in Asheville - Wicked Weed, New Belgium, Hi-Wire, Green Man and Pisgah, to name a few. Good beer - but not nearly as good as Maine beer.

ǂ

CHAPTER 65

SATURDAY, FEBRUARY 9, 2019

John E. Melhorn's funeral was held at the Immaculate Heart of Mary Catholic Church in Abbottsville, Pennsylvania at 10:00 a.m. He had passed away on SUNDAY, FEBRUARY 3, 2019, at the age of 76, leaving behind Janice, his wife of 58 years, and five children. John Melhorn was the father of Julia Strong and the father-in-law of Joe Strong, our longtime friends. Joe was the second person who saw Nixon in the clouds when we were playing softball for St. Gregory's at Sterling High School.

I drove part of the way down from Maine on FRIDAY, FEBRUARY 8, 2019, planning to drive the final 2½ or 3 hours on Saturday morning. I stayed at a hotel, I think it was a Hampton Inn in Bordentown, New Jersey. It was an uneventful ride, but it was still a lot of driving to get from Maine to southern Pennsylvania. Joe and Julia had both attended the services for my mother and father, as well as Nancy's mother. Joe had driven up from Pennsylvania to attend Nancy's father's Celebration of Life. Nancy and I decided that she would stay home and take care of the dogs while I drove down to Pennsylvania for the service.

I woke up early on Saturday morning at the Hampton Inn, put on some good clothes for the funeral, and headed off for Abbottsville, a place that I had never heard of, much less been to. When I arrived just before the service began, there were a lot of people already there, so I took a seat ten or fifteen rows back in the church. John Melhorn had been active in his church, in scouting, and had a large family, hence the large turnout. Joe and Julia were sitting down in the front with family, so they didn't even know that I was there. We hadn't told them that either of us were going in case we changed our minds or the weather was too bad to travel.

After the service, I went to the reception in the basement of the church, saw Julia and Joe, grabbed a quick bite to eat, and headed out so that I could get most of my driving in before dark. I was planning on driving as far as southern Connecticut after the service, staying the night at another budget motel, and driving the rest of the way on Sunday morning. About an hour after leaving the service, I felt a little itch on my back, naturally in a spot that was difficult to reach while driving. I finally managed to locate it and gave it a little scratch. I figured that maybe I had gotten a spider bite or something, since it was February, and not really mosquito season.

By the time I reached my second hotel, I was pretty itchy. This is what I get for staying at budget hotels. When I called Nancy that evening, I told her that I was afraid that I might have gotten bed bugs. I was immediately instructed not to bring anything into the house when I got home the next day, but to leave the suitcase and all of my clothing outside. I stripped as soon as I got home, immediately took a shower, and showed Nancy the marks. Yes, I did indeed have bed bug bites. The thought of those creepy little things crawling all over me and munching away on my flesh as I slept is disgusting. The itching was pretty nasty - but not nearly as nasty as poison ivy - and made for a couple of fitful nights sleeping.

Nearly 15 years earlier, I had also attended the service for Robert A. Strong (TUESDAY, FEBRUARY 17, 1925 - MONDAY, JUNE 28, 2004), although I didn't have to drive as far and I didn't end up with bed bugs. Joe's father had been ill for some time. Joe, Kevin and I were in Boston for the weekend series between the Red Sox and Phillies and Joe kept checking in to see how his father was doing. We went to the Friday night game, and again on SATURDAY, JUNE 26, 2004, a 1:30 p.m. game, which the Phillies surprisingly won, 9-2. It was after that game that we saw the man wearing the Smarty Jones head. Of course, we went out for a couple of beers after the game. When Joe checked on his father later that night, it seemed that his dad had taken a serious turn for the worse. It didn't take long for us to decide that we would head back home as soon as possible.

We would have left immediately and driven through the night, but given our beer intake throughout the day, even we knew that that would not be the smartest decision. So we tried to get some sleep, woke up very early on SUNDAY, JUNE 27, 2004, and started the 6 ½ hour drive south. We didn't miss much of a baseball game, as the Red Sox pummelled the Phillies 12-3, behind the pitching of former Phillie Curt Schilling. Schilling is apparently a world-class horse's ass (sorry, Smarty). The general manager of one team he played for once said something like, "He's a horse every fifth day and a horse's ass the other four." On the night of January 6, 2021, after the insurrection, he tweeted:

You cowards sat on your hands, did nothing while liberal trash looted rioted and burned for air Jordan's and big screens, sit back, stfu, and watch folks start a confrontation for shit that matters like rights, democracy and the end of gvt

corruption.

Obviously, he's a very deep thinker, but not so keen on grammar and punctuation. Anyway, we made it home safely on Sunday and Joe's father passed away the next day. Thank goodness we made it home in time.

A month after he passed away, a memorial service was held at Blair Memorial Park. Robert Strong served as a First Lieutenant in the United States Army during World War II and was awarded both a Bronze Star and a Purple Heart for his service. On FRIDAY, JULY 30, 2004, I drove to Bellwood, Pennsylvania, a nearly four-hour drive, for his memorial service. Joe and Julia were there, of course, along with only a handful of other people. It was sad.

CHAPTER 66

SATURDAY, SEPTEMBER 14, 2019

Each year, on the second Saturday of September, Maine hosts Maine Open Lighthouse Day. Not too far from us, in Cape Elizabeth, is Fort Williams, a beautiful park and home to Portland Head Light. By many accounts, it is the most-photographed lighthouse in America. Completed in 1791, the lighthouse was commissioned by George Washington. Nearly everyone who has come to visit us in Maine has been treated to a trip to Portland Head Light. We have sailed by many times on the schooner *Windameen* and on our 30th anniversary cruise.

We went to the lighthouse on SATURDAY, MAY 26, 2018, with Jane and Ray Carlin, our neighbors from Abbey Road, and again on FRIDAY, JULY 13, 2018, with Linda and Billy Tierney and three of their grandchildren. Nancy and I went by ourselves on THURSDAY, DECEMBER 10, 2020, when the lighthouse was adorned with a giant wreath for Christmas. We have visited Fort Williams literally dozens of times since we moved to Maine.

Maine is home to some 65 lighthouses, and I think that we have seen most of them, although many are only accessible by boat. We have been to Portland Breakwater Light ("Bug Light") a number of times, including on SATURDAY, JULY 6, 2019, with Dylan while he was up visiting over the holiday. We saw Cuckolds Lighthouse in Newagen on FRIDAY, MAY 18, 2018.

One of my favorite lighthouses is Owl's Head Light Station near Rockland. We have been to Owl's head three or four times, but have never seen any ghosts, even though the lighthouse is believed to be haunted. The last time we visited was on MONDAY, MAY 10, 2021, while on our way to Camden, Maine for a quick vacation. One of the first things you see before climbing the stairs to the lighthouse is a grave marker for one of the keeper's dogs, who is said to have saved passing ships by pulling on the bell's rope to alert them to danger. The lighthouse stands high above the harbor, 100 feet above sea level. The views from the lighthouse are spectacular, although I have never been up in the tower itself.

Our favorite lighthouse is Pemaquid Point Lighthouse in Bristol. The views are amazing, and the rocks are made for clambering. We have been to Pemaquid a number of times, including on FRIDAY, MAY 11, 2018. At Pemaquid, we were able to climb up into the light tower and to tour the Fishermen's Museum below. We have visited, or at least gotten as close as we could, to many other lighthouses in Maine. We have been to Doubling Point Lighthouse in Arrowsic, Squirrel Point Light in Phippsburg, Marshall Point Lighthouse in St. George, Bass Harbor Head Light Station in Bass Harbor, Cape Neddick Nubble Lighthouse in York, West Quoddy Head Light in South Lubec, East Light and West Light in Cape Elizabeth, Spring Point Ledge Lighthouse in South Portland, Curtis Island Lighthouse in Camden, and Egg Rock Lighthouse in Bar Harbor. We see Wood Island Lighthouse in Biddeford Pool from the beach in Ocean Park. We have sailed by Ram Island Ledge Light Station in Portland, as well as Ram Island Island Light and Burnt Island Light in Boothbay. I'm sure that there are many others, too. I even took the treacherous, windy walk down 4,346 feet of granite breakwater rocks to the Rockland Breakwater Lighthouse on WEDNESDAY, MAY 12, 2021.

Maine Open Lighthouse Day is the only day of the year when the public can climb the tower of Portland Head Light. Tickets to go up into the tower are free, but they are on a first-come, first-served basis on Lighthouse Day. Since we expected demand to be high, and with the lighthouse only open for six hours, we got up very early and went to get our tickets. Luckily, we got there early enough and secured two timed tickets for a couple of hours later. We killed some time by going to the best doughnut shop in the world, The Cookie Jar, just up the road in Cape Elizabeth, for coffee and a doughnut. There is no doubt that I bought a few extras to bring home.

Although the weather was windy and overcast, we had fun climbing the stairs and taking in the view from atop Portland Head Light. Maine Open Lighthouse Day was cancelled in 2020 because of the ongoing pandemic, and Nancy was in Massachusetts shopping for a dress for Dylan's wedding for the SATURDAY, SEPTEMBER 11, 2021, event, but we will definitely be visiting another lighthouse in 2022. The only question is which one.

CHAPTER 67

The Eagles were in Green Bay for *Thursday Night Football*. Nancy and I had been planning a trip to Acadia National Park and Lubec for some time. We left on MONDAY, SEPTEMBER 23, 2019, and drove to Southwest Harbor, where we had reserved two nights at the Harbor Cottage Inn. Southwest Harbor is on Mount Desert Island, on what they refer to as "the quiet side" of the island, a little bit off of the tourist-beaten path.

On Monday night, we got some takeout from Beal's Lobster Pier in Southwest Harbor and ate on the porch at the inn. We had the entire porch to ourselves and chilled out on seafood and beer. On TUESDAY, SEPTEMBER 24, 2019, we spent the entire day at Acadia National Park. Acadia is absolutely beautiful - stunning, really. From the Porcupine Islands to Jordan Pond to Thunder Hole to Sand Beach, it is awash with stunning views of almost everything that is great about Maine - mountains, rocky coast, lakes, and sandy beaches. We went to the top of Cadillac Mountain, the first place in the U.S. on which to see the sunrise (although we didn't get there that early). Much of Maine, and Acadia, was shaped by the glaciers that moved across Maine during the Ice Age. As recently as 15,000 years ago, Maine was covered by a mile-deep sheet of ice. When it finally receded, it was kind enough to leave behind what we are now so richly blessed with.

When we finally left Acadia, we drove through Ellsworth, looking for MoMo's, which Nancy had read about in our favorite tour book. MoMo is short for "motormouth," since the owner apparently likes to talk. MoMo's is a self-service cheesecake shop (yes, a self-service cheesecake shop) in the owner's garage, operating completely on the honor system, where you stop, walk in, help yourself to a slice or two (or more) of cheesecake, and drop your money in a cashbox. Nancy and I got ourselves a couple of slices, and headed back to enjoy them on what had become our private porch at the inn.

On WEDNESDAY, SEPTEMBER 25, 2019, we left Mount Desert Island for the rest of our trip up to Lubec. On the way, we drove up and down the Schoodic Peninsula, still part of Acadia National Park, but nowhere near as crowded. Schoodic was just as beautiful as parts of Mount Desert Island, and we spent a couple of hours taking it all in, before departing up what is called the "Bold Coast" of Maine toward Lubec. The Bold Coast is wild Maine, with fishing villages, harbors, blueberry barrens and rivers leading to the Bay of Fundy. The Bay of Fundy is one of the seven North American "Wonders of Nature" (along with the Grand Canyon, Yellowstone, Niagara Falls, Yosemite, the Everglades and Mount McKinley), with tides that rise and fall by up to 50 feet in some places.

Finally arriving in Lubec on Wednesday afternoon, our first stop was West Quoddy Head Lighthouse, located on the easternmost tip of the continental United States, first built in 1808, and the only candy-striped lighthouse in the United States. For a couple of minutes, Nancy and I were the easternmost people in America. We looked across the bay to Canada, took a stroll around the park, at first engulfed by an incredibly dense fog, then headed into town to Cohill's Inn, where we would be staying. I chose Cohill's, at least partly (or perhaps, mainly), because of the Philadelphia Eagles logo in one of their pictures.

With our penchant for visiting breweries, after checking in, we walked down the street to Lubec Brewing Company for a beer before supper. There weren't too many people there on a late Wednesday afternoon in September, and we enjoyed a beer and chatted up Gale White, the founder and owner. Lubec Brewing was pretty informal, and seemed to stay open as long as there were people inside. By now, we were getting hungry, and decided to try the Fisherman's Wharf, a classic New England seafood place, with lots of fried food and lobster. I decided on fried clams, and when the waitress came over, I asked for the fried clam dinner. Much to my disappointment, the waitress told me that they were out of clams. Dejectedly, I had to settle for fish 'n' chips.

As we were eating, a man in hip waders came walking into the restaurant and went to the kitchen. A minute or two later, the clammer or the waitress came out of the kitchen and announced to all of the diners, "We have clams!" We should have had another beer at Lubec Brewing. Then I could have had a really fresh fried clam dinner.

Our upstairs room at the Cohill Inn overlooked the narrows and was directly across from Campobello Island and Canada. When we woke up on Thursday morning and looked out, there were already fishing boats heading out and a group of seals (either a herd or bob or harem or rookery) bobbing in and out of the water, presumably either fishing or playing. And it was an absolutely gorgeous, warm, sunny day, topping out at around 70 degrees - not bad for late September in northeastern Maine. It was about to become one of my favorite days.

We were headed to Campobello Island for the day, so we drove across the little two-lane bridge, showed our passports to Canadian Customs, and headed for our first stop, Roosevelt Campobello International Park. Campobello Island is surprisingly small, only nine miles long and three miles wide, so we could see pretty much the whole thing in a day. As a child, Franklin Delano Roosevelt had spent many summers on Campobello. It was there that he first experienced symptoms, and was diagnosed with, infantile paralysis, or polio, at the age of 31. We took the tour of Roosevelt Cottage, if by "cottage" you mean 34 rooms, including 18 bedrooms and 6 bathrooms. In 1908, his mother gave Roosevelt Cottage to Franklin and Eleanor Roosevelt as a belated wedding present. Nancy and I received no such wedding presents, even belatedly.

 We headed north from Roosevelt Cottage toward the far northern end of the island, taking in the coast and the bay. At the far end of the island, at the very end of Lighthouse Road, we stopped. In front of us was Head Harbour Lightstation, built in 1829. The problem, of course, is that Head Harbour Lightstation is on a different island than Campobello. With a little patience, you can actually get to the lighthouse if you time things right. With the tide rising and falling so significantly in the Bay of Fundy, there are a few hours when you can walk across the floor of the bay from Campobello Island to the lighthouse. You don't want to stay too long, however, or you will be spending the night there if you don't come back before the tide rises again. I accepted the challenge, but had to wait for the tide to go out.

We walked around the area, watching the porpoises and eagles, waiting for the tide to ebb and expose the floor, which was covered with slippery rocks, sand and mud. Finally, Nancy and I climbed down the metal ladder built into the cliff. Nancy decided to pass on traversing to seabed, but I scrabbled across to the other side and the lighthouse. While I was celebrating my success at the lighthouse, Nancy met a middle-aged couple from Wisconsin and chatted with them while I walked around the lighthouse grounds. Finally, having seen enough, I made the trek back to Campobello as the tide started to rise again.

As the sun got lower, we made a couple of other stops along the shore of Campobello, at Herring Cove and Raccoon Beach, not really wanting to leave, but finally heading back across the bridge to Lubec. After a long day outdoors, we decided to head back to Lubec Brewing Company for a beer before dinner. While there, Nancy spotted the Wisconsin couple at one of the tables and shouted, "Hey, Wisconsin!" The guy then started talking about some Wisconsin beers that he had in his camper and invited us to try one (or rather *insisted* that we try one). We agreed to meet across the street in a lot next to what appeared to be a long-abandoned sardine canning facility. At one time, there were more than 20 sardine processors in Lubec, but they are all gone. There is a sardine museum, though, but we didn't have time to visit it. Anyway, our new friends from Wisconsin brought some beers from their camper, and the guy was very determined to let us know that these beers, from New Glarus Brewing, could NOT, I repeat, could NOT be purchased outside of Wisconsin. He pointed out several times the writing on the label to that effect. Nancy and I each had one, *Spotted Cow Farmhouse Ale*, I believe, and chatted. Being from Maine, we are generally not overly impressed by other states' beer, with the possible exception of Vermont.

Having finished our Wisconsin beers, and the sun having set, we were ready for dinner, and headed for a nice little restaurant across the street from where we were staying. Of course, I was going to have seafood, and asked the waitress which were better, the clams or the scallops. "Oh, honey, the clams," she said. And so I ordered what I must admit were the best fried clams I have ever had, before or since.

By the time dinner was over, the Eagles-Packers game had started and I was ready to head back to our room to watch on the little television. Originally, we had planned to eat supper that night at Cohill's, where we were staying, but when we left that morning there was a sign in the window saying that the restaurant would be closed that night for a private event. As we approached the Cohill Inn after dinner, I peered through the glass and saw about a dozen people, mostly women, watching the Eagles game on a large flat-screen TV inside. There were also a couple of young border collies running around. Nancy said, "We have to knock on the door." Since it was game day, I was wearing my Eagles hat, and I knocked on the door, pointed to my hat, and they let us in. I knew from the website that Ellen Cohill, one of the owners, was an Eagles fan, and they knew that we were staying there. Glenn Charles, the other owner, poured me a Guiness and we watched the game, a scintillating 34-27 Eagles win, with complete strangers in the far reaches of northeastern Maine. We also played with the dogs. Seals, porpoises, lighthouses, FDR's cottage, beaches, fried clams, Wisconsin and Maine beer, eagles and Eagles, border collies, all in one day. Everyone should be that rich.

CHAPTER 68

I drove myself to ClearChoiceMD Urgent Care on Payne Road in Scarborough, where I saw Dr. Anna Schmid. The drive was far easier than the one I had made with a broken kneecap and ruptured patellar tendon. Nancy was in Dracut visiting her sisters when I went. The left side of my face had been swollen for a few days, right near the jaw hinge. The area was hard, and it was very difficult to open my mouth, chew, or eat. It wasn't excruciating, but it hurt.

Naturally, I had chosen to treat the condition myself, without any nettlesome medical intervention. I tend to under-engage with the medical community. I took Advil and aspirin, applied cold packs and hot packs, and massaged the area. Sometimes it seemed like it was improving, but that was mostly just wishful thinking. After close to a week, I finally broke down and saw a doctor, who quickly diagnosed a salivary gland infection.

I had never heard of a salivary gland infection, but apparently it's a thing. It seems that we have three sets of salivary glands - the sublingual glands below the tongue, the submandibular glands under the jaw, and the parotid glands in the upper cheeks near the ears. Who knew that we have to salivate so much? It was my left parotid gland that had somehow become infected.

I hoped that the 10-day course of antibiotics - Clindamycin, to be exact - worked, because the alternative was having a needle stuck in my mouth to drain the gland, which didn't sound at all like a fun exercise. I took the pills religiously, and, mercifully, they worked. Compared to bed bugs, poison ivy, a ruptured patellar tendon, broken collarbone, food poisoning, or getting hit in the nuts with a frozen Snickers bar, I highly recommend the salivary gland infection.

CHAPTER 69

WEDNESDAY, MARCH 11, 2020

Nancy and I ate lunch at Duckfat, a small restaurant on Middle Street in Portland. Duckfat gets its name from one of its signature items, Belgian fries cooked in duck fat. It was the first and only time that we have eaten there. I had "The Original Duckfat Milkshake," made with vanilla gelato, creme anglais, and Tahitian vanilla beans. Nancy, being a french fries aficionado, ordered fries. I have implored her to write a book about the 500 or 600 best places on the East Coast for fries, but so far she has balked at the idea. I, being a big fan of meatloaf, ordered a meatloaf sandwich. One sure sign of being old is feeling compelled to describe what you had for lunch or dinner.

The only other time I ordered meatloaf at a restaurant, that I can remember, was at the Maine Diner in Wells. Nancy and I had been on a day trip down the coast on a Monday, and were headed home when we approached the Maine Diner. It is either (a) the best diner in the world, or (b) an overpriced tourist trap, depending on which reviews you believe. Nancy is not a big fan of diners, probably because she didn't grow up in New Jersey, where every city and town has at least one fantastic diner. In order to qualify as a real diner, there must be a counter; chrome, bolt-down, backless swivel stools with red cushioned seats; at least one dessert display full of cake, pie and doughnuts on the counter; a waitress who calls you either "hon" or "sweetie;" and a jukebox in each booth. Regardless, we stopped in, and to my surprise it was "Meatloaf Madness Monday" at the diner. That sounded just impossible to pass up, so I ordered the meatloaf special. Madness hardly did it justice.

The meatloaf special arrived at our table via forklift from the kitchen, 20 or 30 pounds of ground meat, filler, and gravy the consistency of snot hanging over the edges of an oversized dinner plate. And only $10.99! I tried my best, ate maybe 10 or 15% of it, and took the rest home to enjoy on Meatloaf Madness Tuesday . . . and Wednesday . . . and Thursday . . . It didn't last as long as the leftover lobster mac from our anniversary cruise, but I got several good meals out of it.

I used to make fun of my father as he got older, because every time he went out to eat and ordered prime rib, which he often did, the slice was thicker than the time before. "Dave," he would tell me, "The prime rib was *this* thick," spreading his thumb and index finger farther apart each time he told me. And now here I am, telling you how big my meatloaf was.

Our visit to Duckfat was the last time that we would eat inside of a restaurant for nearly two years. The pandemic was coming to Maine.

CHAPTER 70

TUESDAY, MARCH 24, 2020

Two weeks into the pandemic, we needed to go grocery shopping. The last time we had gone before COVID-19 struck was on THURSDAY, MARCH 5, 2020, when we had gone together to Trader Joe's in Portland. Grocery shopping may not sound like too nerve-wracking a chore, but it was at the end of March in 2020. Market Basket in Biddeford usually opened at 7:00 a.m., but had just started opening at 6:00 a.m. for seniors, who were at the highest risk of getting seriously ill from the coronavirus. It was still very much unknown exactly how the virus spread, and there was quite a bit of uncertainty about whether or not you could get it from touching surfaces, and, if so, what kind of surfaces. It was also unknown how long the virus survived on various materials and at what temperatures. Touching a shopping cart or a door handle seemed fraught with unknown danger.

Nancy and I decided that I would go alone to Market Basket on Tuesday morning, since there was no sense in two of us risking it. I set my alarm for 5:00 a.m., woke up, had a cup of coffee, and headed out in the cold and the dark for Biddeford. There were a fair number of people there and I went through the store with my list as fast as I possibly could. It was actually a bit frightening, since I really didn't know how serious the risk was as I tried to shop, keep a good distance from other shoppers, and follow the one-way arrows in the aisles. I finally checked out, using plastic store bags, since shoppers were not allowed to bring their own bags into the store at that time. I spent $285.27 and headed home.

We had decided that we would not bring the grocery bags into the house for fear that they might be crawling with the virus, so I left all of the bags on the porch. Wearing rubber gloves, Nancy wiped every grocery item with a disinfecting wipe before we brought anything into the house. Only perishables came inside - everything else could stay outside on the porch for a day or two, just in case. We repeated this process for the first couple of months of the pandemic. I went back to Market Basket at 6:00

a.m. on MONDAY, APRIL 6, 2020; MONDAY, APRIL 20, 2020; FRIDAY, MAY 1, 2020; and WEDNESDAY, MAY 13, 2020.

One of the things that we had concluded was relatively safe was to pick up craft beer at some of the great breweries in Maine. During the first six months of the pandemic, I went to a lot of breweries to pick up beer (and support the local economy, of course). I went to Lone Pine Brewing in Portland the most often, picking up beer (*Oh-J, Hot Fudge Monday*, and *Choco Tuesday*, mainly) on SUNDAY, MARCH 29, 2020; TUESDAY, APRIL 14, 2020; SATURDAY, MAY 2, 2020; WEDNESDAY, MAY 13, 2020; FRIDAY, MAY 22, 2020; SUNDAY, MAY 31, 2020; SUNDAY, JUNE 7, 2020; TUESDAY, JUNE 30, 2020; and TUESDAY, AUGUST 4, 2020. I went to Maine Beer Company in Freeport, mainly to pick up *Dinner* and pizza for Nancy, on FRIDAY, APRIL 17, 2020; FRIDAY, APRIL 24, 2020; FRIDAY, JULY 24, 2020; THURSDAY, JULY 30, 2020; and FRIDAY, AUGUST 14, 2020. I went to Mast Landing Brewing in Westbrook on SATURDAY, APRIL 25, 2020; SATURDAY, MAY 9, 2020; and FRIDAY, JULY 31, 2020. I stopped by Bissell Brothers Brewing in Portland on FRIDAY, APRIL 17, 2020 (probably for *Swish* or *The Substance*); and again on WEDNESDAY, JUNE 3, 2020; and SATURDAY, JUNE 13, 2020. SoMe Brewing in York got visits on FRIDAY, MAY 1, 2020; WEDNESDAY, MAY 6, 2020; THURSDAY, JUNE 18, 2020; SATURDAY, JULY 4, 2020; and THURSDAY, JULY 16, 2020. The brewery complex on Industrial Way in Portland got a few pandemic visits to pick up some beer. I stopped at Definitive Brewing on FRIDAY, JULY 3, 2020, and WEDNESDAY, AUGUST 12, 2020. On THURSDAY, JULY 16, 2020, I went with Nancy to their location in Kittery for their version of *Black Is Beautiful*, an imperial stout whose proceeds went to social justice causes. I became quite the connoisseur of *Black Is Beautiful*, having tried the versions released by Definitive, Allagash, Flight Deck (on THURSDAY, JULY 30, 2020), Austin Street (on SATURDAY, JULY 25, 2020), and Mast Landing. Any cans that we brought home were always wiped down with disinfectant before coming inside.

On THURSDAY, AUGUST 20, 2020, Nancy and I decided to drive to East Boothbay and take a walk along the coastal trail. It was a beautiful day, and there were plenty of rocks to climb on, which I always find impossible to resist. We spent a couple of hours walking, climbing and staring out to sea before deciding to head into Boothbay to try a new brewery, Footbridge Brewing, in the heart of tourist country. We were still pretty nervous about being amongst people, but we masked up, went inside and ordered, and found seats outside. We weren't particularly impressed with the beer, and everything was just a bit too tight, so we finished pretty quickly and took off. On the way home, we stopped at Boothbay Brewing for another beer, and were pretty much the only people there, which was much more relaxing.

On two occasions, SUNDAY, APRIL 19, 2020, and THURSDAY, MAY 14, 2020, I drove as far as Newington, New Hampshire to go to Stoneface Brewing and pick up some wings and beer. The Sunday stop may have been on my way home from my Sunday morning softball league in Haverhill, Massachusetts. I love Stoneface's Russian Imperial Stout, *RIS*, which was recently named the best stout in New Hampshire.. I made yet another trip to New Hampshire in search of craft beer when I drove to Garrison City Beerworks in Dover on WEDNESDAY, MAY 27, 2020. To round out the COVID summer of 2020, I went to Battery Steele Brewing on FRIDAY, JULY 17, 2020; went with Nancy to Bunker Brewing and Battery Steele Brewing on WEDNESDAY, JULY 22, 2020; went to NU Brewing with Nancy on WEDNESDAY, AUGUST 12, 2020; and to Oxbow Brewing on FRIDAY, AUGUST 21, 2020.

We made a very intentional visit to Stars & Stripes Brewing Company on THURSDAY, JULY 23, 2020. We really wanted to offer our support to Stars & Stripes, because they were closed the day before and had lost a little bit of business, courtesy of grifter Lara Trump and the oxymoronic "Women for Trump" tour. The campaign had asked the brewery if the bus could stop there on Wednesday for lunch and a beer. That seemed like no problem to Stars & Stripes. Well, it turned out that the campaign was planning on a full-blown campaign event, which the owners of Stars & Stripes wanted no part of, nor did they appreciate being "misled" by the campaign. "Due to an an authorized political event being held at our brewery we will not open our doors tomorrow. Stars & Stripes Brewing was created to support veterans, service members, and the community. We do not support or take sides in political agendas," the owners said. Nancy and I wanted to help them out a little bit, and stopped in for a drink the day after.

One might get the impression that Nancy and I like beer. I prefer to look at it as supporting small, local businesses that we like. Buy local, they say. But yes, we do like beer. When Nancy and I moved to Maine, there were around 75 breweries in the state, or one for every 17,747 people. That number has more than doubled since we arrived, so that there is now one brewery for every 8,806 people. We've done our part to grow the industry.

Here is the list of the Maine breweries that we've patronized:

Allagash Brewing Company

Atlantic Brewing Company

Austin Street Brewing (both Portland locations)

Banded Brewing Company

Barreled Souls Brewing

Batson River Brewing

Battery Steele Brewing

Baxter Brewing Company (both Lewiston locations)

Bear Bones Beer Company

Belleflower Brewing

Bissell Brothers Brewing Company

Black Pug Brewing Company

Blaze Brewing Company

Boothbay Craft Brewery

Brickyard Hollow Brewing Company

Bunker Brewing Company

Definitive Brewing Company (Portland and Kittery)

Dirigo Brewing Company

Federal Jack's Brewpub

Flight Deck Brewing

Footbridge Brewery

Fore River Brewing Company

Foulmouthed Brewing

Foundation Brewing Company

Funky Bow Brewery

Geary Brewing Company

Gneiss Brewing Company

Goodfire Brewing Company

Gritty's

Island Dog Brewing

Liberator Brewing Company

Liquid Riot Bottling Company

Lone Pine Brewing Company (Portland and Gorham)

Lubec Brewing Company

Maine Beer Company

Mast Landing Brewing Company (Westbrook and Freeport)

Moderation Brewing

Nonesuch River Brewing

Norway Brewing Company

NU Brewery

Odd Alewives Farm Brewery

Odd by Nature Brewing

Oxbow Brewing Company (Portland and Newcastle)

Penobscot Bay Brewery

Rising Tide Brewing Company

Saco River Brewing

Sebago Brewing Company (Kennebunk and Gorham)

Shipyard Brewing Company

SoMe Brewing Company

Stars & Stripes Brewing Company

Strong Brewing Company

Sunday River Brewing Company*

The Run of the Mill

Tributary Brewing Company

Urban Farm Fermentory

Woodland Farms Brewery

YES Brewing

York Beach Beer Company

XOTA Brewing Company

---

*I apologize for having frequented Sunday River Brewing Company long before the pandemic. The brewery illegally remained open during the early stages of the pandemic, despite the state requiring it to remain closed. The owners, probably expecting just a slap on the wrist from the state, found both their health and liquor licenses stripped. Still refusing to comply, the court ordered the place closed and fined the owners $34,000. They have since sold the company. Regardless, I feel bad about having given them my business.

It was just a couple of weeks into the pandemic, but I knew that I was going to go crazy spending months on end inside, reading, building jigsaw puzzles, doing crosswords, and watching television without any sports. I have learned over the years that if I bug Nancy long enough and frequently enough, that she will eventually give up and let me have my way. On occasion, I had talked with her about painting the house, but it never really got off the ground. The pandemic seemed like a good time to bring the subject up again, but I was rebuffed each time. About five or six weeks in, after my daily suggestion that I paint the house, she gave up and very reluctantly agreed to let me try it.

Wasting no time out of fear that she would change her mind and that I would lose my window of opportunity, I raced over to Home Depot, got a bunch of blue paint chips, and pressed for a decision. We agreed on Behr Starless Night, a very deep blue. And for the next six months, with a scraper, sandpaper and brushes, I prepped and painted the entire outside of our house, which had once been a monochrome gray. It isn't perfect, but it's an awful lot nicer than it was, and I had a big pandemic project to keep me from going crazy. Nancy says it looks good.

CHAPTER 71

SATURDAY, MAY 9, 2020

For a couple of years, Nancy and I had been playing bar trivia at Champions Sports Bar in Biddeford. *Brainbusting Trivia with Caleb* was on Thursday nights at 7:30. We usually played with some combination of Rob and Lisa Kenderdine; their daughter, Sydney Bridges; Jim and Julie Clark; and Paul Mason. We were a pretty good team, often finishing in the top three, although only the top two teams won prizes. Our team was "Kong's Krew." Not nearly as good a name as "The Cunning Stunts," "Uncles with Benefits," or the one-man team "The Lorax," with whom we competed. In March, Champions closed because of the pandemic. Although Champions has re-opened and *Brainbusting Trivia* is back, we still haven't quite wrapped our heads around going back into a small, windowless bar with low ceilings. Maybe someday.

A small scandal arose within our team over one question at Champions. Caleb Biggers, the host, had asked which department store was the original sponsor of *Rudolph the Red-Nosed Reindeer*. Nancy, Lisa and I (Nancy, mostly) had come up with the answer of Montgomery Ward. Rob and Paul thought that it was Gimbels. Even though the team vote was 3-2 in favor of Montgomery Ward, which we *knew* to be correct, Rob, as "captain," submitted Gimbels as our answer. Montgomery Ward, of course, is the correct answer, and we lost. There has been the occasional discussion of Rob's impeachment over his malfeasance, but we have never been able to secure the ⅔ vote needed to convict.

On another night, our team answered all 15 questions correctly, but through some poor wagering, only managed second place. Perhaps my finest moment came in response to a one-hit wonder question: "Who had a hit with the song 'Brandy'?" I am not very good at this category, but somehow knew that it was Looking Glass. I did *not* know the Run DMC was the first rap group to appear on the cover of *Rolling Stone*.

I love a good trivia question and a good puzzle. One of my favorites is the Monty Hall Dilemma, because the answer is so counterintuitive, and seems so wrong, that even mathematicians have been confounded by it. If you remember *Let's Make a Deal,* the old game show hosted by Monty Hall, the show always ended the same way. One audience member was asked to choose one of three closed doors on the stage. Behind one door was something great, like a car. Behind the other two were gag prizes, like chickens or goats. The contestant was asked to choose one of the doors. Monty would then open one of the other two doors, always one with one of the gag prizes. Monty, of course, knew what was behind each of the three doors.

That meant that there were now two doors left, one with a car and one with a chicken (or goat). Monty then asked the contestant if they wanted to stick with the door they had originally selected or switch to the other door. The Monty Hall Dilemma asks the question, "What should the contestant do?" Obviously, it doesn't matter, because with two doors left, there's a 50/50 chance which door the car is behind, right? Wrong!

Surprisingly, the contestant actually doubles the chance of winning by switching doors. There is probably a mathematical formula to prove that this is true, but I most likely wouldn't understand it and certainly couldn't explain it. But there are two simple ways to look at it. First, there is only a ⅓ chance that the original choice was correct, meaning that there is a ⅔ chance that the original choice is *incorrect.* Second, there are only nine possible combinations of choice and outcome, illustrated below:

Choice: (Door #1): Winning Door (1) - Switch (Lose)/Stay (Win)
Choice: (Door #1): Winning Door (2) - Switch (Win)/Stay (Lose)
Choice: (Door #1): Winning Door (3) - Switch (Win)/Stay (Lose)
Choice: (Door #2): Winning Door (1) - Switch (Win)/Stay (Lose)
Choice: (Door #2): Winning Door (2) - Switch (Lose)/Stay (Win)
Choice: (Door #2): Winning Door (3) - Switch (Win)/Stay (Lose)
Choice: (Door #3): Winning Door (1) - Switch (Win)/Stay (Lose)
Choice: (Door #3): Winning Door (2) - Switch (Win)/Stay (Lose)
Choice: (Door #3); Winning Door (3) - Switch (Lose)/Stay (Win)

As you can see, by switching doors, you win in six of the nine scenarios, or ⅔ of the time. I know and appreciated that you still don't believe me, but it's true.

With the pandemic raging, I came up with the idea later in March of playing from home amongst ourselves via text. That idea quickly morphed into playing on Zoom, which I hadn't even heard of before the pandemic. Although at first we simply asked the questions verbally, we quickly learned that we could do it far better with Powerpoint or Slides, with answers sent via the Chat feature. People take turns asking the questions from week-to-week.

The number of teams quickly grew with the additions of Scotte Mason, Paul's wife; Rich and Vivian Bucich from Florida; Barb and John

Jakubowski from New Jersey; Joe and Julia Strong from Pennsylvania; and Fred and Gina Raper, and their daughter, Katie Wilson, from Florida.

On MAY 9, 2020, Nancy and I were in charge of asking the questions, and I prepared our first Slides presentation. The questions were as follows:

Category: (*Cause of Death*)

What was the cause of death of George Castanza's fiancée Susan?

Category: (*Dogs*)

What is the name of the Darling family's dog in *Peter Pan*?

Category: (*Multi-Hit Wonders*)

What is the only song recorded and released by both the Rolling Stones and the Beatles?

Category: (*Where in the World*)

In what city/town is the world's largest rotating globe located?

Bonus Category: (*Games*)

How many squares are on a standard *Scrabble* board?

Category: (*Movies*)

Who played Judge Chamberlain Haller in the 1992 movie *My Cousin Vinny*?

Category: (*15-Letter Words*)

What is a "prestidigitator?"

Category: (*Brains*)

Who was the Executive Producer of this TV show? (video of *Animaniacs*)

Category: (*The Arctic Circle*)

What would you find in the "Doomsday Vault" on the island of Spitsbergen in Norway?

Bonus Category: (*Fake Money*)

How much money does each player start with in *Monopoly*?

Category: (*Packs*)

Name 4 members of the "Brat Pack."

Category: *(Mottos)*

What does "Dirigo" mean?

Category: *(Travel)*

MSY is the three-letter code for what United States airport?

Category: *(Trains)*

Name the first two people to play the role of "Mr. Conductor" in the children's show named for the character on the left. (picture of Thomas the Tank Engine)

Bonus Category: *(Pandemics)*

The word "Quarantine" derives from an Italian word meaning what?

Answers:

(Cause of Death): Poisoned by glue on cheap wedding invitations

(Dogs): Nana

(Multi-Hit Wonders): "I Wanna be Your Man"

(Where in the World): Yarmouth, Maine

(Games): 225

(Movies): Fred Gwynne

(15-Letter Words): A magician

(Brains): Steven Spielberg

(The Arctic Circle): Seeds

(Fake Money): $1,500

(Packs): Rob Lowe, Judd Nelson, Emilio Estevez, Molly Ringwald, Anthony Michael Hall, Andrew McCarthy, Demi Moore, and Ally Sheedy

(Mottos): I direct

(Travel): Louis Armstrong New Orleans International

Airport

(Trains): Ringo Starr and George Carlin

(Pandemics): 40 days

Rob is more than a little bit of a train geek. He loves trains, and has even gone to Utah for the 150th anniversary celebration of the "Golden Spike." Paul and I tease him mercilessly about his train fetish. So when it was my turn to make up and ask the questions on SATURDAY, OCTOBER 24, 2020 (our 33rd wedding anniversary), I had the following categories and questions designed to get in Rob's head:

<u>Category</u>: *(Trains)*

The heavy rail and elevated system serving the San Francisco/Oakland area is known by the acronym "BART." What does "BART" stand for?

<u>Category</u>: *(Trains)*

In the animated Christmas special, *Rudolph the Red-Nosed Reindeer*, where would you find the following characters: Charlie-in-the-Box, a spotted elephant, a cowboy who rides an ostrich, and a train with square wheels on its caboose?

<u>Category</u>: *(Trains)*

The Woody Guthrie folk song, "This Train is Bound for Glory" contains the following lyrics: "This train is bound for glory, this train; This train is bound for glory, this train; This train is bound for glory, don't carry nothin' but the _____ and the _____; This train is bound for glory, this train." What are the two missing words?

<u>Category</u>: *(Trains)*

If I were to roll twelve on a pair of dice in a craps game, what is the nickname for what I rolled? (Hint: The answer is NOT "12."

<u>Bonus Category</u>: *(Trains)*

What is this railroad car carrying in the tank? [Picture of

tank car with "LNG" on its side]

Category: *(Trains)*

What movie, later a TV show, had a theme song with the following lyrics: "Looks like we're comin' into town, seems like this train is slowin' down, can't help but wonder what's in store, could be I've been here once before, a-driftin' the world is my friend, I'm travelin' along the road without end"?

Category: *(Trains)*

Lecil Travis Martin (1931-1999), who owned a theater, museum, and two hotels in Branson, Missouri which bear his stage name, was better known as who?

Category: *(Trains)*

What was the nickname of the NFL player (pictured below) with the following on his resume: 7-time All-Pro, Named to the NFL's 100th Anniversary All-Time team, Holds the NFL record with 14 interceptions in one season, Member of the NFL Hall of Fame, Highest-ranked defensive back on *The Sporting News* list of the greatest players of all time?

Category: *(Trains)*

Who was the creator and original host of the syndicated television show *Soul Train*?

Bonus Category: *(Trains)*

If I were to mix the following ingredients, what potent potable would I be making? 4 oz. Gin, 1 oz. grand marnier, 1 oz. lemon juice, .5 oz grenadine, 1 egg white.

Category: *(Training)*

What kind of training involves a series of high-intensity workouts interspersed with rest or relief periods? The high-intensity periods are typically at or close to anaerobic exercise, while the recovery periods involve activity of lower intensity.

<u>Category</u>: *(Railroads)*

The northernmost site in the United States on the National Underground Railroad Network to Freedom list of historic underground railroad sites is located in what state?

<u>Category</u>: Trains

In the children's book, "The Little Engine That Could," what was the broken-down train rescued by the little engine carrying?

<u>Category</u>: *(Railroads)*

Who is the huckster pictured below [picture of the Good 'n' Plenty engine]?

<u>Bonus Category</u>: *(Nothing to do with Trains or Railroads)*

How many cubic inches are in a ten-foot long 2x4 piece of lumber?

<u>Answers</u>:

(Trains): Bay Area Rapid Transit

(Trains): The Island of Misfit Toys

(Trains): "Righteous" and "holy"

(Trains): Boxcars

(Trains): Liquefied Natural Gas - LNG

(Trains): *The Littlest Hobo*

(Trains): Boxcar Willie

(Trains): Dick "Night Train" Lane

(Trains): Don Cornelius

(Trains): A Boxcar

(Training): Interval Training

(Railroads): New York

(Trains): Toys for all the good girls and boys on the other side of the mountain

(Railroads): Choo Choo Charlie

(Nothing to do with Trains or Railroads): 1.5" x 3.5" x 120" =
630 cubic inches

We continued with Zoom trivia every Saturday night, except for one or
two holidays, throughout the pandemic. By June of 2021, after nearly 15
months of Zoom trivia, most people were getting a little bored and
restless, so we elected to take the summer largely off. We're back at it again,
although only twice a month. One day, hopefully, maybe, we will return to
trivia at Champions, although without Rob and Lisa, who moved to
Florida in December, 2020. It just won't be the same.

CHAPTER 72

It was never going to end any other way. Almost exclusively white - and the vast majority male - the mob rampaged through the Capitol in a vain attempt to keep their Dear Leader in power. God knows how unfair this country has been to white men. No wonder they were so angry.

Certainly, the insurrection must have been his second choice. I'm guessing that he would have preferred to have actually won the election, but I'm pretty sure that egging on and unleashing a mob to try to violently overthrow the election and reinstall himself in power was an acceptable alternative. There was one, and only one, person who could have stopped what happened that day. And he wasn't nearly big enough to do that. I'm sure that he enjoyed watching it on TV while scarfing down a few Big Macs and Cokes.

And so the president, only the fifth incumbent since 1888 to lose a re-election bid, spent his final days in office as the leader of a failed coup, attempted because his daddy always told him there were two kinds of people - winners and losers. And he was a loser.

CHAPTER 73

The inauguration was at noon. The United States Capitol had been repaired and the staging readied following the failed *coup d'etat* two weeks earlier. Donald Trump had left for Mar-a-Lago earlier in the morning, petulantly refusing to attend Joe Biden's swearing-in and never having spoken to the president-elect after the election. It is hard to imagine a more immature, whiny, ignorant, ungracious, childish, moronic, shallow, asinine, petty man - and those are just off the top of my head.

At 11:45 a.m, I opened a bottle of champagne, which Nancy and I shared and savored. We don't usually drink before noon, but we made an exception today.

CHAPTER 74

WEDNESDAY, MARCH 10, 2021

Nancy and I finally got our first dose of the COVID-19 vaccine. We were scheduled to receive it at 1:40 and 1:50 p.m., respectively, at the Scarborough Downs Racetrack. After filling out the paperwork and going through a few lines, we were seated. Nancy went first, and took the first of two doses of the Pfizer mRNA in her left arm. I chose to get it in the right. After waiting the mandatory 15 minutes, we headed home. There was finally some hope. In three weeks, we would return for the second shot.

At 2:35 p.m. on WEDNESDAY, MARCH 31, 2021, we returned to Scarborough Downs. Nancy went first, again in the left arm, and this one hurt a bit. I went next with no issues. At 2:53 p.m., we exited the old racetrack and headed home. It took two weeks after the second dose for the Pfizer vaccine to become fully effective, and on WEDNESDAY, APRIL 14, 2021, we became as immune to COVID-19 as we could be (or so we thought). As it turned out, the vaccines tended to weaken over time, and by the fall, it was recommended that old folks, like us, get a booster shot. With Dylan's wedding approaching, I decided that I wanted to be at peak COVID-fighting strength come the wedding day, so on FRIDAY, OCTOBER 15, 2021, I went to Walgreen's and got a COVID booster shot and a flu shot at the same time, both in my right arm. Although I hadn't had any reaction to the first two shots, I didn't feel great for the next 24 hours. It was a small price to pay for some added sense of security.

Plus ça change, plus c'est la même chose. "The more things change, the more they stay the same." John Finnegan, the lawyer who had arranged my adoption by Charlie and Marge, argued against requiring vaccination against polio before the Maple Shade Board of Education on TUESDAY, NOVEMBER 24, 1959, claiming that it was "against American principles." He lost by a unanimous vote.

In the interim between my COVID shot and my booster, I came to a sad, but all-too-predictable realization. The anti-vaxxers and anti-factsers had spread enough manure and lied to enough people that we were never going to get to the 75 or 80% vaccination rate that we needed to beat the disease. Had we gotten there when we had the chance, before the anti-vaxxers won the day, we would probably be back to normal lives. Now, I'm pretty sure that we will never be.

I came to this realization slowly, not wanting to believe it. One of my Facebook "friends" is an extreme anti-vaxxer and posts anti-vaccine "information" weekly, if not daily. At first I would respond, generally pointing out that her "sources," such as the American Association of Physicians and Surgeons, are largely ultra-conservative political groups, and are anti-choice, anti-Medicare, AIDS-denying, Trump-loving, fringe groups. Rand Paul was a member, so . . . But then I stopped - because it was pointless.

It wasn't even a COVID post that brought the point home to me, though. This Facebook "friend" posted a picture of where the Atlantic and Pacific oceans supposedly "meet," showing two distinctly different colors of water. I pointed out to her that the picture was not, in fact, where those two oceans "meet," but rather something quite different. Even a moment's thought would lead to the recognition that all of the oceans are really just one continuous body of water, and that their "meeting" place is just the label that we have put on them for convenience. To the right is the Atlantic, to the left is the Pacific. They "meet" only where we draw the line on a globe. When I pointed out to her that her post was simply wrong, her response was basically, "Ha, ha. You're right."

All of that may seem perfectly harmless, and in and of itself, I guess that it is. But that picture has been posted and shared by thousands and thousands of people, who now believe that what it falsely purports to be is true. Just look at the string of comments in the thread - "Wow, that's amazing," "Awesome," "I never knew this," etc. And that's how innocently people come to believe nonsense. They see it, they "like" it, they re-post it, and suddenly millions of people think that it's true. But it's not. And that's how the anti-vaxxers won.

It would all be just harmless fun if people weren't dying. If.

CHAPTER 75

SUNDAY, MARCH 21, 2021

For the first time in more than a year, there was curling. In mid-March of 2019, while I was on the Board of Directors, we had cancelled the remainder of the Pine Tree Curling Club's winter league, just before the Troubh Arena closed down because of the COVID-19 outbreak.

On Sunday night, March 21, 2021, I curled with Emily Lozeau, Garrett Gustafson and Rachel Peterson against Dave Peterson, John Scammon, Nancy Filliter and Scott Dube. Our team scored one in the first end, two in the second, two more in the third, and three in the fifth en route to a 13-3 win in seven ends.

Curling, for those of you who aren't familiar with the sport, involves sliding 42-pound granite curling stones down 140 feet of ice so that they stop in a particular place, a little bit like shuffleboard or bocce, only on ice and on a much grander scale. I had wanted to try curling for years, but there wasn't any curling club in New Jersey or Pennsylvania close enough for me to do it. When I got to Maine, I did a little research and found that there was, indeed, a curling club in Portland. On a lark, I signed up, joined a league, and threw my first stone without any practice or training in an actual game. I've been curling ever since, although most of my friends and acquaintances can't understand why.

I was actually the president of the Pine Tree Curling Club for a year or so from 2020-2021. I didn't have any particular interest in running an arena curling club, but I did have an interest in building a dedicated curling facility. There are basically three ways to curl - outdoors on a lake, like it was originally done; indoors at an ice arena; and at a facility dedicated only to curling. Of those three, the only way to go is with a dedicated curling facility.

Shortly after I joined the club, I met with some of the leaders for breakfast one morning and proposed that we try to build our own facility by February, 2022, when the Winter Olympics would be held and interest in curling would be at its highest. That gave us more than three years. I set out to write a detailed business plan and to start looking at buildings that we might be able to adapt for curling. I won't bore you with all of the details of what is required in a curling building, but suffice it to say that they are pretty technical and specific. Finding a building where you can lay down 10,000 square feet of ice, while simultaneously controlling the temperature and humidity, is tricky. Using my experience from *WePAC*, I started sending out press releases about what we were looking to do. My main goal was to find someone with a building we could use.

The reason that real curling needs its own building is the ice. Now, you may think that ice is ice, but it's not. Arena ice isn't flat, is full of divots and gouges from hockey and figure skates, and isn't pebbled. Everyone knows that you can't curl without pebbled ice.

On WEDNESDAY, JANUARY 9, 2019, the *Maine Business Journal* ran an article entitled, "Portland curling club seeks home of its own in tight real estate market." I met with the reporter, Maureen Milliken, at the Troubh Arena for the interview. The club was featured on the Maine television show *207*, a local news and features show. On WEDNESDAY, SEPTEMBER 9, 2020, the *Portland Forecaster* ran an article entitled, "Curlers set on sweeping in new ice rink." In the meantime, the president of our club stepped down, and I volunteered to take over, thinking that having the title of "President" would give me a little more clout when talking to funders, reporters and real estate agents. I spoke with many of our club members, secured around $125,000 in pledges toward a new facility, and raised another $7,000 by holding a "Buildspiel" at the beautiful Broomstones Curling Club in Wayland, Massachusetts, on SATURDAY, DECEMBER 7, 2019, and SUNDAY, DECEMBER 8, 2019. I spent literally hundreds of hours running different membership structures and financial projections.

After looking at a lot of buildings, I finally found one that would work in the Saco Industrial Park. The timing was right, the layout was right, parking was right, and the price was right. I visited the building a number of times with some other Board members and an ice technician. Everyone seemed to agree that the building in Saco could be a great curling venue. There were some zoning issues, but it seemed like they could be overcome. The Saco Economic Development Commission recommended that our club be permitted to operate in the Industrial Park, and I participated in the City Council hearings on MONDAY, JANUARY 11, 2021, and MONDAY, FEBRUARY 1, 2021. Saco was ready to approve the curling club.

In the midst of all the excitement about having a substantial amount of our funding in place, as well as finding a place for our facility, all hell broke loose within the Board over membership structure and fees. The Board voted not to pursue the opportunity in Saco, I stepped down as president, and now, more than a year later, we're still curling at 10:00 at night at the hockey arena. Maybe that will change, maybe not.

I love curling, and I have some great guys - Rich Campbell, Lee Cyr and Jim Ford - as teammates. Plus, curling breaks up what can be pretty long and lonely winters in Maine. On some days, the sun goes down before 4:00 p.m.. Nancy tried curling once, on WEDNESDAY, APRIL 4, 2018. It wasn't the most successful experience, and I don't think that she will try it again, although she claims to have had fun. For Christmas, 2021, we gave Dylan and Elizabeth a Learn-to-Curl night at the dedicated curling facility run by the Charlotte Curling Association. Despite my urging, I don't think that anyone in my family loves curling as much as I do. That's OK, because I don't love guacamole as much as they do. To each their own.

CHAPTER 76

FRIDAY, APRIL 9, 2021

We saw a puffin today, at least we think we did, on Tibbetts Pond while hiking in the Ocean Point Preserve in East Boothbay. As far as I know, it was the first time that I actually saw a puffin. It was alone, swimming in the pond across from where Nancy and I were walking.

Whether the bird at Tibbetts Pond was a puffin or not, we definitely saw puffins, and lots of them, on MONDAY, JULY 5, 2021. Dylan and Elizabeth had come to Maine for a visit over the Fourth of July holiday, and on their last day here we decided to go on a puffin watch aboard Cap'n Fish's Audubon Puffin Cruise out of Boothbay. It was a beautiful, sunny day for the boat ride out to Eastern Egg Rock to a puffin colony.

Although Atlantic puffins are a pretty good size, roughly the size of chickens, they aren't that easy to get a good look at. And they fly like bats, furiously beating their wings up to 400 times a minute. From a boat a few hundred yards from the little island, the ones that aren't flying or swimming are hard to see amongst the rocks and vegetation. But we saw quite a few flying over the water on fishing trips, and some more just swimming or floating on the water. Their distinctive orange beaks make them a little easier to distinguish from all of the other birds flying around the little island.

While Dylan and Elizabeth were visiting, we drove down to New Hampshire on THURSDAY, JULY 1, 2021, intending to play some disc golf at an alleged disc golf course at Smuttynose Brewing Company. We took our discs, the hostess pointed us toward the course, and off we went. Our disc golf outing lasted but one hole. The course was not maintained at all, and proved to be nearly impossible to navigate, with branches, thickets, debris, and lots and lots of ferocious-looking poison ivy. We decided to turn around and not sabotage the visit, so we had a beer at Smuttynose and headed over to another fine brewery, Stoneface, in Newington, New Hampshire, where we enjoyed some great beer and even greater Shishito peppers.

It was rainy for most of Dylan and Elizabeth's visit, but we managed to get in a few non-brewery activities. We had fried seafood at the Portland Lobster Company in Portland on SATURDAY, JULY 3, 2021; had more fried seafood at Harraseeket Lunch & Lobster in South Freeport; had fries from the Duckfat Frites Shack in Portland; went shopping at L.L. Bean; stopped in at the Garmin building in Yarmouth to see Eartha, the world's largest rotating globe; and played *Qwixx* at our kitchen table. All too soon, the long weekend was over. We set our alarms for 4:00 a.m. on TUESDAY, JULY 6, 2021, and drove Dylan and Elizabeth to the Portland International Jetport for their flight back home to Charlotte.

It was the last time that I would see them until *The Wedding*.

Chapter 77

Saturday, November 6, 2021

Dylan and Elizabeth finally got married on November 6th. The wedding was supposed to be on SATURDAY, NOVEMBER 7, 2020, but was postponed for a year because of the pandemic. Nancy and I flew down to Charlotte on THURSDAY, NOVEMBER 4, 2021, and were picked up at the airport in Dylan's rental car. It was a rental car because earlier in the week, just three days before the wedding, Dylan's Jeep Renegade was totaled when a car made an illegal left turn in front of Elizabeth, who was driving. No one was hurt, but the car was totaled. Pretty bad timing.

Dylan proposed to Elizabeth on my 65th birthday, SATURDAY, MAY 4, 2019. That was an unexpected present.

We met Elizabeth's mother for the first time on Thursday at Noble Smoke, a barbecue restaurant in Charlotte not nearly as good as Midwood Smokehouse or Mac's Speed Shop. Dylan and I planned to go golfing on the day before his wedding, FRIDAY, NOVEMBER 5, 2021. Dylan's friend, Cameron Dougherty, would play with us, too. Because there were lots of other things for Dylan to be doing that day, he reserved an early, 8:00 a.m. tee time at Eagle Ridge. At 8:00, it was 36 degrees, the ground was covered with frost, and steam was rising into the frigid air from the warm ponds on the course. Nevertheless, we played all 18 holes, each of us in horrendous fashion, and I don't think that we bothered to tally up the final scores. I'm going to blame my play on the rented clubs which I used, lack of golf shoes, the cold weather, and an unfamiliar course. Dylan and Cameron can make their own excuses.

On the way home, we dropped Cameron off, stopped at the jeweler to pick up Dylan's wedding ring, grabbed some fast food, and Dylan dropped me off at our hotel. That evening, we went to rehearsal and then to a welcome party for everyone who was already in town at Heist Brewery/Barrel Arts. My only official duty for the weekend was to give a little welcome speech to everyone, which I mercifully made brief. My unofficial duty was as beer procurement liaison for Ray Carlin, Joe and Julia Strong, and Kevin Schildt. Heist didn't have any stouts on tap, which was both surprising and disappointing, since they had a long tap list, and I asked the manager if he could scare some up for us. He went to the basement and procured a delicious coconut, bourbon barrel aged, imperial stout, which I delighted in sharing with the cohort longing for stout. It was one of, if not the, best stouts I have ever had, with a rather steep ABV of around 15%. The manager made a couple more trips for me, until he said he was out, and we had to settle for another great, but not quite as delicious, stout from the basement. Great beer is always meant to be shared.

The wedding went off without a hitch on Saturday, although the maid of honor nearly placed the train of Elizabeth's gown into one of the candles. Nancy and I sat in front, of course, as our only son exchanged vows and entered into matrimony. Even Felix, Elizabeth and Dylan's dog, was there. If their lives are as full and rich and blessed as mine has been, they're in for a great ride.

We spent all of Sunday lounging at Dylan's house, eating Bossy Bites from Bossy Beulah's Chicken Shack and watching the Eagles lose 27-24 to the Los Angeles Chargers. Most of Nancy's family had gone tailgating (although without the benefit of a car) and to the football game. By a random stroke of luck, the Patriots were in town that day to play the Panthers, and the extended MacDonald clan attended. Unlike the Eagles, the Cheatin' Patriots won.

Nancy and I flew home to Maine on MONDAY, NOVEMBER 8, 2021, tired but happy that the wedding had gone off without a hitch. I'm pretty sure that that was the last time that anyone will see me in a tux.

EPILOGUE

This book could have gone on endlessly. Just about everything reminded me of something else. But I got a little bored after ten months of reliving and reliving my life, and some of the things just didn't seem to fit in anywhere, so I just left them out. For example, when I was very young, in the early 1960's, my father took me, and maybe Dennis, to an NBA doubleheader. The Sixers played somebody in one game, and the Celtics played somebody else in the other. I don't even know where the game was played, although it was most likely in either Camden Convention Hall or Philadelphia Convention Hall. Although the details are lost to time, at least I got to see Wilt Chamberlain and Bill Russell play on the same day, albeit not against each other.

Charlie and Marge took us to the New York World's Fair in Queens in 1964 or 1965. I still have a token from the World's Fair with a radioactive dime in the center. Thanks, Atomic Energy Commission.

In high school, we celebrated the first Earth Day, WEDNESDAY, APRIL 22, 1970. I vaguely remember cleaning trash and debris from Saddler's Woods behind the high school near MacArthur Boulevard. I doubt that we did it exactly on Earth Day. It was more likely on Saturday, but who knows.

Kevin and I went to the Villanova-Georgetown basketball game on MONDAY, JANUARY 31, 1983, at the Palestra in Philadelphia. This game was played at the height of the two schools' basketball rivalry and by all accounts was a great game, which Villanova won 68-67. The college kids were merciless, and racist, toward Patrick Ewing. We had stayed at Happy Hour at a bar with an Irish name near the Palestra for a bit too long, so the details are a little murky.

Nor did I include the time that I broke Bob Thomas's nose at Faneuil Hall in Boston one winter night in the 1990's. We were messing around throwing snow and ice at each other, not hard, just for giggles. As I lobbed a chunk of ice at him, he bent over to pick up one of his own. As fate would have it, he lowered his head just in time for the ice to hit him in the nose. Bob actually went to the hospital that night, and I'm not sure that he has ever forgiven me for it. He was kind enough to send me an 8 x 10 black and white glossy of his swollen face.

When Dylan was six years old, we went to Washington, D.C. for the weekend. We did most of the Washington tourist stuff, including going to the National Air and Space Museum on FRIDAY, JANUARY 23, 1998. For me, though, as cool as the Smithsonian is, nothing tops the Lincoln Memorial, Arlington National Cemetery or the Vietnam Veterans Memorial.

I like watching meteors and wanted Dylan to share the experience. The Leonid shower happens every November. The Leonids are not as good as the Perseids, but they can put on a decent show. In order to get a really good look at meteors, you need to find as dark a spot as you can. Voorhees was pretty developed and crowded, with lots of light - not great for meteor-watching. In the middle of the night, I woke Dylan up, we got dressed, grabbed a couple of lawn chairs, stopped at Wawa for something hot to drink, and drove to Kresson Golf Course. We set up our chairs on the third fairway, leaned back, and watched the show together.

On Tuesday, June 20, 2006, we went to Dylan's Voorhees Middle School graduation; on Monday, October 27, 2008, we watched the beginning of Game 5 of the World Series between the Phillies and Tampa Bay and watched the conclusion two days later, on Wednesday, October 29, 2008, because of two solid days of rain in Philadelphia. After a lot of bickering and arguing, we reluctantly let Dylan go to the championship parade in Philly (along with around 2 million other people) on Friday, October 31, 2008.

In 2015, Dylan came home for Thanksgiving and ran in the Philadelphia Marathon, something that I personally think is insane. Nobody looks happy when running a marathon, nor for several days thereafter. Nonetheless, we dropped him off on the morning of SUNDAY, NOVEMBER 22, 2015, wished him luck, and headed back to the comforts of home. We were able to track his time from home, and as he got close to the finish, we headed back to Philly to pick him up. Somewhat to my surprise, we saw him cross the finish line, and in a time of 3 hours and 59 minutes. He said that he wanted to beat four hours. We went home and watched Mark Sanchez throw three interceptions as the Eagles were routed by Tampa Bay 45-17.

Ray and Jane Carlin came up to Maine to visit over Memorial Day weekend in 2018. Of course, we visited some breweries, went to Fort Williams to see Portland Head Light, as we do with all of our guests, and took a sunset cruise on the schooner *Wendameen* on FRIDAY, MAY 25, 2018. As we sailed past a green bell buoy, one of the mates announced that it was good luck to throw a coin and land it on top of the buoy. Unable to resist almost any kind of competition or challenge, I grabbed some change and tossed it. I don't want to brag, but you can guess where it landed. I've had nothing but good luck since.

On THURSDAY, SEPTEMBER 27, 2018, we left Maine and drove to the Finger Lakes in New York to meet up with Joe and Julia and hang around in New York's wine country. Our first stop was at the Women's Rights National Historical Park and Wesleyan Chapel in Seneca Falls, the site of the first Women's Rights Convention in 1848, the beginning of the suffrage movement which ultimately led to the ratification of the 19th Amendment, granting women the right to vote. We bought a Suffrage Flag, which we fly on our house every year at election time. It was a five-hour drive to the Finger Lakes, but the time passed quickly, since it happened to be the day that Dr. Christine Blasey Ford gave her damning testimony against Bret Kavanaugh during his Supreme Court confirmation hearing. We listened to her entire testimony on the car radio. McConnell, of course, didn't care, and made sure that Kavanaugh was confirmed regardless. And Senator Susan Collins (R-ME), once again, was duped.

On FRIDAY, DECEMBER 29, 2017, we met Dylan and Elizabeth in Winter Park, Colorado, for a few days of skiing; on SATURDAY, MARCH 17, 2018, Nancy and I went to Féile Irish Pub in Wells to celebrate St. Patrick's Day with a black and tan and some Irish music; on SATURDAY, APRIL 28, 2018, three of Nancy's sisters - Linda, Donna and Cindy - drove up for a visit; Nancy and I took a day trip to Bristol, Maine and Pemaquid on FRIDAY, MAY 11, 2018, and to Barter Island and Newagen on FRIDAY, MAY 18, 2018; I drove down to Philly and went to see the Eagles-Cowboys game with Joe on SUNDAY, NOVEMBER 11, 2018, a 27-20 loss, although Zach Ertz caught an amazing 14 passes for 145 yards and two touchdowns; the day before the game, on SATURDAY, NOVEMBER 10, 2018, I attended a Manta and Welge reunion in King of Prussia, Pennsylvania; Nancy and I spent Christmas Eve, MONDAY, DECEMBER 24, 2018, at Cindy and Dave's in Dracut, as we did many other Christmas Eves, including TUESDAY, DECEMBER 24, 2019, when we went with Dylan and Elizabeth and where Donna presented everyone with "This is Us Family Christmas 2019" shirts; on TUESDAY, FEBRUARY 26, 2019, Nancy and I ate at Pedro's in Kennebunkport, with Nancy having the obligatory margarita for her birthday; Dylan came up to visit over the Fourth of July in 2019, and on SATURDAY, JULY 6, 2019, we went to Bug Light in Portland and did the cliff walk at Black Point in Scarborough; on the first day of school for Haddon Township in 2019, TUESDAY, SEPTEMBER 3, 2019, Nancy and I went to the beach and took a picture of Nancy sitting in the sun to send to her still-working teacher friends.

Nowhere did I even mention my three pet raccoons - Hector, April and Roscoe. Nor did I have the time and space to muse on a couple of things that have confounded me through the years, like, "When did Tastykake

Butterscotch Krimpets get so damn small?" and "Why does the frosting stick to the cellophane and not the krimpet when you open them?" I would also like to know why, oh why, can't I get a decent cheesesteak anywhere outside of the Philadelphia area?

One of the things that struck me in writing all of this is that some people who were once a significant part of my life aren't even mentioned, like Denise Murphy, who worked with me at Meehan, Boyle and Cohen in Boston and who was a good, smart and funny friend. Denise went on to become the President of the Massachusetts Bar Association. Or Harry Lee and Kevin Fitzgerald, with whom I worked at Foley, Hoag & Eliot in Boston. We went golfing together a couple of times, spent hours talking about sports, and at one time played a serious game of Prisoner's Dilemma with a couple of other folks at the firm, where everyone would make one move a day against each of the other players. Harry, I think, had a doctorate, or was working on his doctorate in philosophy and organized the game. Kevin was the son of legendary *Boston Globe* sportswriter Ray Fitzgerald, a 12-time Massachusetts Sportswriter of the Year honoree.

One of the other things that struck me is how fortunate I have been to have met and befriended so many amazing, kind, generous, irreverent and wonderful people in my life. By my count, I have mentioned 1,049 different people. Many, of course, are people that I have only watched, like athletes; or distant relatives that I have never met; or politicians I have observed or met fleetingly. Many, though, are people who, at one time or another, were a large part of my life and who shaped, for better or worse, who I am. In *almost* all instances, I have been fortunate to have known them and to have shared my life with them.

As I mentioned at the very beginning of this project, it has been a rather ordinary life. I have been extremely lucky never to have really wanted for anything; never to have suffered from poverty, nor known homelessness, abuse, food insecurity, racism or bullying. I have never been seriously ill, can eat what I want, and am not on any medications. I try my best to be grateful every day for those things.

To those of you who have read this far, thank you. Take some time to tell your own stories, because they are all important and bind us all together.

Lastly, as I said at the outset, I don't think that I have learned any grand, universal truths about life, nor do I offer any advice on how others should live their lives. What I do know is that I have been blessed to know the people that I have known, that I have been remiss in not telling them that, and that I hope that when they think of me, if they ever do, it is with a little bit of a smile.

Chronological listing of all dates cited herein. Dates in **Bold** are Chapter headings.

MONDAY, APRIL 17, 1815 (Charles Lowden born)
FRIDAY, FEBRUARY 20, 1818 (Hannah Fish Lowden born)
SUNDAY, SEPTEMBER 1, 1822 (Jacob Barnes born)
SATURDAY, JUNE 14, 1823 (Hannah Barnes born)
SUNDAY, APRIL 21, 1833 (Franz John Bernhardt born)
TUESDAY, FEBRUARY 9, 1836 (Anna Catharina Debos born)
THURSDAY, MAY 19, 1836 (Johann Adam Florig born)
TUESDAY, JULY 27, 1841 (Henrike Ziegler born)
THURSDAY, DECEMBER 1, 1854 (Frederick Lowden born)
SATURDAY, NOVEMBER 16, 1861 (Anna Hazeltine Barnes Lowden born)
MONDAY, NOVEMBER 10, 1862 (Jacob Barnes joins the army)
FRIDAY, AUGUST 7, 1863 (Jacob Barnes discharged from army)
THURSDAY, FEBRUARY 11, 1866 (Adolph Florig born)
TUESDAY, OCTOBER 14, 1879 (Anna Catharina Bedos dies)
FRIDAY, FEBRUARY 14, 1890 (Jacob Barnes drowns)
SATURDAY, JANUARY 13, 1894 (Marjorie Lowden Scott born)
SUNDAY, SEPTEMBER 2, 1894 (Thomas Scott born)
MONDAY, NOVEMBER 29, 1897 (John Florig born)
MONDAY, DECEMBER 29, 1902 (Hannah Fish Lowden dies)
THURSDAY, FEBRUARY 18, 1904 (Charlies Lowden dies)
SATURDAY, MARCH 18, 1905 (Franz John Bernhardt dies)
SATURDAY, MARCH 9, 1907 (Thomas Birrane dies)
TUESDAY, MAY 31, 1910 (Thomas B. Scott born)
MONDAY, AUGUST 26, 1912 (Hannah Barnes dies)
WEDNESDAY, APRIL 7, 1915 (Henrike Ziegler dies)
TUESDAY, DECEMBER 21, 1915 (Frederick Lowden dies)
THURSDAY, AUGUST 8, 1918 (Thomas Scott buys furniture for home)
WEDNESDAY, SEPTEMBER 25, 1918 (Thomas Scott/Marjorie Lowden married)
WEDNESDAY, DECEMBER 4, 1918 (Letter to Thomas Scott from Ireland)
SUNDAY, AUGUST 1, 1920 (Reverend Belting gambling sermon)
WEDNESDAY, OCTOBER 20, 1920 (Marge born)
WEDNESDAY, MAY 18, 1921 (John Joseph Florig dies)
WEDNESDAY, JUNE 1, 1921 (Charlie born)
SUNDAY, JUNE 5, 1921 (Charlie baptized)
SUNDAY, JUNE 12, 1921 (Marge baptized)
SATURDAY, JANUARY 7, 1922 (Robert Scott born)
SATURDAY, FEBRUARY 24, 1923 (Thomas John Florig born)
WEDNESDAY, DECEMBER 3, 1924 (215 Burrwood Avenue sold to Pleibel)
TUESDAY, FEBRUARY 15, 1925 (Robert Strong born)
TUESDAY, JANUARY 25, 1927 (William Scott born)

FRIDAY, JUNE 10, 1927 (Marge finishes 1st grade)
FRIDAY, JUNE 8, 1928 (Marge finishes 2nd grade)
SUNDAY, OCTOBER 7, 1928 (Marge promoted to Primary Department)
SUNDAY, OCTOBER 21, 1928 (James Scott born)
FRIDAY, JUNE 14, 1929 (Marge finishes 3rd grade)
TUESDAY, FEBRUARY 11, 1930 (Stephen Florig born)
TUESDAY, JUNE 3, 1930 (Jim born)
FRIDAY, JUNE 13, 1930 (Marge finishes 4th grade)
SATURDAY, SEPTEMBER 6, 1930 (Mary Bernhardt Florig dies)
FRIDAY, MAY 22, 1931 (Marge 4-H Award of Merit)
FRIDAY, JUNE 19, 1931 (Marge finishes 5th grade)
WEDNESDAY, AUGUST 26, 1931 (Doris born)
FRIDAY, JUNE 17, 1932 (Marge finishes 6th grade)
MONDAY, JUNE 27, 1932 (Marge starts Vacation Church School)
FRIDAY, JULY 22, 1932 (Marge finishes Vacation Church School)
FRIDAY, JUNE 15, 1934 (Marge finishes 8th grade)
SATURDAY, JANUARY 26, 1935 (Marge completes Palmer Method of Business Writing)
THURSDAY, JUNE 6, 1935 (Charlie graduates 8th grade)
FRIDAY, JUNE 7, 1935 (Charlie Honorably Discharged from safety patrol)
WEDNESDAY, JUNE 12, 1935 (Marge Certificate of Admission to high school)
FRIDAY, JUNE 14, 1935 (Marge finishes 9th grade)
MONDAY, SEPTEMBER 9. 1935 (Marge starts high school)
WEDNESDAY, SEPTEMBER 9, 1936 (Marge starts 11th grade)
THURSDAY, MARCH 11, 1937 (Adolph Florig dies)
THURSDAY, JUNE 16, 1938 (Marge graduates high school)
SATURDAY, JULY 20, 1940 (Charlie saves sisters from drowning)
TUESDAY, OCTOBER 28, 1941 (Charlie/Marge engagement in *Courier-Post*)
SATURDAY, OCTOBER 10, 1942 (Charlie and Marge get married)
SATURDAY, AUGUST 26, 1944 (Charlie inducted into U.S. Marines)
MONDAY, MAY 28, 1945 (Charlie arrives in Hawaii) (John Fogerty born)
WEDNESDAY, AUGUST 7, 1946 (Charlie Honorably Discharged from U.S. Marines)
WEDNESDAY, APRIL 16, 1947 (Texas City explosion)
TUESDAY, JULY 22, 1947 (Westmont Baptist 11, Audubon Lutheran 2)
SUNDAY, JULY 23, 1950 (Dennis Florig born)
SUNDAY, MARCH 25, 1951 (Dennis baptized)
TUESDAY, FEBRUARY 26, 1952 (Nancy MacDonald born)
WEDNESDAY, MARCH 5, 1952 (Nancy baptized)
THURSDAY, JANUARY 15, 1953 (Anna Hazeltine Barnes Lowden dies)
TUESDAY, MAY 4, 1954 (I was born)
SUNDAY, JUNE 13, 1954 (I was baptized Methodist)
MONDAY, AUGUST 2, 1954 (I was enrolled in Cradle Roll Department)

SATURDAY, MARCH 5, 1955 (215 Burrwood Avenue sold to Hansons)

WEDNESDAY, APRIL 27, 1955 (I got vaccinated for smallpox)

TUESDAY, OCTOBER 11, 1955 (Charlie and Marge get my birth certificate)

SATURDAY, NOVEMBER 19, 1955 (I got PDT booster)

FRIDAY, SEPTEMBER 14, 1956 (Charlie and Marge enter Agreement of Sale for 215 Burrwood Avenue)

SATURDAY, FEBRUARY 9, 1957 (I completed polio vaccine series)

FRIDAY, MARCH 29, 1957 (Charlie/Marge settlement on 215 Burrwood Avenue)

SUNDAY, FEBRUARY 23, 1958 (Thomas Scott dies)

SATURDAY, JANUARY 31, 1959 (I get PDT booster)

TUESDAY, NOVEMBER 24, 1959 (John Finnegan opposes polio vaccination)

FRIDAY, DECEMBER 25, 1959 (Lassie for Christmas)

WEDNESDAY, APRIL 5, 1961 ("Travelin' Man" video on *Ozzie and Harriett*)

THURSDAY, MAY 25, 1961 (JFK moon speech)

MONDAY, JUNE 12, 1961 (I get promoted to 2nd grade)

TUESDAY, FEBRUARY 20, 1962 (John Glenn Mercury flight)

THURSDAY, MARCH 1, 1962 (John Glenn parade)

THURSDAY, MAY 24, 1962 (Scott Carpenter Mercury flight)

TUESDAY, JUNE 5, 1962 (Scott Carpenter parade)

FRIDAY, JUNE 8, 1962 (I get promoted to 3rd grade)

WEDNESDAY, MAY 15, 1963 (Gordon Cooper Mercury flight)

WEDNESDAY, MAY 22, 1963 (Gordon Cooper parade)

THURSDAY, JUNE 13, 1963 (I get promoted to 4th grade)

FRIDAY, NOVEMBER 22, 1963 (JFK assassination)

SUNDAY, FEBRUARY 9, 1964 (Beatles on the *Ed Sullivan Show*)

SUNDAY, APRIL 26, 1964 (Charlie and Marge art studio loan)

FRIDAY, JUNE 12, 1964 (I get promoted to 5th grade)

SUNDAY, JUNE 21, 1964 (Jim Bunning's perfect game)

TUESDAY, JULY 7, 1964 (Callison home run in All-Star game)

MONDAY, SEPTEMBER 21, 1964 (Chico Ruiz steals home)

SUNDAY, OCTOBER 4, 1964 (Phillies lose pennant)

SUNDAY, NOVEMBER 1, 1964 (Redskins-Eagles at Franklin Field)

MONDAY, MARCH 29, 1965 (Gus Grissom parade)

SATURDAY, MAY 29, 1965 (Dick Allen 529-foot home run)

THURSDAY, JUNE 17, 1965 (I get promoted to 6th grade)

SUNDAY, JULY 25, 1965 (Bob Dylan at Newport Folk Festival)

FRIDAY, JUNE 17, 1966 (I get promoted to 7th grade)

SUNDAY, JUNE 26, 1966 (Woody Fryman shuts out Phillies)

SATURDAY, AUGUST 1, 1966 (University of Texas shooting)

SATURDAY, SEPTEMBER 24, 1966 (Jim Bunning's 18th win)

SUNDAY, OCTOBER 2, 1966 (Koufax, Drysdale and Bunning pitch at Connie Mack)

FRIDAY, JANUARY 16, 1967 (Dennis elected to National Honor Society)

FRIDAY, JANUARY 27, 1967 (Gus Grissom dies)
MAY 1, 1967 (Nancy Weil moves)
FRIDAY, JUNE 23, 1967 (Hollybush summit)
SUNDAY, JANUARY 14, 1968 (Thomas B. Scott dies)
SATURDAY, MARCH 16, 1968 (Robert Kennedy announces candidacy)
SUNDAY, MARCH 31, 1968 (LBJ announcements he won't seek re-election)
MONDAY, APRIL 1, 1968 (Robert Kennedy in Camden)
THURSDAY, APRIL 4, 1968 (Robert Kennedy in Indianapolis) (Martin Luther King, Jr. assassinated)
TUESDAY, MAY 7, 1968 (Robert Kennedy wins Indiana primary)
TUESDAY, JUNE 4, 1968 (Robert Kennedy assassinated) (NJ/CA primaries)
WEDNESDAY, JUNE 5, 1968 (Robert Kennedy dies)
THURSDAY, JUNE 13, 1968 (Dennis graduates HTHS)
SATURDAY, SEPTEMBER 21, 1968 (Richard Nixon at Cherry Hill Mall)
MONDAY, SEPTEMBER 23, 1968 (*Charly* released)
TUESDAY, OCTOBER 8, 1968 (*Romeo and Juliet* released)
SUNDAY, DECEMBER 15, 1968 (Eagles fans boo Santa)
SUNDAY, MAY 4, 1969 (Lorne Greene autograph) (15th birthday)
WEDNESDAY, MAY 28, 1969 (*The April Fools* released)
FRIDAY, JUNE 13, 1969 (*True Grit* released)
MONDAY, JUNE 30, 1969 (*Sports Illustrated* with Ron Santo autograph)
WEDNESDAY, JULY 16, 1969 (Blind Faith with Becky)
SUNDAY, JULY 20, 1969 (Moon landing)
SUNDAY, AUGUST 17, 1969 (First day of NEBYC) (Last day of Woodstock)
MONDAY, SEPTEMBER 1, 1969 (John Florig dies)
WEDNESDAY, SEPTEMBER 24, 1969 (*Butch Cassidy and the Sundance Kid* released)
WEDNESDAY, OCTOBER 22, 1969 (*The Sterile Cuckoo* released)
SATURDAY, NOVEMBER 1, 1969 (Haddon Heights 71, Haddon Twp. 0)
WEDNESDAY, DECEMBER 10, 1969 (*They Shoot Horses, Don't They?* released)
SUNDAY, FEBRUARY 8, 1970 (Pete Seeger at Academy of Music)
TUESDAY, MARCH 17, 1970 (*The Boys in the Band* released)
THURSDAY, MARCH 26, 1970 (*Woodstock* released)
WEDNESDAY, APRIL 22, 1970 (First Earth Day)
MONDAY, JUNE 15, 1970 (Tony Black's first win)
THURSDAY, OCTOBER 1, 1970 (Last game at Connie Mack Stadium)
MONDAY, MARCH 8, 1971 (Ali/Frazier I) (Alan Shepard parade)
WEDNESDAY, APRIL 21, 1971 (Audubon 4 - Haddon Twp. 2 in golf)
THURSDAY, APRIL 22, 1971 (Haddon Heights 4 - Haddon Twp. 2 in golf)
MONDAY, MAY 3, 1971 (*Sports Illustrated* with Jim Fregosi autograph)
TUESDAY, MAY 4, 1971 (Student council election speech) (I get my driver's license) (17th birthday)
TUESDAY, MAY 11, 1971 (Haddon Twp. 3 1/2 - Paulsboro 2 1/2 in golf)

FRIDAY, MAY 14, 1971 (Haddon Twp. 3 - Eastern 3 in golf)

WEDNESDAY, JUNE 9, 1971 (*Hawker* student council election story)

MONDAY, JULY 5, 1971 (26th Amendment becomes law)

SUNDAY, AUGUST 1, 1971 (Concert for Bangladesh)

MONDAY, AUGUST 9, 1971 (Leon Russell/Freddie King concert in Conshohocken)

FRIDAY, AUGUST 20, 1971 (Fire at Connie Mack Stadium)

THURSDAY, AUGUST 26, 1971 (Left for Haiti)

TUESDAY, SEPTEMBER 6, 1971 (Left for Port-Au-Prince)

WEDNESDAY, SEPTEMBER 7, 1971 (Arrived home from Haiti)

MONDAY, NOVEMBER 8, 1971 (Elvis at the Spectrum)

SATURDAY, NOVEMBER 27, 1971 (Army-Navy game at JFK Stadium)

FRIDAY, DECEMBER 10, 1971 (*The Man Who Came to Dinner* Opens)

SATURDAY, DECEMBER 11, 1971 (*The Man Who Came to Dinner* Closes)

WEDNESDAY, DECEMBER 22, 1971 (Dennis graduates American University)

WEDNESDAY, MARCH 22, 1972 (Joe Cocker/Dave Mason at Spectrum)

WEDNESDAY, APRIL 12, 1972 (Haddon Twp. 6 - Haddon Heights 0 in golf)

MONDAY, APRIL 17, 1972 (Paulsboro 4 - Haddon Twp. 2 in golf)

FRIDAY, APRIL 21, 1972 (Haddon Twp. 3 1/2 - Audubon 2 1/2 in golf)

MONDAY, APRIL 24, 1972 (Haddonfield 4, Haddon Twp. 2 in golf)

TUESDAY, MAY 2, 1972 (Haddon Twp. 4 1/2 - Gloucester Catholic. 1 1/2 in golf)

FRIDAY, MAY 5, 1972 (Lenape 4 1/2 - Haddon Twp. 1 1/2 in golf)

MONDAY, MAY 8, 1972 (Haddon Twp. 3 1/2 - Haddon Heights 2 1/2 in golf)

FRIDAY, MAY 12, 1972 (My senior prom with Leona) (Haddon Twp. 4, Haddonfield 2 in golf)

WEDNESDAY, MAY 17, 1972 (Haddon Twp. 3 1/2 - Gloucester Catholic 2 1/2 in golf)

MONDAY, MAY 22, 1972 (*Sports Illustrated* with Willie Mays autograph) (Woodbury 4, Haddon Twp. 2 in golf)

TUESDAY, MAY 23, 1972 (Haddon Twp. 3 1/2 - Paulsboro 2 1/2 in golf)

FRIDAY, MAY 26, 1972 (Haddon Twp. 4 - Audubon 2 in golf)

TUESDAY, MAY 30, 1972 (Haddon Twp. 3 1/2 - Haddonfield 2 1/2 for golf championship)

THURSDAY, JUNE 15, 1972 (HTHS graduation)

SUNDAY, JULY 2, 1972 (Badfinger/Faces at Spectrum)

WEDNESDAY, SEPTEMBER 13, 1972 (McGovern rally in Philadelphia)

TUESDAY, NOVEMBER 7, 1972 (Nixon/McGovern election)

FRIDAY, JANUARY 5, 1973 (*Courier-Post* Board of Education election preview)

TUESDAY, FEBRUARY 13, 1973 (Haddon Townshipp. Board of Education election)

SUNDAY, JANUARY 6, 1974 (Bob Dylan/The Band at Spectrum)

MONDAY, JANUARY 28, 1974 (Ali-Frazier II)
SATURDAY, JUNE 8, 1974 (Nancy gets Massachusetts teaching certificate)
WEDNESDAY, JULY 10, 1974 (Portland Storm at Philadelphia Bell)
TUESDAY, OCTOBER 15, 1974 (First Ronald McDonald House opens in Philadelphia)
FRIDAY, APRIL 18, 1975 (John Denver at Spectrum)
Wednesday, October 1, 1975 (Ali-Frazier III)
Saturday, October 11, 1975 (*Saturday Night Live* debuts)
Monday, July 12, 1976 (California State University - Fullerton shooting)
Tuesday, July 13, 1976 (Connie Mack Stadium demolition completed)
Tuesday, November 2, 1976 (Carter/Ford election)
Thursday, April 14, 1977 (Garden State Park fire)
Wednesday, July 27, 1977 (YMBC 8, Christ the King 3)
Tuesday, December 6, 1977 (Billy Joel concert with Dottie Schroeder)
Tuesday, October 5, 1978 (Dodgers beat Phillies in playoffs)
Sunday, November 19, 1978 (Dottie Schroeder "date") (Miracle at the Meadowlands)
Saturday, April 21, 1979 (Rick Nelson at Pitman Theater)
Wednesday, May 9, 1979 (YMBC 20, Audubon Mormon 4)
Friday, May 25, 1979 (YMBC 13, Westmont Methodist 8)
Monday, May 28, 1979 (*Sports Illustrated* autographed by Pete Rose)
Friday, June 8, 1979 (YMBC 19, Emmanuel Methodist 8)
Friday, June 15, 1979 (*Rocky II* released)
Friday, June 22, 1979 (YMBC 11, St. Gregory's 10)
Wednesday, July 11, 1979 (YMBC 27, Haddonfield Baptist 3)
Saturday, November 10, 1979 (Rick Nelson in Pitman)
Saturday, November 17, 1979 (First Philadelphia Fox game)
Friday, November 23, 1979 (St. Louis Streak at Philadelphia Fox)
Tuesday, December 18, 1979 (Last Philadelphia Fox game)
Thursday, March 13, 1980 (Charlie retires)
Tuesday, May 6, 1980 (St. Gregory's 22, Christ the King 6)
Friday, May 16, 1980 (Lakers defeat Sixers 4-2 for championship)
Monday, May 19, 1980 (St. Gregory's 16, Martin Luther 5)
Saturday, May 24, 1980 (Islanders defeat Flyers 4-2 for Stanley Cup)
Monday, June 23, 1980 (St. Gregory's 13, YMBC 4)
Thursday, July 31, 1980 (St. Gregory's 7, Haddonfield Presbyterian 6)
Friday, August 1, 1980 (St. Gregory's 9, Haddonfield Presbyterian 2)
Thursday, August 7, 1980 (St. Gregory's 3, St. John's 0)
Friday, August 8, 1980 (St. Gregory's beats St. Johns 14-2 for championship)
Saturday, September 27, 1980 (Expos defeat Phillies)
Monday, October 6, 1980 (Astros clinch NL West)
Tuesday, October 7, 1980 (Phillies/Astros Game 1)
Saturday, October 11, 1980 (Phillies/Astros Game 4)
Sunday, October 12, 1980 (Phillies/Astros Game 5)

Tuesday, October 21, 1980 (Phillies win World Series)
Wednesday, October 22, 1980 (*Philadelphia Inquirer* w/Carlton autograph)
Tuesday, November 4, 1980 (Carter/Reagan election)
Saturday, January 3, 1981 (Eagles defeat Vikings in playoffs)
Sunday, January 11, 1981 (Eagles defeat Cowboys in NFC championship)
Sunday, January 25, 1981 (Eagles lose *Super Bowl XV*)
Tuesday, May 5, 1981 (St. Gregory's 16, Gibbsboro Methodist 3)
Friday, May 22, 1981 (St. Gregory's 9, St. Andrew's 2)
Monday, June 8, 1981 (*Sports Illustrated* autographed by Greg Luzinski)
Wednesday, June 17, 1981 (St. Gregory's 18, Westmont Methodist 1)
Thursday, July 16, 1981 (St. Gregory's 7, Haddonfield Baptist 2 and St. Gregory's 5, Haddonfield Baptist 4 in doubleheader)
Friday, August 14, 1981 (St. Gregory's over YMBC for championship)
Tuesday, September 15, 1981 (Marjorie Lowden Scott dies)
Tuesday, April 27, 1982 (Dennis lecture notice in *The Cowl*)
Sunday, May 2, 1982 (Dennis lecture at Providence)
Friday, May 14, 1982 (St. Gregory's 9, Martin Luther 2)
Friday, May 21, 1982 (St. Gregory's 21, Temple Lutheran 2)
Tuesday, May 25, 1982 (St. Gregory's 17, St. Andrew's 8)
Thursday, June 24, 1982 (St. Gregory's 18, Haddonfield Baptist 9)
Friday, July 9, 1982 (Haddonfield Presbyterian 11, St. Gregory's 5; and Haddonfield Presbyterian 11, St. Gregory's 5 doubleheader)
Friday, July 16, 1982 (St. Gregory's 16, Gibbsboro Methodist 15)
Monday, July 19, 1982 (St. John's 4, St. Gregory's 2)
Tuesday, July 27, 1982 (St. Gregory's 13, Haddonfield Presbyterian 12)
Friday, July 30, 1982 (St. Gregory's 5, Haddonfield Presbyterian 3)
Wednesday, August 4, 1982 (St. Gregory's 9, YMBC 8)
Thursday, August 5, 1982 (YMBC 7, St. Gregory's 4)
Friday, August 6, 1982 (YMBC 10, St. Gregory's 8)
Tuesday, August 10, 1982 (St. Gregory's 9, YMBC 3)
Wednesday, August 11, 1982 (St. Gregory's 9, YMBC 0 for championship)
Monday, March 14, 1983 (*Sports Illustrated* autographed by Joe Morgan)
Monday, January 31, 1983 (Villanova-Georgetown at Palestra)
Thursday, July 21, 1983 (St. Gregory's 5, Haddonfield 3)
Monday, July 25, 1983 (St. Gregory's 17, Haddonfield Baptist 5)
Wednesday, August 10, 1983 (Haddonfield Presbyterian 9, St. Gregory's 8 for championship)
Sunday, October 23, 1983 (Jessica Savitch dies)
Friday, February 24, 1984 (49th Street Elementary School shooting)
Thursday, September 20, 1984 (Steve Goodman dies)
Tuesday, October 2, 1984 (Chicago Cubs playoff game)
Tuesday, November 6, 1984 (Reagan/Mondale election)
Thursday, May 30, 1985 (Oilers beat Flyers for Stanley Cup)

Monday, September 23, 1985 (*Sports Illustrated* autographed by Ozzie Smith)
Thursday, November 7, 1985 (Pelle Lindbergh's last game)
Friday, November 8, 1985 (Pistons-Celtics at Boston Garden)
Sunday, November 10, 1985 (Colts-Patriots at Sullivan Stadium)
Monday, November 11, 1985 (Pelle Lindbergh dies)
Tuesday, November 26, 1985 (Spanaway Junior High School shooting)
Tuesday, January 28, 1986 (*Challenger* explosion)
Sunday, September 14, 1986 (John Fogerty at Great Woods)
Saturday, October 4, 1986 (Nancy and I meet at Mr. Tipps)
Wednesday, October 8, 1986 ("The Letter" to Nancy)
Friday, October 24, 1986 (First date with Nancy)
Tuesday, October 27, 1986 (Second date with Nancy at Johnny's Bench)
Sunday, December 21, 1986 (Jingle Bell run in Boston)
Saturday, October 24, 1987 (My Wedding)
Thursday, December 24, 1987 (I got Jesse for Christmas)
Friday, January 15, 1988 (Purchased 211 East Palmer Avenue)
Sunday, January 24, 1988 (Letter from Albert Riester)
Tuesday, February 23, 1988 (Pennsylvania bar exam essays)
Wednesday, February 24, 1988 (Multistate bar exam)
Thursday, February 25, 1988 (New Jersey bar exam essays)
Friday, April 29, 1988 (Passed Pennsylvania bar exam)
Thursday, May 5, 1988 (*Intelligencer* publishes Pennsylvania bar results)
Monday, May 9, 1988 (*Law Journal-Reporter* publishes Pennsylvania bar results)
Thursday, May 12, 1988 (St. Gregory's 17, Haddonfield Baptist 7)
Thursday, May 19, 1988 (*New Jersey Law Journal* publishes bar results)
Thursday, June 2, 1988 (New Jersey bar admission ceremony)
Friday, June 3, 1988 (Admitted to Pennsylvania bar)
Tuesday, July 19, 1988 (St. Gregory's 15, Martin Luther 12)
Thursday, August 11, 1988 (St. Gregory's 4, Haddonfield Presbyterian 3 to reach finals)
Tuesday, August 16, 1988 (St. Gregory's 8, St. John's 7 in playoffs)
Thursday, August 18, 1988 (St. Gregory's 19, St. John's 2 for championship)
Tuesday, November 8, 1988 (Dukakis/Bush election)
Wednesday, December 21, 1988 (Pan Am 103)
Saturday, December 31, 1988 (Fog Bowl) (Mooney/Brenner wedding)
Tuesday, January 17, 1989 (Cleveland Elementary School shooting)
Friday, September 29, 1989 (Moved to Abbey Road)
Friday, January 5, 1990 (*Town & Country Fine Furniture v. WCAB* decided by Pennsylvania Supreme Court)
Wednesday, June 6, 1990 (St. Gregory's 4, Haddonfield Presbyterian 3)
Sunday, June 10, 1990 (Cubs 7, Phillies 3 at Wrigley Field)
Saturday, June 16, 1990 (Red Sox autographs in Baltimore)

Sunday, June 17, 1990 (Red Sox at Orioles)
Wednesday, July 25, 1990 (St. Gregory's 7, Haddonfield Presbyterian 6)
Friday, August 24, 1990 (St. Gregory's 9, Martin Luther 4 for championship)
Wednesday, May 29, 1991 (St. Gregory's 20, Holy Trinity 1)
Friday, June 28, 1991 (Red Sox at Orioles)
Saturday June 29, 1991 (Red Sox at Orioles)
Sunday, June 30, 1991 (Red Sox at Orioles)
Monday, August 19, 1991 (St. Gregory's 11, Martin Luther 9 for championship)
Saturday, September 28, 1991 (Dylan's due date)
Tuesday, October 8, 1991 (Dylan born)
Wednesday, October 9, 1991 (Golf with Charlie at Iron Rock CC)
Sunday, October 13, 1991 (Rosebud at First Baptist Church)
Friday, November 1, 1991 (University of Iowa shooting)
Monday, November 11, 1991 (Dylan's birth announcement in *Courier-Post*)
Friday, May 1, 1992 (Lindhurst High School shooting)
Tuesday, May 12, 1992 (Cardinals 6, Reds 4 at Busch Stadium)
Tuesday, May 19, 1992 (Dan Quayle's *Murphy Brown* speech)
Tuesday, June 23, 1992 (St. Gregory's 10, KOAG 0)
Saturday, June 27, 1992 (Phillies 5, Cubs 4 at Wrigley Field)
Sunday, June 28, 1992 (Cubs 5, Phillies 2 at Wrigley Field)
Wednesday, July 1, 1992 (St. Gregory's 17, Westmont Methodist 5)
Thursday, July 9, 1992 (St. Gregory's 6, Haddonfield Presbyterian 5)
Thursday, August 13, 1992 (St. Gregory's 8, Grace Baptist 7)
Saturday, October 24, 1992 (20th HS reunion) (5th wedding anniversary)
Sunday, November 1, 1992 (Bill Clinton at Garden State Park)
Tuesday, November 3, 1992 (Clinton/Bush election)
Wednesday, January 20, 1993 (In Jonesboro, Arkansas) (Bill Clinton inaugurated)
Friday, January 22, 1993 (Got on wrong plane, wound up in Indianapolis)
Friday, April 9, 1993 (Cubs 11, Phillies 7 in home opener)
Wednesday, April 14, 1993 (Phillies 9, Reds 2)
Tuesday, May 11, 1993 (Roger Clemens vs. Orioles at Camden Yards)
Saturday, June 12, 1993 (Rockies 14, Astros 11 at Mile High Stadium)
Friday, July 9, 1993 (Durham Bulls at Wilmington Blue Rocks)
Sunday, July 11, 1993 (San Francisco Giants 10, Phillies 2)
Friday, May 13, 1994 (Angels 11, Mariners 1 at Kingdome)
Tuesday, July 12, 1994 (*Mealey's Litigation Reports (Insurance)* article)
Tuesday, September 20, 1994 (*Mealey's Litigation Reports (Insurance)* article)
Saturday, November 5, 1994 (Mary Chapin Carpenter/John Gorka at Tower Theater)
Wednesday, April 12, 1995 (Marge dies)

Friday, April 14, 1995 (Marge cremated) (Marge's obituary in *Courier-Post*)

Saturday, April 15, 1995 (Marge's obituary in *Courier-Post*)

Monday, April 17, 1995 (Marge's memorial service)

Thursday, August 3, 1995 (Mary Chapin Carpenter/Mavericks at Mann Music Center)

Friday, February 2, 1996 (Frontier Middle School shooting)

Wednesday, July 3, 1996 (*Gearing v. Nationwide Insurance Company* decided by Supreme Court of Ohio)

Wednesday, July 31, 1996 (Ruptured patella tendon)

Friday, August 2, 1996 (Patella surgery)

Thursday, August 15, 1996 (San Diego State University shooting)

Tuesday, November 5, 1996 (Clinton/Dole election)

Wednesday, December 4, 1996 (Charlie sells 215 Burrwood Avenue)

Friday, August 8, 1997 (*Princeton Insurance Company v. Chunmuang* decided by Supreme Court of New Jersey)

Monday, December 1, 1997 (Heath High School shooting)

Friday, January 23, 1998 (National Air and Space Museum)

Tuesday, March 24, 1998 (Jonesboro, Arkansas school shooting)

Thursday, May 21, 1998 (Thurston High School shooting)

Sunday, June 7, 1998 (James Byrd, Jr. murdered)

Saturday, December 5, 1998 (Flyers v. Capitals at Wells Fargo Center)

Friday, February 26, 1999 (*Physicians Insurance Company v. Pistone* decided by Supreme Court of Pennsylvania)

Tuesday, April 20, 1999 (Columbine High School shooting)

Friday, September 24, 1999 (Bruce Springsteen concert at the Spectrum)

Friday, October 29, 1999 (Rose Murray dies)

Saturday, January 1, 2000 (Y2K)

Wednesday, May 3, 2000 (Supreme Court of Canada cites *Tort & Insurance Law Journal* article)

Tuesday, November 7, 2000 (Bush/Gore election)

Friday, November 10, 2000 (Baseball Hall of Fame)

Sunday, December 31, 2000 (Eagles-Bucs in last NFL game of century)

Sunday, January 7, 2001 (Giants 20, Eagles 10)

Friday, April 20, 2001 (Thomas John Florig dies)

Thursday, May 3, 2001 (Last race at Garden State Park)

Thursday, July 12, 2001 (Pirates 2, Royals 0 at PNC Park)

Tuesday, September 11, 2001 (Terrorist attacks)

Friday, October 12, 2001 (Bennetts/Martine arrive for Great Adventure)

Saturday, October 13, 2001 (Great Adventure)

Sunday, October 14, 2001 (Frisbee football/green eggs and ham)

Wednesday, January 16, 2002 (Appalachian School of Law shooting) (*St. Paul Fire and Marine Insurance Company v. Engelmann* decided by Supreme Court of South Dakota)

Wednesday, April 3, 2002 (*United Fire and Casualty Co. v. Shelly Funeral*

Home decided by Iowa Supreme Court)
Monday, October 28, 2002 (Univ. of Arizona School of Nursing shooting)
Friday, November 1, 2002 (*R.W. v. Schrein* decided)
Sunday, November 17, 2002 (McNabb breaks ankle in Eagles win)
Monday, November 25, 2002 (Eagles-Niners on *Monday Night Football*)
Sunday, January 19, 2003 (Eagles lose NFC championship to Bucs)
Thursday, August 28, 2003 (Jets-Eagles preseason game at the Linc)
Sunday, September 14, 2003 (Patriots defeat Eagles at Linc)
Monday, September 29, 2003 (Sandy Campbell dies)
Friday, November 21, 2003 (Dar Williams in Collingswood)
Sunday, January 11, 2004 (Fourth and 26)
Sunday, January 18, 2004 (Panthers-Eagles NFC Championship game)
Sunday, March 21, 2004 (Vet implosion)
Saturday, May 1, 2004 (Smarty Jones wins Kentucky Derby)
Saturday, June 5, 2004 (Smarty Jones loses Belmont Stakes)
Friday, June 25, 2004 (Red Sox 12, Phillies 1 at Fenway Park)
Saturday, June 26, 2004 (Phillies 9, Red Sox 2)
Sunday, June 27, 2004 (Driving home from Boston)
Monday, June 28, 2004 (Robert Strong dies)
Wednesday, June 30, 2004 (Expos 6, Phillies 3 at Citizens Bank Park)
Friday, July 30, 2004 (Robert Strong memorial service)
Sunday, October 17, 2004 (Red Sox defeat Yankees in Game 4 of ALCS)
Wednesday, October 27, 2004 (Red Sox win *World Series*)
Tuesday, November 2, 2004 (Bush/Kerry election)
Sunday, February 6, 2005 (Patriots defeat Eagles in *Super Bowl XXXIX*)
Monday, February 7, 2005 (The Fours named Best Sports Bar)
Monday, March 21, 2005 (Red Lake Senior High School shooting)
Friday, July 15, 2005 (John Fogerty/John Mellencamp at Tweeter Center)
Monday, August 29, 2005 (Hurricane Katrina makes landfall)
Friday, November 25, 2005 (Flyers at Bruins) (Nachos at The Fours)
Tuesday, June 20, 2006 (Voorhees Middle School graduation)
Saturday, September 24, 2006 (Hurricane Rita)
Monday, October 2, 2006 (West Nickel Mines School shooting)
Sunday, October 29, 2006 (Eagles - Jaguars at the Linc)
Wednesday, December 6, 2006 (Robert Scott dies)
Saturday, March 17, 2007 (Erin born)
Thursday, April 5, 2007 (JV versus Cherokee)
Tuesday, April 10, 2007 (JV at Cherry Hill East)
Thursday, April 12, 2007 (JV at Clearview)
Saturday, April 14, 2007 (JV versus Washington Township)
Monday, April 16, 2007 (JV versus Rancocas Valley) (Virginia Tech shooting)
Wednesday, April 18, 2007 (JV at St. Augustine Prep)
Tuesday, April 24, 2007 (JV at Washington Township)

Thursday, April 26, 2007 (JV at Cherokee)
Saturday, April 28, 2007 (JV at Lenape)
Wednesday, May 2, 2007 (JV versus Cherry Hill East)
Friday, May 4, 2007 (JV at Rancocas Valley)
Saturday, May 5, 2007 (JV versus Holy Cross)
Monday, May 7, 2007 (JV at Seneca)
Wednesday, May 9, 2007 (JV versus Lenape)
Thursday, May 10, 2007 (JV at Cherry Hill West)
Friday, May 11, 2007 (Del Val Pool Maintenance contract)
Wednesday, May 16, 2007 (JV versus Camden Catholic)
Friday, May 18, 2007 (JV at Shawnee)
Sunday, September 9, 2007 (Patriots illegally videotape Jets)
Saturday, September 15, 2007 (Patriots punished for "Spygate")
Saturday, November 3, 2007 (John Fogerty at the Tower Theater)
Sunday, November 25, 2007 (Eagles at Patriots)
Friday, February 8, 2008 (Louisiana Technical College shooting)
Thursday, February 14, 2008 (Northern Illinois University shooting)
Wednesday, April 2, 2008 (Eastern 12, Kingsway 0)
Thursday, April 3, 2008: (Eastern 12, Cherry Hill West 10)
Saturday, April 5, 2008: (Eastern 8, Cherokee 5)
Tuesday, April 8, 2008: (Eastern 14, Cherry Hill East 5)
Thursday, April 10, 2008: (Eastern 11, Clearview 8)
Monday, April 14, 2008: (Eastern 15, Rancocas Valley 1)
Wednesday, April 16, 2008: (Eastern 9, Holy Cross 2)
Monday, April 21, 2008: (Eastern 12, Washington Township 7)
Thursday, April 24, 2008: (Cherokee 13, Eastern 6)
Saturday, April 26, 2008: (Lenape 7, Eastern 6)
Tuesday, April 29, 2008: (Eastern 9, West Deptford 5)
Wednesday, April 30, 2008: (Eastern 16, Cherry Hill East 0)
Friday, May 2, 2008: (Eastern 17, Rancocas Valley 2)
Sunday, May 4, 2008 (54th birthday at Lone Star)
Monday, May 5, 2008: (Eastern 12, Seneca 5)
Wednesday, May 7, 2008 (Eastern 12, Lenape 5)
Thursday, May 8, 2008 (Eastern 17, Washington Township 5)
Monday, May 12, 2008 (St. Augustine 8, Eastern 5)
Wednesday, May 14, 2008 (Eastern 14, Camden Catholic 4)
Friday, May 16, 2008 (Shawnee 8, Eastern 6)
Wednesday, May 21, 2008 (Eastern 7, Toms River North 4)
Friday, May 23, 2008 (Montclair 9, Eastern 3)
Sunday, May 25, 2008 (Charlie dies)
Monday, May 26, 2008 (Charlie's arrangements at funeral home)
Wednesday, May 28, 2008 (Charlie cremated)
Thursday, May 29, 2008 (Charlie's memorial service)
Tuesday, June 3, 2008 (Eastern Athletic awards)

Friday, June 20, 2008 (Appointed Executor of Charlie's estate)
Monday, July 28, 2008 (Chris Surran goalie camp begins)
Thursday, July 31, 2008 (Chris Surran goalie camp ends)
Saturday, August 30, 2008 (Kelly/Patrick wedding in Vermont)
Thursday, September 4, 2008 (Leona Miller dies)
Sunday, September 7, 2008 (Eagles - Rams at the Linc)
Monday, October 27, 2008 (World Series Game 5 starts)
Wednesday, October 29, 2008 (World Series Game 5 ends)
Friday, October 31, 2008 (Phillies parade)
Tuesday, November 4, 2008 (Obama/McCain election)
Wednesday, April 1, 2009 (Eastern 14, Bishop Eustace 4)
Saturday, April 4, 2009 (St. Augustine 10, Eastern 2)
Wednesday, April 8, 2009 (Eastern 9, Lenape 1)
Saturday, April 11, 2009 (Cherokee 8, Eastern 6)
Tuesday, April 14, 2009 (Eastern 3, Clearview 2)
Friday, April 17, 2009 (Shawnee 15, Eastern 4)
Friday, April 24, 2009 (Eastern 15, Cherry Hill East 0)
Monday, April 27, 2009 (Cherokee 5, Eastern 1)
Wednesday, April 29, 2009 (Eastern 16, West Deptford 3)
Monday, May 4, 2009 (Moorestown 8, Eastern 7)
Wednesday, May 6, 2009 (Eastern 9, Seneca 2)
Thursday, May 7, 2009 (Eastern 9, Washington Township 2)
Monday, May 11, 2009 (West Windsor-Plainsboro 6, Eastern 4)
Wednesday, May 13, 2009 (Peddie 8, Eastern 7
Friday, May 15, 2009 (Eastern 7, Washington Township 3)
Monday, May 18, 2009 (Eastern 9, Lenape 5)
Wednesday, May 20, 2009 (Eastern 10, Jackson 3)
Saturday, May 23, 2009 (Bridgewater-Raritan 11, Eastern 3)
Wednesday, June 3, 2009 (Eastern Academic awards)
Wednesday, June 24, 2009 (Top 205 camp begins)
Saturday, June 27, 2009 (Top 205 camp ends) (Elite 180 camp begins)
Tuesday, June 30, 2009 (Elite 180 camp ends)
Wednesday, September 16, 2009 (Stephen Florig dies)
Sunday, September 20, 2009 (Eagles - Saints at the Linc)
Friday, October 2, 2009 (23rd Lee-Jackson Classic)
November 27, 2009 (Sue Glennon dies)
Saturday, December 12, 2009 (Sue Glennon funeral mass)
Saturday, March 13, 2010 (F&M 7, W&L 5 in Lancaster)
Thursday, April 1, 2010 (Eastern 13, Bishop Eustace 2)
Tuesday, April 6, 2010 (Shawnee 11, Eastern 10)
Wednesday, April 7, 2010 (Eastern 10, Cherry Hill West 3)
Friday, April 9, 2010 (Eastern 10, Cherokee 2)
Monday, April 12, 2010 (Eastern 11, Cherry Hill East 0)
Wednesday, April 14, 2010 (Eastern 11, Clearview 1)

Monday, April 19, 2010 (Eastern 14, Holy Cross 0)
Wednesday, April 21, 2010 (Eastern 7, Lenape 4)
Thursday, April 22, 2010 (Washington Township 6, Eastern 5)
Tuesday, April 27, 2010 (Eastern 13, Cherokee 6)
Thursday, April 29, 2010 (Eastern 13, West Deptford 5)
Friday, April 30, 2010 (Peddie 7, Eastern 6)
Tuesday, May 4, 2010 (Eastern 13, Cherry Hill East 1)
Wednesday, May 5, 2010 (Moorestown 9, Eastern 2)
Friday, May 7, 2010 (Eastern 8, Seneca 7)
Tuesday, May 11, 2010 (Lenape 5, Eastern 2)
Tuesday, May 18, 2010 (Eastern 7, Clifton 1)
Thursday, May 20, 2010 (Eastern 12, North Hunterdon 7)
Saturday, May 22, 2010 (Montclair 12, Eastern 4)
Wednesday, June 9, 2010 (Eastern Academic awards II)
Wednesday, June 23, 2010 (Dylan graduates from Eastern High School)
Tuesday, August 10, 2010 (Black woman calls Dr. Laura)
Saturday, October 23, 2010 (24th Lee-Jackson Classic)
Saturday, November 6, 2010 (Parents' Weekend at W&L)
Tuesday, December 28, 2010 (Eagles - Vikings at the Linc)
Saturday, March 5, 2011 (W&L 5, Washington College 4)
Wednesday, March 23, 2011 (Dylan plays versus Guilford College)
Tuesday, March 29, 2011 (Middlebury 5, W&L 4 at Georgetown)
Saturday, April 2, 2011 (Dylan plays versus Randolph College)
Monday, June 6, 2011 (*Impact100* grant presentation)
Tuesday, October 4, 2011 (*Impact100* report at Bala Golf Club)
Wednesday, October 5, 2011 (Longstreth library opening)
Friday, October 21, 2011 (25th Lee-Jackson Classic)
Sunday, November 27, 2011 (Patriots defeat Eagles at the Linc)
Sunday, December 18, 2011 (Eagles - Jets at the Linc)
Monday, February 27, 2012 (Chardon High School shooting)
Saturday, March 31, 2012 (W&L 21, Randolph 2)
Monday, April 2, 2012 (Oikos University shooting)
Monday, April 9, 2012 (National Library Week begins)
Friday, April 13, 2012 (National Library Week ends)
Wednesday, April 18, 2012 (W&L 14, Greensboro 4)
Thursday, June 28, 2012 (Chris Sanderson dies)
Tuesday, July 24, 2012 (Phillies 7, Brewers 6 at Citizens Bank Park)
Friday, October 12, 2012 (McMichael School library opening)
Friday, October 26, 2012 (26th Lee-Jackson Classic)
Saturday, November 3, 2012 (Certificate from NELI)
Tuesday, November 6, 2012 (Obama/Romney election)
Friday, December 14, 2012 (Sandy Hook Elementary School shooting)
Tuesday, January 15, 2013 (Hazard Community and Technical College shooting)

Wednesday, January 16, 2013 (Possible Molly birthday)

Thursday, January 24, 2013 (Possible Molly birthday)

Monday, February 4, 2013 (*WePAC* named "*GameChanger*")

Tuesday, February 12, 2013 (Dylan plays versus Ferrum College)

Saturday, February 16, 2013 (W&L 12, Christopher Newport 9)

Wednesday, February 20, 2013 (W&L 7, Salisbury 6)

Friday, March 1, 2013 (Possible Molly birthday)

Saturday, March 2, 2013 (Washington College 8, W&L 4)

Wednesday, March 20, 2013 (W&L 9, Mary Washington 4)

Saturday, March 23, 2013 (Guilford at W&L)

Wednesday, April 3, 2013 (Dylan plays versus Bridgewater College)

Saturday, April 13, 2013 (Dylan plays versus Randolph College)

Thursday, April 18, 2013 (*WePAC* fundraiser at Simeone Museum)

Monday, April 22, 2013 (National Library Week begins)

Wednesday, April 24, 2013 (Dylan plays versus Shenandoah University)

Friday, April 26, 2013 (National Library Week ends)

Saturday, April 27, 2013 (W&L at Hampden-Sydney College at 1:00 pm)

Saturday, May 4, 2013 (Lynchburg v. W&L in ODAC semifinal)

Sunday, May 5, 2013 (W&L loses to Roanoke in ODAC championship)

Wednesday, May 8, 2013 (W&L defeats Sewanee in NCAA tournament)

Saturday, May 11, 2013 (Salisbury 7, W&L 4)

Friday, June 7, 2013 (Santa Monica College shooting)

Thursday, June 20, 2013 (*Philadelphia Inquirer* open letter from *WePAC*)

Sunday, June 23, 2013 (*Main Line Times* open letter from *WePAC*)

Friday, August 30, 2013 (Sara "Sally" Miller dies)

Saturday, September 7, 2013 (Fenway euthanized)

Tuesday, September 10, 2013 (Fenway cremated)

Monday, September 16, 2013 (*WePAC* Volunteer Kick-Off)

Wednesday, September 25, 2013 (William Scott dies)

Sunday, September 29, 2013 (*Breaking Bad* finale)

Thursday, January 16, 2014 (Molly picked up in Decatur, Georgia)

Monday, January 20, 2014 (MLK Day of Service at *WePAC*)

Friday, January 24, 2014 (Molly arrives at Voorhees Animal Orphanage)

Saturday, January 25, 2014 (Molly adopted)

Saturday, March 8, 2014 ("Literacy is Not an Elective" in *Philadelphia Inquirer*) (Board strategic planning retreat)

Sunday, March 9, 2014 (Started writing *WePAC* exit memos)

Friday, March 14, 2014 (*WePAC* Separation Agreement signed)

Wednesday, April 9, 2014 (*WePAC* fundraising gala)

Tuesday, April 15, 2014 (Last day at *WePAC*)

Wednesday, May 14, 2014 (Ray Miller, Sr. dies)

Wednesday, May 21, 2014 (W&L luncheon and reception)

Thursday, May 22, 2014 (W&L graduation)

Saturday, June 28, 2014 (Charlotte Hounds v. Boston Cannons)

Friday, October 24, 2014 (Marysville Pilchuck High School shooting)
Thursday, November 6, 2014 (Nancy and I purchased house in Maine)
Sunday, January 18, 2005 (Patriots deflate footballs)
Tuesday, May 19, 2015 (Ray Miller, Jr. dies)
Thursday, May 21, 2015 (Haddon Twp. Board of Education Resolution)
Saturday, June 27, 2015 (John Fogerty at Mann Music Center)
Saturday, July 4, 2015 (Doris dies)
Tuesday, July 7, 2015 (Doris' Celebration of Life)
Wednesday, July 8, 2015 (Doris' funeral)
Saturday, July 25, 2015 (Cole Hamels no-hitter)
Friday, July 31, 2015 (Cole Hamels traded)
Thursday, October 1, 2015 (Umpqua Community College shooting)
Sunday, October 25, 2015 (Eagles at Panthers in Charlotte)
Sunday, November 22, 2015 (Philadelphia Marathon)
Thursday, March 10, 2016 (Abbey Road listed for sale)
Monday, March 14, 2016 (Bachs make offer on Abbey Road)
Wednesday, March 16, 2016 (Agreement of Sale for Abbey Road)
Thursday, May 19, 2016 (Abbey Road sold)
Friday, May 20, 2016 (Moved to Maine)
Saturday, May 28, 2016 (Dennis dies)
Monday, May 30, 2016 (Jim visits us in Maine)
Friday, June 3, 2016 (Jim in hospital)
Saturday, June 4, 2016 (Dylan Facetime with Jim)
Sunday, June 5, 2016 (Jim dies)
Tuesday, June 7, 2016 (Jim's Celebration of Life)
Wednesday, June 8, 2016 (Jim's funeral)
Friday, June 17, 2016 (Letter from Meyoung re Dennis' death)
Friday, July 1, 2016 (James Scott dies)
Tuesday, November 8, 2016 (Clinton/Trump election)
Friday, January 20, 2017 (Trump inauguration)
Sunday, March 26, 2017 (Maine Maple Sunday)
Thursday, May 4, 2017 (Cowshit Corner)
Friday, June 16, 2017 (Bailey Island and Orr's Island)
Sunday, August 6, 2017 (Mary Chapin Carpenter at Stone Mountain)
Saturday, September 16, 2017 (Anniversary cruise)
Thursday, October 19, 2017 (Fort Popham)
Tuesday, November 14, 2017 (Rancho Tehama Elementary School shooting)
Saturday, November 18, 2017 (The Lost Kitchen with Becky and David)
Thursday, December 7, 2017 (Aztec High School shooting)
Friday, December 29, 2017 (Skiing in Winter Park)
Saturday, January 13, 2018 (Eagles beat Falcons in playoffs)
Sunday, January 21, 2018 (Eagles beat Vikings in playoffs)
Sunday, February 4, 2018 (Eagles defeat Patriots in *Super Bowl LII*)

Thursday, February 8, 2018 (Eagles' *Super Bowl* parade)
Wednesday, February 14, 2018 (Marjory Stoneman Douglas HS shooting)
Friday, March 9, 2018 (Ed Hutto dies)
Saturday, March 17, 2018 (Féile)
Saturday, March 24, 2018 (March for Our Lives in Portland)
Saturday, April 7, 2018 (Waterford)
Tuesday, April 10, 2018 (*Horace Mann Insurance Co. v. Barney* decided by U.S. District Court for the Western District of Virginia)
Wednesday, April 4, 2018 (Nancy tries curling)
Saturday, April 28, 2018 (Sisters here)
Friday, May 4, 2018 (National Whitewater Center in Charlotte)
Friday, May 11, 2018 (Agnes Florig Sheldon dies) (Bristol/Pemaquid)
Friday, May 18, 2018 (Santa Fe High School shooting) (Barter Island/Newagen/Cuckolds Lighthouse]
Friday, May 25, 2018 (Cruise with Carlins)
Saturday, May 26, 2018 (Portland Head Light with Carlins)
Friday, June 22, 2018 (John Fogerty at Bank of New Hampshire Pavilion)
Friday, July 13, 2018 (Portland Head LIght with Linda and Billy)
Sunday, July 22, 2018 (Mary Chapin Carpenter at Stone Mountain Arts Center with Donna and Roy)
Sunday, August 5, 2018 (John Sebastian at Jonathan's)
Thursday, September 27, 2018 (Left for Finger Lakes/Blasey Ford)
Saturday, November 10, 2018 (Manta and Welge reunion)
Sunday, November 11, 2018 (Eagles-Cowboys with Joe)
Monday, December 24, 2018 (Christmas Eve at Cindy and Dave's)
Wednesday, January 9, 2019 (Curling Club in *Maine Business Journal*)
Sunday, February 3, 2019 (John Melhorn dies)
Friday, February 8, 2019 (I got bed bugs)
Saturday, February 9, 2019 (John Melhorn funeral)
Tuesday, February 26, 2019 (Pedro's in Kennebunkport)
Saturday, March 30, 2019 (Milt Ryder dies)
Saturday, May 4, 2019 (Dylan and Elizabeth engaged) (My 65th birthday)
Saturday, May 18, 2019 (Milt Ryder memorial service)
Saturday, June 22, 2019 (Reading Phils at Portland Sea Dogs)
Saturday, July 6, 2019 (Black Point Inn/Bug Light with Dylan)
Sunday, August 11, 2019 (John Fogerty at Rock Row in Maine)
Tuesday, September 3, 2019 (First Day of School - Nancy at beach)
Saturday, September 14, 2019 (Maine Open Lighthouse Day)
Monday, September 23, 2019 (Leave for Southwest Harbor)
Tuesday, September 24, 2019 (Acadia National Park)
Wednesday, September 25, 2019 (Schoodic)
Thursday, September 26, 2019 (Watched Eagles-Packers in Lubec)
Friday, November 1, 2019 (Nancy and I drive to New Jersey)
Saturday, November 2, 2019 (Flyers-Maple Leafs shootout)

Sunday, November 3, 2019 (Eagles-Bears at the Linc)
Monday, November 4, 2019 (Dylan to airport/Drive home to Maine)
Thursday, November 14, 2019 (Saugus High School shooting)
Saturday, December 7, 2019 (Broomstones Buildspiel)
Sunday, December 8, 2019 (Broomstones Buildspiel)
Tuesday, December 24, 2019 (This is Us Christmas Eve at Cindy's)
Friday, January 17, 2020 (Salivary gland infection)
Thursday, March 5, 2020 (Trader Joe's)
Wednesday, March 11, 2020 (Lunch at Duckfat)
Tuesday, March 24, 2020 (First pandemic trip to Market Basket)
Sunday, March 29, 2020 (Lone Pine Brewing)
Monday, April 6. 2020 (Market Basket)
Tuesday, April 7, 2020 (John Prine dies)
Tuesday, April 14, 2020 (Lone Pine Brewing)
Friday, April 17, 2020 (Maine Beer Company) (Bissell Brothers Brewing)
Sunday, April 19, 2020 (Stoneface Brewing)
Monday, April 20, 2020 (Market Basket)
Friday, April 24, 2020 (Maine Beer Company)
Saturday, April 25, 2020 (Mast Landing Brewing)
Friday, May 1, 2020 (Market Basket) (SoMe Brewing)
Saturday, May 2, 2020 (Lone Pine Brewing)
Wednesday, May 6, 2020 (SoMe Brewing)
Saturday, May 9, 2020 (Trivia) (Mast Landing Brewing)
Wednesday, May 13, 2020 (Market Basket) (Lone Pine Brewing)
Thursday, May 14, 2020 (Stoneface Brewing)
Friday, May 22, 2020 (Lone Pine Brewing)
Wednesday, May 27, 2020 (Garrison City Beerworks)
Sunday, May 31, 2020 (Lone Pine Brewing)
Wednesday, June 3, 2020 (Bissell Brothers Brewing)
Sunday, June 7, 2020 (Lone Pine Brewing)
Saturday, June 13, 2020 (Bissell Brothers Brewing)
Thursday, June 18, 2020 (SoMe Brewing)
Tuesday, June 30, 2020 (Lone Pine Brewing)
Friday, July 3, 2020 (Definitive Brewing)
Saturday, July 4, 2020 (SoMe Brewing)
Thursday, July 16, 2020 (SoMe Brewing) (Definitive Brewing)
Friday, July 17, 2020 (Battery Steele Brewing)
Wednesday, July 22, 2020 (Bunker Brewing) (Battery Steele Brewing)
Thursday, July 23, 2020 (Stars & Stripes Brewing Company)
Friday, July 24, 2020 (Maine Beer Company)
Saturday, July 25, 2020 (Austin Street Brewing)
Thursday, July 30, 2020 (Maine Beer Company) (Flight Deck Brewing)
Friday, July 31, 2020 (Mast Landing Brewing)
Tuesday, August 4, 2020 (Lone Pine Brewing)

Wednesday, August 12, 2020 (Definitive Brewing) (NU Brewing)
Friday, August 14, 2020 (Maine Beer Company)
Thursday, August 20, 2020 (Boothbay)
Friday, August 21, 2020 (Oxbow Brewing)
Monday, August 31, 2020 (The Fours closes)
Wednesday, September 9, 2020 (Curling Club in *Portland Forecaster*)
Saturday, October 24, 2020 (Train trivia) (33rd wedding anniversary)
Tuesday, November 3, 2020 (Biden/Trump election)
Saturday, November 7, 2020 (Dylan/Elizabeth original wedding date)
Thursday, December 10, 2020 (Portland Head Light)
Wednesday, January 6, 2021 (Insurrection)
Monday, January 11, 2021 (Saco City Council)
Wednesday, January 20, 2021 (Biden inauguration)
Monday, February 1, 2021 (Saco City Council)
Wednesday, March 10, 2021 (First COVID vaccine shot)
Sunday, March 21, 2021 (Curling)
Sunday, March 28, 2021 (Maine Maple Sunday)
Wednesday, March 31, 2021 (Second COVID vaccine shot)
Friday, April 9, 2021 (Saw a puffin in East Boothbay)
Wednesday, April 14, 2021 (Fully immune)
Tuesday, April 27, 2021 (Mary Hutto dies)
Monday, May 10, 2021 (Owl's Head Light Station)
Wednesday, May 12, 2021 (Rockland Breakwater Light)
Tuesday, May 25, 2021 (Hartford Yard Goats at Portland Sea Dogs)
Thursday, July 1, 2021 (Smuttynose/Stoneface breweries with Dylan/Elizabeth)
Saturday, July 3, 2021 (Portland Lobster Company)
Monday, July 5, 2021 (Puffin cruise)
Tuesday, July 6, 2021 (Dylan and Elizabeth to airport)
Friday, July 16, 2021 (Quebe Sisters at Stone Mountain Arts Center)
Wednesday, August 11, 2021 (Branchy's Brood wins championship)
Monday, August 16, 2021 (Visited pet cemetery on Mackworth Island)
Sunday, August 29, 2021 (Shaughnessy proclaims Newton Patriots' starter)
Saturday, September 11, 2021 (Nancy shopping for wedding dress)
Wednesday, September 29, 2021 (Mary Chapin Carpenter scheduled to play in Portland)
Tuesday, October 5, 2021 (Scattered Mary Hutto's ashes)
Friday, October 8, 2021 (Dylan turned 30)
Friday, October 15, 2021 (COVID booster)
Thursday, November 4, 2021 (Nancy and I fly to Charlotte)
Friday, November 5, 2021 (Golf with Dylan)
Saturday, November 6, 2021 (Dylan got married)
Monday, November 8, 2021 (Nancy and I fly home to Portland)
Tuesday, November 30, 2021 (Oxford High School school shooting)

A lphabetical listing of every person mentioned herein.

Brian Adams . . . Jeff Adams . . . Kirk Adams . . . Wayne Adams . . . Steve Adelman . . . Lynne Adkins . . . Aeschylus . . . Spiro Agnew . . . David Akers . . . . Susan Albino . . . Dorothy Albrecht . . . Kermit Alexander . . . Muhammad Ali . . . Anita Allen . . . Dick Allen . . . Reverend Benjamin Allgood . . . Steve Amadio . . . Ruben Amaro . . . Glenn Anderson . . . John Anderson . . . Lee Andrews . . . Rob Andrews . . . Luis Aparicio . . . Neil Armstrong . . . Marion Ashmore . . . Isaac Asimov . . . Marjorie B. . . . James Bach . . . Tara Bach . . . Dr. Robert Bachman . . . Jeff Bagwell . . . Paul Bailey . . . Ginger Baker . . . Frank Banecker . . . Ronde Barber . . . Matt Barkley . . . Franklin Barnes . . . Hannah Barnes . . . Jacob L. Barnes . . . Joseph Barnes . . . Martin Barnes . . . Marty Barrett . . . Gene Barretta . . . Percival P. Baxter . . . Frank Beard . . . Katie Bedard . . . Arlene Bednarczyk . . . Anna Catharina Bedos . . . Bill Belichick . . . Christine Bell . . . Reverend Herbert J. Belting . . . Carole Bennett . . . Peter Bennett . . . Warren Berenis . . . Candace Bergen . . . Bill Bergey . . . Franz John Bernhardt . . . Yogi Berra . . . Chuck Berry . . . Shawn Allen Berry . . . Beyoncé . . . Anthony Bezich . . . Joe Biden . . . Dante Bichette . . . Caleb Biggers . . . Craig Biggio . . . Brian Biggs . . . Wayne Bikuieli . . . Elizabeth McAndrew Birrane . . . Thomas Birrane . . . Becky Birtha . . . Barbara Bisbing . . . Bernice Bisbing . . . Willard Bisbing . . . Blaine Bishop . . . Matt Bittner . . . Chester Bixby . . . Lorna Bixby . . . Clint Black . . . Tony Black . . . Mike Boddicker . . . Barbara Boenning . . . Debbie Boenning . . . Rob Boenning . . . Sue Boettcher . . . Ann Bogar . . . Wade Boggs . . . Usain Bolt . . . Barry Bonds . . . Bob Boone . . . John Wilkes Booth . . . Robert Bork . . . Lee Bouggess . . . Bob Bowdoin . . . Dorothy Bowker . . . Phil Boyle . . . Sam Bradford . . . Tom Brady . . . Drew Brees . . . David Brenner . . . Julie K. Bressler . . . Joseph Bretschneider . . . Lawrence Russell Brewer . . . Sydney Bridges . . . Rod Brind'Amour . . . Garth Brooks . . . Edna Brown . . . Reverend Floyd Brown . . . Ken Brown . . . Paul Brown . . . Sheldon Brown . . . Dave Brownlow . . . Tom Brunansky . . . Barry Bruner . . . Sue Bruner . . . Mary Beth Bryant . . . Tom Bryant . . . Mica Brzezinski . . . Rich Bucich . . . Vivian Bucich . . . Jimmy Buffett . . . Norm Bulaich . . . Jim Bunning . . . Ellis Burks . . . Don Burroughs . . . Trey Burton . . . George H.W. Bush . . . George W. Bush . . . Jeb Bush . . . Marie Butler . . . Marty Butler . . . James Byrd, Jr. . . . William Cahill . . . Johnny Callison . . . Rich Campbell . . . Sandy Campbell . . . Brendan Canavan . . . Don Cannon . . . Mike Caravana . . . Deborah Carey . . . George Carlin . . . Jane Carlin . . . Patrick Carlin . . . Ray Carlin . . . Sean Carlin . . . Carl Carlson . . . Lorraine Carlson . . . Steve Carlton . . . Harold Carmichael . . . Mary Chapin Carpenter . . . Scott Carpenter . . . Jon Carroll . . . Gary Carter . . . Jimmy Carter . . . Joe Carter . . . Pete Case . . . Joe Casole . . . Fran Catando . . . Joe Catando . . . Karenellen Cechvala . . . Wilt Chamberlain . . . Mark David

Chapman . . . Glenn Charles . . . Chris Christie . . . Jeff Chute . . . Pam
Chute . . . Joe Cielia . . . Jim Cilento . . . Eric Clapton . . . Dave Clark . . . Jim
Clark . . . Julie Clark . . . Eldridge Cleaver . . . Mr. Clegg . . . Roger Clemens .
. . Mike Clifford . . . Patsy Cline . . . Bill Clinton . . . Hillary Clinton . . . Kurt
Cobain . . . Donna Cochrane . . . Roy Cochrane . . . Joe Cocker . . . Paul
Coffey . . . Ellen Cohill . . . Al Coleman . . . Doug Collins . . . Joan Collins . . .
Sue Comeforo . . . Jay Cook . . . Gordon Cooper . . . Linda Cooper . . . Don
Cornelius . . . Tyler Costantino . . . Eva Couillard . . . Ovid Couillard . . .
John Courtney . . . Sean Couturier . . . Wes Covington . . . Stephanie
Cowans . . . Ted Coyle . . . Bryan Cranston . . . Beverly Crawl . . . Walter
Cronkite . . . Cindy Cunningham . . . Dave Cunningham . . . Randall
Cunningham . . . Lee Cyr . . . Nick Dadarrio . . . Debbie Dadey . . . Tom
Daley . . . Clay Dalrymple . . . Pamela Dalton . . . Jennifer Darby . . . Debbie
Darling . . . Dr. Albert B. Davis . . . John H. "Jack" Davis . . . Andre Dawson .
. . Ed Day . . . Joseph Day . . . Mike DeLuca . . . Tom Dempsey . . . Judi
Dench . . . Joe Denote . . . John Denver . . . Eric Desjardins . . . Koy Detmer . .
. Dave Diano . . . Emily Dickinson . . . G.R. Digby . . . Wayne Dilugi . . .
Chris DiNote . . . Charles DiPietropolo . . . Ricky Divis . . . Joseph Dixon . . .
Lauren Dodington . . . Joe Doe . . . Tom Doe . . . Jim Doherty . . . Michael
Dolich . . . Mike D'Olio . . . Mike Dominick . . . Susan Donahue . . . Fyoder
Dostoevsky . . . Cameron Dougherty . . . Larry Drexler . . . Don Drysdale . . .
Scott Dube . . . Joyce Dudley . . . Michael Dukakis . . . Bill Dunstan . . . John
Durst . . . Francqis "Papa Doc" Duvalier . . . Jean-Claude "Baby Doc"
Duvalier . . . Bob Dylan . . . Roy Earnest . . . John Eberle . . . Ken Ecklund . . .
Marie Ecklund . . . Marion Eddy . . . Douglas Edwards . . . Herman Edwards
. . . Tamala Edwards . . . Maggie Ellery . . . Charles Epley . . . Mary Erhard . . .
Emilio Estevez . . . Lady Eugenia . . . Dick Evans . . . Dwight Evans . . . Linda
Evans . . . Patrick Ewing . . . Tom Fanelli . . . Joel Farabee . . . Orval Faubus . .
. Marshall Faulk . . . Brett Favre . . . Tony Fazzie . . . Lee Federline . . . A.J.
Feeley . . . Mike Feldberg . . . Lee Felheimer . . . Frank X. Feller . . . Al Ferrari
. . . Vince Ferrari . . . Ed Ferren . . . Nancy Filliter . . . Edna Fineberg . . .
Larry Fink . . . David L. Finnegan . . . John Finnegan . . . John J. Finnegan,
Jr. . . . Kevin Fitzgerald . . . Ray Fitzgerald . . . Tom Fitzgerald . . . Shane
Flannery . . . Isabel Bogorad Fleiss . . . Shirley J. Fletcher . . . Adolph Florig .
. . Charlie Florig . . . Dennis Florig . . . Dylan Florig . . . John Florig . . . John
Joseph Florig . . . Marie Florig . . . Marjorie Florig . . . Mary Bernhardt
Florig . . . Meyoung Lee Florig . . . Nancy MacDonald Florig . . . Stephen
Florig . . . Thomas John Florig . . . C. Maria Flynn . . . John Fogerty . . .
Shane Fogerty . . . John Walsh Folcarelli . . . Nick Foles . . . Lin Foley . . . Dr.
Christine Blasey Ford . . . Jim Ford . . . George Foreman . . . Peter Forsberg .
. . Ken Forsch . . . Kim Forsyth . . . Marian Foster . . . Dylan Fox . . . John
Franciotti . . . Tony Franklin . . . Joe Frazier . . . Jim Fregosi . . . Erin French . .
. Adam Friedant . . . Marc Friedant . . . Woody Fryman . . . Grant Fuhr . . .
Annette Funicello . . . Roman Gabriel . . . Simon Gagne . . . Michael

Gallagher . . . Oscar Gamble . . . Mahatma Gandhi . . . Rich Gant . . . Lori Garber . . . Kate Garchinsky . . . Wes Gardner . . . David Garrard . . . George Gehring . . . George Geist . . . Andy Gelman . . . Tom Genetta . . . Hon. John F. Gerry . . . Billy Gibbons . . . Harry Giberson . . . Roger Gill . . . Clark Gillies . . . Newt Gingrich . . . Claude Giroux . . . Debbie Gizelbach . . . Bonnie Glaser . . . Emma Gleason . . . John Glenn . . . Dave Glennon . . . Sue Glennon . . . Kim Glovas . . . Carl Glover . . . Georgia Glover . . . Hannah Godfrey . . . Stan Golas . . . Tony Gonzalez . . . Rodman Goode . . . Virginia Goode . . . Dwight Gooden . . . Jake Goodman . . . Steve Goodman . . . Bob Gordon . . . Al Gore . . . Heather Gorham . . . John Gorka . . . Shane Gostisbehere . . . David Gottlieb . . . Bob Grabiak . . . Jeff Grabowski . . . Dave Graham . . . Ric Grech . . . Lorne Greene . . . Cherri Gregg . . . Wayne Gretzky . . . Ken Griffey, Jr. . . . John Grisham . . . Gus Grissom . . . Greg Gross . . . Mike Grossman . . . Linda Grote . . . Mark Grussenmeyer . . . Jay Gunn . . . Riley Gunnels . . . Garrett Gustafson . . . Arlo Guthrie . . . Woody Guthrie . . . Dan Gutman . . . Jack Gwillam . . . Fred Gwynne . . . Reverend Ivan H. Hagedorn . . . Laurie Haines . . . Dr. W. H. Haines . . . Ronald Hales . . . Anthony Michael Hall . . . Monty Hall . . . Eileen Halloran . . . Pete Ham . . . Cole Hamels . . . Heidi Hamels . . . Michal Handzus . . . Bruce V. Hanson . . . Greg Harris . . . Richard Harris . . . George Harrison . . . Lauren Hart . . . John Havlicek . . . Reverend George Hawthorne . . . Kevin Hayes . . . Richie Hebner . . . Danny Heep . . . Luke Heinsohn . . . Theresa Florig Helmuth . . . Jimi Hendrix . . . Alexandria Hensleigh . . . Audrey Hepburn . . . Reverend William J. Herman . . . Elizabeth Florig Hettmannsperger . . . Ron Hextall . . . Faith Hill . . . Fred Hill . . . Kim Hill . . . King Hill . . . Gladys Hillman . . . Sue Holcombe . . . J.D. Holiday . . . Buddy Holly . . . Santonio Holmes . . . Anthony Hopkins . . . Ryan Howard . . . Ed Hyrniewicz . . . Jan Hyrniewicz . . . Jim Hudson . . . Claude Humphrey . . . Hubert H. Humphrey . . . Bob Hunsberger . . . Lawrence Hutcherson . . . Becky Hutto . . . Carol Hutto . . . Chris Hutto . . . Ed Hutso . . . Mary Hutto . . . Steve Ibbeken . . . Amy Ignatow . . . Barbara Ilgenfritz . . . Bob Ilgenfritz . . . Michael Irvin . . . Barry Jackman . . . Lynne Jackman . . . Alan Jackson . . . Bo Jackson . . . Desean Jackson . . . Janet Jackson . . . Reverend Jesse Jackson . . . Larry Jackson . . . Stephen Jackson . . . Thomas "Stonewall" Jackson . . . Audrey Jacobsen . . . Anne Jacobs . . . Barbara Jacobs . . . Barb Jakubowski . . . John Jakubowski . . . Gregory Jarvis . . . Ron Jaworski . . . John Jennings . . . Patrick Jennings . . . Mike Jevic . . . Billy Joel . . . Tommy John . . . Keyshawn Johnson . . . Lyndon B. Johnson . . . Magic Johnson . . . Rich Johnson . . . Davy Jones . . . Kenney Jones . . . Mac Jones . . . Janis Joplin . . . Joe Jurevicius . . . Nancy Justice . . . Patricia Justice . . . Jackie Kahane . . . Robin Kaigh . . . James M. Kauffman . . . Bret Kavanaugh . . . Margie Keefe . . . Jim Kelley . . . Chip Kelly . . . Ulysses Kendall . . . Lisa Kenderdine . . . Rob Kenderdine . . . Ethyl Kennedy . . . Jackie Kennedy . . . John F. Kennedy . . . John F. Kennedy, Jr. . . . Robert F. Kennedy . . . Ted Kennedy . . . Diane

Kerr . . . Herbert Kerr . . . John Kerry . . . Howard Keys . . . Ruth Kille . . .
Yoo Lin Kim . . . Albert King . . . B.B. King . . . Billie Jean King . . . Carole
King . . . Freddie King . . . John William King . . . Martin Luther King, Jr. . .
. Ms. Kirk . . . Levan Kirkland . . . Peggy Klang . . . Johnny Klippstein . . .
Darold Knowles . . . Donald Koehler . . . Kevin Kolb . . . Travis Konecny . . .
Alexei Kosygin . . . Sandy Koufax . . . Jeff Kowalczyk . . . Vanessa Kowalczyk
. . . Christian Kramer . . . Elizabeth Krayer . . . Mike Kruger . . . Jari Kurri . . .
John Kuswara . . . Randy Kutcher . . . Donna Lackman . . . Bob Landry . . .
Dick "Night Train" Lane . . . Mike Lane . . . Ronnie Lane . . . Izzy Lang . . .
Barry Larkin . . . Patty Larkin . . . Don Larsen . . . Anna A. Latimer . . . Joe
Lavender . . . Inez Lear . . . Harry Lee . . . Robert E. Lee . . . Mike LeFever . . .
Ron Lemanowicz . . . John Lennon . . . David Letterman . . . Michael
Leung . . . Diane Lewis . . . Jerry Lee Lewis . . . Tom Lichtman . . . Dick
Lillich . . . Abraham Lincoln . . . Wendy Anne Lincoln . . . Brad Lindberg . .
. Charles Lindberg . . . Charlie Lindberg . . . Pelle Lindbergh . . . Oskar
Lindblom . . . Tom Lingo . . . Earl R. Lippincott . . . Hy Lit . . . Dave Lloyd .
. . Meat Loaf . . . Mrs. Long . . . Patrick Longley . . . Kathryn Loux . . . Ron
Love . . . Susan Lovitt . . . Anna Hazeltine Lowden . . . Charles Lowden . . .
Frederick Lowden . . . Hannah Fish Lowden . . . Harrison Lowden . . . Rob
Lowe . . . Emily Lozeau . . . Greg Luzinski . . . Doris MacDonald . . . Jim
MacDonald . . . Joseph MacDonald . . . Mark MacDonald . . . Mary
MacDonald . . . Bill "Red" Mack . . . Catherine Mack . . . Carol MacKenzie .
. . Garry Maddox . . . Raul Malo . . . Peyton Manning . . . Ricky Manning,
Jr. . . . Kevin Manns . . . Gary Mansfield . . . Bob Marley . . . Lecil Travis
"Boxcar Willie" Martin . . . Rod Martin . . . Edgar Martinez . . . Pedro
Martinez . . . John Marzano . . . Dave Mason . . . Paul Mason . . . Scotte
Mason . . . Manya Matyka . . . Gene Mauch . . . Jim Maxwell . . . Sherri May
. . . Arlene Mayer . . . Willie Mays . . . Christa McAuliffe . . . Martina
McBride . . . Gene McCabe . . . Andrew McCarthy . . . Eugene McCarthy . .
. John McCarthy . . . Tim McCarthy . . . Paul McCartney . . . Tim
McCarver . . . Reverend William R. McClelland . . . William J.
McClyment, Jr. . . . Mitch McConnell . . . Tommy McDonald . . . Reba
McEntire . . . Bill McGinn . . . George McGovern . . . Colin McGrath . . .
Kevin McGrath . . . Mrs. McGrath . . . Ali McGraw . . . Tim McGraw . . .
Tug McGraw . . . Fred McGriff . . . Marlin McKeever . . . Ian McLagan . . .
Bob McLeod . . . Cal McLish . . . Donovan McNabb . . . Ronald McNair . . .
John Meacham . . . Timmy Mead . . . Janice Melhorn . . . John E. Melhorn .
. . Dr. Harold Mellby, Jr. . . . John Mellencamp . . . Burgess Meredith . . .
Mark Messier . . . Derek Metallo . . . Jack Meyer . . . John Meyers . . . George
Michael . . . Michaelangelo . . . Leona Miller . . . Mary Miller . . . Ray
Miller, Jr. . . . Ray Miller, Sr. . . . Sally Miller . . . Sara Miller . . . Maureen
Milliken . . . Joe Milo . . . Doug Misarti . . . Brian Mitchell . . . Freddie
Mitchell . . . Joni Mitchell . . . Dorothy Moldoff . . . Walter Mondale . . .
Wilbert Montgomery . . . Chris Mooney . . . Demi Moore . . . Joe Morgan . .

. Joe Morgan . . . Mike Morgan . . . John Moser . . . Denise Murphy . . . Evelyn Murphy . . . Greg Murphy . . . John Murray . . . John Murray . . . John Murray, Jr. . . . Rose Murray . . . Gary Murza . . . Stan Musial . . . Dr. Rade R. Musulin . . . Andy Myer . . . Steve Mygatt . . . Stu Nahan . . . Donna Jo Napoli . . . . Martina Navratilova . . . Judd Nelson . . . Rick Nelson . . . Jim Nettleton . . . Cam Newton . . . Joe Niagara . . . Catherine Nichols . . . Jack Nicklaus . . . Sal Nicosia . . . Julie Nixon . . . Richard Nixon . . . Tricia Nixon . . . Mark Nordquist . . . Earl Norman . . . Michael Nutter . . . Barack Obama . . . Victor Oberg . . . Jim O'Brien . . . Phil Ochs . . . Zach O'Hora . . . Bob Oldis . . . Greg Oliver . . . Laurence Olivier . . . Ryan O'Neal . . . Ellison Onizuka . . . Roy Orbison . . . David Ortiz . . . Annie Osteen . . . Lee Harvey Oswald . . . Debbie Ott . . . Alice Ozma . . . Jeffrey Packer . . . Marisa de Jesus Paolicelli . . . Vince Papale . . . Dick Parker . . . Kelly Parker . . . Patricia Parker . . . Christine Parsells . . . Arthur Allen Patterson . . . Rand Paul . . . Helen Paxon . . . Tom Paxton . . . Dale Payne . . . Doug Pederson . . . Charlie Peffall . . . Bruce Pellnitz . . . Phyllis Pelouze . . . Mike Pence . . . Michael Penney . . . Ross Perot . . . Joe Perrone . . . Luke Perry . . . Dave Peterson . . . Rachel Peterson . . . Blane Petterson . . . Betty Ann Petterson . . . Ed Pfeifer . . . Matt Phelan . . . Nick Philippi . . . Bobby Phillips . . . Linda Lee Phillips . . . Steve Picot . . . Robert Pinto . . . Greg Pizzoli . . . Elissa Plasky . . . George Pleibel . . . Ray Poage . . . Anne Polak . . . Frank Polak . . . Donna Polidora . . . Sandra Poots . . . Bob Porter . . . Boog Powell . . . Miller Preston . . . Elvis Presley . . . John Prine . . . Ivan Provorov . . . Rex Putnal . . . Dan Quayle . . . Gary Rab . . . Dick Radatz . . . Michael Raffl . . . Bonnie Raitt . . . Manny Ramirez . . . V. Randall . . . Fred Raper . . . Gina Raper . . . Kevin Rapp . . . James Earl Ray . . . Jeff Reardon . . . Siobhan Reardon . . . John Reaves . . . Jim Reed . . . Josh Reese . . . Andy Reid . . . Anne Remick . . . Ed Rendell . . . Judith Resnick . . . Pete Retzlaff . . . Ethan Reynolds . . . Little Richard . . . Bobby Richards . . . Willard Richman . . . James van Riemsdyk . . . Dr. Albert Riester . . . Lora Riester . . . LeAnn Rimes . . . Molly Ringwald . . . Cal Ripken, Jr. . . . . Luis Rivera . . . Mary Roach . . . Brooks Robinson . . . Frank Robinson . . . Jackie Robinson . . . Laurie Robinson . . . Roger Roble . . . Mara Rockliff . . . Marie Rod . . . Fred Rogers . . . Joan Rogers . . . Roy Rogers . . . Jimmy Rollins . . . Mitt Romney . . . Eleanor Roosevelt . . . Franklin Delano Roosevelt . . . William Rosborough . . . Pete Rose . . . Steve Rosenberg . . . Tim Rossovich . . . Jack Ruby . . . Wayne Rudolph . . . Carlos Ruiz . . . Chico Ruiz . . . Max Ruiz . . . Helen Russ . . . Bill Russell . . . Leon Russell . . . Dick Ruthven . . . Buddy Ryan . . . Nolan Ryan . . . Reverend Milt Ryder . . . Julius Sacchetti . . . Pete Sacchetti . . . Antoine de Saint-Exupery . . . Martin St. Louis . . . Asante Samuel . . . Mark Sanchez . . . Ryne Sandberg . . . Chris Sanderson . . . Fernando Santiago . . . Reverend Robert Santilli . . . Ron Santo . . . Rick Santorum . . . Linda Saun . . . Jessica Savitch . . . Clifton Saxton . . . John Scammon . . . Joe Scarborough . . . Judy Schachner . . . Frances Schaevitz . . .

Frank Scherer . . . Kevin Schildt . . . Curt Schilling . . . Laura Schlessinger . . . Dr. Anna Schmid . . . Jim Schmidt, Jr. . . . Jim Schmidt, Sr. . . . Karen Schmidt . . . Mike Schmidt . . . Sandy Schmidt . . . Doug Schmitt . . . Jim Schrader . . . Dorothy Schroeder . . . Ken Schroeder . . . Col. Herbert Norman Schwartzkopf . . . Gen. Norman Schwarzkopf, Jr. . . . Francis Scobee . . . Bill Scott . . . Bob Scott . . . Duane Scott . . . Jim Scott . . . Joanne Scott . . . Marjorie Lowden Scott . . . Mary Scott . . . Thomas Scott . . . Thomas B. Scott . . . Will Scott . . . John Sebastian . . . Pete Seeger . . . Dr. Seuss . . . Milton Shapp . . . Omar Sharif . . . Dan Shaughnessy . . . Ally Sheedy . . . Agnes Florig Sheldon . . . Alan Shepard . . . Jack Shibe . . . Lynne Shindle . . . Talia Shire . . . Walter Shirra . . . Chris Short . . . Sargent Shriver . . . Lee Shute . . . Shel Silverstein . . . Bob Siman . . . Joe Simkins . . . Kenny Simpkins . . . Margaret Simpson . . . O.J. Simpson . . . Frank Sinatra . . . Betty Siner . . . Frank Sirch . . . Virginia Sirolli . . . David Skidmore . . . Bob Skinner . . . Deke Slayton . . . Harriet Smelker . . . Michael Smerconish . . . Joyce Smith . . . Lee Smith . . . Lonnie Smith . . . Michael Smith . . . Ozzie Smith . . . Reed Smith . . . Steve Smith . . . Connie Smolsky . . . Norm Snead . . . Bob Snow . . . Dylan Snow . . . John Sodaski . . . Aleksandr Solzhenitsyn . . . Lori Sotland . . . Steven Spielberg . . . Eileen Spinelli . . . Bruce Springsteen . . . Rita Stabler . . . Alexander Stadler . . . Duce Staley . . . Sylvester Stallone . . . Ringo Starr . . . Sally Starr . . . John Stelmach . . . John Stephenson . . . Alvin Stern . . . Clifford Stetler . . . Richard Stevens . . . Dave Stewart . . . Rod Stewart . . . Sarah Stewart . . . Leon Stickle . . . Michael Stoner . . . Doris String . . . Phyllis String . . . Elizabeth Strohminger . . . Joe Strong . . . Julia Strong . . . Robert A. Strong . . . Dick Stuart . . . Eddie Stubits . . . Ed Sullivan . . . Tom Sullivan . . . Chris Surran . . . Dave Swisher . . . Dr. James Talarico . . . Al Tanner . . . Jay Taraschi . . . Alex Tarbell . . . Carl Tarbell . . . Martine Taylor . . . Tony Taylor . . . Jo Tedesco . . . Helen Thayer . . . Bob Thomas . . . Frank Thomas . . . Jim Thome . . . Emma Thompson . . . Billy Tierney . . . Kelly Tierney . . . Linda Tierney . . . J.D. Tippet . . . Rich Toll . . . Mike Tomczak . . . Tom Torillo . . . Rich Townsend . . . Pat Trainer . . . R. James Tredinnick . . . Manny Trillo . . . Camy Trinidad . . . Mike Trout . . . Harry Truman . . . Donald J. Trump . . . Donald Trump, Jr. . . . Paul Tsongas . . . Pamela Tuck . . . Robert M. Tull, Jr. . . . Ivan Turgenev . . . Joyce Turkelson . . . Agnes Sligh Turnbull . . . Betty Turner . . . Bret Turner . . . Kip Turner . . . Shania Twain . . . Dean Tyler . . . David Tyree . . . Chase Utley . . . J.C. Valore . . . Bob Van Osten . . . George Washington Vanderbilt II . . . Lance Vernon . . . Michael Vick . . . Shane Victorino . . . Leonardo da Vinci . . . Jakub Voracek . . . Mike Wahl . . . Nicolle Wallace . . . Denny Walling . . . Bobby Walston . . . Adele Walton . . . George Washington . . . Carl Weathers . . . Joe Webb . . . Nancy Weil . . . Elaine Welden . . . Scott Weldon . . . Carson Wentz . . . Richard Wesolowski . . . Frank White . . . Gale White . . . Al Widmar . . . David Wiesner . . . Hon. Robert N. Wilentz . . . Kathy Wiley . . . Charlotte Wilkins . . . Dar Williams . . . Mitch Williams . . .

Serena Williams . . . Katie Wilson . . . Lori Wilson . . . Willie Wilson . . . Steve Winwood . . . Rick Wise . . . Tom Wisely . . . Geoffrey Wolf . . . William Wolf . . . Ronnie Wood . . . Sam Wood . . . Tom Woodeshick . . . Bertha Woodrow . . . Adrienne Wright . . . Burt Young . . . Charlie Young . . . Rich Young . . . Vince Young . . . Al Yourich . . . Steve Zabel . . . Henrike Ziegler . . . Don Zimmerman

About the Author

David Florig is the author of . . . well, nothing, really. No novels, poems, biographies, graphic novels or even novellas. He did have a couple of short stories published in his high school literary magazine and a couple of legal articles published in trade journals, though, if that counts. And he still doesn't know who his natural parents are.

The product of a teenage out-of-wedlock pregnancy, and growing up on the mean streets of Haddon Township, New Jersey, he misguidedly set out to see if he could figure out what he was doing on each and every day of his life, which is nearly 25,000 days. That attempt failed miserably. The result is *A Life of Dates*, a stream-of-consciousness journey through an extraordinarily normal life, full of great joy, overwhelming sadness, sheer stupidity, some poison ivy and a fall off of a roof.

David practiced law for far too long and left the practice before it claimed what was left of his soul. He recently took up curling.

He lives in Maine with his adoring wife of 34 years, Nancy, and their two ill-mannered dogs, Erin and Molly. They sometimes share their yard with a family of foxes. Their son, Dylan, is the best boy in the world. Dylan lives in North Carolina with his wife, Elizabeth, way too far away.

* * *

You can contact David Florig at david.florig207@gmail.com.

If you would care to leave a review, please do so at the Amazon book page for "*A Life of Dates*." I would love to know what you think. All reviews are greatly appreciated.

Made in the USA
Middletown, DE
20 March 2022

62967385R00239